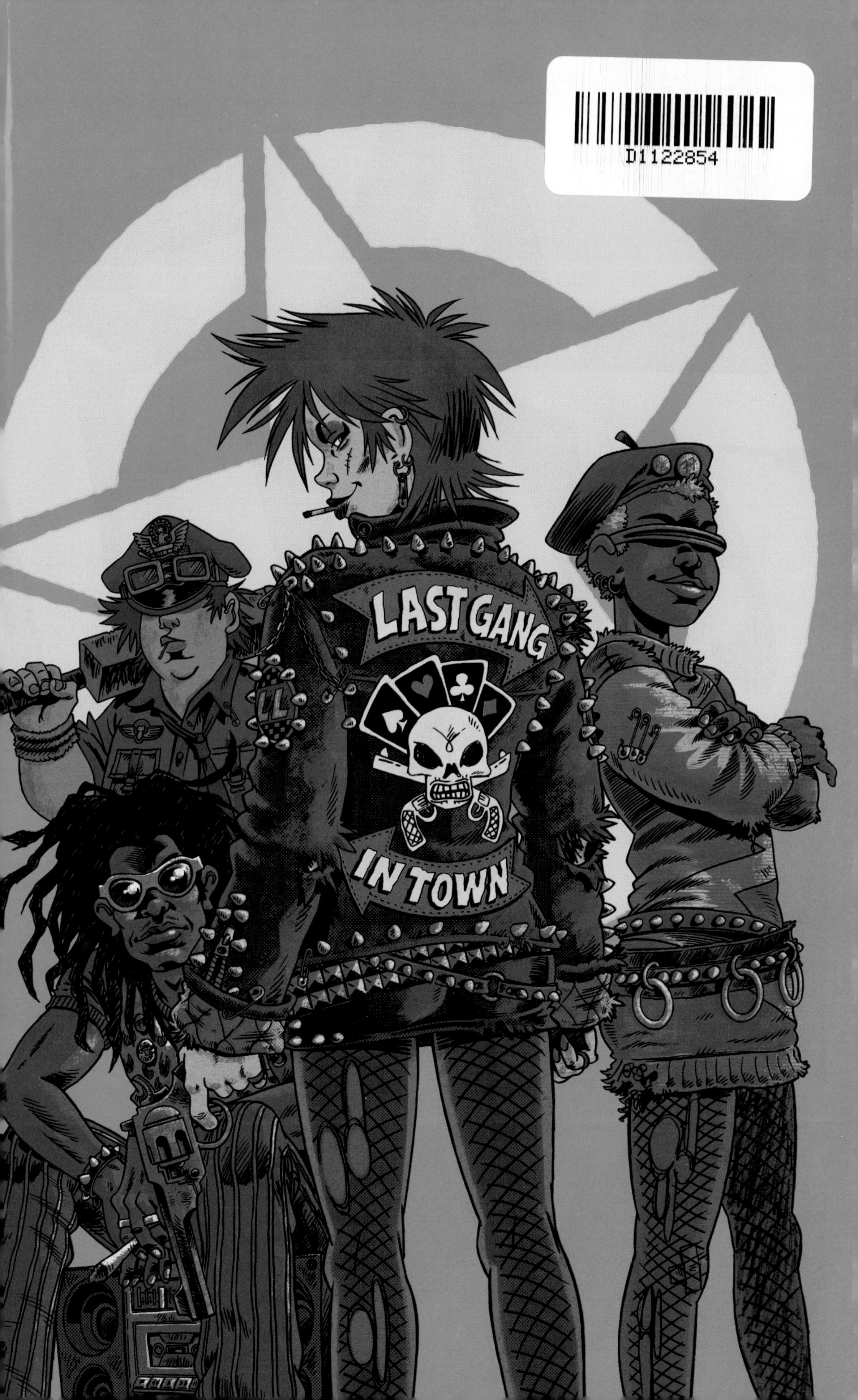
LAST GANG
IN TOWN

LAST
GANG
IN
TOWN

SIMON OLIVER
WRITER

RUFUS DAYGLO
ARTIST

ADAM CADWELL
FINISHES (CHAPTERS 3 & 4)

GIULIA BRUSCO
WITH DEE CUNNIFFE (CHAPTER 6)
COLORISTS

STEVE WANDS
LETTERER

RUFUS DAYGLO
COVER ART

ROB DAVIS
ORIGINAL SERIES COVERS

LAST GANG IN TOWN
CREATED BY SIMON OLIVER
AND RUFUS DAYGLO

GOD save

RUFUS DAYGLO

GOD save

SIMON OLIVER

JAMIE S. RICH Editor – Original Series
MOLLY MAHAN Associate Editor – Original Series
JEB WOODARD Group Editor – Collected Editions
SCOTT NYBAKKEN Editor – Collected Edition
STEVE COOK Design Director – Books
LOUIS PRANDI Publication Design

SHELLY BOND VP & Executive Editor – Vertigo

DIANE NELSON President
DAN DIDIO AND JIM LEE Co-Publishers
GEOFF JOHNS Chief Creative Officer
AMIT DESAI Senior VP – Marketing & Global Franchise Management
NAIRI GARDINER Senior VP – Finance
SAM ADES VP – Digital Marketing
BOBBIE CHASE VP – Talent Development
MARK CHIARELLO Senior VP – Art, Design & Collected Editions
JOHN CUNNINGHAM VP – Content Strategy
ANNE DEPIES VP – Strategy Planning & Reporting
DON FALLETTI VP – Manufacturing Operations
LAWRENCE GANEM VP – Editorial Administration & Talent Relations
ALISON GILL Senior VP – Manufacturing & Operations
HANK KANALZ Senior VP – Editorial Strategy & Administration
JAY KOGAN VP – Legal Affairs
DEREK MADDALENA Senior VP – Sales & Business Development
JACK MAHAN VP – Business Affairs
DAN MIRON VP – Sales Planning & Trade Development
NICK NAPOLITANO VP – Manufacturing Administration
CAROL ROEDER VP – Marketing
EDDIE SCANNELL VP – Mass Account & Digital Sales
COURTNEY SIMMONS Senior VP – Publicity & Communications
JIM (SKI) SOKOLOWSKI VP – Comic Book Specialty & Newsstand Sales
SANDY YI Senior VP – Global Franchise Management

Logo design by RIAN HUGHES

LAST GANG IN TOWN

Published by DC Comics. Compilation, cover, and all new material
Copyright © 2016 Simon Oliver and Rufus Dayglo. All Rights Reserved.
Originally published in single magazine form as LAST GANG IN
TOWN 1-6. Copyright © 2016 Simon Oliver and Rufus Dayglo. All
Rights Reserved. All characters, their distinctive likenesses and
related elements featured in this publication are trademarks of
Simon Oliver and Rufus Dayglo. VERTIGO is a trademark of DC
Comics. The stories, characters and incidents featured in this
publication are entirely fictional. DC Comics does not read or
accept unsolicited submissions of ideas, stories or artwork.

DC Comics
2900 West Alameda Avenue
Burbank, CA 91505
Printed in the USA. First Printing.
ISBN: 978-1-4012-6473-4

Library of Congress Cataloging-in-Publication Data is available.

PEFC Certified
Printed on paper from
sustainably managed
forests and controlled
sources
PEFC/29-31-75   www.pefc.org

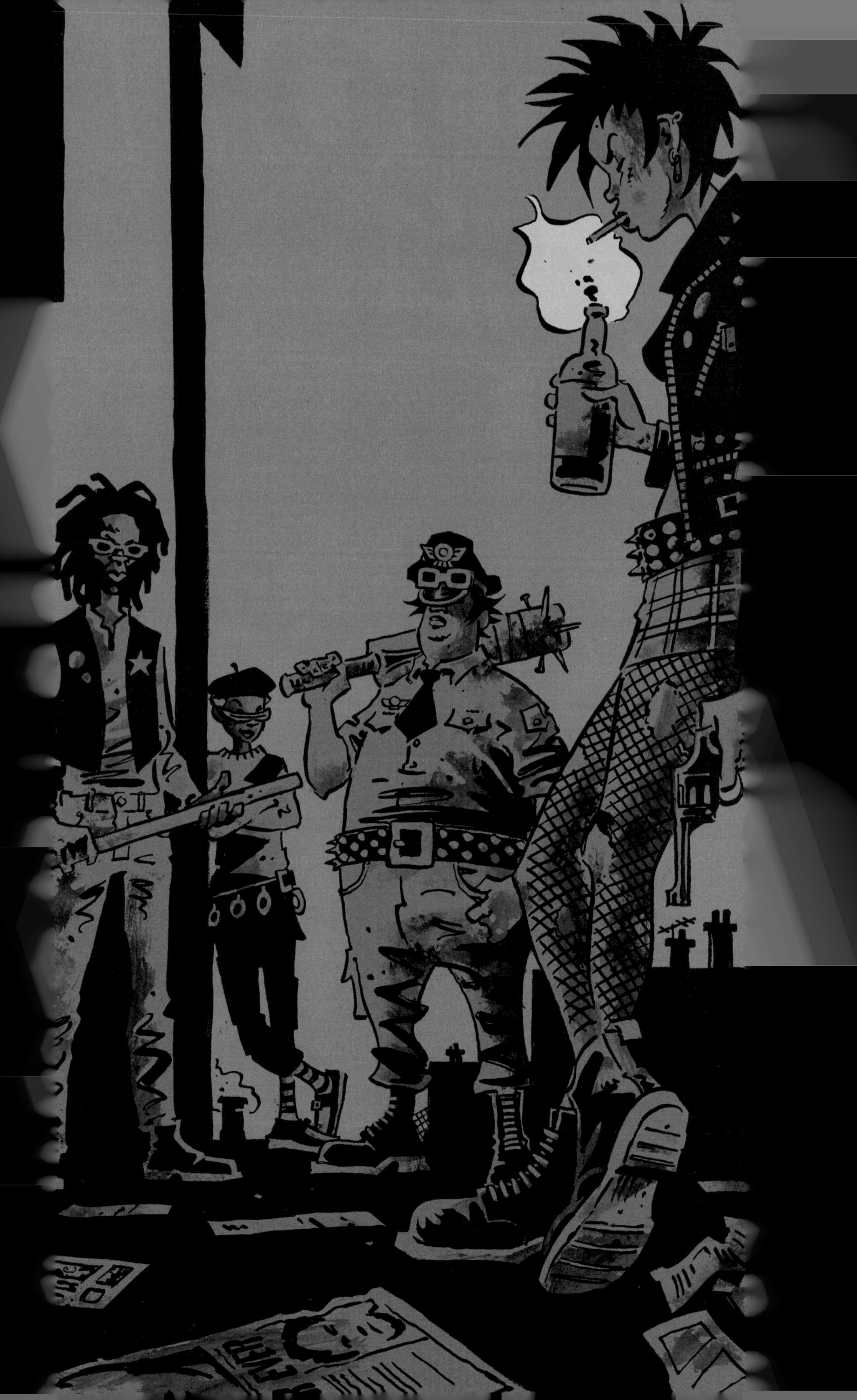

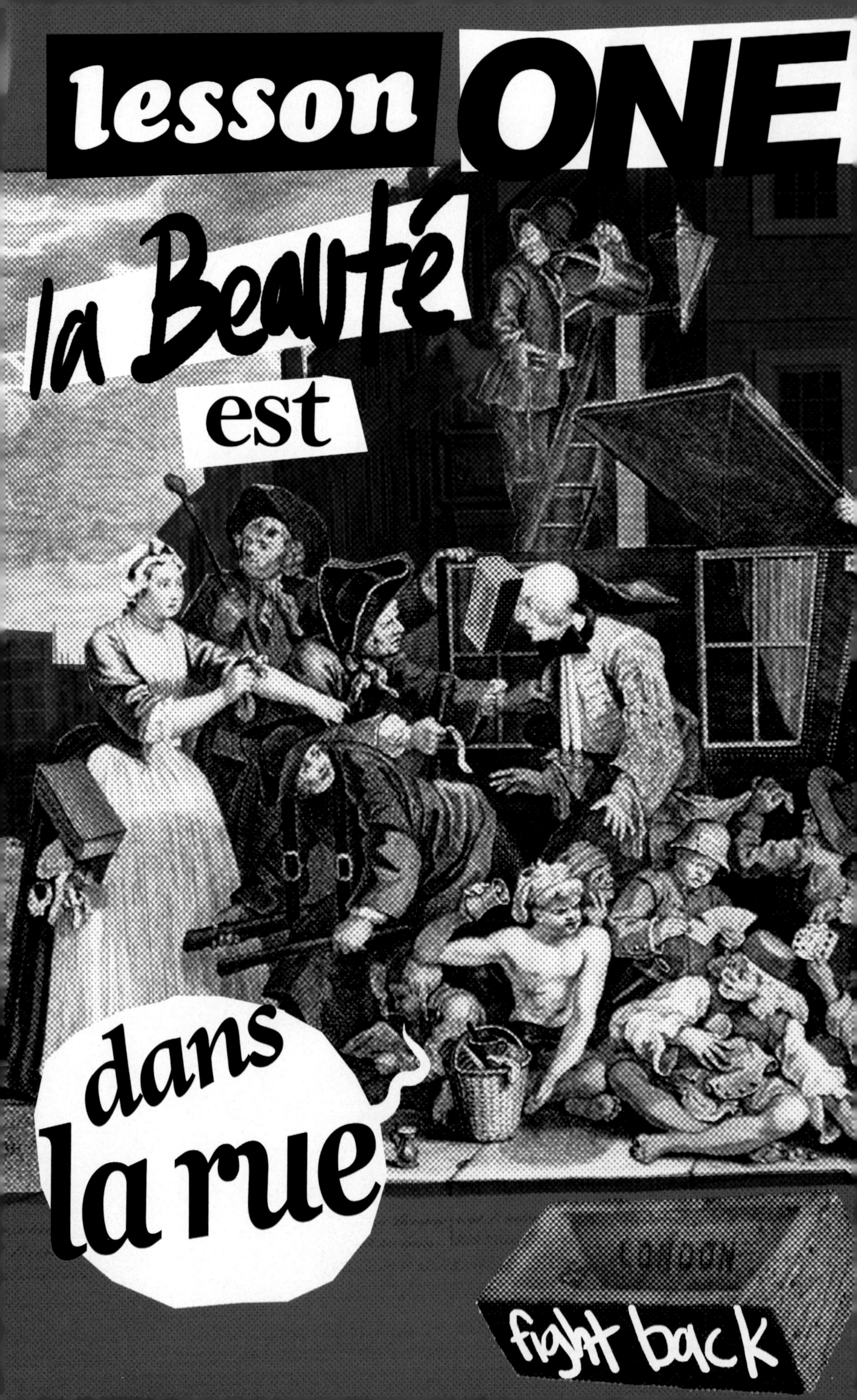

lesson ONE
la Beauté
est
dans
la rue
fight back

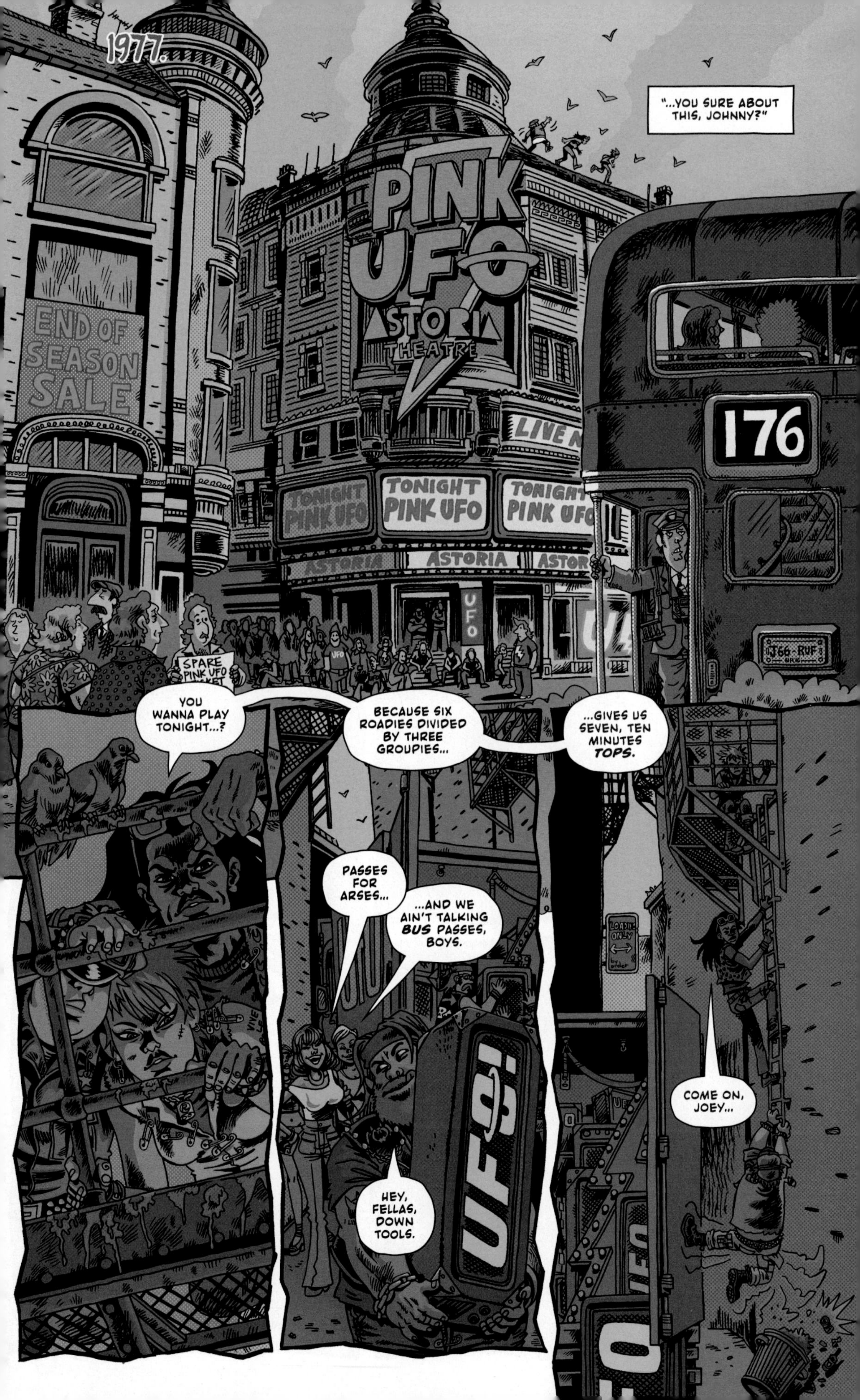
1977.
"...YOU SURE ABOUT THIS, JOHNNY?"
PINK UFO
ASTORIA THEATRE
END OF SEASON SALE
LIVE
TONIGHT PINK UFO
TONIGHT PINK UFO
TONIGHT PINK UFO
ASTORIA
ASTORIA
ASTOR
176
SPARE PINK UFO TICKET
YOU WANNA PLAY TONIGHT...?
BECAUSE SIX ROADIES DIVIDED BY THREE GROUPIES...
...GIVES US SEVEN, TEN MINUTES *TOPS.*
PASSES FOR ARSES...
...AND WE AIN'T TALKING *BUS* PASSES, BOYS.
LOADING ONLY
HEY, FELLAS, DOWN TOOLS.
COME ON, JOEY...

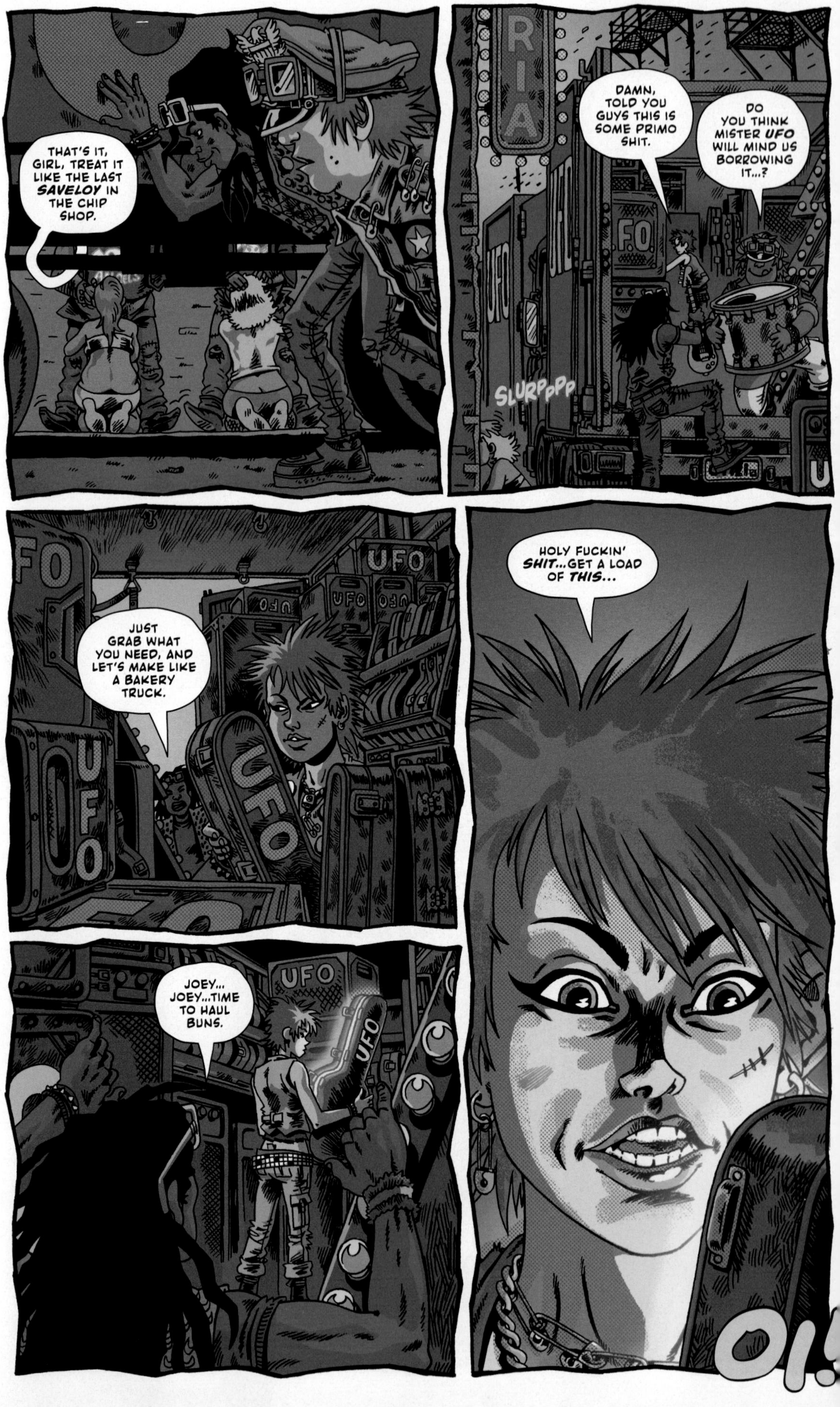
THAT'S IT, GIRL, TREAT IT LIKE THE LAST *SAVELOY* IN THE CHIP SHOP.
DAMN, TOLD YOU GUYS THIS IS SOME PRIMO SHIT.
DO YOU THINK MISTER *UFO* WILL MIND US BORROWING IT...?
SLURPPPP
JUST GRAB WHAT YOU NEED, AND LET'S MAKE LIKE A BAKERY TRUCK.
JOEY... JOEY...TIME TO HAUL BUNS.
HOLY FUCKIN' *SHIT*...GET A LOAD OF *THIS*...
OI!

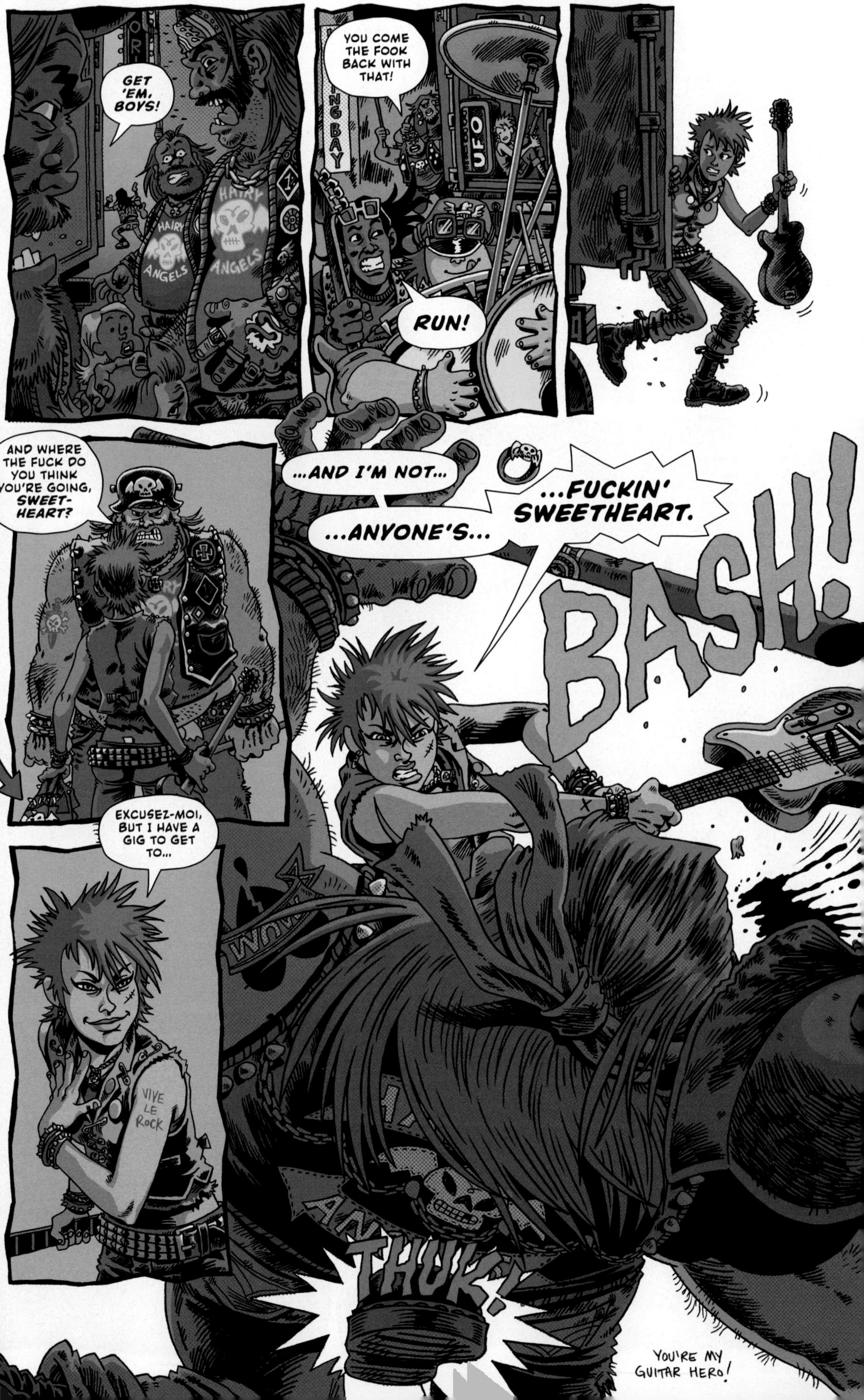
GET 'EM, BOYS!
HAIRY ANGELS
HAIRY ANGELS
YOU COME THE FOOK BACK WITH THAT!
UFO
RUN!
AND WHERE THE FUCK DO YOU THINK YOU'RE GOING, SWEET-HEART?
...AND I'M NOT...
...ANYONE'S...
...FUCKIN' SWEETHEART.
BASH!
EXCUSEZ-MOI, BUT I HAVE A GIG TO GET TO...
VIVE LE ROCK
THUK!
YOU'RE MY GUITAR HERO!

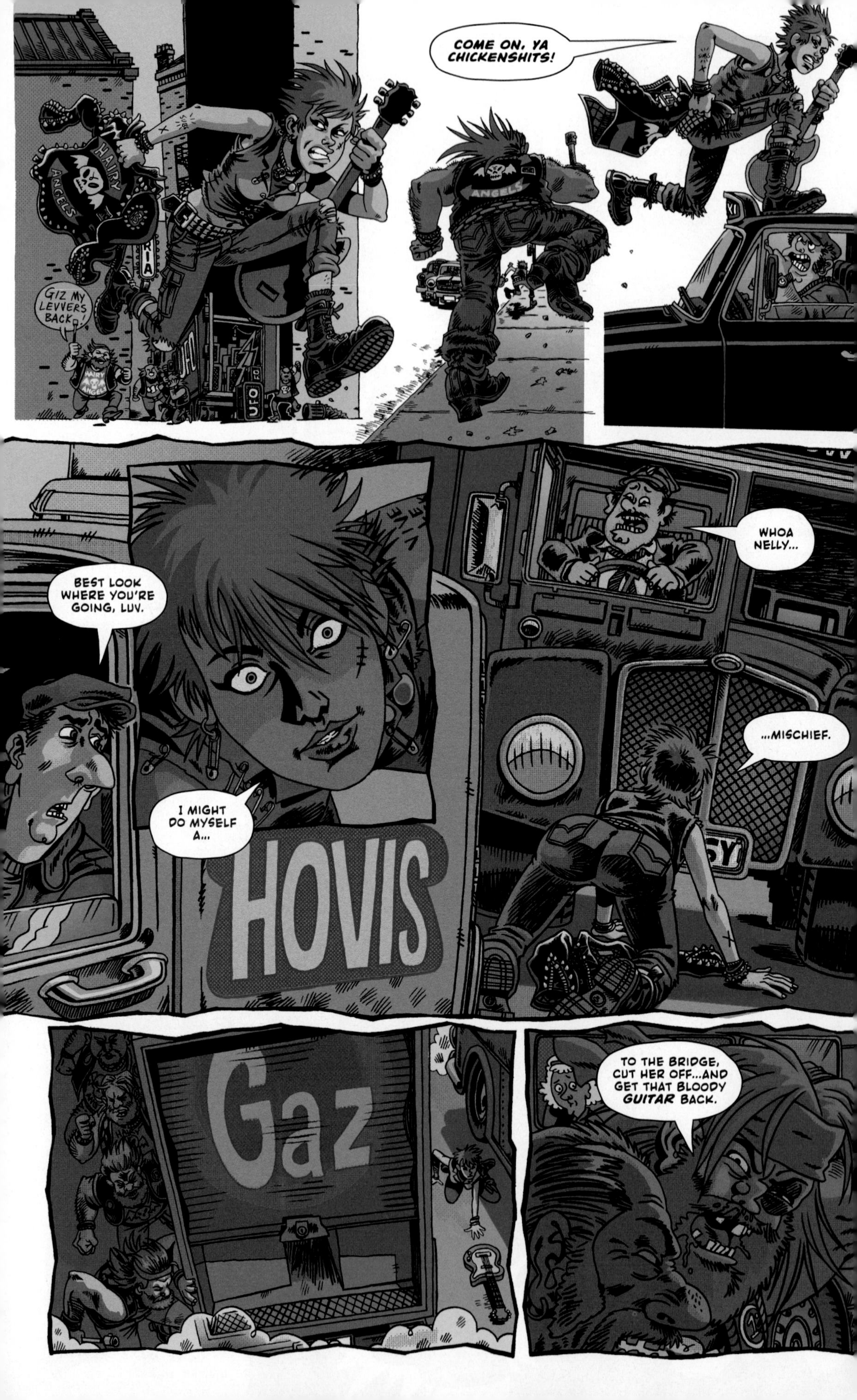
GIZ MY LEVVERS BACK!
COME ON, YA CHICKENSHITS!
BEST LOOK WHERE YOU'RE GOING, LUV.
WHOA NELLY...
I MIGHT DO MYSELF A...
...MISCHIEF.
HOVIS
Gaz
TO THE BRIDGE, CUT HER OFF...AND GET THAT BLOODY GUITAR BACK.

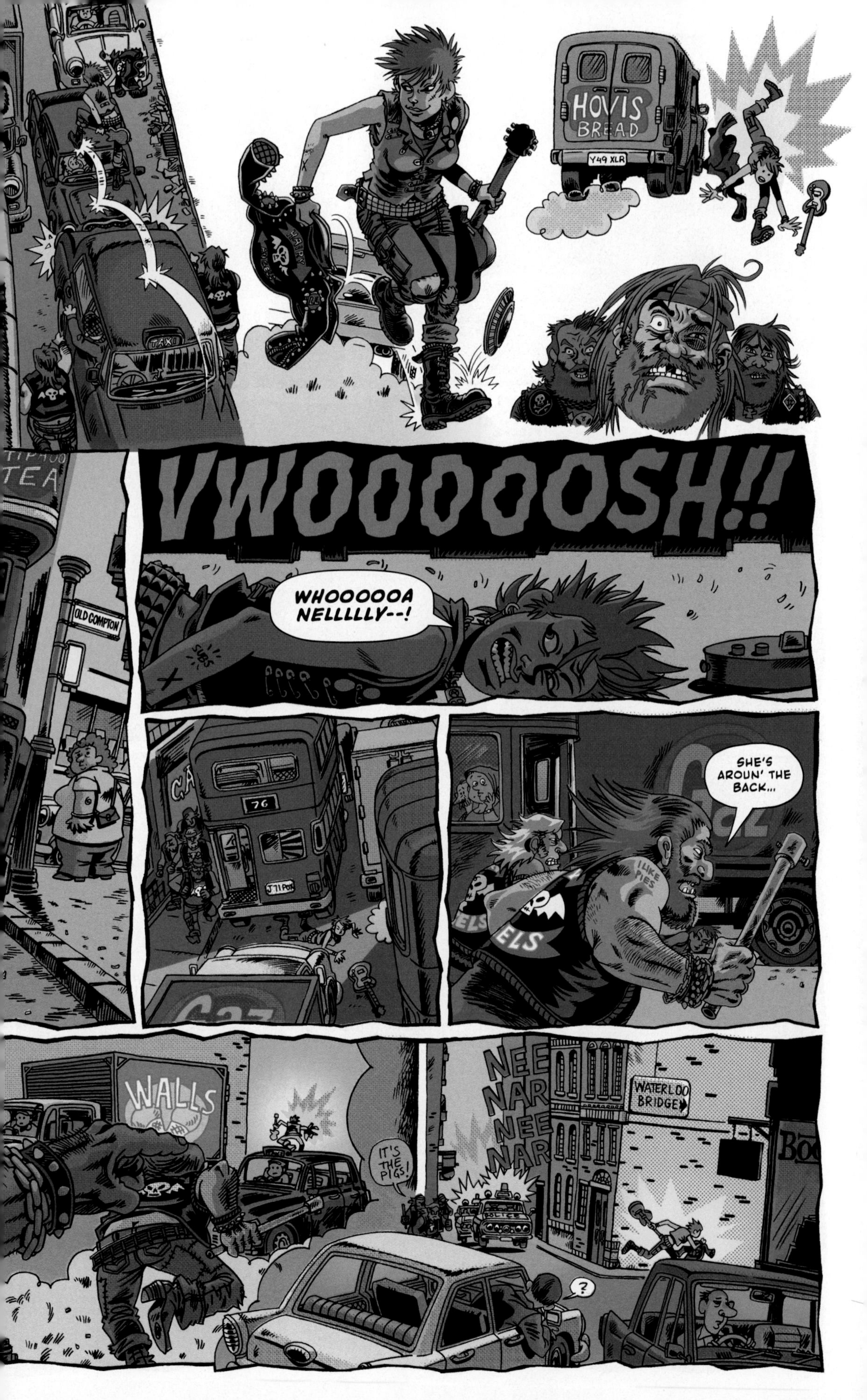
HOVIS
BREAD
Y49 XLR
TAXI
VWOOOOOSH!!
WHOOOOOA NELLLLLY--!
OLD COMPTON
TIPHOO
TEA
76
SHE'S AROUN' THE BACK...
I LIKE PIES
WALLS
IT'S THE PIGS!
NEE NAR NEE NAR
WATERLOO BRIDGE
POLICE
?

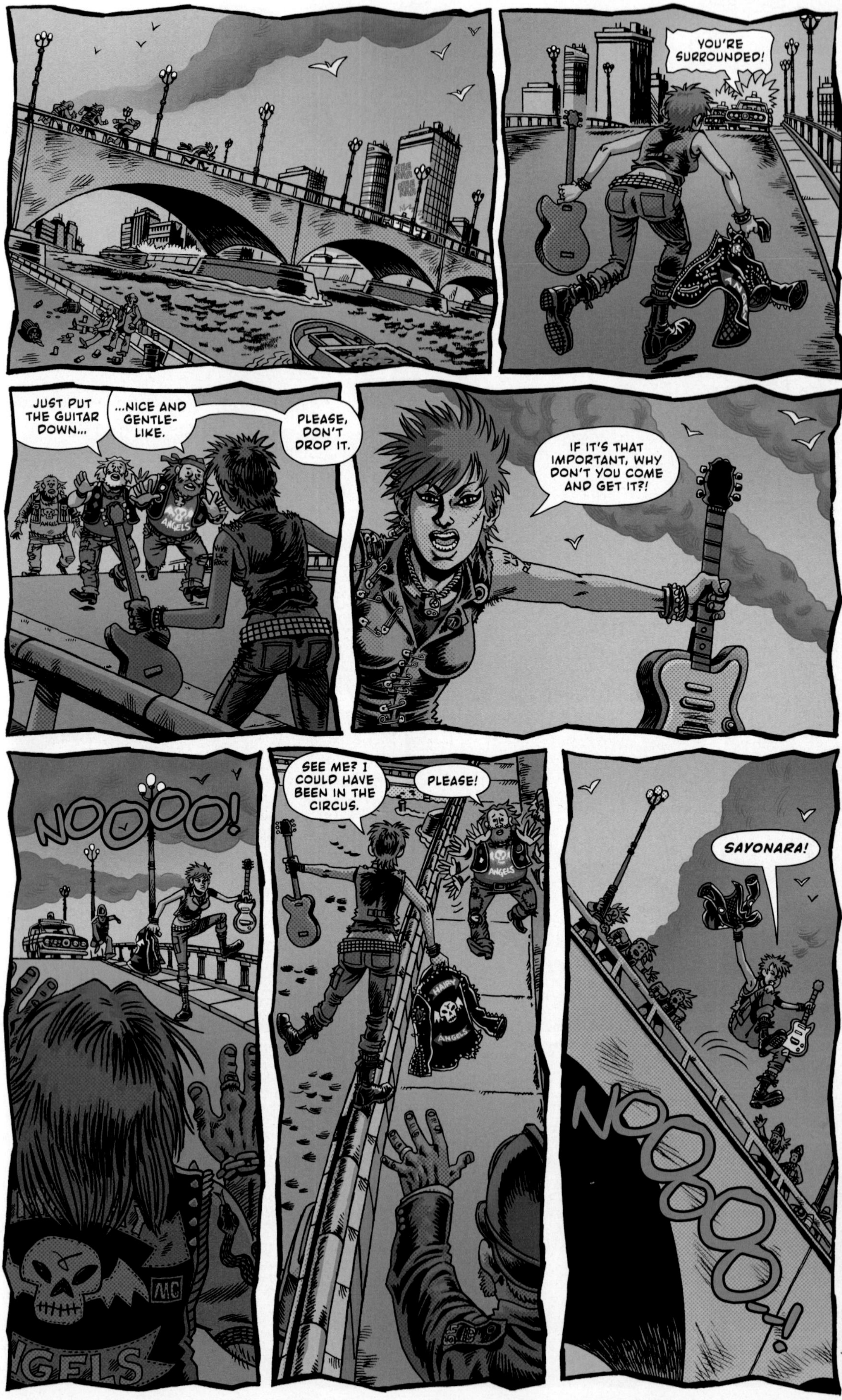
YOU'RE SURROUNDED!
JUST PUT THE GUITAR DOWN...
...NICE AND GENTLE-LIKE.
PLEASE, DON'T DROP IT.
IF IT'S THAT IMPORTANT, WHY DON'T YOU COME AND GET IT?!
NOOOOO!
SEE ME? I COULD HAVE BEEN IN THE CIRCUS.
PLEASE!
SAYONARA!
NOOOOO...!

LOOK OUT BELOW!

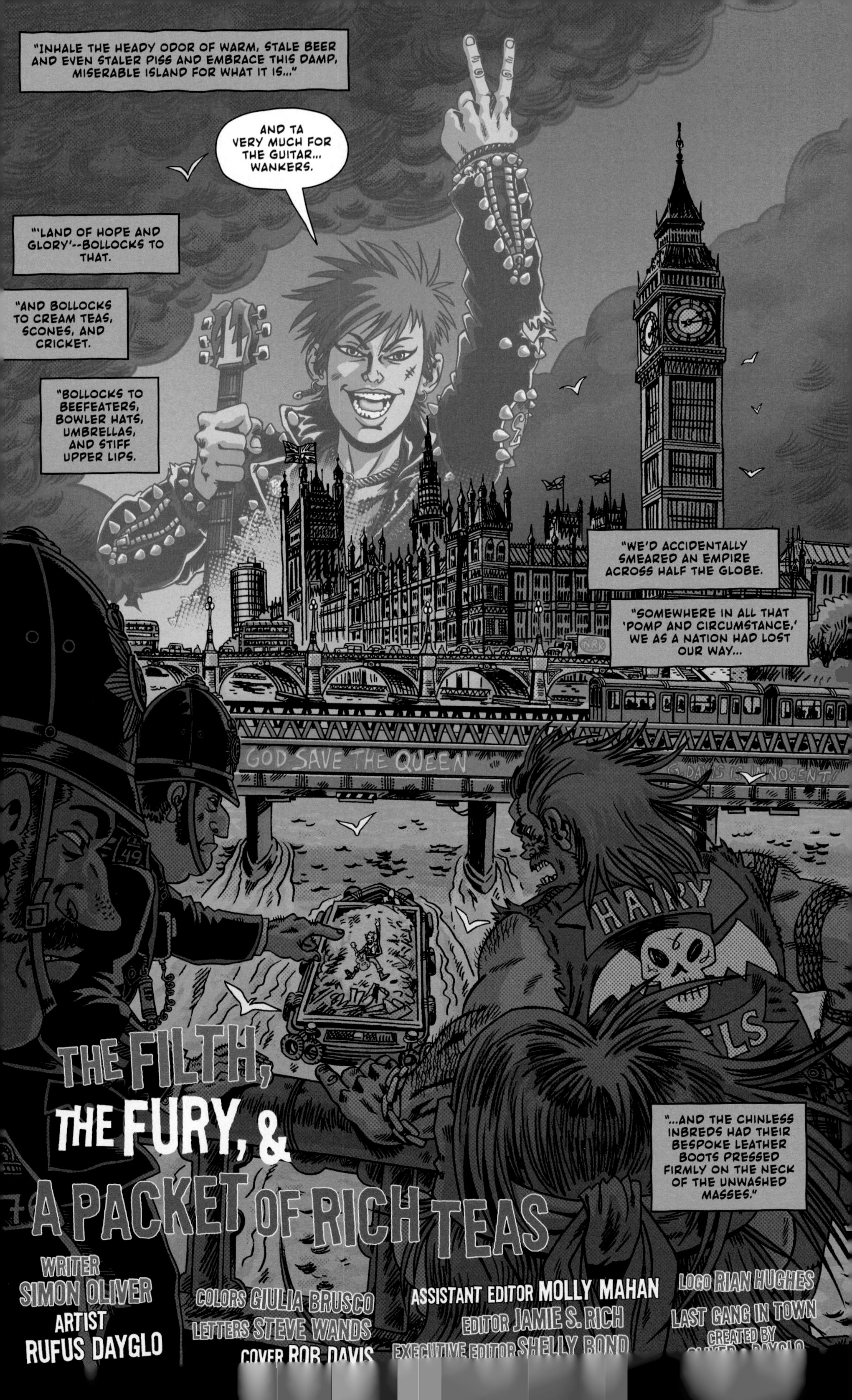

"INHALE THE HEADY ODOR OF WARM, STALE BEER AND EVEN STALER PISS AND EMBRACE THIS DAMP, MISERABLE ISLAND FOR WHAT IT IS..."
AND TA VERY MUCH FOR THE GUITAR... WANKERS.
"'LAND OF HOPE AND GLORY'--BOLLOCKS TO THAT.
"AND BOLLOCKS TO CREAM TEAS, SCONES, AND CRICKET.
"BOLLOCKS TO BEEFEATERS, BOWLER HATS, UMBRELLAS, AND STIFF UPPER LIPS.
"WE'D ACCIDENTALLY SMEARED AN EMPIRE ACROSS HALF THE GLOBE.
"SOMEWHERE IN ALL THAT 'POMP AND CIRCUMSTANCE,' WE AS A NATION HAD LOST OUR WAY...
GOD SAVE THE QUEEN
HAIRY
"...AND THE CHINLESS INBREDS HAD THEIR BESPOKE LEATHER BOOTS PRESSED FIRMLY ON THE NECK OF THE UNWASHED MASSES."
THE FILTH, THE FURY, & A PACKET OF RICH TEAS
WRITER SIMON OLIVER
ARTIST RUFUS DAYGLO
COLORS GIULIA BRUSCO
LETTERS STEVE WANDS
COVER ROB DAVIS
ASSISTANT EDITOR MOLLY MAHAN
EDITOR JAMIE S. RICH
EXECUTIVE EDITOR SHELLY BOND
LOGO RIAN HUGHES
LAST GANG IN TOWN CREATED BY

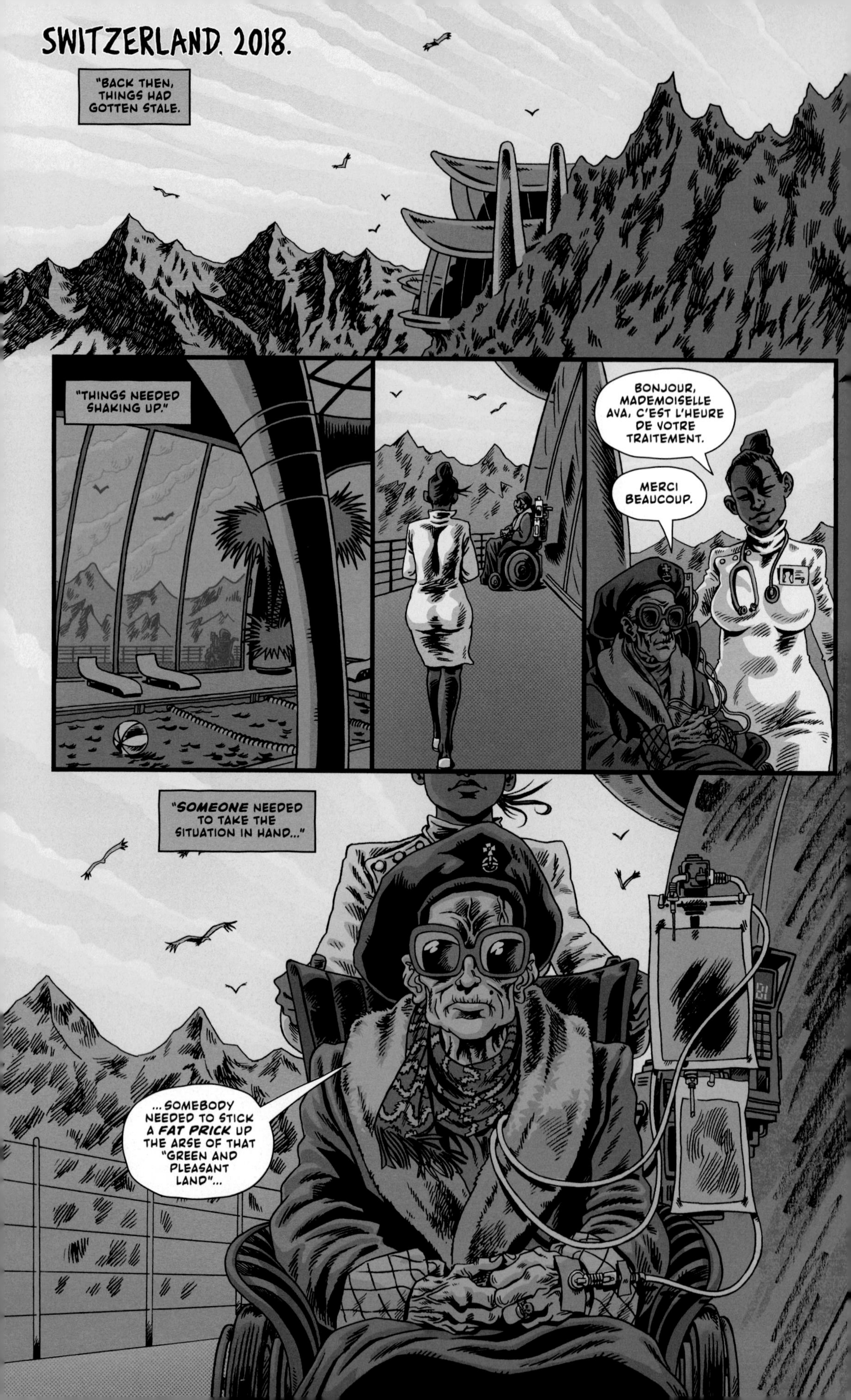
SWITZERLAND, 2018.
"BACK THEN, THINGS HAD GOTTEN STALE.
"THINGS NEEDED SHAKING UP."
BONJOUR, MADEMOISELLE AVA, C'EST L'HEURE DE VOTRE TRAITEMENT.
MERCI BEAUCOUP.
"SOMEONE NEEDED TO TAKE THE SITUATION IN HAND..."
...SOMEBODY NEEDED TO STICK A FAT PRICK UP THE ARSE OF THAT "GREEN AND PLEASANT LAND"...

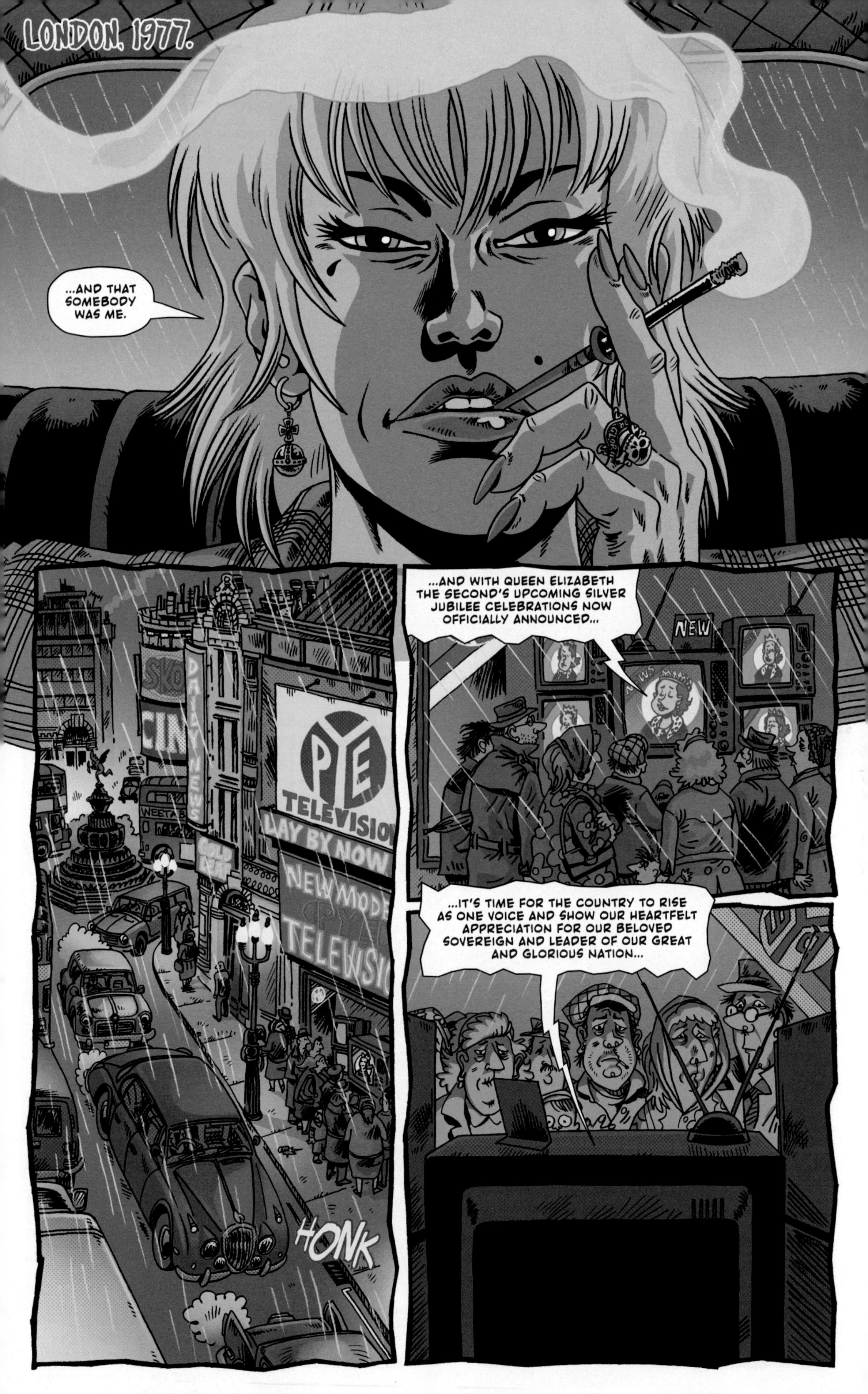
LONDON, 1977.
...AND THAT SOMEBODY WAS ME.
DAILY NEWS
PYE TELEVISION
LAY BY NOW
NEW MODEL PYE TELEVISION
GOLD LEAF
HONK
...AND WITH QUEEN ELIZABETH THE SECOND'S UPCOMING SILVER JUBILEE CELEBRATIONS NOW OFFICIALLY ANNOUNCED...
NEW
NEWS
...IT'S TIME FOR THE COUNTRY TO RISE AS ONE VOICE AND SHOW OUR HEARTFELT APPRECIATION FOR OUR BELOVED SOVEREIGN AND LEADER OF OUR GREAT AND GLORIOUS NATION...

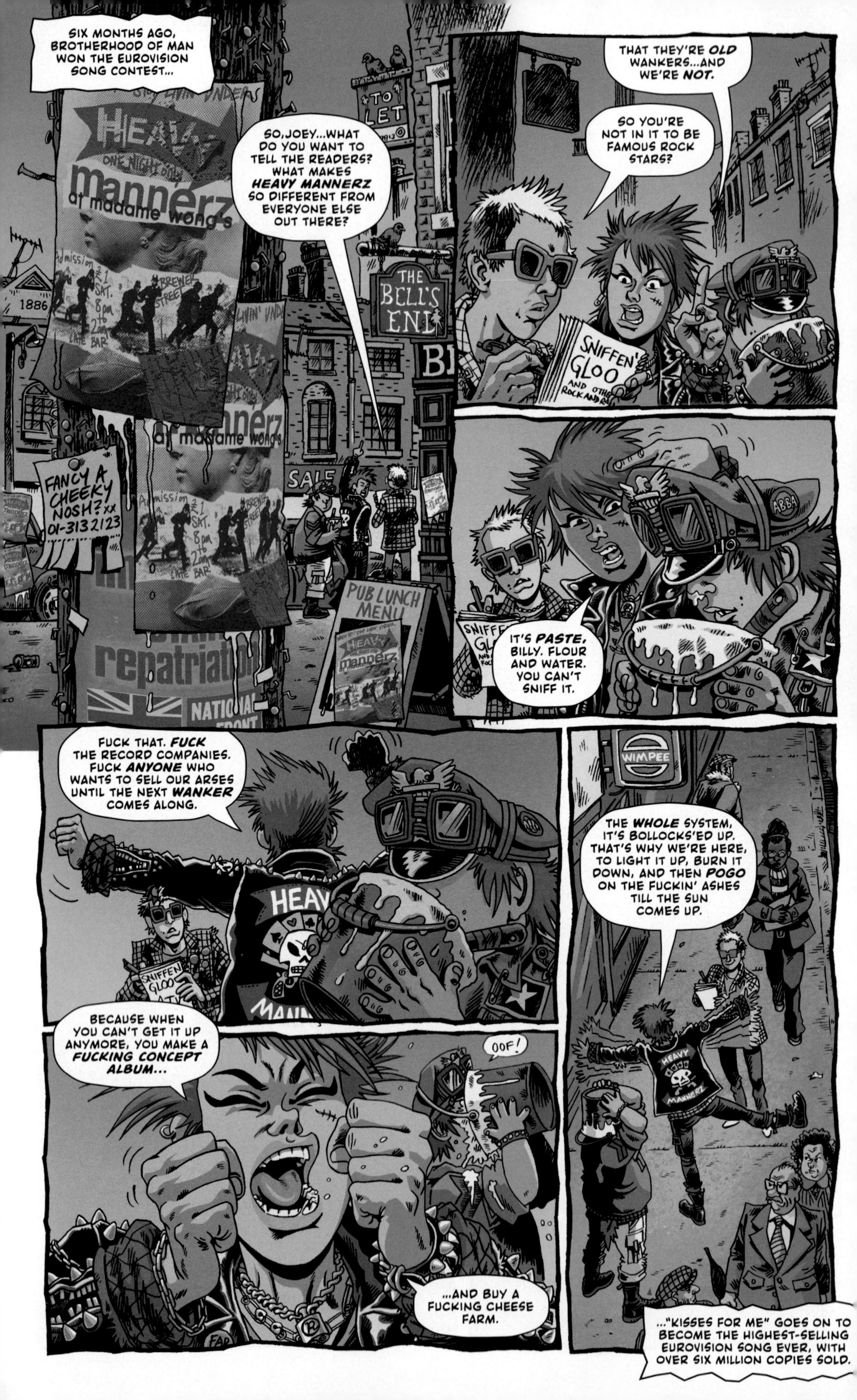
SIX MONTHS AGO, BROTHERHOOD OF MAN WON THE EUROVISION SONG CONTEST...
HEAVY manner'z at madame wong's
Admission £1 SAT. 8pm to 2am LATE BAR
BREWER STREET
FANCY A CHEEKY NOSH? xx 01-313 2123
TO LET
THE BELL'S END
PUB LUNCH MENU
repatriation
NATIONAL FRONT
SO, JOEY...WHAT DO YOU WANT TO TELL THE READERS? WHAT MAKES HEAVY MANNERZ SO DIFFERENT FROM EVERYONE ELSE OUT THERE?
THAT THEY'RE OLD WANKERS...AND WE'RE NOT.
SO YOU'RE NOT IN IT TO BE FAMOUS ROCK STARS?
SNIFFEN' GLOO AND OTHER ROCK AND R...
ABBA
IT'S PASTE, BILLY. FLOUR AND WATER. YOU CAN'T SNIFF IT.
FUCK THAT. FUCK THE RECORD COMPANIES. FUCK ANYONE WHO WANTS TO SELL OUR ARSES UNTIL THE NEXT WANKER COMES ALONG.
BECAUSE WHEN YOU CAN'T GET IT UP ANYMORE, YOU MAKE A FUCKING CONCEPT ALBUM...
OOF!
...AND BUY A FUCKING CHEESE FARM.
WIMPEE
THE WHOLE SYSTEM, IT'S BOLLOCKS'ED UP. THAT'S WHY WE'RE HERE, TO LIGHT IT UP, BURN IT DOWN, AND THEN POGO ON THE FUCKIN' ASHES TILL THE SUN COMES UP.
HEAVY MANNERZ
..."KISSES FOR ME" GOES ON TO BECOME THE HIGHEST-SELLING EUROVISION SONG EVER, WITH OVER SIX MILLION COPIES SOLD.

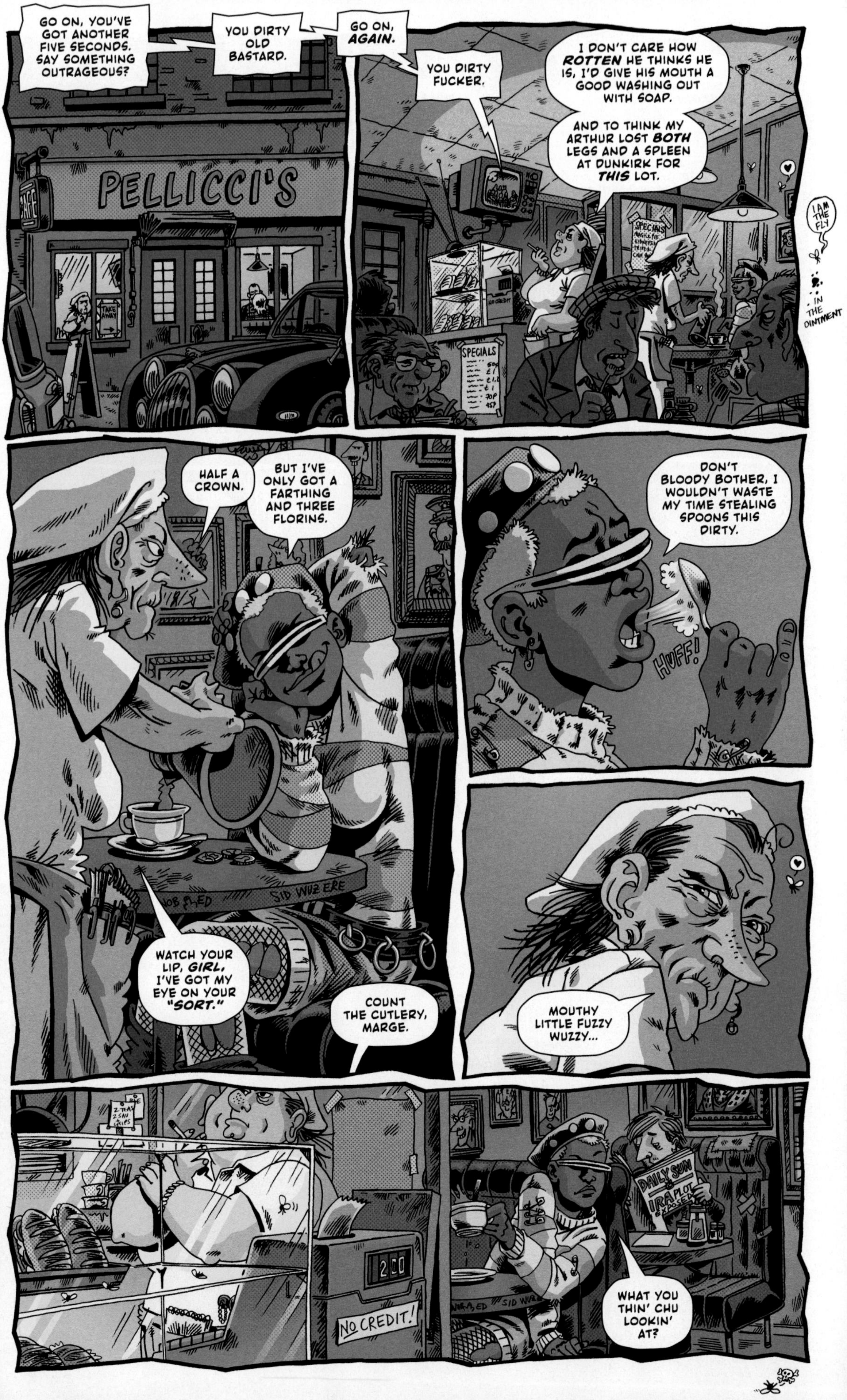
GO ON, YOU'VE GOT ANOTHER FIVE SECONDS. SAY SOMETHING OUTRAGEOUS?
YOU DIRTY OLD BASTARD.
GO ON, AGAIN.
YOU DIRTY FUCKER.
PELLICCI'S
I DON'T CARE HOW ROTTEN HE THINKS HE IS, I'D GIVE HIS MOUTH A GOOD WASHING OUT WITH SOAP.
AND TO THINK MY ARTHUR LOST BOTH LEGS AND A SPLEEN AT DUNKIRK FOR THIS LOT.
SPECIALS
I AM THE FLY
IN THE OINTMENT
HALF A CROWN.
BUT I'VE ONLY GOT A FARTHING AND THREE FLORINS.
SID WUZ ERE
WATCH YOUR LIP, GIRL, I'VE GOT MY EYE ON YOUR "SORT."
COUNT THE CUTLERY, MARGE.
DON'T BLOODY BOTHER, I WOULDN'T WASTE MY TIME STEALING SPOONS THIS DIRTY.
HUFF!
MOUTHY LITTLE FUZZY WUZZY...
NO CREDIT!
DAILY SUN
IRA PLOT EXPOSED
WHAT YOU THIN' CHU LOOKIN' AT?

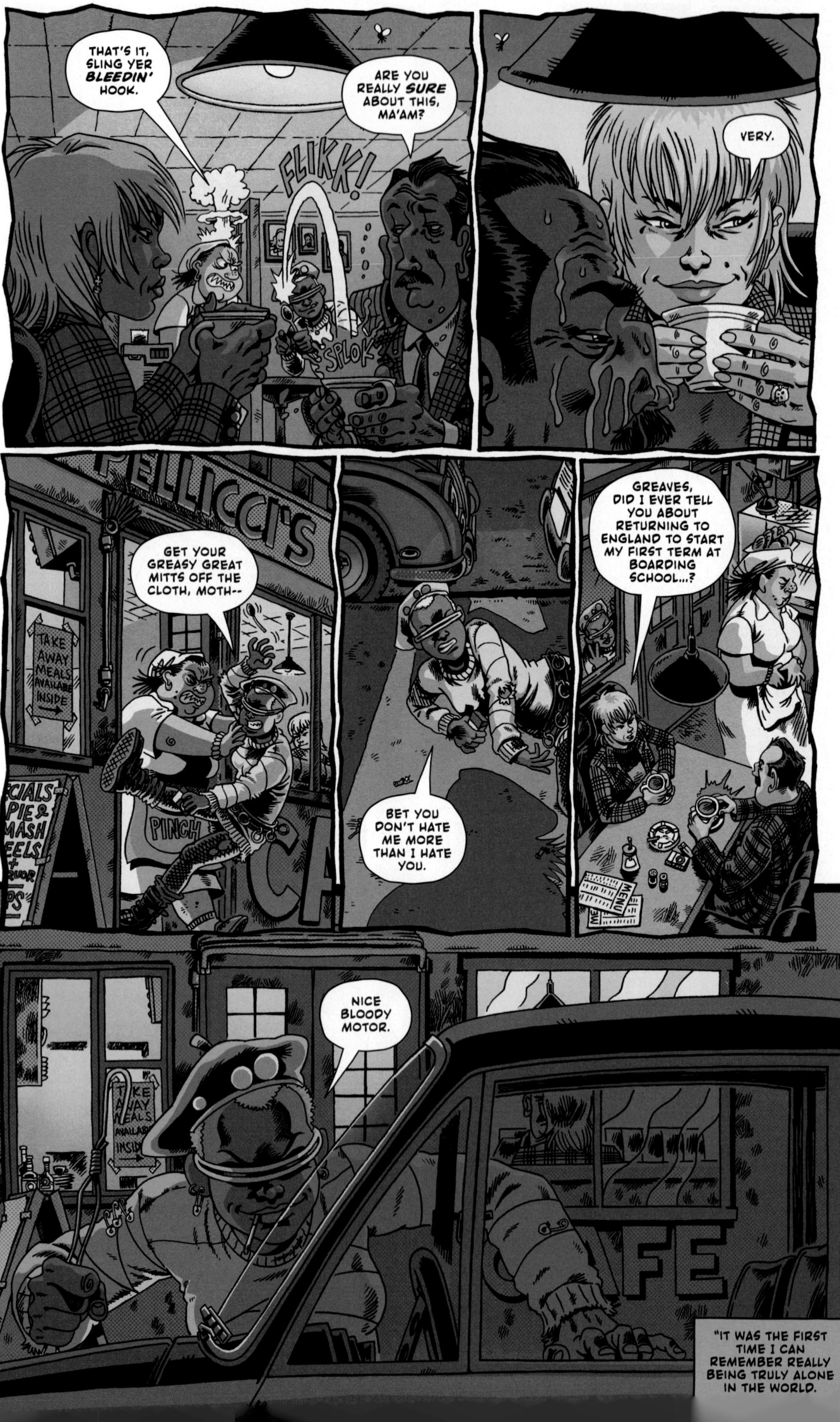
THAT'S IT, SLING YER BLEEDIN' HOOK.
ARE YOU REALLY SURE ABOUT THIS, MA'AM?
FLIKK!
SPLOK
VERY.
PELLICCI'S
TAKE AWAY MEALS AVAILABLE INSIDE
GET YOUR GREASY GREAT MITTS OFF THE CLOTH, MOTH--
PINCH
BET YOU DON'T HATE ME MORE THAN I HATE YOU.
GREAVES, DID I EVER TELL YOU ABOUT RETURNING TO ENGLAND TO START MY FIRST TERM AT BOARDING SCHOOL...?
MENU
NICE BLOODY MOTOR.
"IT WAS THE FIRST TIME I CAN REMEMBER REALLY BEING TRULY ALONE IN THE WORLD.

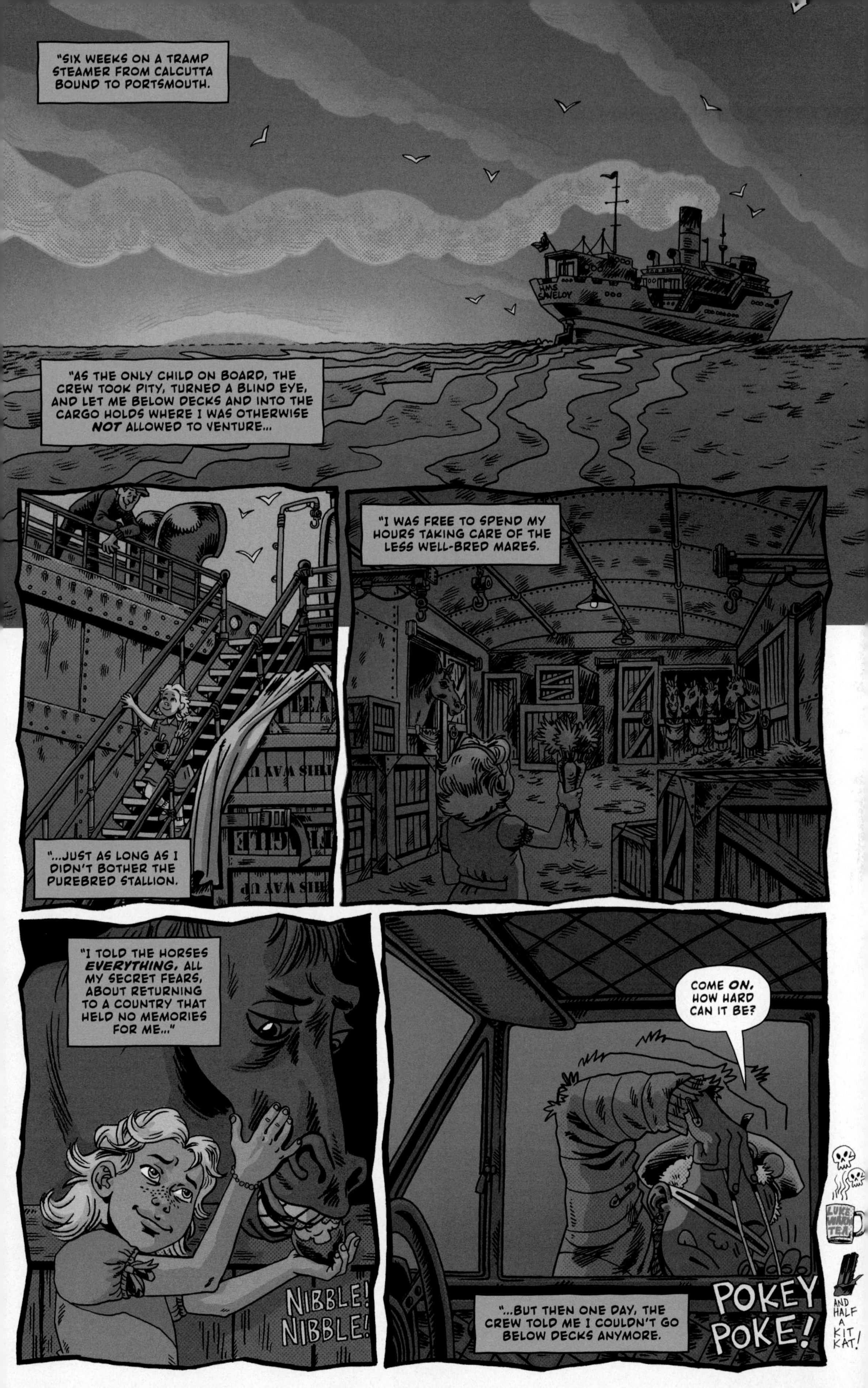
"SIX WEEKS ON A TRAMP STEAMER FROM CALCUTTA BOUND TO PORTSMOUTH.
"AS THE ONLY CHILD ON BOARD, THE CREW TOOK PITY, TURNED A BLIND EYE, AND LET ME BELOW DECKS AND INTO THE CARGO HOLDS WHERE I WAS OTHERWISE *NOT* ALLOWED TO VENTURE...
"...JUST AS LONG AS I DIDN'T BOTHER THE PUREBRED STALLION.
"I WAS FREE TO SPEND MY HOURS TAKING CARE OF THE LESS WELL-BRED MARES.
"I TOLD THE HORSES *EVERYTHING*, ALL MY SECRET FEARS, ABOUT RETURNING TO A COUNTRY THAT HELD NO MEMORIES FOR ME..."
NIBBLE! NIBBLE!
COME *ON*, HOW HARD CAN IT BE?
"...BUT THEN ONE DAY, THE CREW TOLD ME I COULDN'T GO BELOW DECKS ANYMORE.
POKEY POKE!
LUKE WARM TEA
AND HALF A KIT KAT!

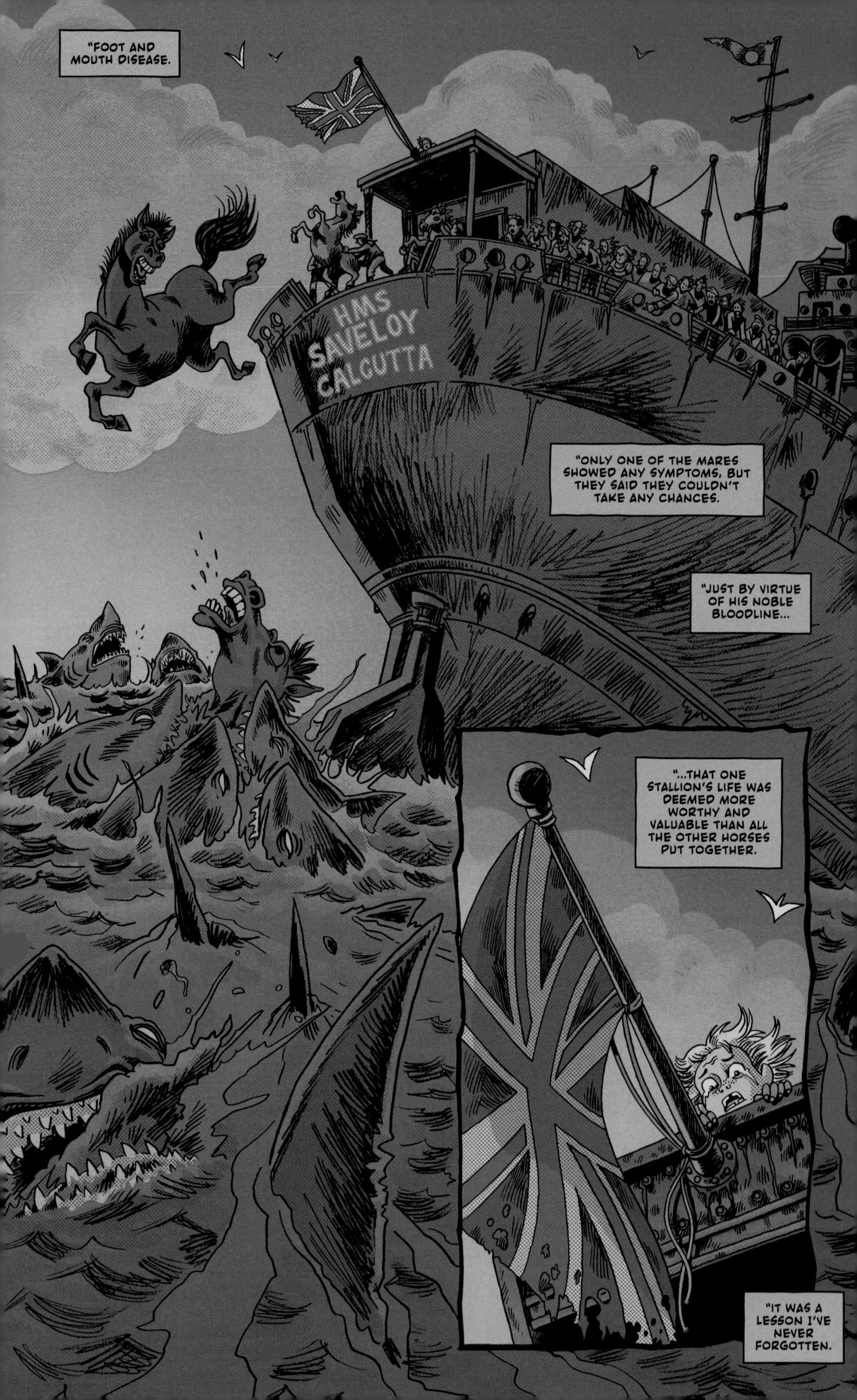
"FOOT AND MOUTH DISEASE.
HMS SAVELOY CALCUTTA
"ONLY ONE OF THE MARES SHOWED ANY SYMPTOMS, BUT THEY SAID THEY COULDN'T TAKE ANY CHANCES.
"JUST BY VIRTUE OF HIS NOBLE BLOODLINE...
"...THAT ONE STALLION'S LIFE WAS DEEMED MORE WORTHY AND VALUABLE THAN ALL THE OTHER HORSES PUT TOGETHER.
"IT WAS A LESSON I'VE NEVER FORGOTTEN.

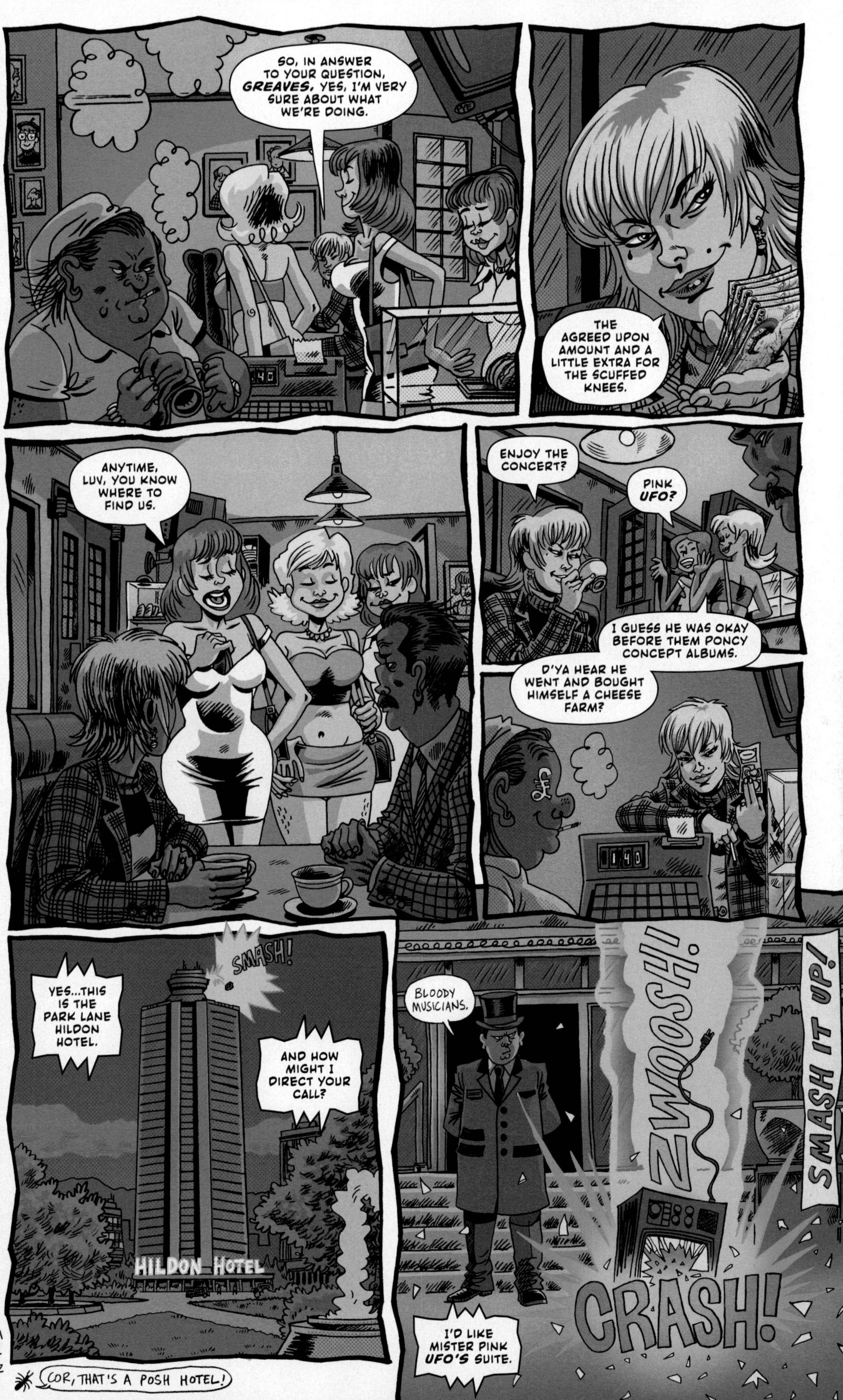

SO, IN ANSWER TO YOUR QUESTION, GREAVES, YES, I'M VERY SURE ABOUT WHAT WE'RE DOING.
140
THE AGREED UPON AMOUNT AND A LITTLE EXTRA FOR THE SCUFFED KNEES.
ANYTIME, LUV, YOU KNOW WHERE TO FIND US.
ENJOY THE CONCERT?
PINK UFO?
I GUESS HE WAS OKAY BEFORE THEM PONCY CONCEPT ALBUMS.
D'YA HEAR HE WENT AND BOUGHT HIMSELF A CHEESE FARM?
140
SMASH!
YES...THIS IS THE PARK LANE HILDON HOTEL.
AND HOW MIGHT I DIRECT YOUR CALL?
HILDON HOTEL
BLOODY MUSICIANS.
ZWOOSH!
SMASH IT UP!
CRASH!
I'D LIKE MISTER PINK UFO'S SUITE.
COR, THAT'S A POSH HOTEL!

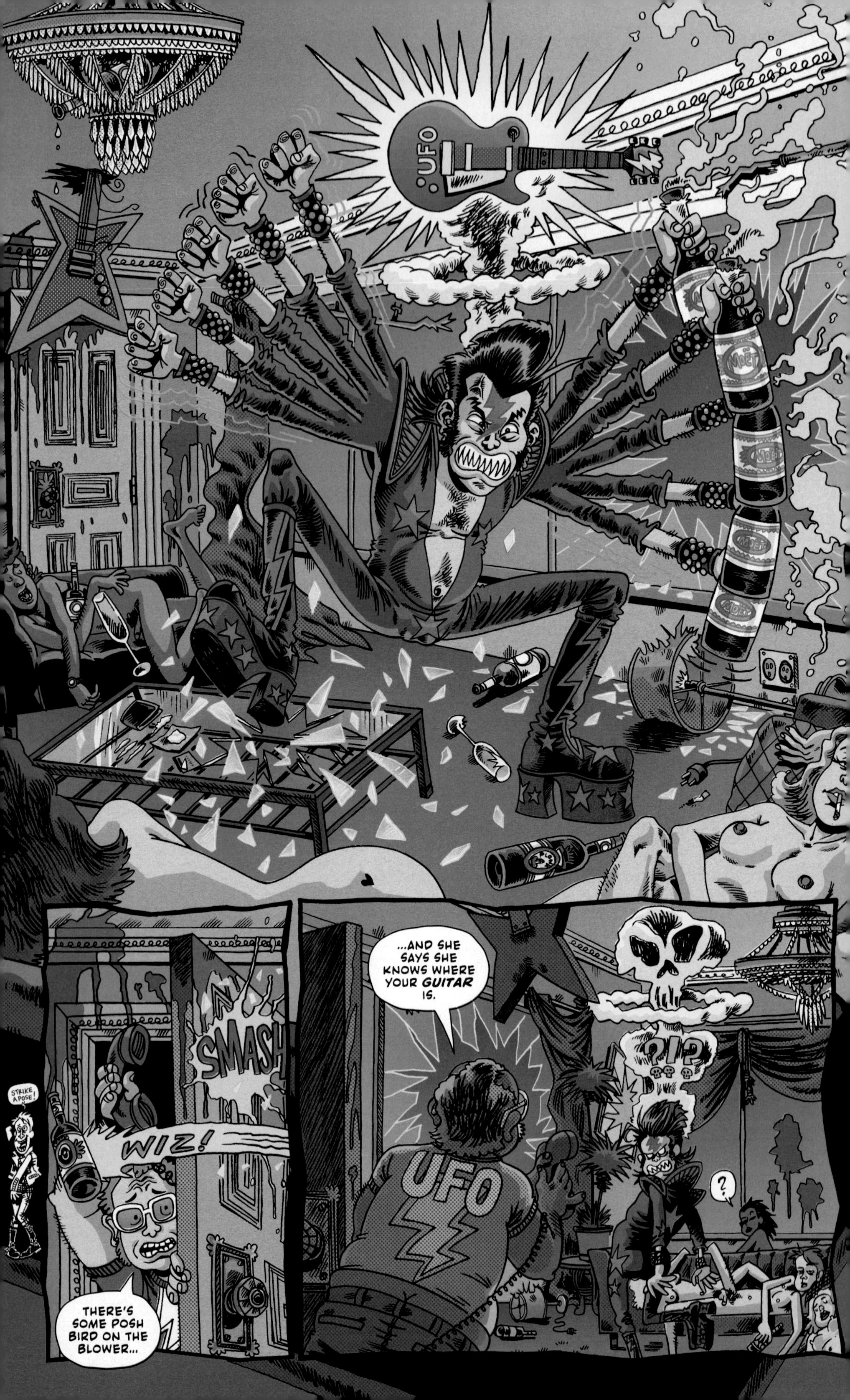
UFO
MOËT
SMASH
WIZ!
STRIKE A POSE!
THERE'S SOME POSH BIRD ON THE BLOWER...
...AND SHE SAYS SHE KNOWS WHERE YOUR GUITAR IS.
UFO
?!?
?

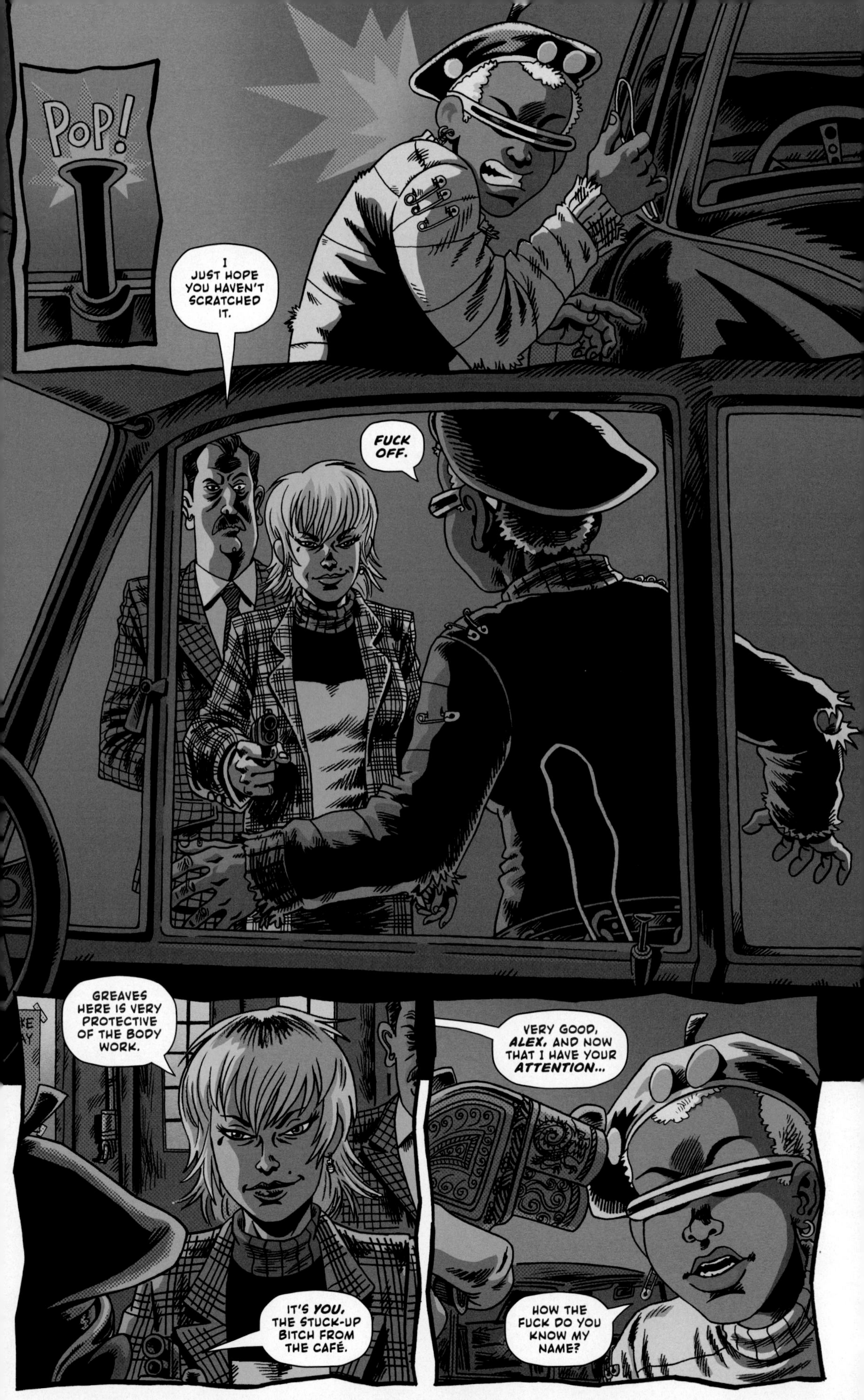
POP!
I JUST HOPE YOU HAVEN'T SCRATCHED IT.
FUCK OFF.
GREAVES HERE IS VERY PROTECTIVE OF THE BODY WORK.
IT'S YOU. THE STUCK-UP BITCH FROM THE CAFÉ.
VERY GOOD, ALEX. AND NOW THAT I HAVE YOUR ATTENTION...
HOW THE FUCK DO YOU KNOW MY NAME?

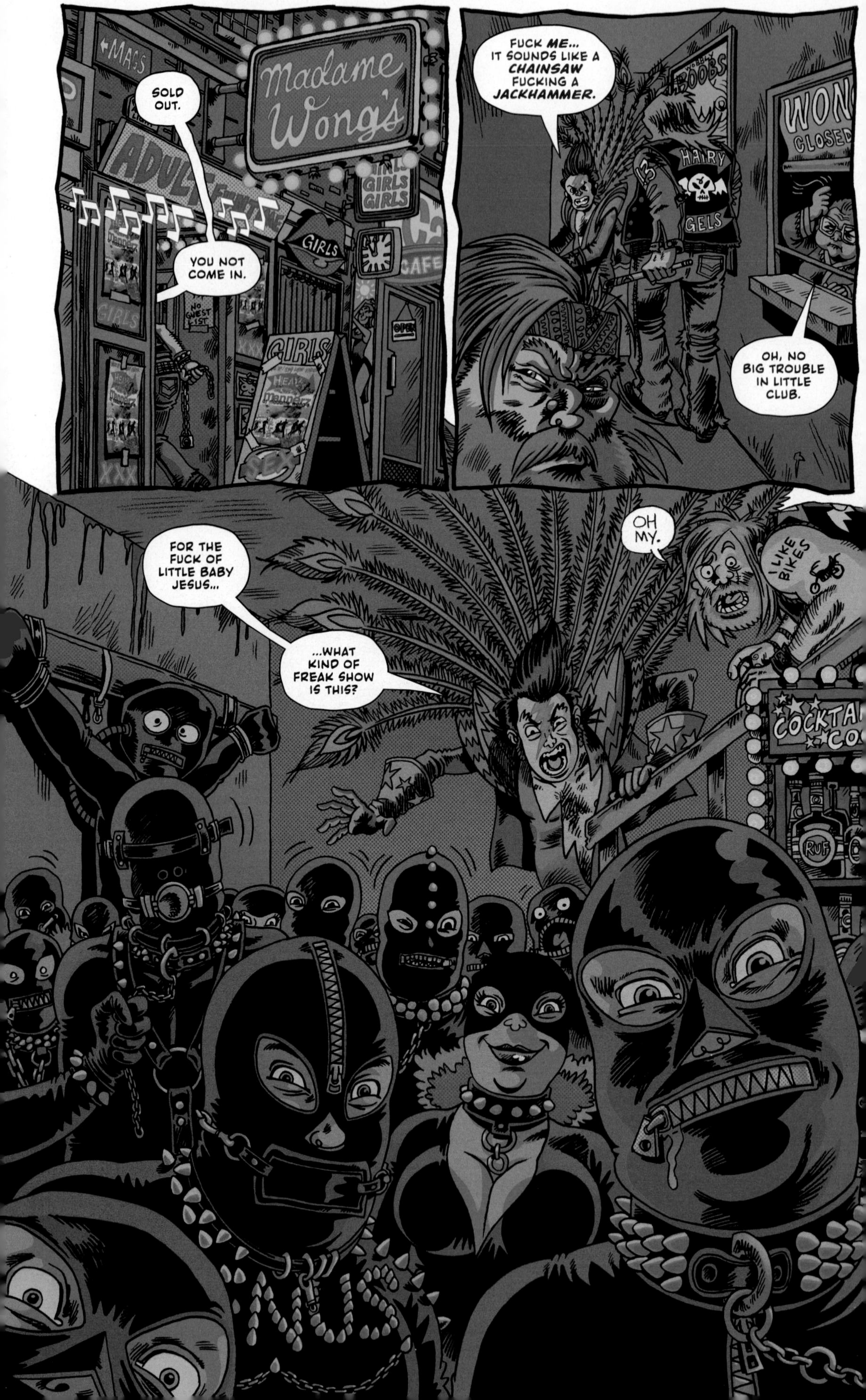
MAGS
Madame Wong's
SOLD OUT.
ADULT
GIRLS GIRLS GIRLS
YOU NOT COME IN.
NO GUEST LIST
GIRLS
CAFE
OPEN
FUCK ME... IT SOUNDS LIKE A CHAINSAW FUCKING A JACKHAMMER.
CLOSED
OH, NO BIG TROUBLE IN LITTLE CLUB.
FOR THE FUCK OF LITTLE BABY JESUS...
...WHAT KIND OF FREAK SHOW IS THIS?
OH MY.
I LIKE BIKES

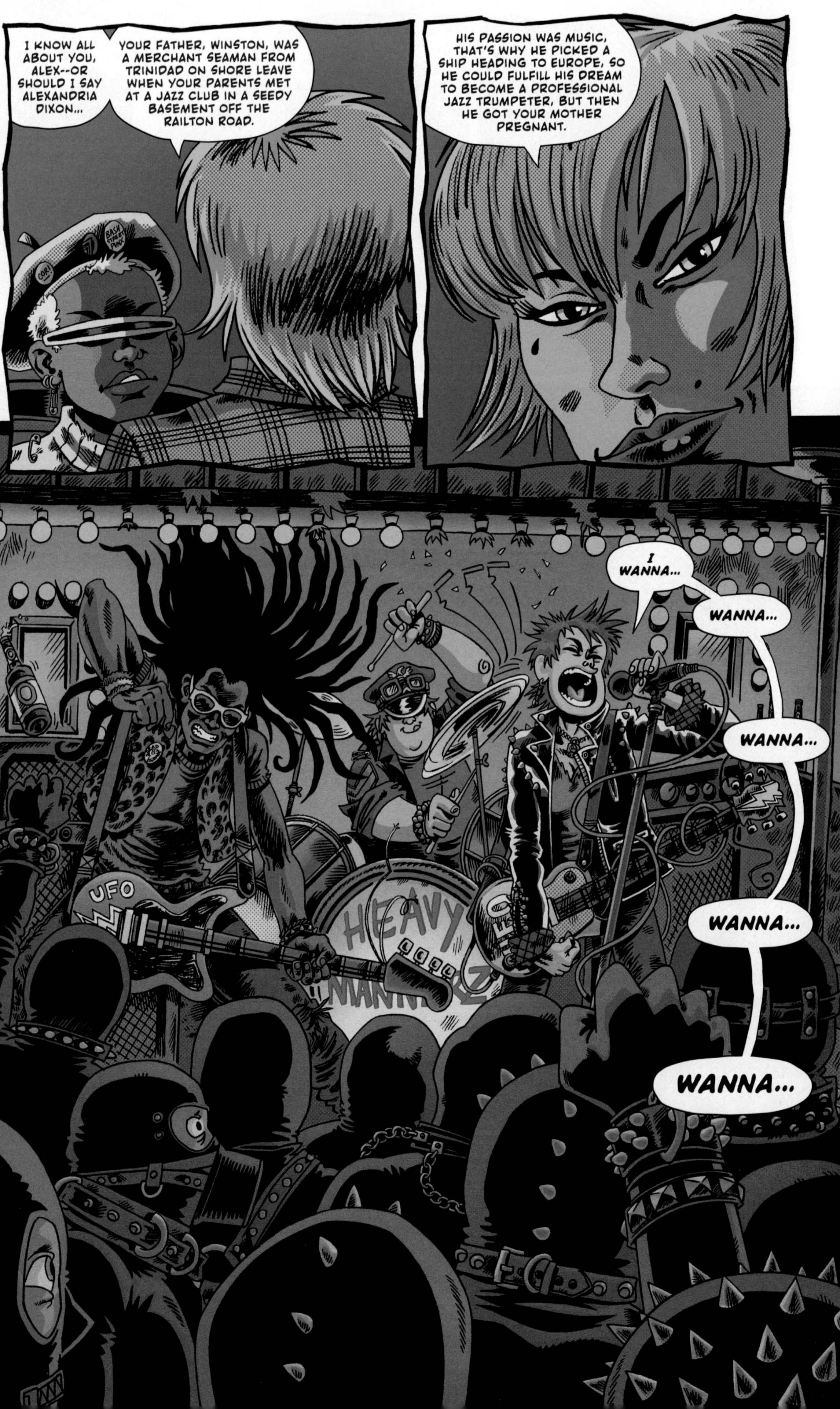
I KNOW ALL ABOUT YOU, ALEX--OR SHOULD I SAY ALEXANDRIA DIXON...
YOUR FATHER, WINSTON, WAS A MERCHANT SEAMAN FROM TRINIDAD ON SHORE LEAVE WHEN YOUR PARENTS MET AT A JAZZ CLUB IN A SEEDY BASEMENT OFF THE RAILTON ROAD.
BASH STREET PUNKS
COR!
HIS PASSION WAS MUSIC, THAT'S WHY HE PICKED A SHIP HEADING TO EUROPE, SO HE COULD FULFILL HIS DREAM TO BECOME A PROFESSIONAL JAZZ TRUMPETER, BUT THEN HE GOT YOUR MOTHER PREGNANT.
I WANNA...
WANNA...
WANNA...
WANNA...
WANNA...
UFO
HEAVY

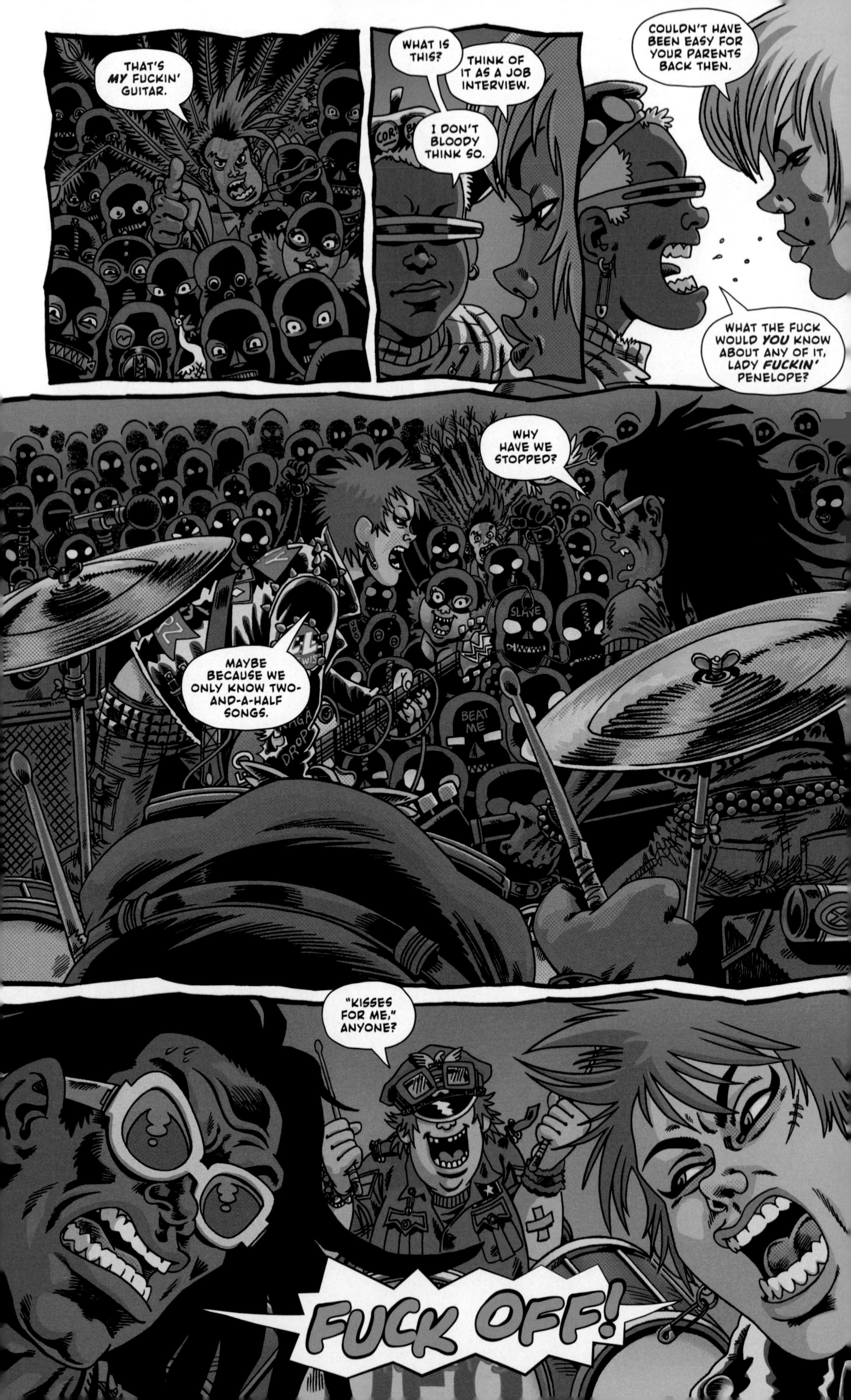
THAT'S *MY* FUCKIN' GUITAR.
WHAT IS THIS?
THINK OF IT AS A JOB INTERVIEW.
I DON'T BLOODY THINK SO.
COULDN'T HAVE BEEN EASY FOR YOUR PARENTS BACK THEN.
WHAT THE FUCK WOULD *YOU* KNOW ABOUT ANY OF IT, LADY *FUCKIN'* PENELOPE?
WHY HAVE WE STOPPED?
MAYBE BECAUSE WE ONLY KNOW TWO-AND-A-HALF SONGS.
SLAVE
BEAT ME
"KISSES FOR ME," ANYONE?
FUCK OFF!

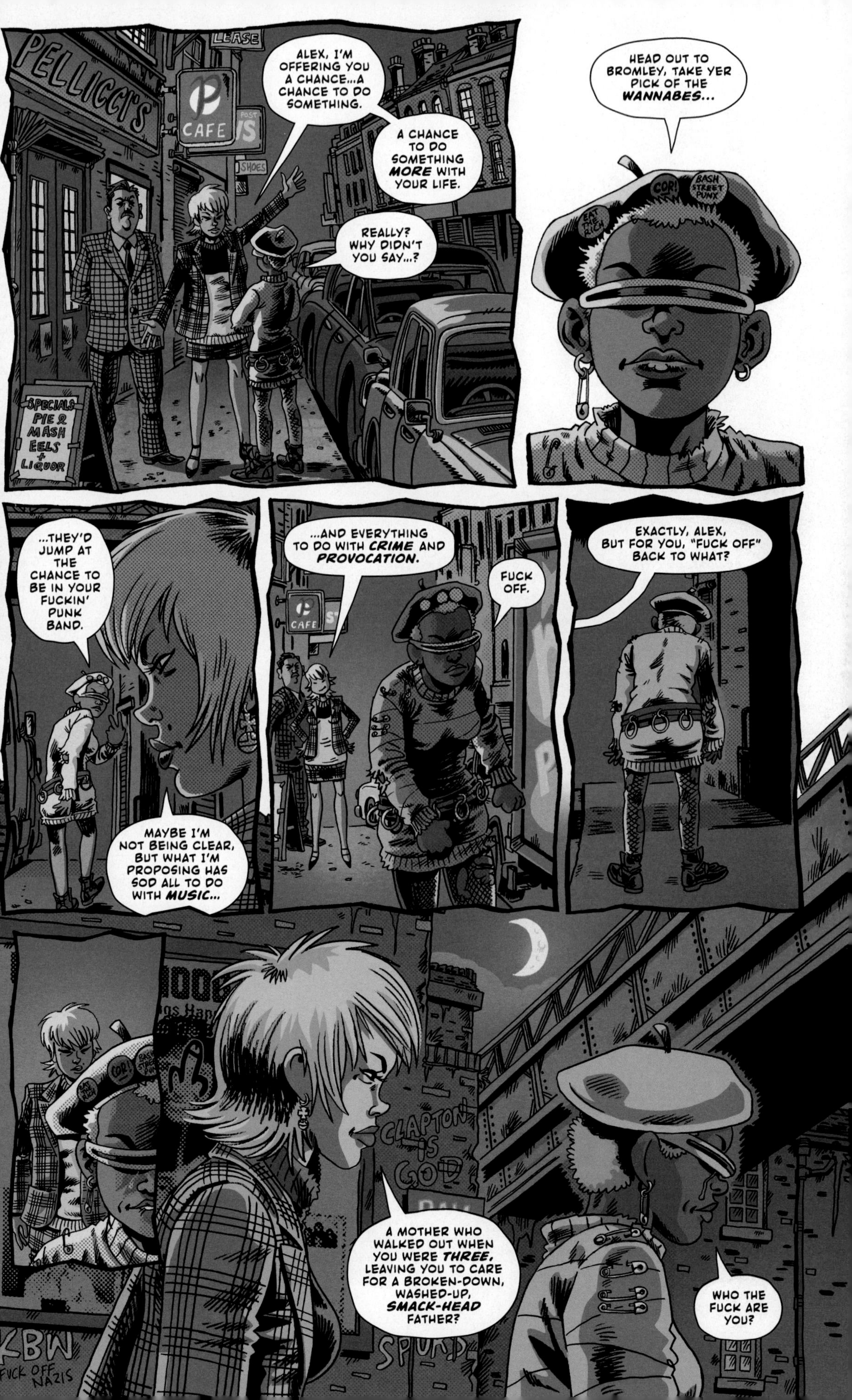
PELLICCI'S
LEASE
CAFE
SHOES
SPECIALS PIE & MASH EELS + LIQUOR
ALEX, I'M OFFERING YOU A CHANCE...A CHANCE TO DO SOMETHING.
A CHANCE TO DO SOMETHING *MORE* WITH YOUR LIFE.
REALLY? WHY DIDN'T YOU SAY...?
HEAD OUT TO BROMLEY, TAKE YER PICK OF THE *WANNABES*...
COR!
BASH STREET PUNX
EAT THE RICH
...THEY'D JUMP AT THE CHANCE TO BE IN YOUR FUCKIN' PUNK BAND.
MAYBE I'M NOT BEING CLEAR, BUT WHAT I'M PROPOSING HAS SOD ALL TO DO WITH *MUSIC*...
...AND EVERYTHING TO DO WITH *CRIME* AND *PROVOCATION.*
CAFE
FUCK OFF.
EXACTLY, ALEX, BUT FOR YOU, "FUCK OFF" BACK TO WHAT?
CLAPTON IS GOD
A MOTHER WHO WALKED OUT WHEN YOU WERE *THREE,* LEAVING YOU TO CARE FOR A BROKEN-DOWN, WASHED-UP, *SMACK-HEAD* FATHER?
WHO THE FUCK ARE YOU?
KBW
FUCK OFF NAZIS

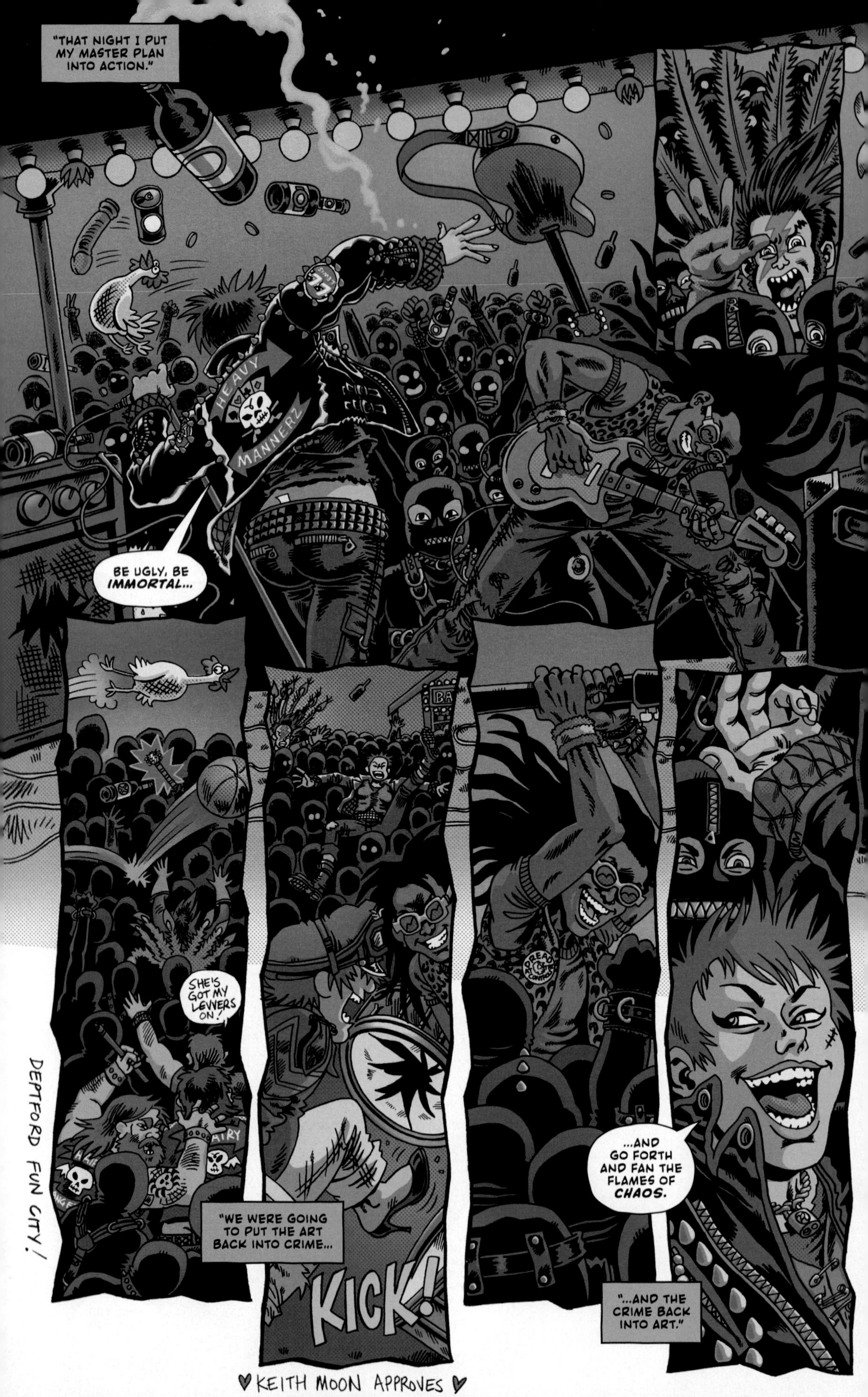
"THAT NIGHT I PUT MY MASTER PLAN INTO ACTION."
HEAVY MANNERZ
BE UGLY, BE *IMMORTAL*...
SHE'S GOT MY LEVVERS ON!
"WE WERE GOING TO PUT THE ART BACK INTO CRIME...
KICK!
...AND GO FORTH AND FAN THE FLAMES OF *CHAOS.*
"...AND THE CRIME BACK INTO ART."

DEPTFORD FUN CITY!

♥ KEITH MOON APPROVES ♥

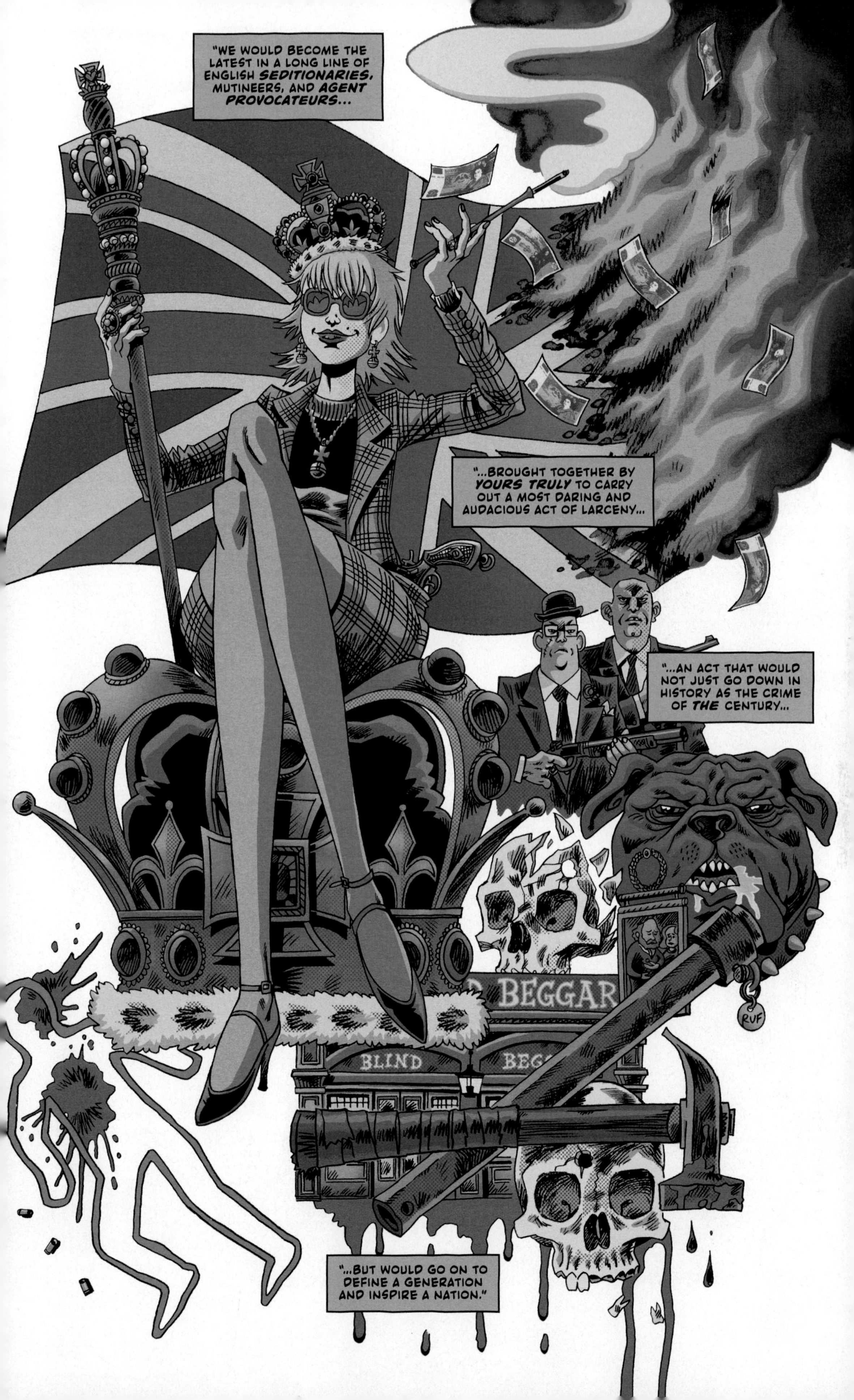
"WE WOULD BECOME THE LATEST IN A LONG LINE OF ENGLISH SEDITIONARIES, MUTINEERS, AND AGENT PROVOCATEURS...
"...BROUGHT TOGETHER BY YOURS TRULY TO CARRY OUT A MOST DARING AND AUDACIOUS ACT OF LARCENY...
"...AN ACT THAT WOULD NOT JUST GO DOWN IN HISTORY AS THE CRIME OF THE CENTURY...
D BEGGAR
BLIND
BEGG
RUF
"...BUT WOULD GO ON TO DEFINE A GENERATION AND INSPIRE A NATION."

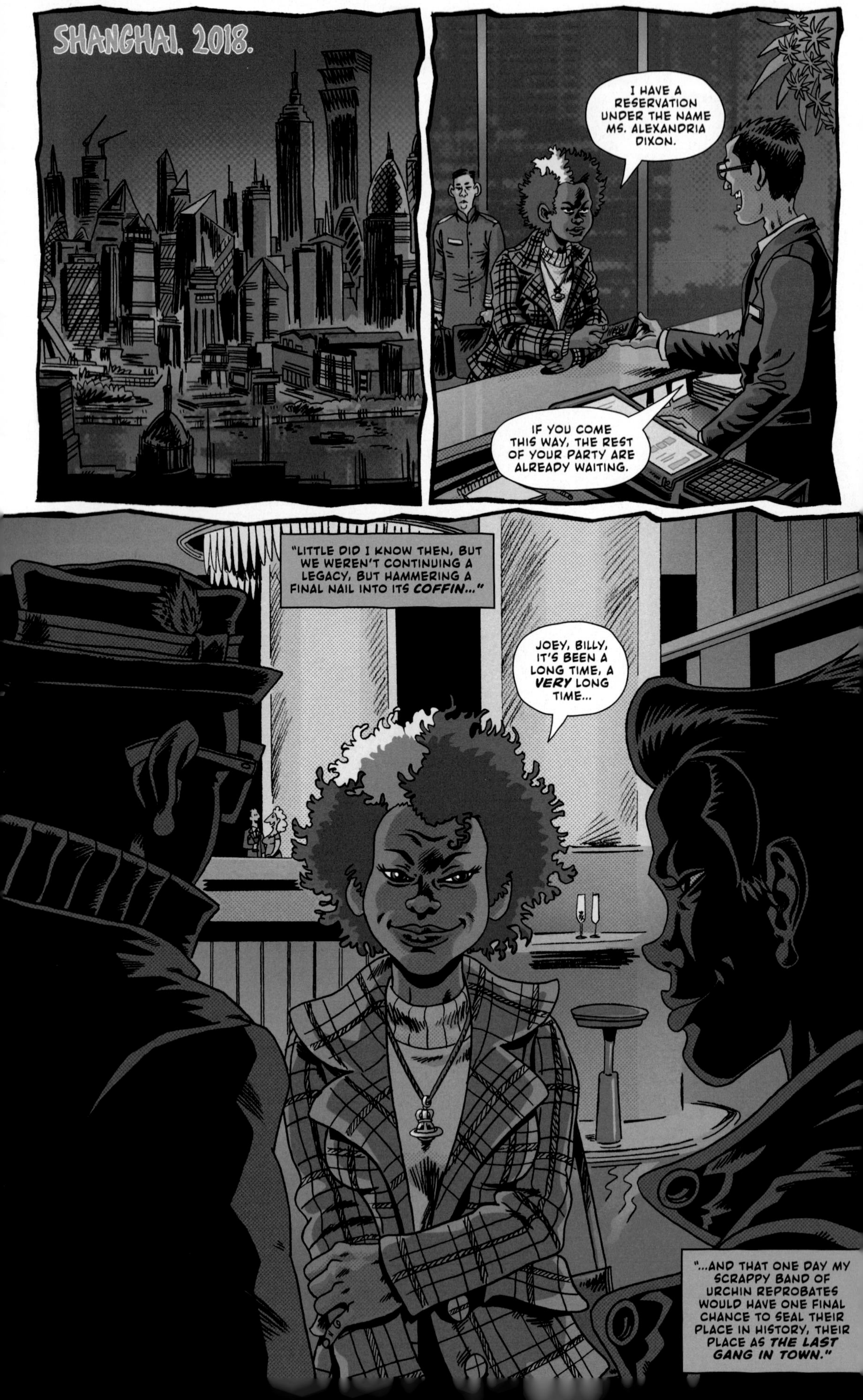
SHANGHAI, 2018.
I HAVE A RESERVATION UNDER THE NAME MS. ALEXANDRIA DIXON.
IF YOU COME THIS WAY, THE REST OF YOUR PARTY ARE ALREADY WAITING.
"LITTLE DID I KNOW THEN, BUT WE WEREN'T CONTINUING A LEGACY, BUT HAMMERING A FINAL NAIL INTO ITS *COFFIN...*"
JOEY, BILLY, IT'S BEEN A LONG TIME, A *VERY* LONG TIME...
"...AND THAT ONE DAY MY SCRAPPY BAND OF URCHIN REPROBATES WOULD HAVE ONE FINAL CHANCE TO SEAL THEIR PLACE IN HISTORY, THEIR PLACE AS *THE LAST GANG IN TOWN.*"

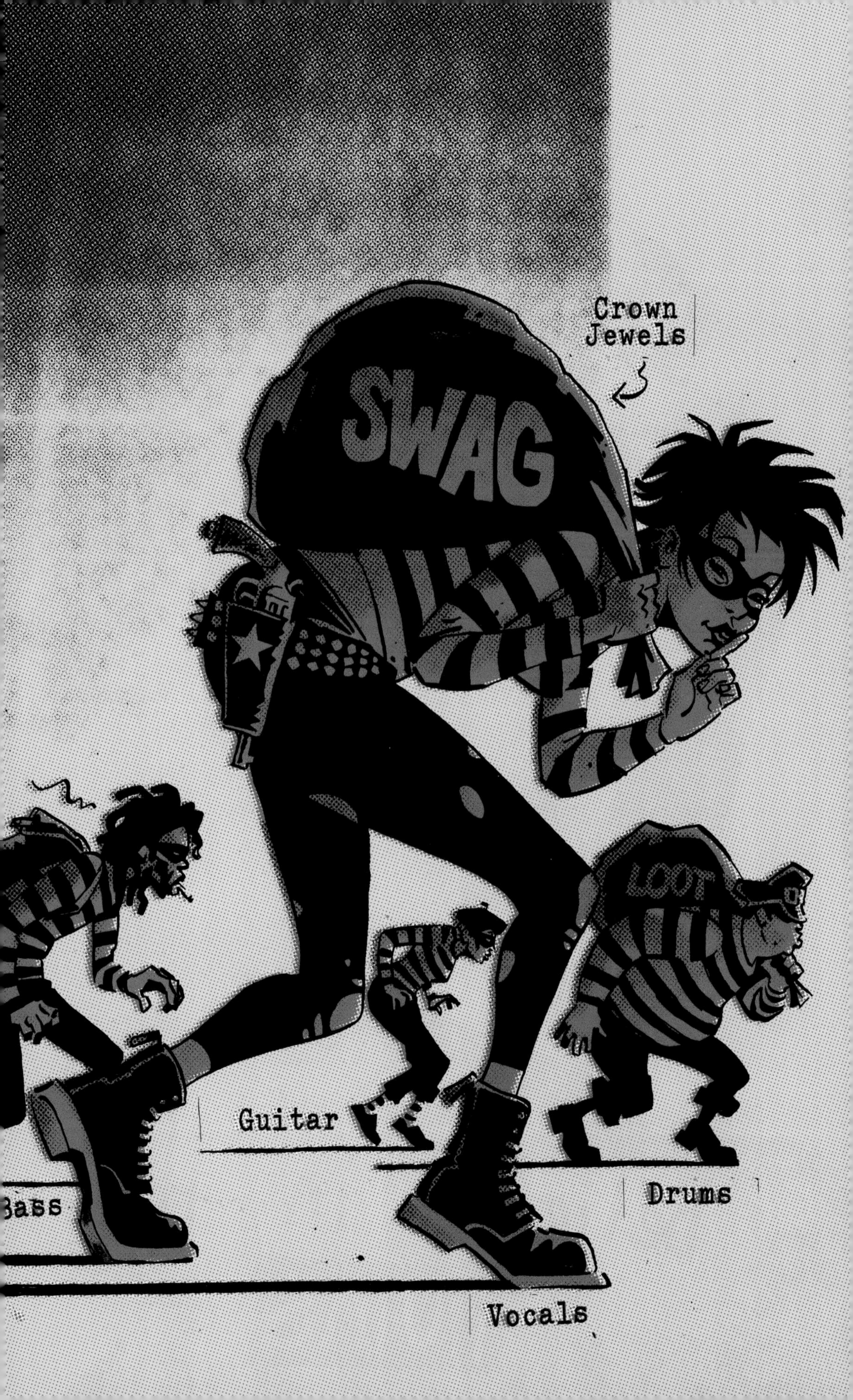
Crown Jewels
SWAG
LOOT
Guitar
Bass
Drums
Vocals

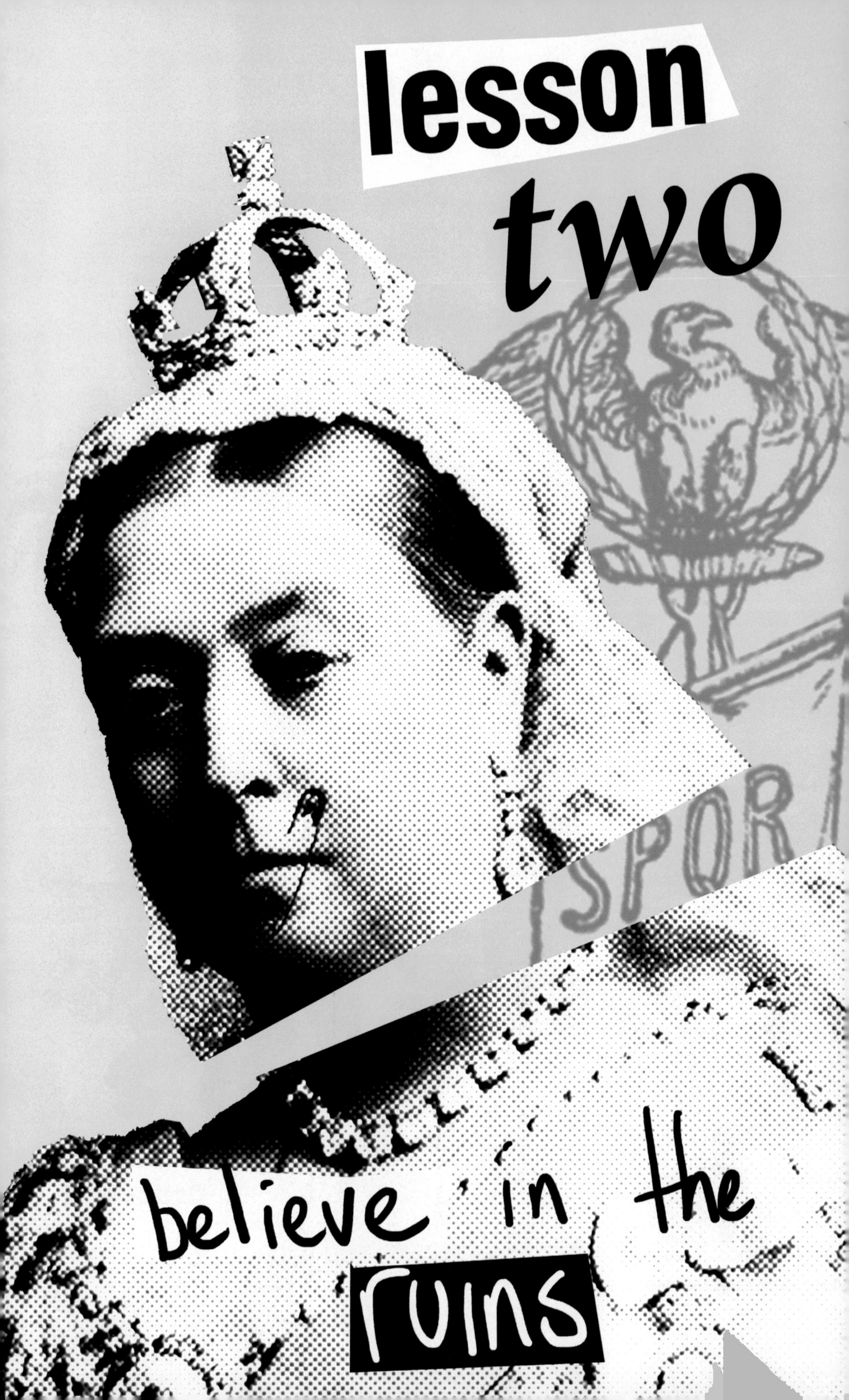
lesson
two
believe in the
ruins

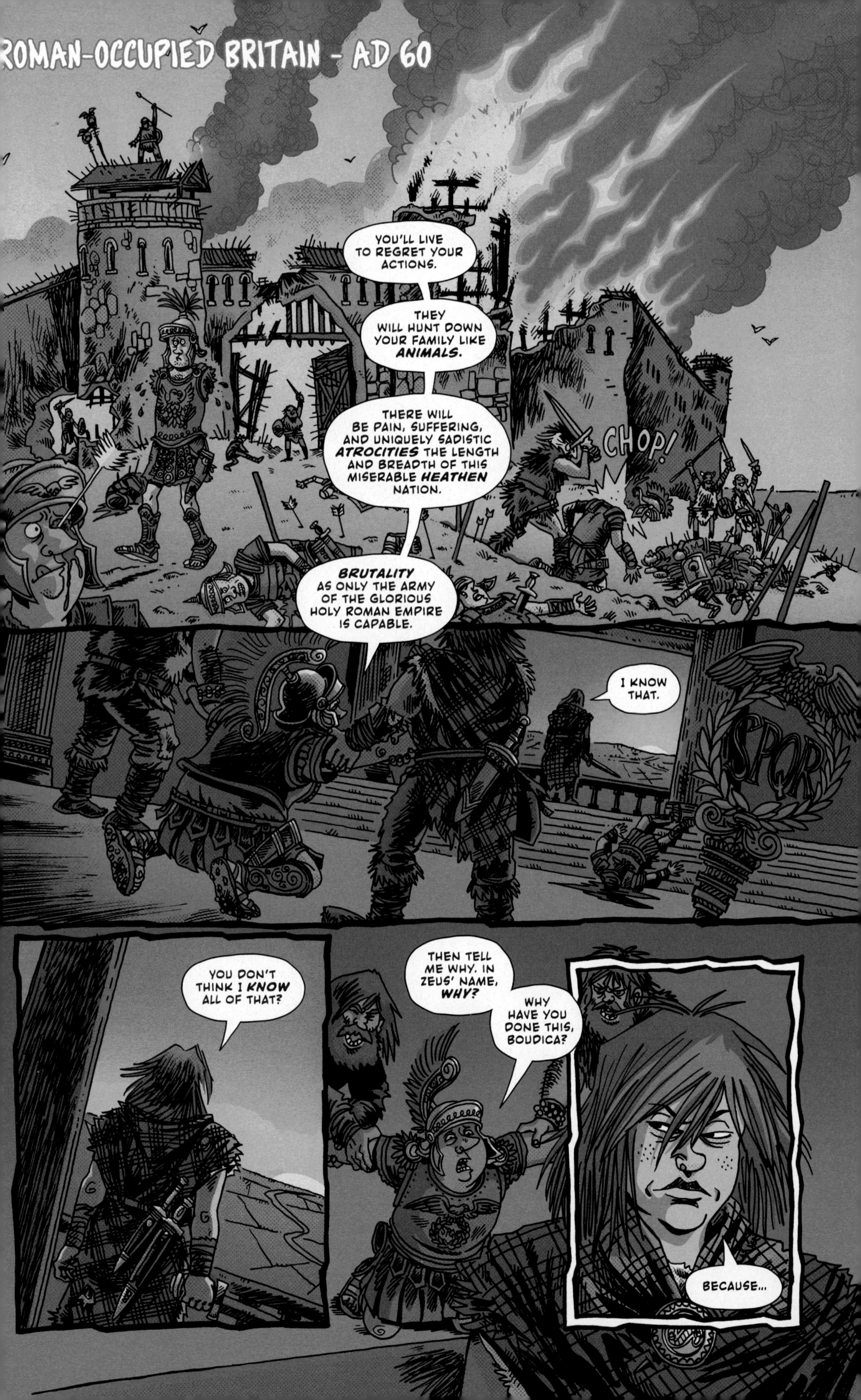
ROMAN-OCCUPIED BRITAIN - AD 60
YOU'LL LIVE TO REGRET YOUR ACTIONS.
THEY WILL HUNT DOWN YOUR FAMILY LIKE ANIMALS.
THERE WILL BE PAIN, SUFFERING, AND UNIQUELY SADISTIC ATROCITIES THE LENGTH AND BREADTH OF THIS MISERABLE HEATHEN NATION.
CHOP!
BRUTALITY AS ONLY THE ARMY OF THE GLORIOUS HOLY ROMAN EMPIRE IS CAPABLE.
I KNOW THAT.
SPQR
YOU DON'T THINK I KNOW ALL OF THAT?
THEN TELL ME WHY. IN ZEUS' NAME, WHY?
WHY HAVE YOU DONE THIS, BOUDICA?
BECAUSE...

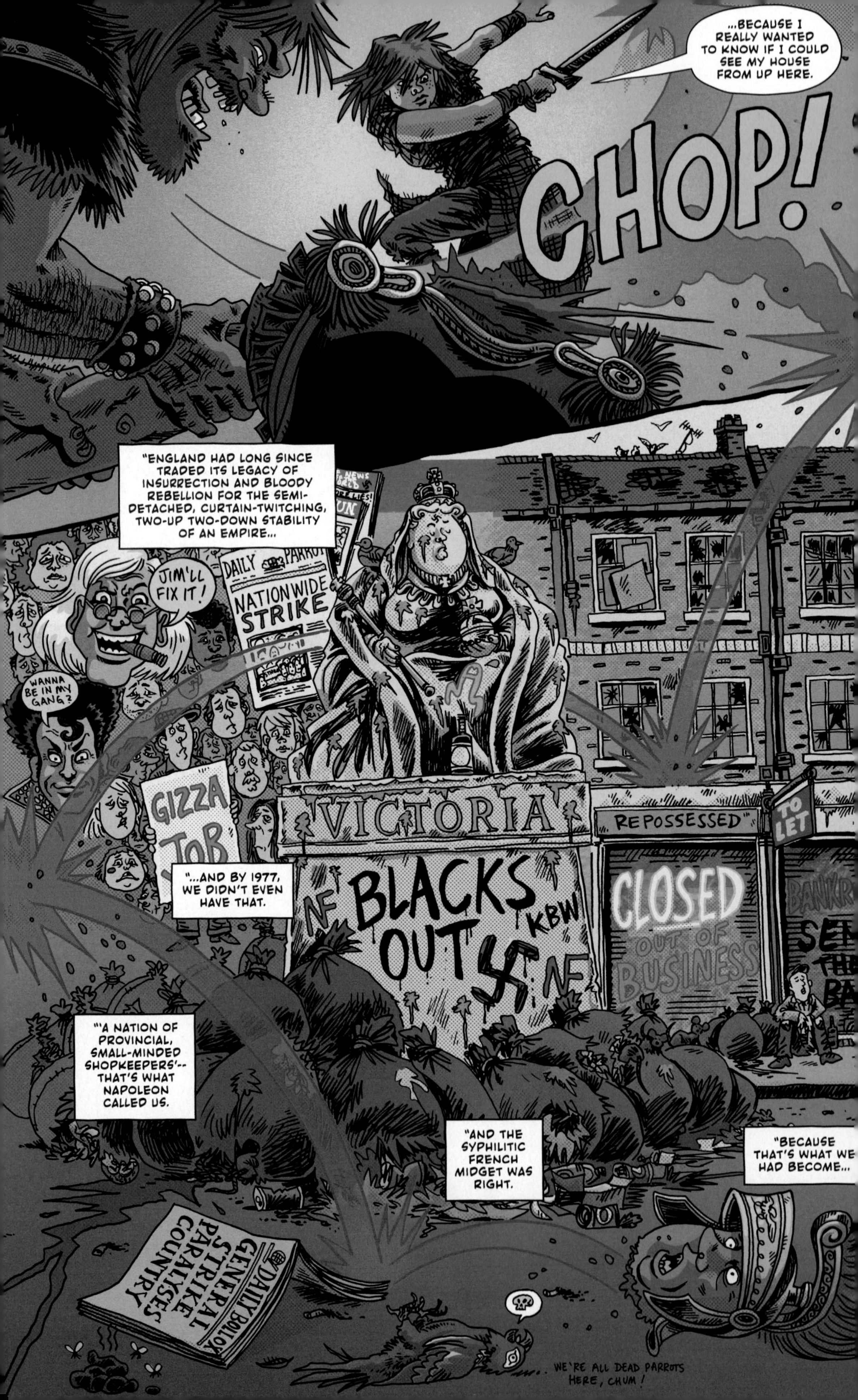
...BECAUSE I REALLY WANTED TO KNOW IF I COULD SEE MY HOUSE FROM UP HERE.
CHOP!
"ENGLAND HAD LONG SINCE TRADED ITS LEGACY OF INSURRECTION AND BLOODY REBELLION FOR THE SEMI-DETACHED, CURTAIN-TWITCHING, TWO-UP TWO-DOWN STABILITY OF AN EMPIRE...
JIM'LL FIX IT!
DAILY PARROT
NATION WIDE STRIKE
WANNA BE IN MY GANG?
GIZZA JOB
VICTORIA
BLACKS OUT
NF
KBW
NF
REPOSSESSED
TO LET
CLOSED
OUT OF BUSINESS
"...AND BY 1977, WE DIDN'T EVEN HAVE THAT.
"'A NATION OF PROVINCIAL, SMALL-MINDED SHOPKEEPERS'-- THAT'S WHAT NAPOLEON CALLED US.
"AND THE SYPHILITIC FRENCH MIDGET WAS RIGHT.
"BECAUSE THAT'S WHAT WE HAD BECOME...
DAILY BOLLOX
GENERAL STRIKE PARALYSES COUNTRY
WE'RE ALL DEAD PARROTS HERE, CHUM!

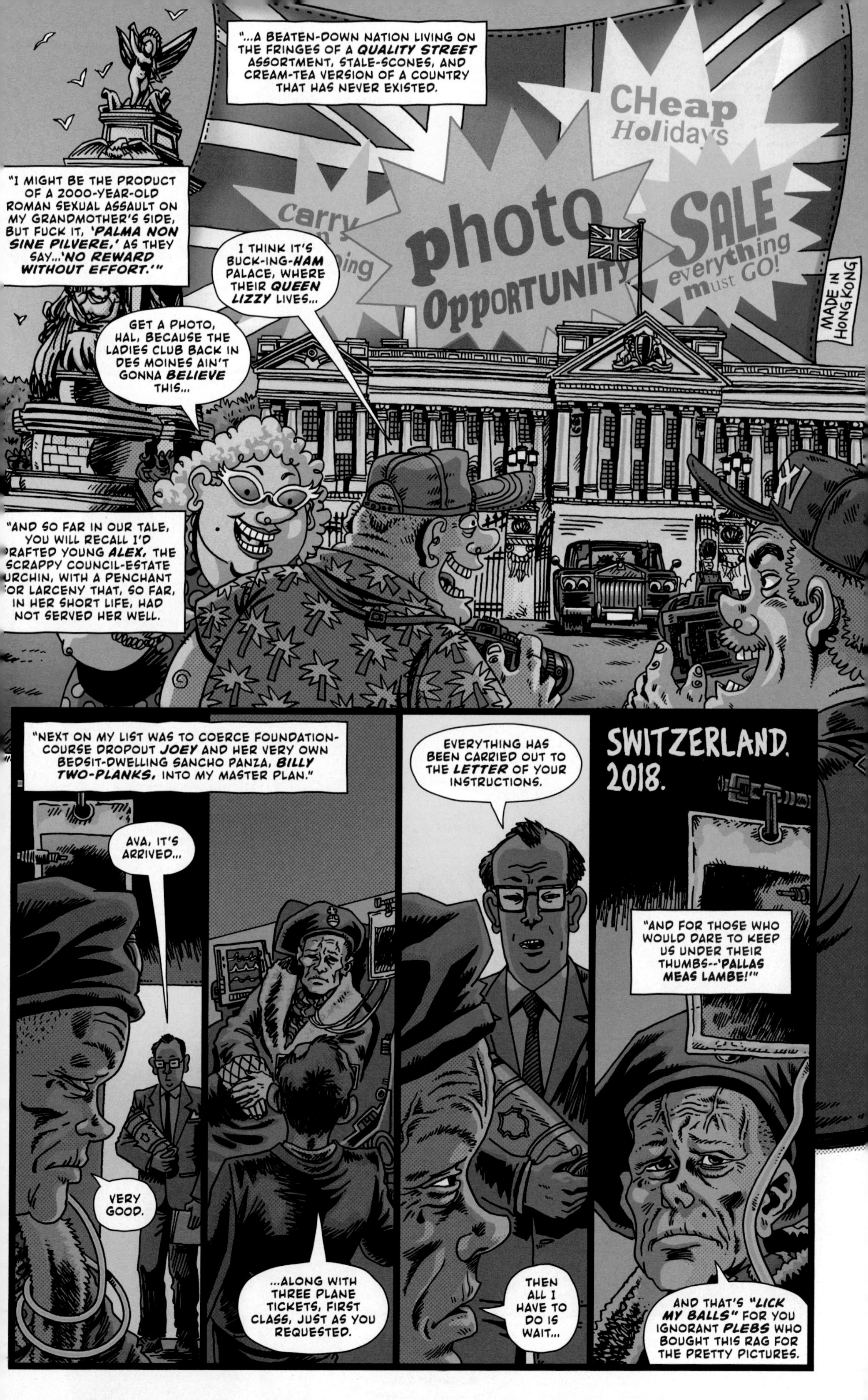
"...A BEATEN-DOWN NATION LIVING ON THE FRINGES OF A QUALITY STREET ASSORTMENT, STALE-SCONES, AND CREAM-TEA VERSION OF A COUNTRY THAT HAS NEVER EXISTED.
CHeap Holidays
photo OppORTUNITY
SALE everything must GO!
MADE IN HONGKONG
"I MIGHT BE THE PRODUCT OF A 2000-YEAR-OLD ROMAN SEXUAL ASSAULT ON MY GRANDMOTHER'S SIDE, BUT FUCK IT, 'PALMA NON SINE PILVERE,' AS THEY SAY...'NO REWARD WITHOUT EFFORT.'"
I THINK IT'S BUCK-ING-HAM PALACE, WHERE THEIR QUEEN LIZZY LIVES...
GET A PHOTO, HAL, BECAUSE THE LADIES CLUB BACK IN DES MOINES AIN'T GONNA BELIEVE THIS...
"AND SO FAR IN OUR TALE, YOU WILL RECALL I'D RAFTED YOUNG ALEX, THE SCRAPPY COUNCIL-ESTATE URCHIN, WITH A PENCHANT OR LARCENY THAT, SO FAR, IN HER SHORT LIFE, HAD NOT SERVED HER WELL.
"NEXT ON MY LIST WAS TO COERCE FOUNDATION-COURSE DROPOUT JOEY AND HER VERY OWN BEDSIT-DWELLING SANCHO PANZA, BILLY TWO-PLANKS, INTO MY MASTER PLAN."
AVA, IT'S ARRIVED...
VERY GOOD.
...ALONG WITH THREE PLANE TICKETS, FIRST CLASS, JUST AS YOU REQUESTED.
EVERYTHING HAS BEEN CARRIED OUT TO THE LETTER OF YOUR INSTRUCTIONS.
THEN ALL I HAVE TO DO IS WAIT...
SWITZERLAND, 2018.
"AND FOR THOSE WHO WOULD DARE TO KEEP US UNDER THEIR THUMBS--'PALLAS MEAS LAMBE!'"
AND THAT'S "LICK MY BALLS" FOR YOU IGNORANT PLEBS WHO BOUGHT THIS RAG FOR THE PRETTY PICTURES.

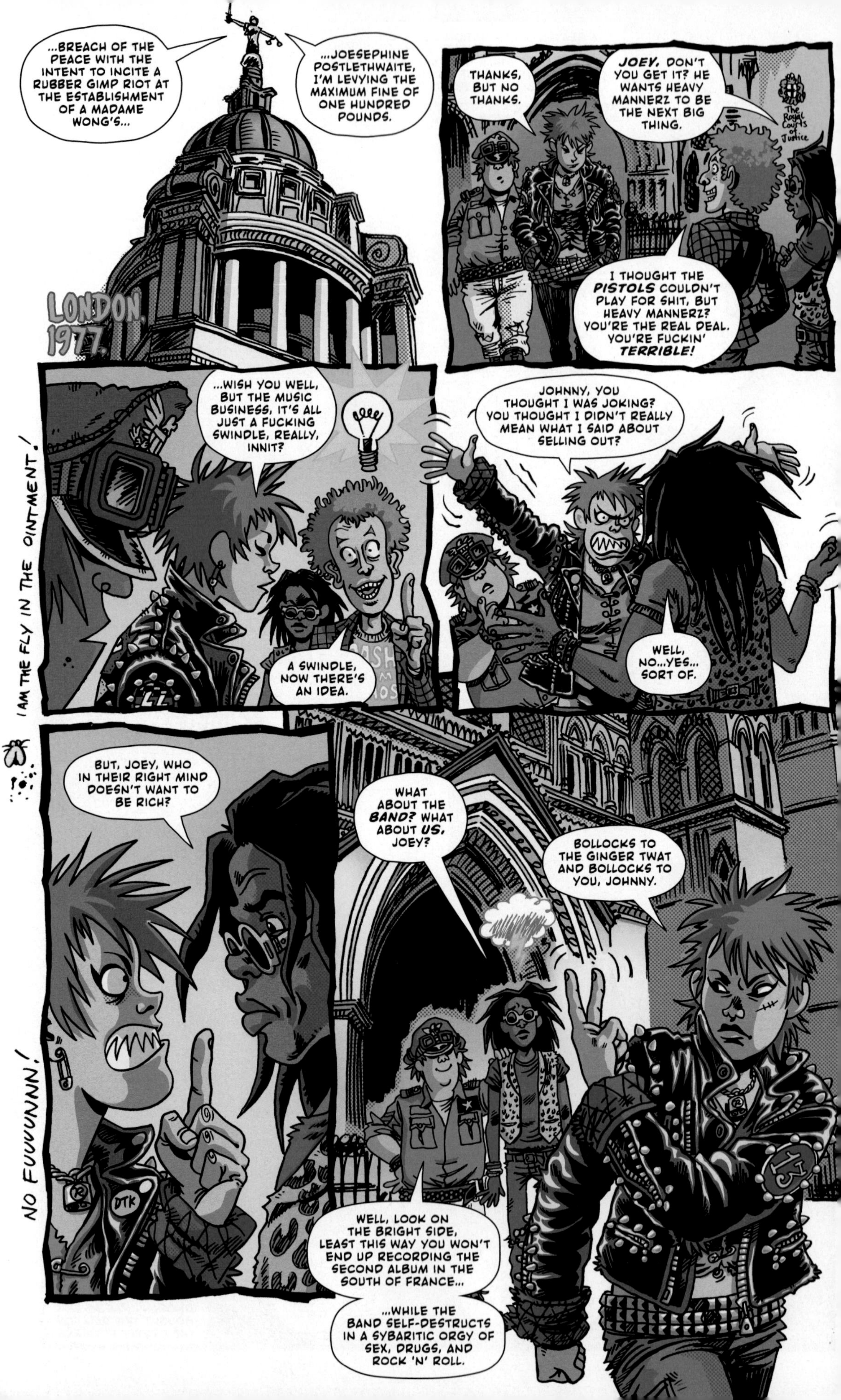
...BREACH OF THE PEACE WITH THE INTENT TO INCITE A RUBBER GIMP RIOT AT THE ESTABLISHMENT OF A MADAME WONG'S...
...JOESEPHINE POSTLETHWAITE, I'M LEVYING THE MAXIMUM FINE OF ONE HUNDRED POUNDS.
LONDON, 1977.
THANKS, BUT NO THANKS.
JOEY. DON'T YOU GET IT? HE WANTS HEAVY MANNERZ TO BE THE NEXT BIG THING.
The Royal Courts of Justice
I THOUGHT THE PISTOLS COULDN'T PLAY FOR SHIT, BUT HEAVY MANNERZ? YOU'RE THE REAL DEAL. YOU'RE FUCKIN' TERRIBLE!
I AM THE FLY IN THE OINTMENT!
...WISH YOU WELL, BUT THE MUSIC BUSINESS, IT'S ALL JUST A FUCKING SWINDLE, REALLY, INNIT?
A SWINDLE, NOW THERE'S AN IDEA.
JOHNNY, YOU THOUGHT I WAS JOKING? YOU THOUGHT I DIDN'T REALLY MEAN WHAT I SAID ABOUT SELLING OUT?
WELL, NO...YES... SORT OF.
NO FUUUNNN!
BUT, JOEY, WHO IN THEIR RIGHT MIND DOESN'T WANT TO BE RICH?
WHAT ABOUT THE BAND? WHAT ABOUT US, JOEY?
BOLLOCKS TO THE GINGER TWAT AND BOLLOCKS TO YOU, JOHNNY.
WELL, LOOK ON THE BRIGHT SIDE, LEAST THIS WAY YOU WON'T END UP RECORDING THE SECOND ALBUM IN THE SOUTH OF FRANCE...
...WHILE THE BAND SELF-DESTRUCTS IN A SYBARITIC ORGY OF SEX, DRUGS, AND ROCK 'N' ROLL.

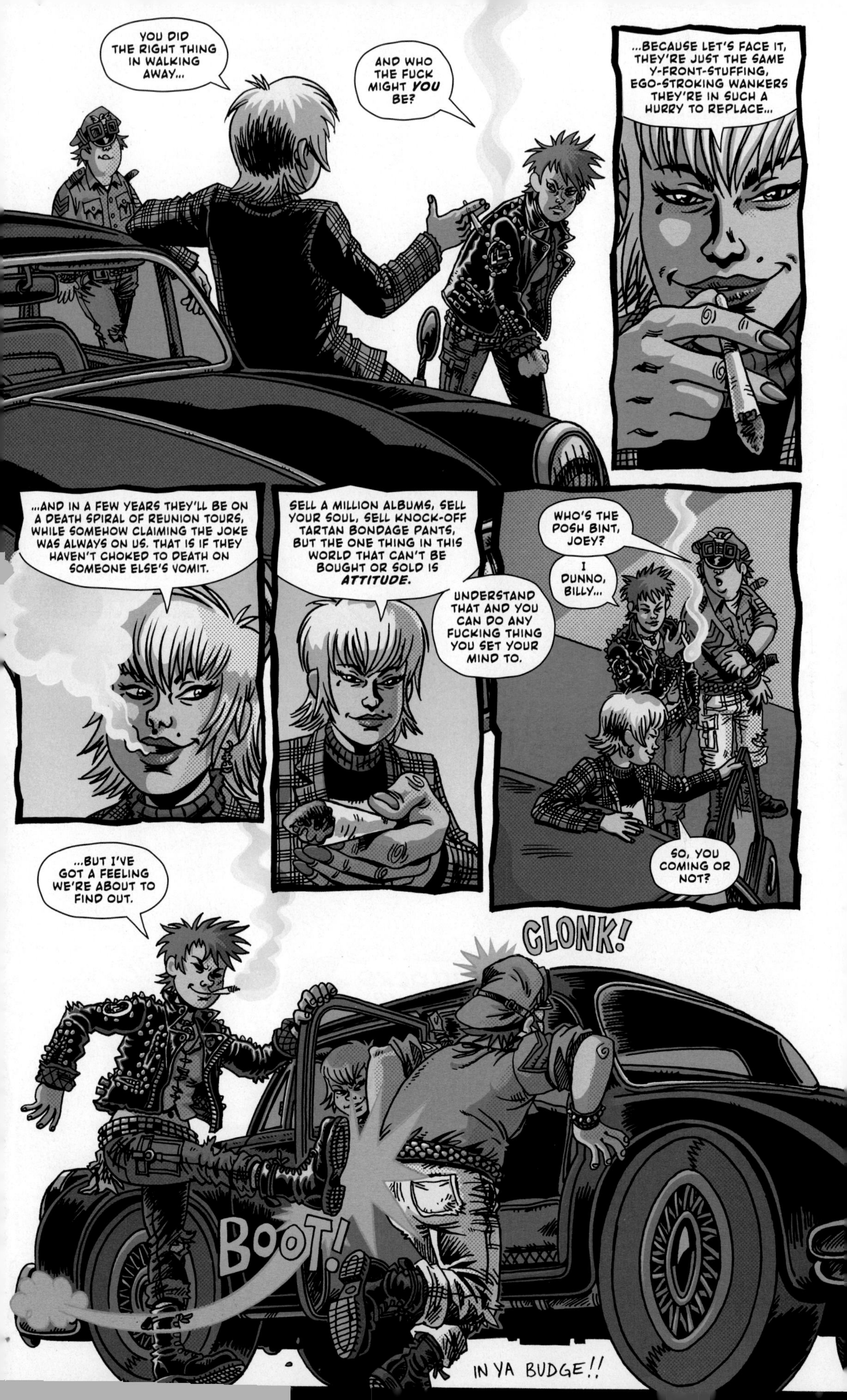

YOU DID THE RIGHT THING IN WALKING AWAY...
AND WHO THE FUCK MIGHT *YOU* BE?
...BECAUSE LET'S FACE IT, THEY'RE JUST THE SAME Y-FRONT-STUFFING, EGO-STROKING WANKERS THEY'RE IN SUCH A HURRY TO REPLACE...
...AND IN A FEW YEARS THEY'LL BE ON A DEATH SPIRAL OF REUNION TOURS, WHILE SOMEHOW CLAIMING THE JOKE WAS ALWAYS ON US. THAT IS IF THEY HAVEN'T CHOKED TO DEATH ON SOMEONE ELSE'S VOMIT.
SELL A MILLION ALBUMS, SELL YOUR SOUL, SELL KNOCK-OFF TARTAN BONDAGE PANTS, BUT THE ONE THING IN THIS WORLD THAT CAN'T BE BOUGHT OR SOLD IS *ATTITUDE.*
UNDERSTAND THAT AND YOU CAN DO ANY FUCKING THING YOU SET YOUR MIND TO.
WHO'S THE POSH BINT, JOEY?
I DUNNO, BILLY...
SO, YOU COMING OR NOT?
...BUT I'VE GOT A FEELING WE'RE ABOUT TO FIND OUT.
CLONK!
BOOT!
IN YA BUDGE!!

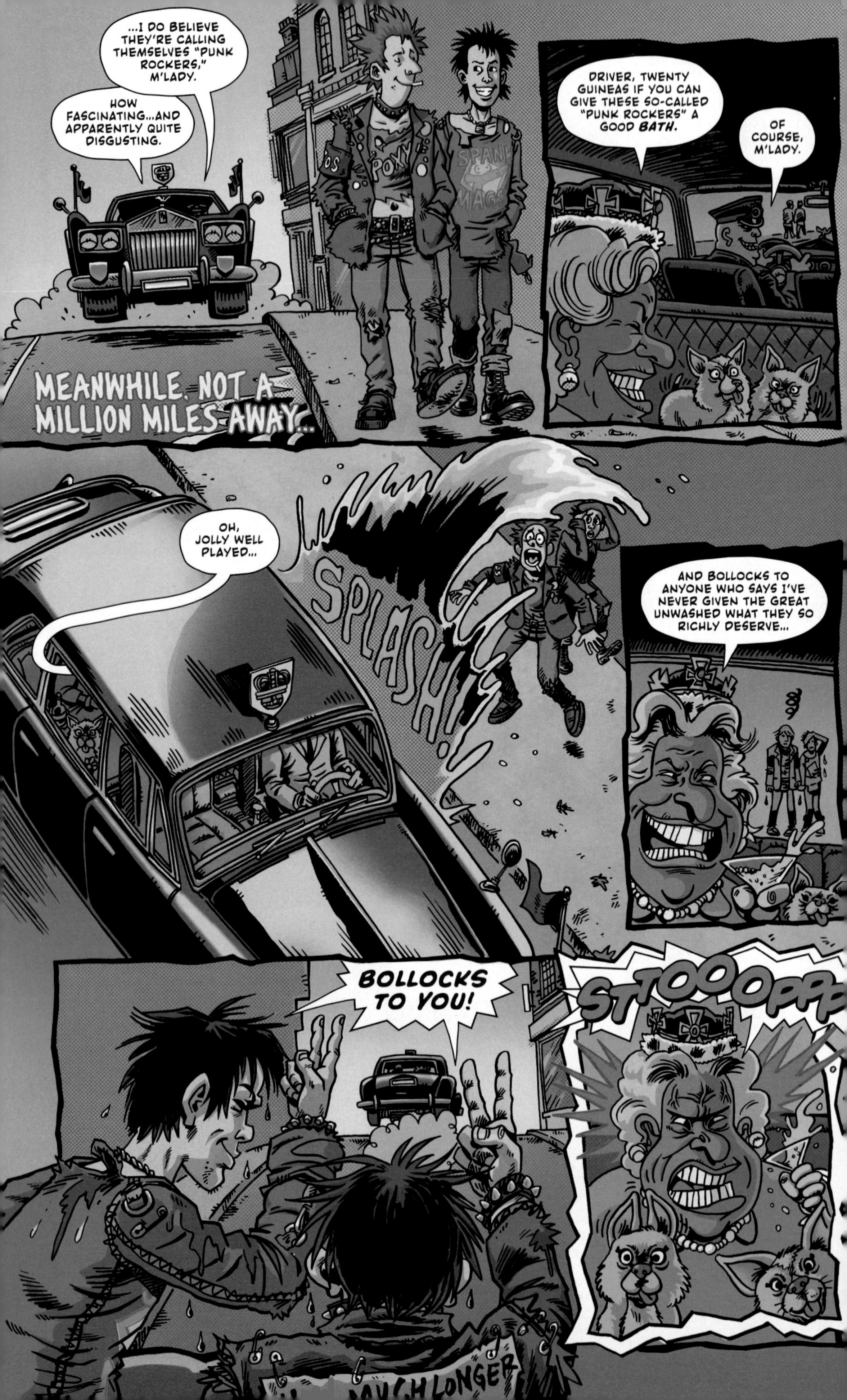
...I DO BELIEVE THEY'RE CALLING THEMSELVES "PUNK ROCKERS," M'LADY.
HOW FASCINATING...AND APPARENTLY QUITE DISGUSTING.
POXY
SPANK MAGS
MEANWHILE, NOT A MILLION MILES AWAY...
DRIVER, TWENTY GUINEAS IF YOU CAN GIVE THESE SO-CALLED "PUNK ROCKERS" A GOOD BATH.
OF COURSE, M'LADY.
OH, JOLLY WELL PLAYED...
SPLASH!!
AND BOLLOCKS TO ANYONE WHO SAYS I'VE NEVER GIVEN THE GREAT UNWASHED WHAT THEY SO RICHLY DESERVE...
BOLLOCKS TO YOU!
STOOOOPPP
MUCH LONGER

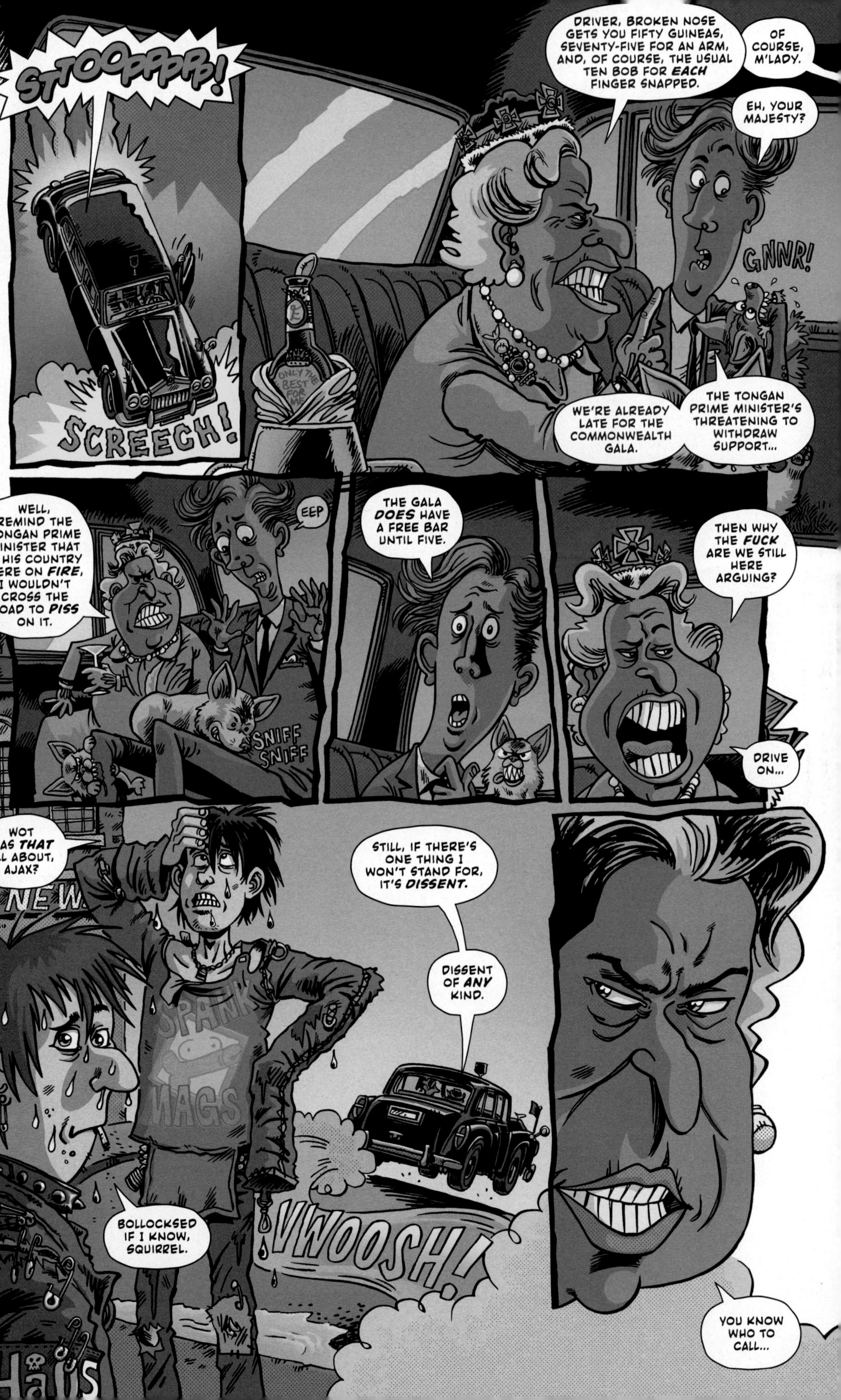
STTOOPPPPP!
SCREECH!
ONLY THE BEST FOR ME
DRIVER, BROKEN NOSE GETS YOU FIFTY GUINEAS, SEVENTY-FIVE FOR AN ARM, AND, OF COURSE, THE USUAL TEN BOB FOR EACH FINGER SNAPPED.
OF COURSE, M'LADY.
EH, YOUR MAJESTY?
GNNR!
WE'RE ALREADY LATE FOR THE COMMONWEALTH GALA.
THE TONGAN PRIME MINISTER'S THREATENING TO WITHDRAW SUPPORT...
WELL, REMIND THE TONGAN PRIME MINISTER THAT IF HIS COUNTRY WERE ON FIRE, I WOULDN'T CROSS THE ROAD TO PISS ON IT.
EEP
SNIFF SNIFF
THE GALA DOES HAVE A FREE BAR UNTIL FIVE.
THEN WHY THE FUCK ARE WE STILL HERE ARGUING?
DRIVE ON...
WOT WAS THAT ALL ABOUT, AJAX?
NEW
SPANK MAGS
BOLLOCKSED IF I KNOW, SQUIRREL.
STILL, IF THERE'S ONE THING I WON'T STAND FOR, IT'S DISSENT.
DISSENT OF ANY KIND.
VWOOSH!
YOU KNOW WHO TO CALL...

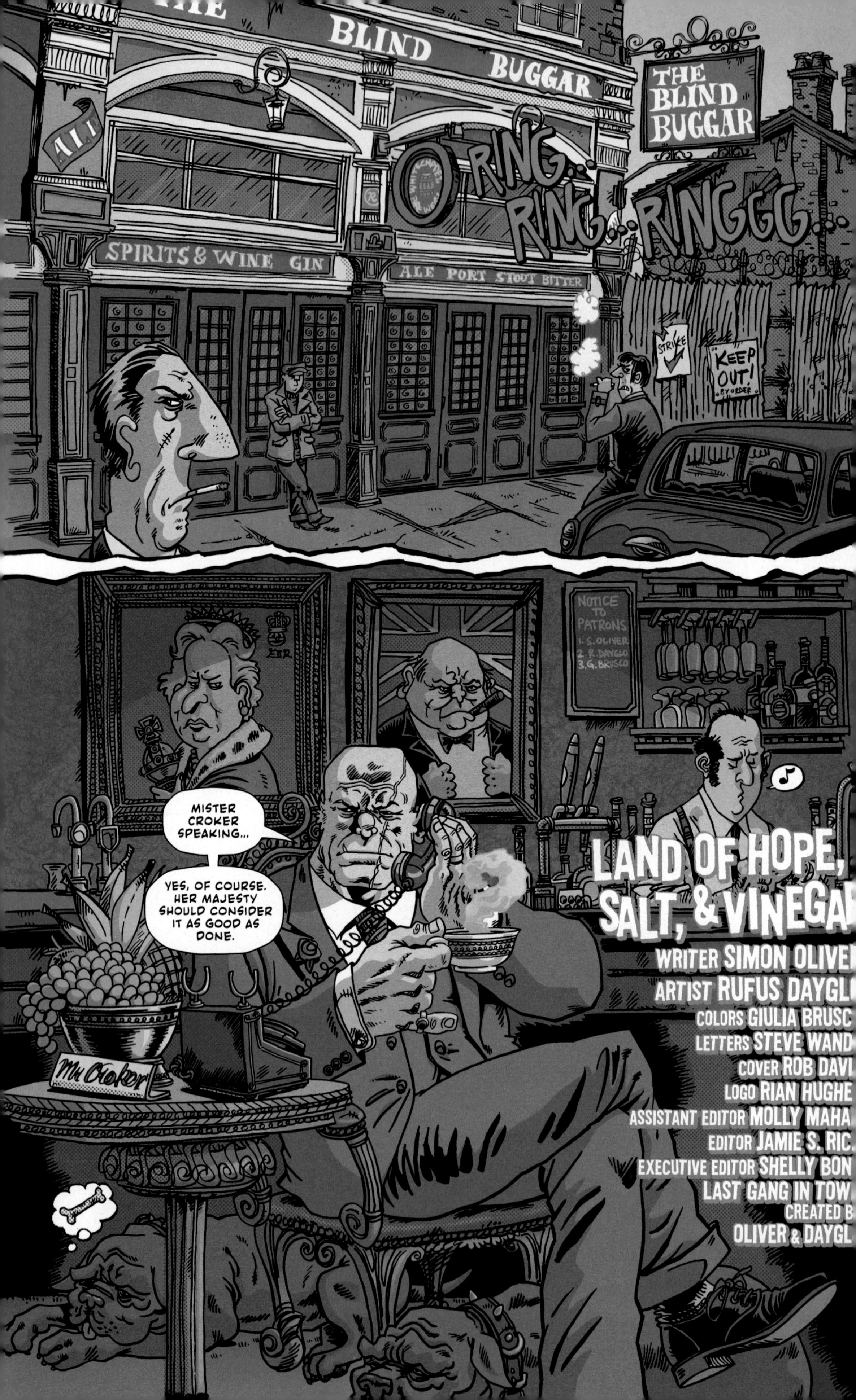

BLIND BUGGAR
THE BLIND BUGGAR
SPIRITS & WINE GIN
ALE PORT STOUT BITTER
RING... RING!... RINGGG...
STRIKE
KEEP OUT! BY ORDER
NOTICE TO PATRONS
1. S. OLIVER
2. R. DAYGLO
3. G. BRUSCO
MISTER CROKER SPEAKING...
YES, OF COURSE. HER MAJESTY SHOULD CONSIDER IT AS GOOD AS DONE.
Mr Croker
LAND OF HOPE,
SALT, & VINEGA
WRITER SIMON OLIVE
ARTIST RUFUS DAYGL
COLORS GIULIA BRUSC
LETTERS STEVE WAND
COVER ROB DAVI
LOGO RIAN HUGHE
ASSISTANT EDITOR MOLLY MAHA
EDITOR JAMIE S. RIC
EXECUTIVE EDITOR SHELLY BON
LAST GANG IN TOW
CREATED B
OLIVER & DAYGL

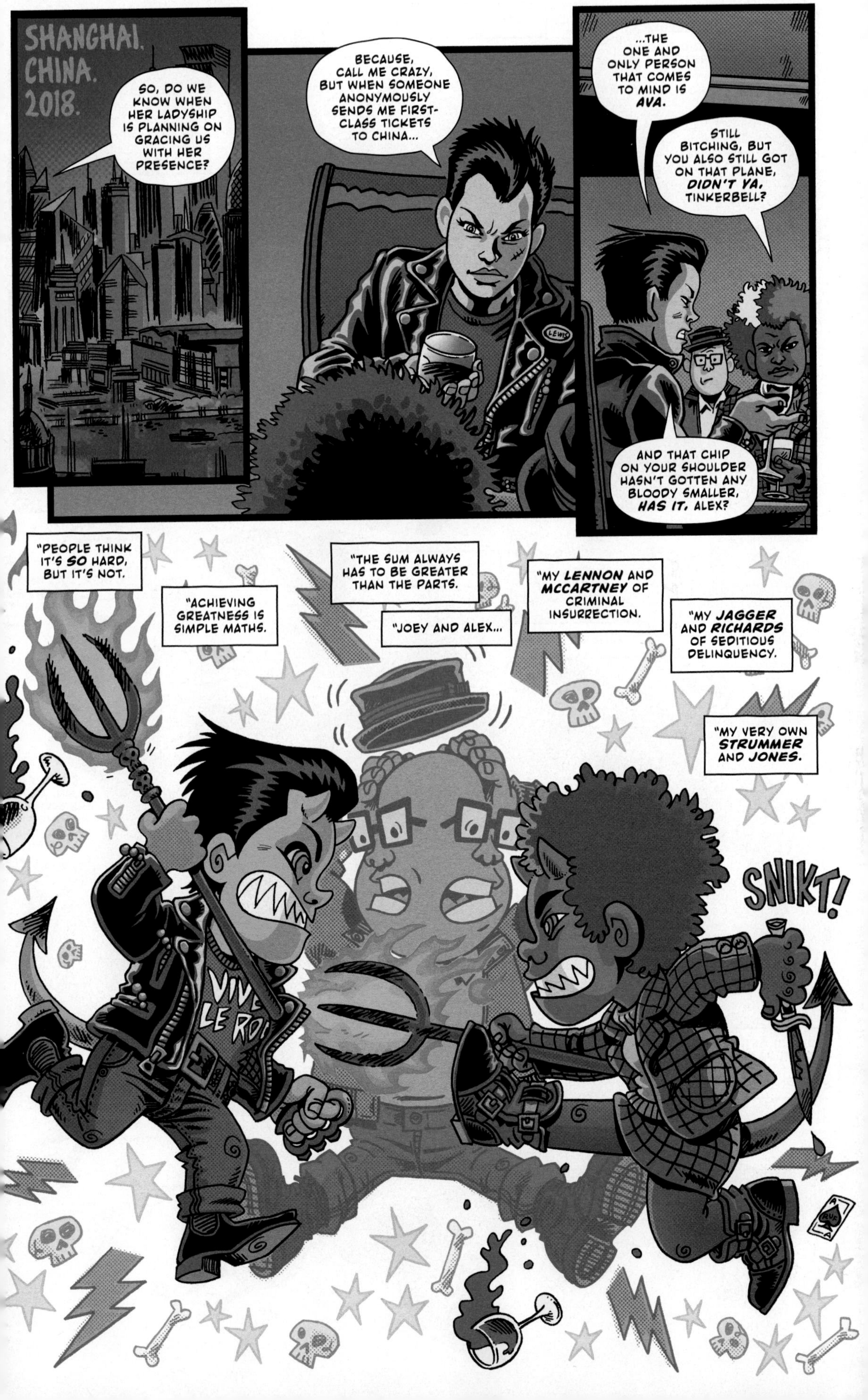
SHANGHAI, CHINA. 2018.
SO, DO WE KNOW WHEN HER LADYSHIP IS PLANNING ON GRACING US WITH HER PRESENCE?
BECAUSE, CALL ME CRAZY, BUT WHEN SOMEONE ANONYMOUSLY SENDS ME FIRST-CLASS TICKETS TO CHINA...
...THE ONE AND ONLY PERSON THAT COMES TO MIND IS AVA.
STILL BITCHING, BUT YOU ALSO STILL GOT ON THAT PLANE, DIDN'T YA, TINKERBELL?
AND THAT CHIP ON YOUR SHOULDER HASN'T GOTTEN ANY BLOODY SMALLER, HAS IT, ALEX?
"PEOPLE THINK IT'S SO HARD, BUT IT'S NOT.
"ACHIEVING GREATNESS IS SIMPLE MATHS.
"THE SUM ALWAYS HAS TO BE GREATER THAN THE PARTS.
"JOEY AND ALEX...
"MY LENNON AND MCCARTNEY OF CRIMINAL INSURRECTION.
"MY JAGGER AND RICHARDS OF SEDITIOUS DELINQUENCY.
"MY VERY OWN STRUMMER AND JONES.
VIVE LE ROC
SNIKT!

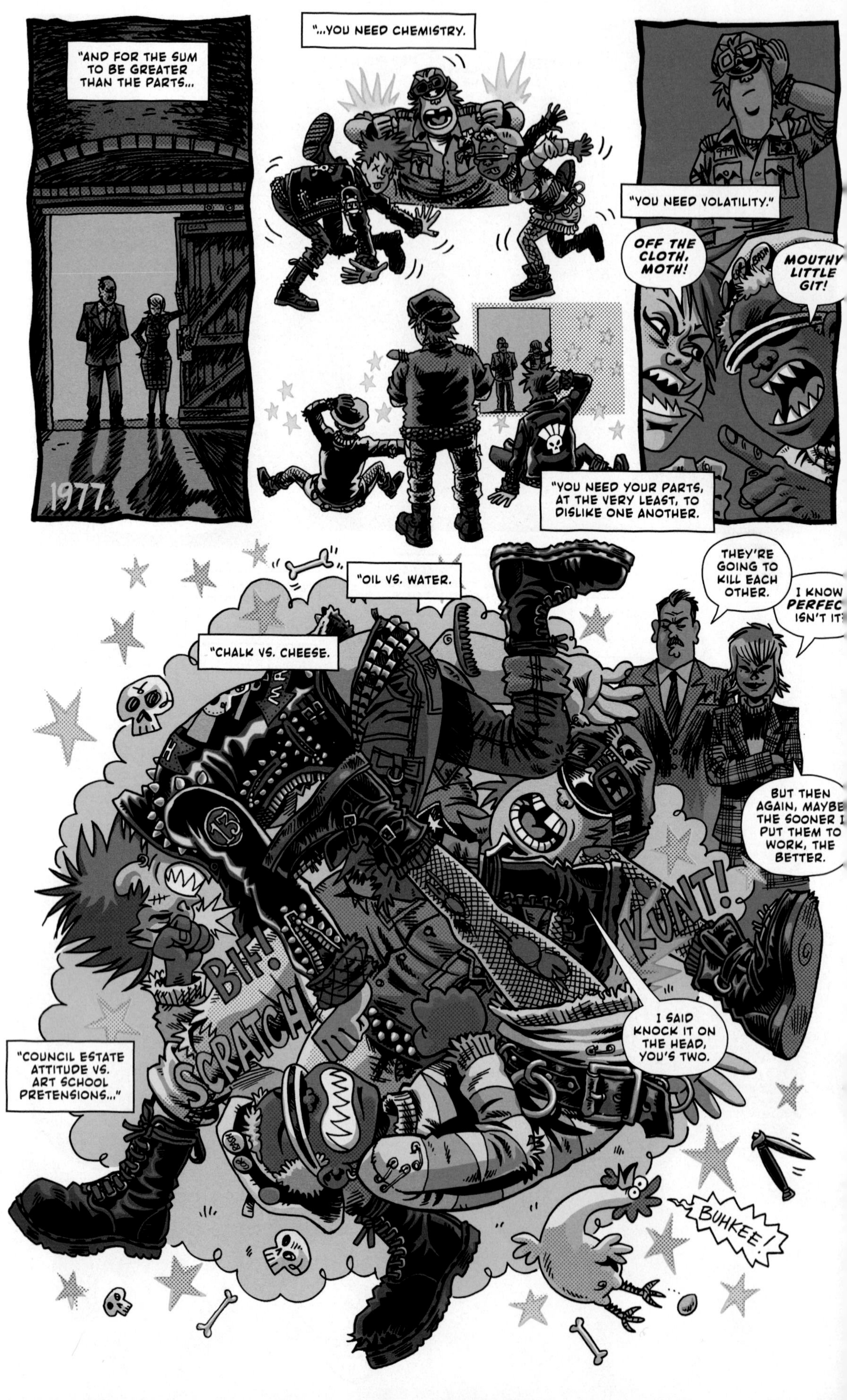
"AND FOR THE SUM TO BE GREATER THAN THE PARTS...
1977.
"...YOU NEED CHEMISTRY.
"YOU NEED VOLATILITY."
OFF THE CLOTH, MOTH!
MOUTHY LITTLE GIT!
"YOU NEED YOUR PARTS, AT THE VERY LEAST, TO DISLIKE ONE ANOTHER.
"OIL VS. WATER.
"CHALK VS. CHEESE.
THEY'RE GOING TO KILL EACH OTHER.
I KNOW. PERFEC ISN'T IT
BUT THEN AGAIN, MAYBE THE SOONER I PUT THEM TO WORK, THE BETTER.
BIF!
SCRATCH
KUNT!
I SAID KNOCK IT ON THE HEAD, YOU'S TWO.
"COUNCIL ESTATE ATTITUDE VS. ART SCHOOL PRETENSIONS..."
BUHKEE!

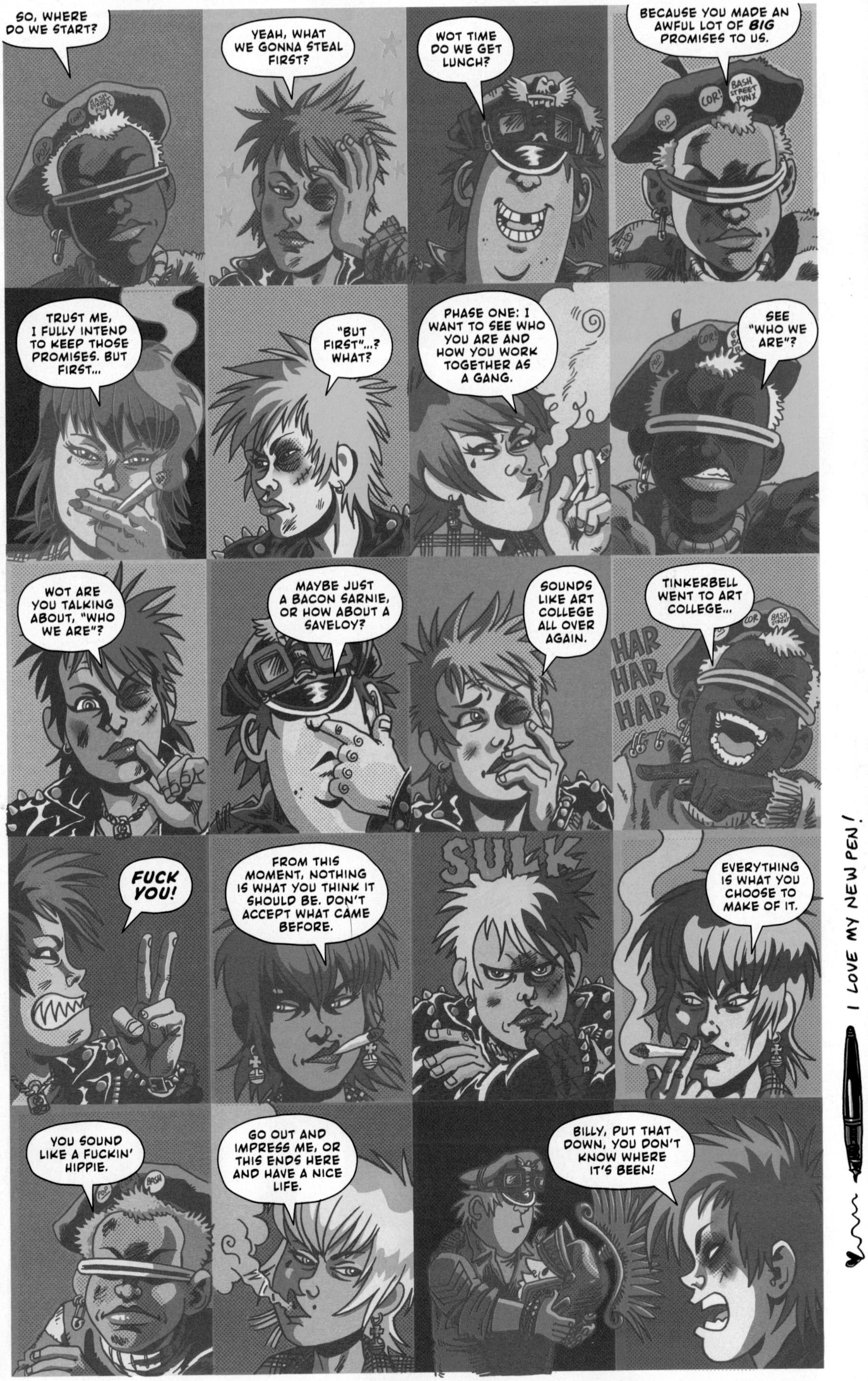
SO, WHERE DO WE START?
YEAH, WHAT WE GONNA STEAL FIRST?
WOT TIME DO WE GET LUNCH?
BECAUSE YOU MADE AN AWFUL LOT OF **BIG** PROMISES TO US.
TRUST ME, I FULLY INTEND TO KEEP THOSE PROMISES. BUT FIRST...
"BUT FIRST"...? WHAT?
PHASE ONE: I WANT TO SEE WHO YOU ARE AND HOW YOU WORK TOGETHER AS A GANG.
SEE "WHO WE ARE"?
WOT ARE YOU TALKING ABOUT, "WHO WE ARE"?
MAYBE JUST A BACON SARNIE, OR HOW ABOUT A SAVELOY?
SOUNDS LIKE ART COLLEGE ALL OVER AGAIN.
TINKERBELL WENT TO ART COLLEGE...
HAR HAR HAR
FUCK YOU!
FROM THIS MOMENT, NOTHING IS WHAT YOU THINK IT SHOULD BE. DON'T ACCEPT WHAT CAME BEFORE.
SULK
EVERYTHING IS WHAT YOU CHOOSE TO MAKE OF IT.
YOU SOUND LIKE A FUCKIN' HIPPIE.
GO OUT AND IMPRESS ME, OR THIS ENDS HERE AND HAVE A NICE LIFE.
BILLY, PUT THAT DOWN, YOU DON'T KNOW WHERE IT'S BEEN!
I LOVE MY NEW PEN!

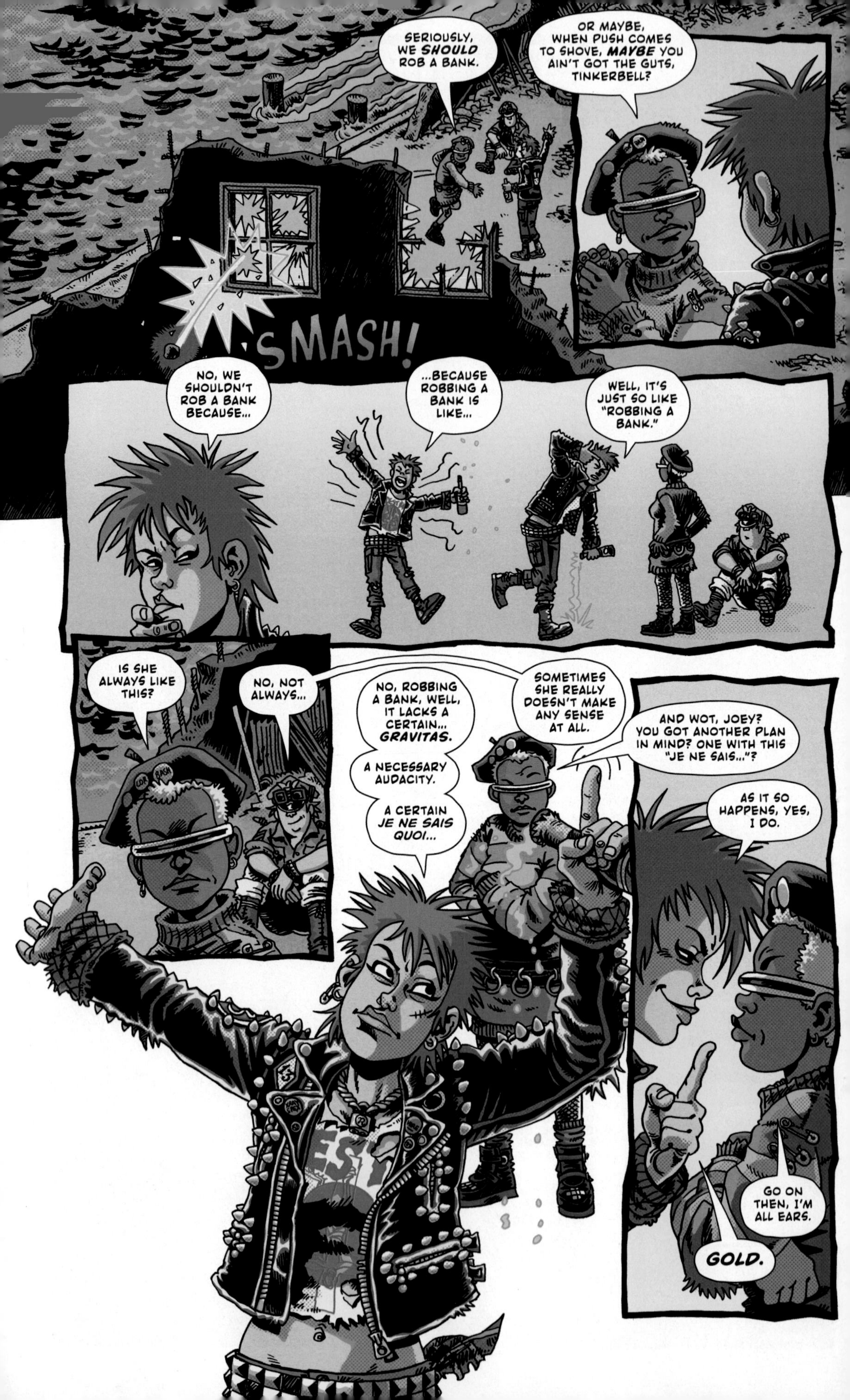
SERIOUSLY, WE SHOULD ROB A BANK.
SMASH!
OR MAYBE, WHEN PUSH COMES TO SHOVE, MAYBE YOU AIN'T GOT THE GUTS, TINKERBELL?
NO, WE SHOULDN'T ROB A BANK BECAUSE...
...BECAUSE ROBBING A BANK IS LIKE...
WELL, IT'S JUST SO LIKE "ROBBING A BANK."
IS SHE ALWAYS LIKE THIS?
NO, NOT ALWAYS...
SOMETIMES SHE REALLY DOESN'T MAKE ANY SENSE AT ALL.
NO, ROBBING A BANK, WELL, IT LACKS A CERTAIN... GRAVITAS.
A NECESSARY AUDACITY.
A CERTAIN JE NE SAIS QUOI...
AND WOT, JOEY? YOU GOT ANOTHER PLAN IN MIND? ONE WITH THIS "JE NE SAIS..."?
AS IT SO HAPPENS, YES, I DO.
GO ON THEN, I'M ALL EARS.
GOLD.

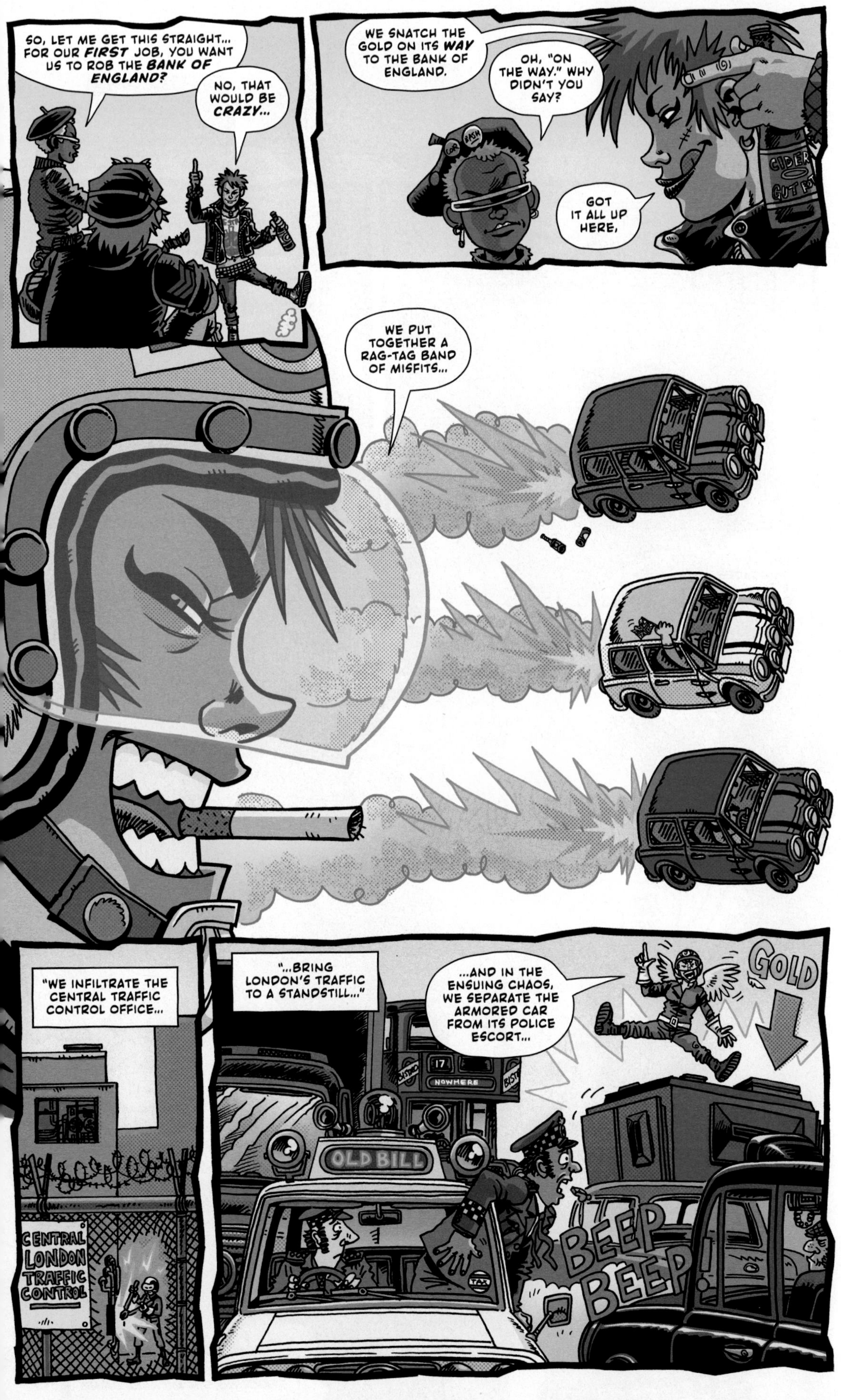
SO, LET ME GET THIS STRAIGHT... FOR OUR FIRST JOB, YOU WANT US TO ROB THE BANK OF ENGLAND?
NO, THAT WOULD BE CRAZY...
WE SNATCH THE GOLD ON ITS WAY TO THE BANK OF ENGLAND.
OH, "ON THE WAY." WHY DIDN'T YOU SAY?
CIDER
GUT ROT
GOT IT ALL UP HERE,
WE PUT TOGETHER A RAG-TAG BAND OF MISFITS...
"WE INFILTRATE THE CENTRAL TRAFFIC CONTROL OFFICE...
CENTRAL LONDON TRAFFIC CONTROL
"...BRING LONDON'S TRAFFIC TO A STANDSTILL..."
...AND IN THE ENSUING CHAOS, WE SEPARATE THE ARMORED CAR FROM ITS POLICE ESCORT...
GOLD
17
NOWHERE
OLD BILL
TAX
BEEP BEEP!

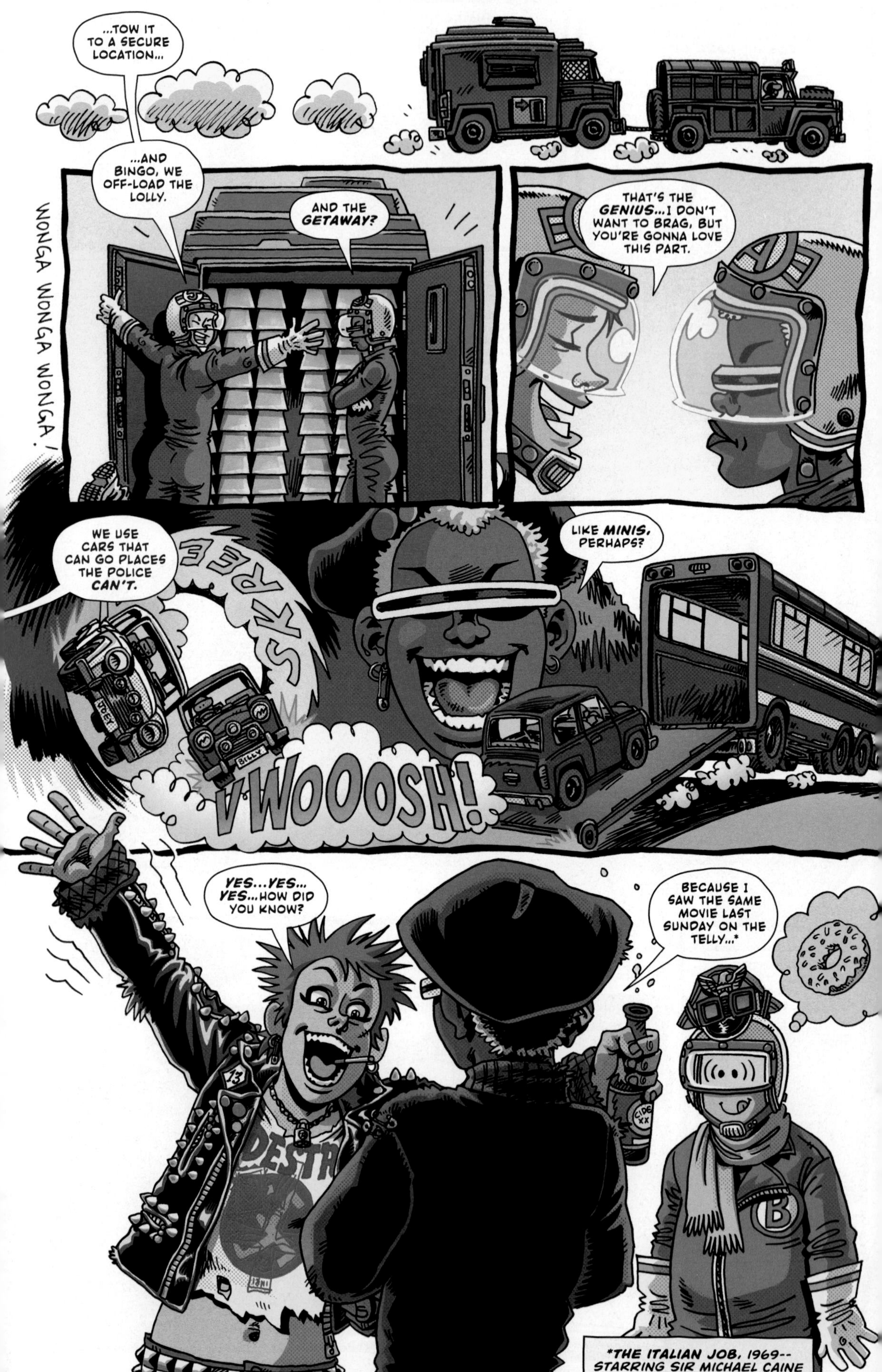
...TOW IT TO A SECURE LOCATION...
...AND BINGO, WE OFF-LOAD THE LOLLY.
AND THE GETAWAY?
WONGA WONGA WONGA!
THAT'S THE GENIUS...I DON'T WANT TO BRAG, BUT YOU'RE GONNA LOVE THIS PART.
WE USE CARS THAT CAN GO PLACES THE POLICE CAN'T.
SKREE
LIKE MINIS, PERHAPS?
VWOOOSH!
YES...YES... YES...HOW DID YOU KNOW?
BECAUSE I SAW THE SAME MOVIE LAST SUNDAY ON THE TELLY...*
*THE ITALIAN JOB, 1969-- STARRING SIR MICHAEL CAINE

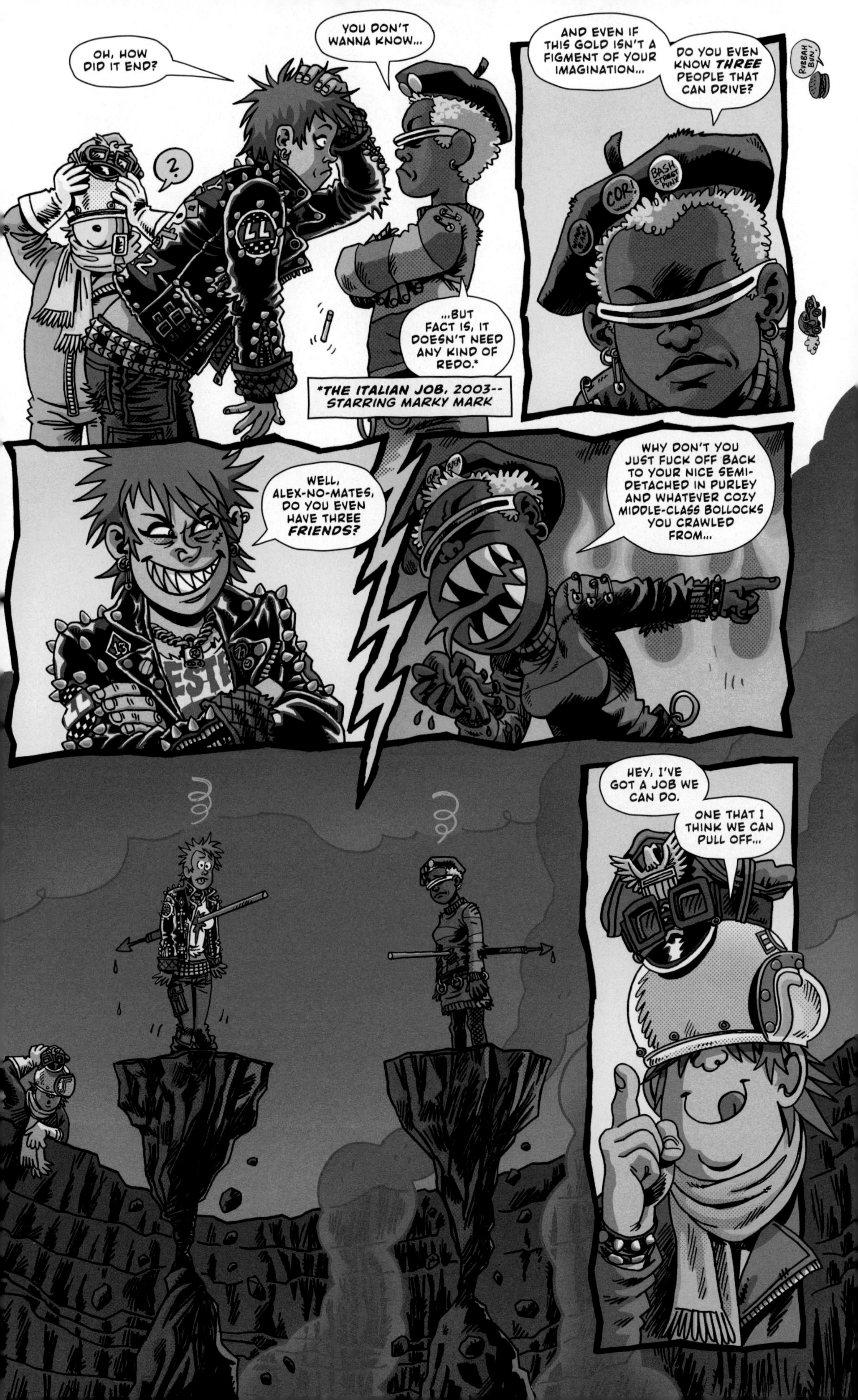
OH, HOW DID IT END?
YOU DON'T WANNA KNOW...
?
...BUT FACT IS, IT DOESN'T NEED ANY KIND OF REDO.*
*THE ITALIAN JOB, 2003-- STARRING MARKY MARK
AND EVEN IF THIS GOLD ISN'T A FIGMENT OF YOUR IMAGINATION...
DO YOU EVEN KNOW THREE PEOPLE THAT CAN DRIVE?
RUBBAH BUN!
COR!
BASH STREET PUNX
WELL, ALEX-NO-MATES, DO YOU EVEN HAVE THREE FRIENDS?
WHY DON'T YOU JUST FUCK OFF BACK TO YOUR NICE SEMI-DETACHED IN PURLEY AND WHATEVER COZY MIDDLE-CLASS BOLLOCKS YOU CRAWLED FROM...
HEY, I'VE GOT A JOB WE CAN DO.
ONE THAT I THINK WE CAN PULL OFF...

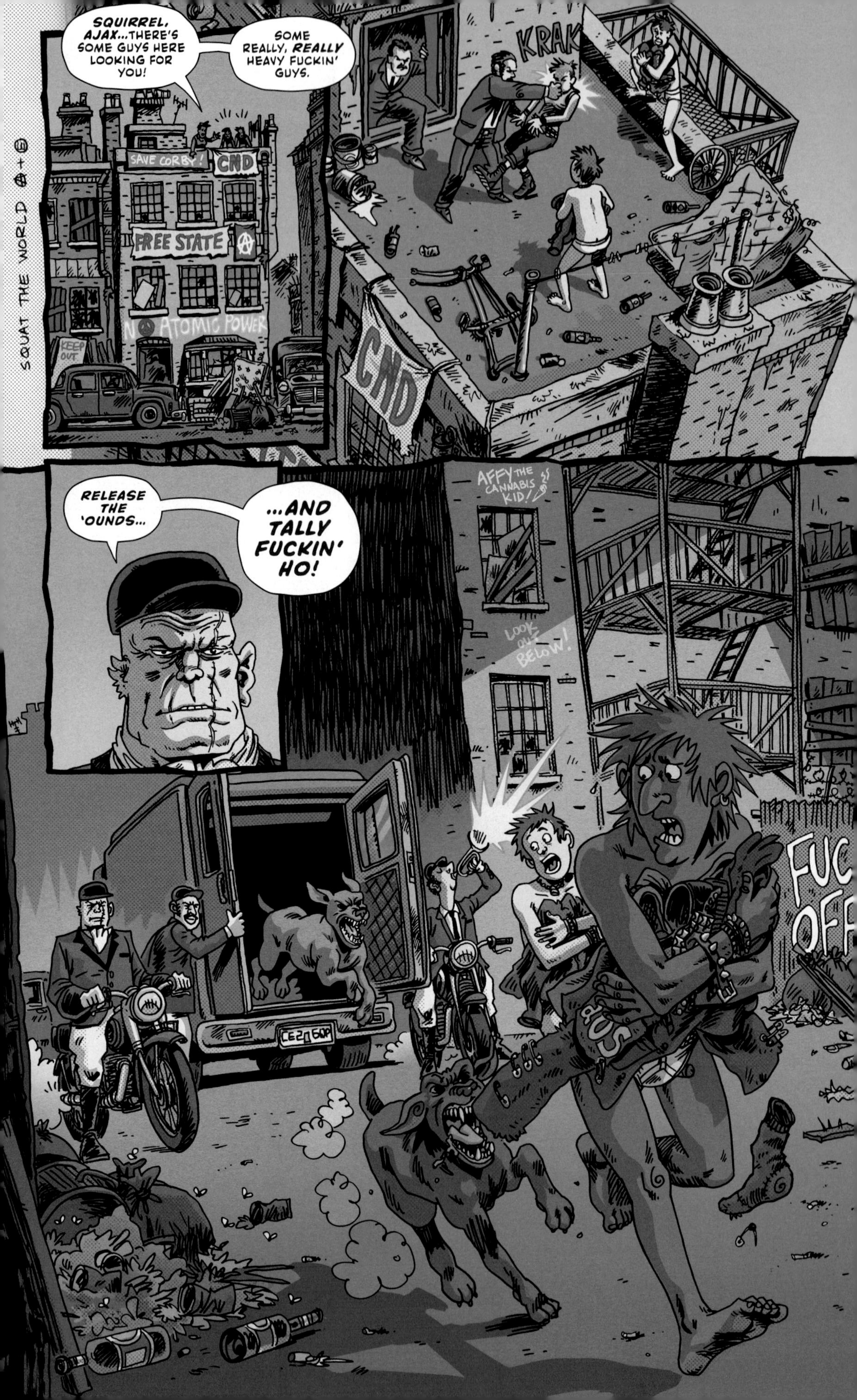
SQUIRREL, AJAX...THERE'S SOME GUYS HERE LOOKING FOR YOU!
SOME REALLY, REALLY HEAVY FUCKIN' GUYS.
KRAK
SAVE CORBY!
CND
FREE STATE
NO ATOMIC POWER
KEEP OUT.
CND
SQUAT THE WORLD
RELEASE THE 'OUNDS...
...AND TALLY FUCKIN' HO!
AFFY THE CANNABIS KID!
LOOK OUT BELOW!
FUC OFF
CE20 60P

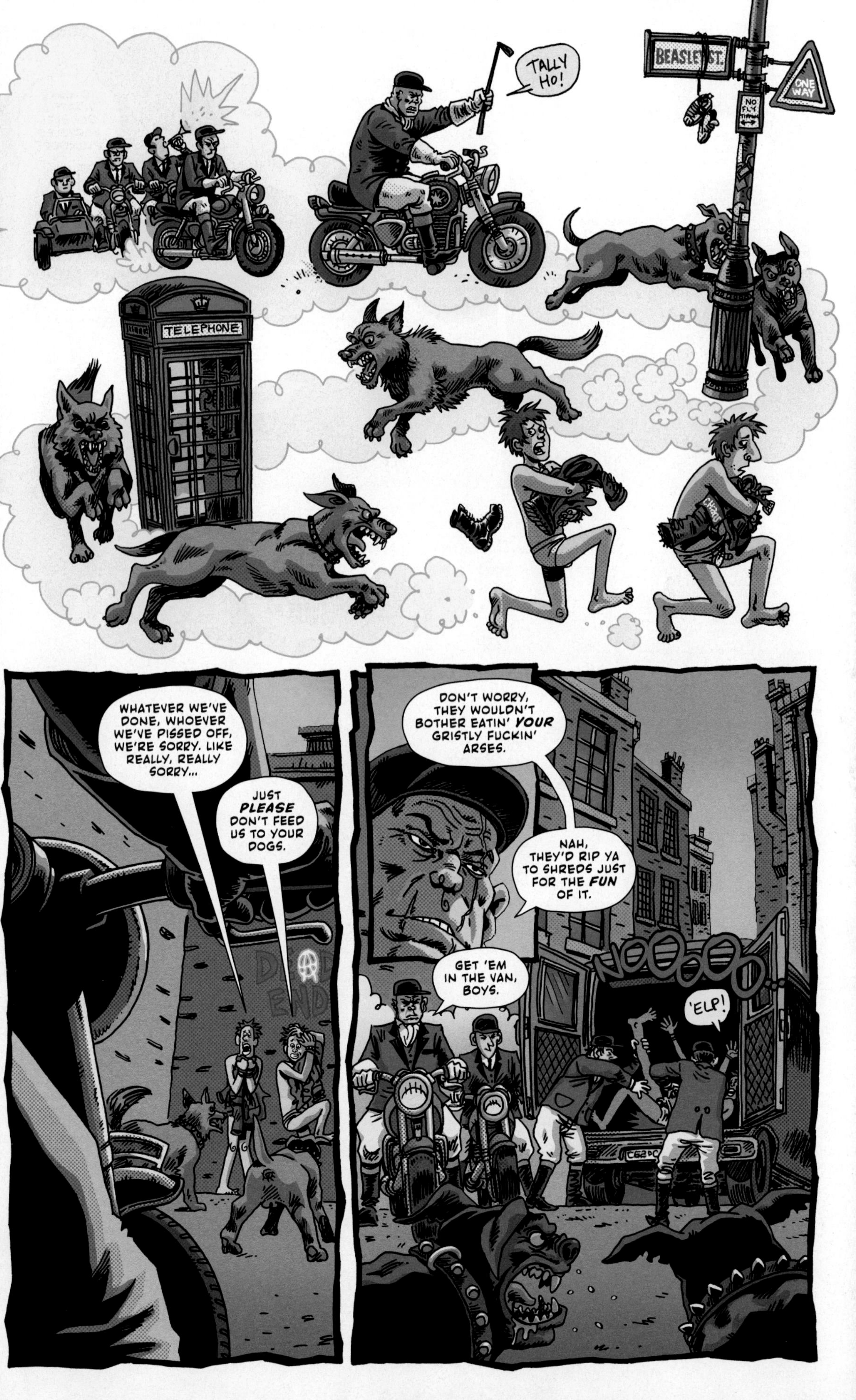
BEASLEY ST.
ONE WAY
TALLY HO!
TELEPHONE
WHATEVER WE'VE DONE, WHOEVER WE'VE PISSED OFF, WE'RE SORRY. LIKE REALLY, REALLY SORRY...
JUST *PLEASE* DON'T FEED US TO YOUR DOGS.
DON'T WORRY, THEY WOULDN'T BOTHER EATIN' *YOUR* GRISTLY FUCKIN' ARSES.
NAH, THEY'D RIP YA TO SHREDS JUST FOR THE *FUN* OF IT.
GET 'EM IN THE VAN, BOYS.
NOOOOOO
'ELP!

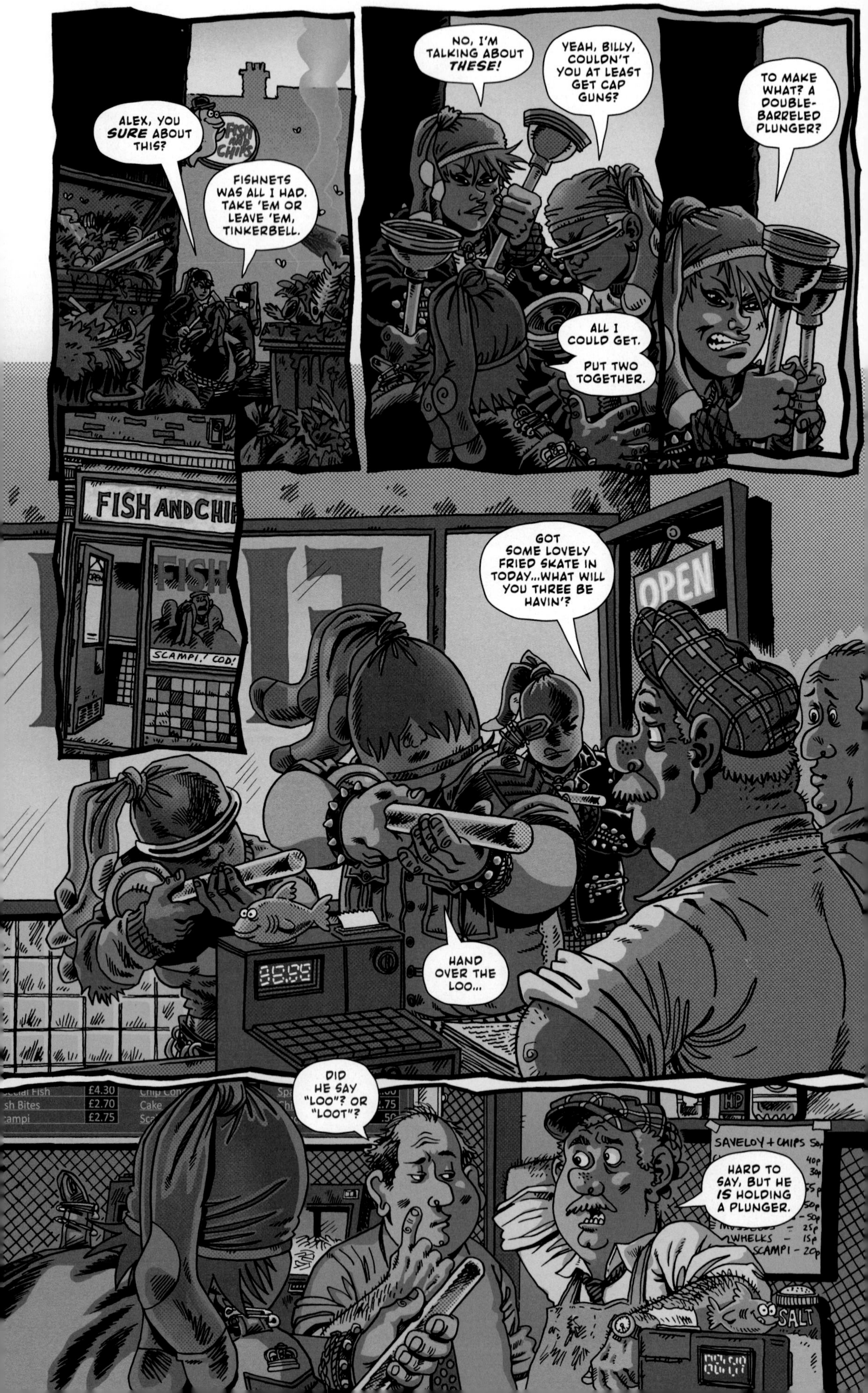
FISH AND CHIPS
ALEX, YOU SURE ABOUT THIS?
FISHNETS WAS ALL I HAD. TAKE 'EM OR LEAVE 'EM, TINKERBELL.
NO, I'M TALKING ABOUT THESE!
YEAH, BILLY, COULDN'T YOU AT LEAST GET CAP GUNS?
ALL I COULD GET.
PUT TWO TOGETHER.
TO MAKE WHAT? A DOUBLE-BARRELED PLUNGER?
FISH AND CHI
SCAMPI! COD!
OPEN
GOT SOME LOVELY FRIED SKATE IN TODAY...WHAT WILL YOU THREE BE HAVIN'?
HAND OVER THE LOO...
DID HE SAY "LOO"? OR "LOOT"?
SAVELOY + CHIPS
HARD TO SAY, BUT HE IS HOLDING A PLUNGER.
WHELKS - 15p
SCAMPI - 20p
SALT

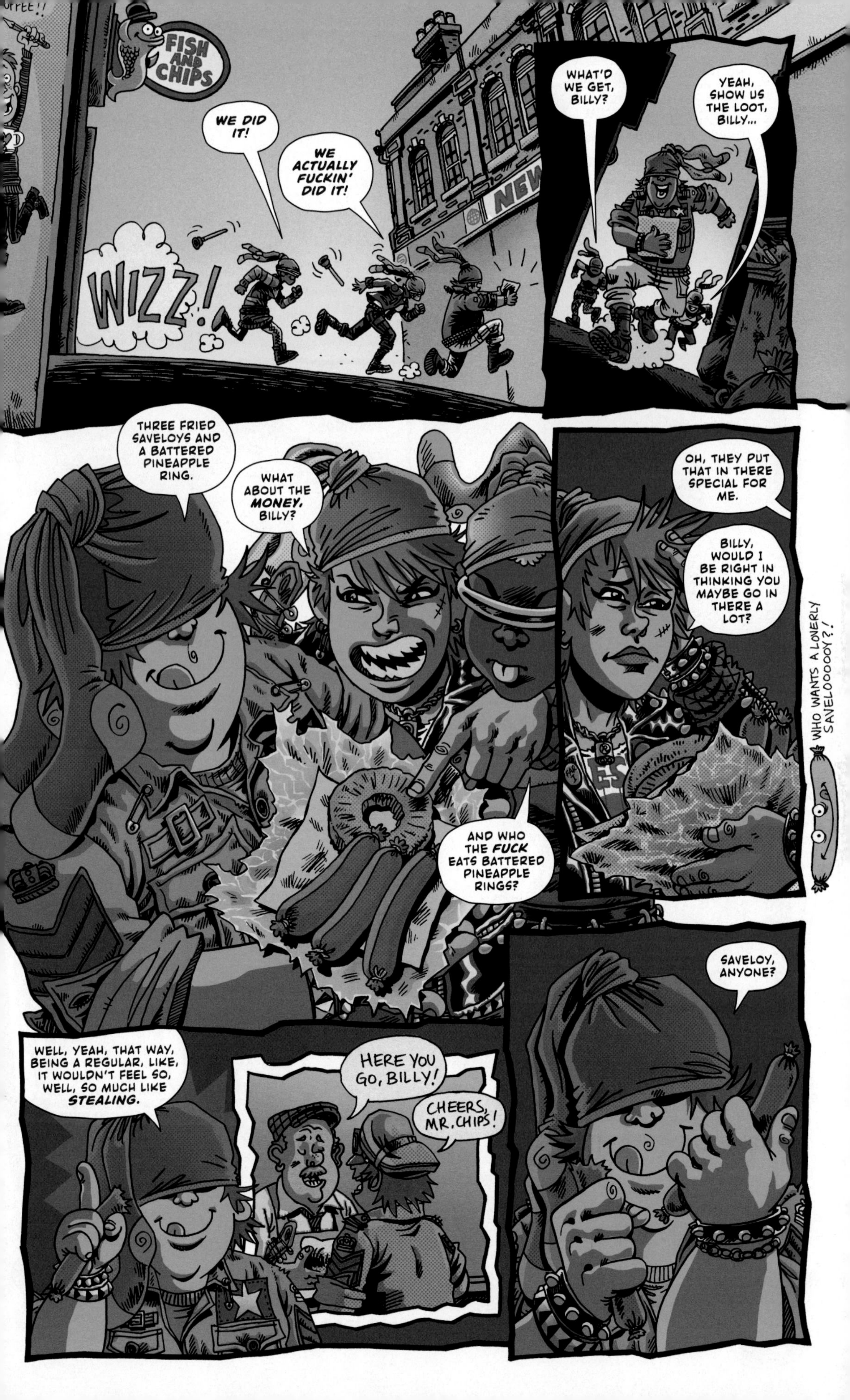
FISH AND CHIPS
WE DID IT!
WE ACTUALLY FUCKIN' DID IT!
WIZZ!
WHAT'D WE GET, BILLY?
YEAH, SHOW US THE LOOT, BILLY...
THREE FRIED SAVELOYS AND A BATTERED PINEAPPLE RING.
WHAT ABOUT THE MONEY, BILLY?
AND WHO THE FUCK EATS BATTERED PINEAPPLE RINGS?
OH, THEY PUT THAT IN THERE SPECIAL FOR ME.
BILLY, WOULD I BE RIGHT IN THINKING YOU MAYBE GO IN THERE A LOT?
WHO WANTS A LOVERLY SAVELOOOOOY?!
WELL, YEAH, THAT WAY, BEING A REGULAR, LIKE, IT WOULDN'T FEEL SO, WELL, SO MUCH LIKE STEALING.
HERE YOU GO, BILLY!
CHEERS, MR. CHIPS!
SAVELOY, ANYONE?

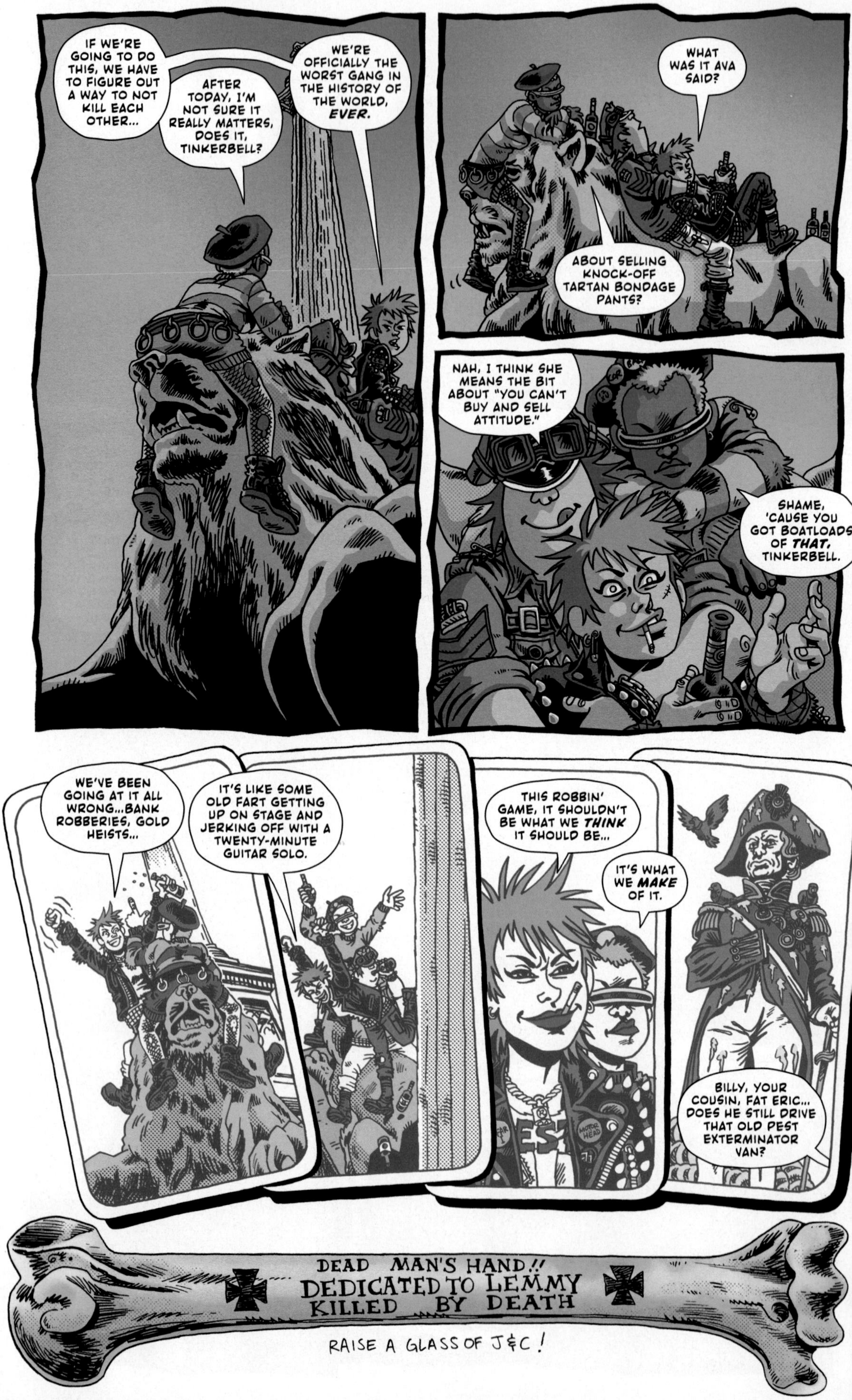
IF WE'RE GOING TO DO THIS, WE HAVE TO FIGURE OUT A WAY TO NOT KILL EACH OTHER...
AFTER TODAY, I'M NOT SURE IT REALLY MATTERS, DOES IT, TINKERBELL?
WE'RE OFFICIALLY THE WORST GANG IN THE HISTORY OF THE WORLD, EVER.
WHAT WAS IT AVA SAID?
ABOUT SELLING KNOCK-OFF TARTAN BONDAGE PANTS?
NAH, I THINK SHE MEANS THE BIT ABOUT "YOU CAN'T BUY AND SELL ATTITUDE."
SHAME, 'CAUSE YOU GOT BOATLOADS OF THAT, TINKERBELL.
WE'VE BEEN GOING AT IT ALL WRONG...BANK ROBBERIES, GOLD HEISTS...
IT'S LIKE SOME OLD FART GETTING UP ON STAGE AND JERKING OFF WITH A TWENTY-MINUTE GUITAR SOLO.
THIS ROBBIN' GAME, IT SHOULDN'T BE WHAT WE THINK IT SHOULD BE...
IT'S WHAT WE MAKE OF IT.
BILLY, YOUR COUSIN, FAT ERIC... DOES HE STILL DRIVE THAT OLD PEST EXTERMINATOR VAN?
DEAD MAN'S HAND!!
DEDICATED TO LEMMY
KILLED BY DEATH
RAISE A GLASS OF J&C!

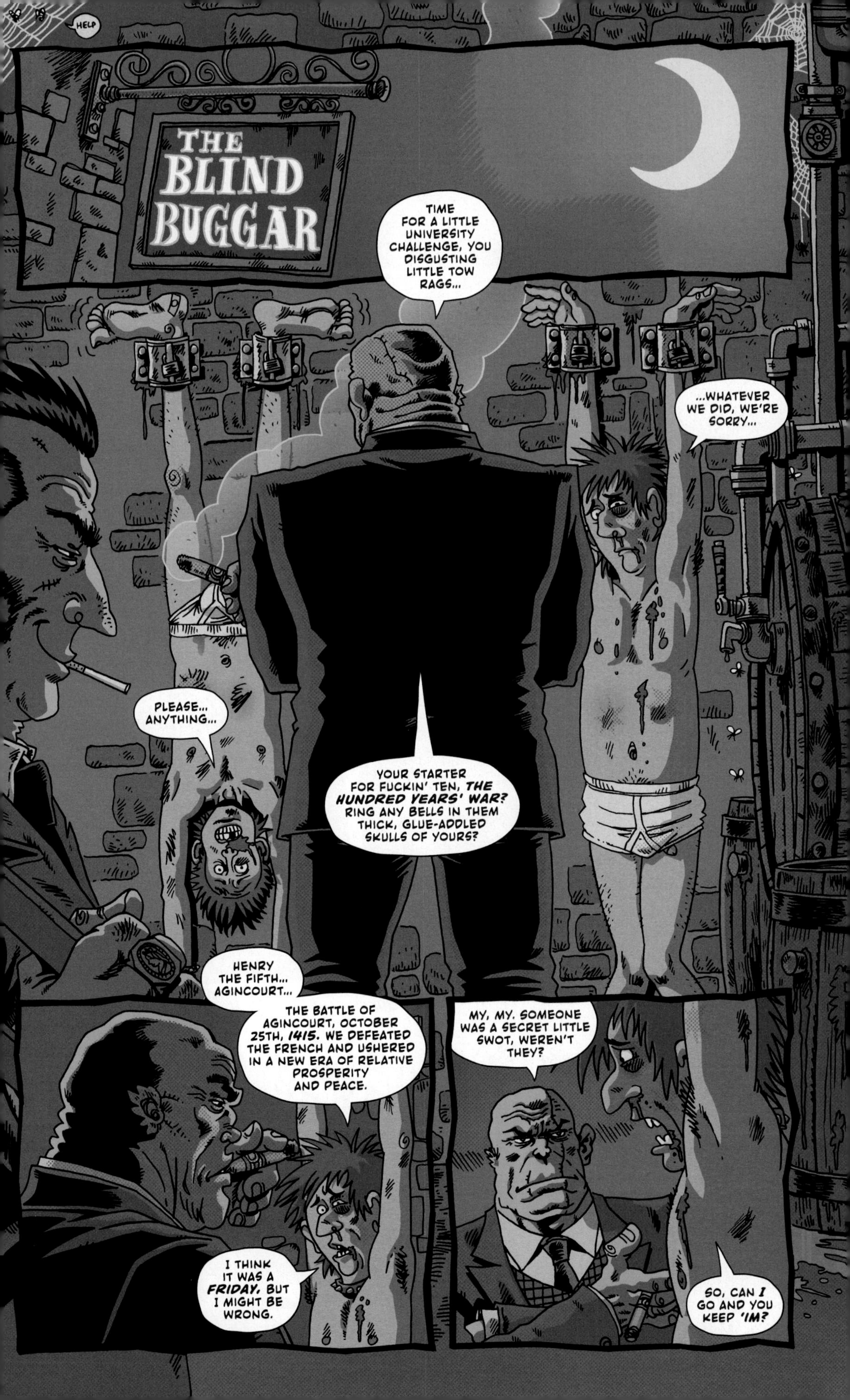
HELP
THE BLIND BUGGAR
TIME FOR A LITTLE UNIVERSITY CHALLENGE, YOU DISGUSTING LITTLE TOW RAGS...
...WHATEVER WE DID, WE'RE SORRY...
PLEASE... ANYTHING...
YOUR STARTER FOR FUCKIN' TEN, THE HUNDRED YEARS' WAR? RING ANY BELLS IN THEM THICK, GLUE-ADDLED SKULLS OF YOURS?
HENRY THE FIFTH... AGINCOURT...
THE BATTLE OF AGINCOURT, OCTOBER 25TH, 1415. WE DEFEATED THE FRENCH AND USHERED IN A NEW ERA OF RELATIVE PROSPERITY AND PEACE.
I THINK IT WAS A FRIDAY, BUT I MIGHT BE WRONG.
MY, MY. SOMEONE WAS A SECRET LITTLE SWOT, WEREN'T THEY?
SO, CAN I GO AND YOU KEEP 'IM?

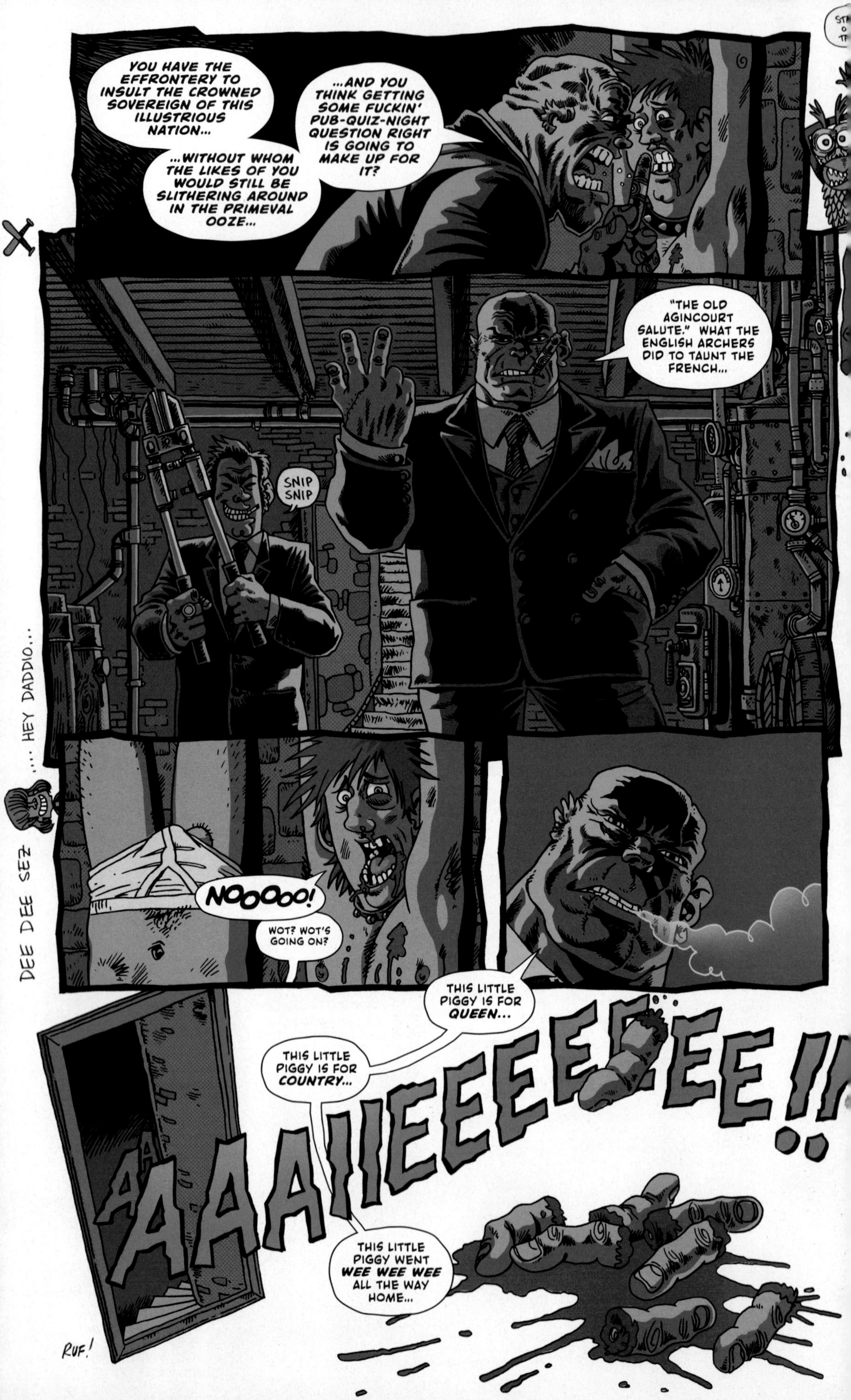
YOU HAVE THE EFFRONTERY TO INSULT THE CROWNED SOVEREIGN OF THIS ILLUSTRIOUS NATION...
...WITHOUT WHOM THE LIKES OF YOU WOULD STILL BE SLITHERING AROUND IN THE PRIMEVAL OOZE...
...AND YOU THINK GETTING SOME FUCKIN' PUB-QUIZ-NIGHT QUESTION RIGHT IS GOING TO MAKE UP FOR IT?
"THE OLD AGINCOURT SALUTE." WHAT THE ENGLISH ARCHERS DID TO TAUNT THE FRENCH...
SNIP SNIP
NOOOOO!
WOT? WOT'S GOING ON?
THIS LITTLE PIGGY IS FOR QUEEN...
THIS LITTLE PIGGY IS FOR COUNTRY...
AAAIIEEEEEEEEE!!
THIS LITTLE PIGGY WENT WEE WEE WEE ALL THE WAY HOME...
RUF!
DEE DEE SEZ .... HEY DADDIO...

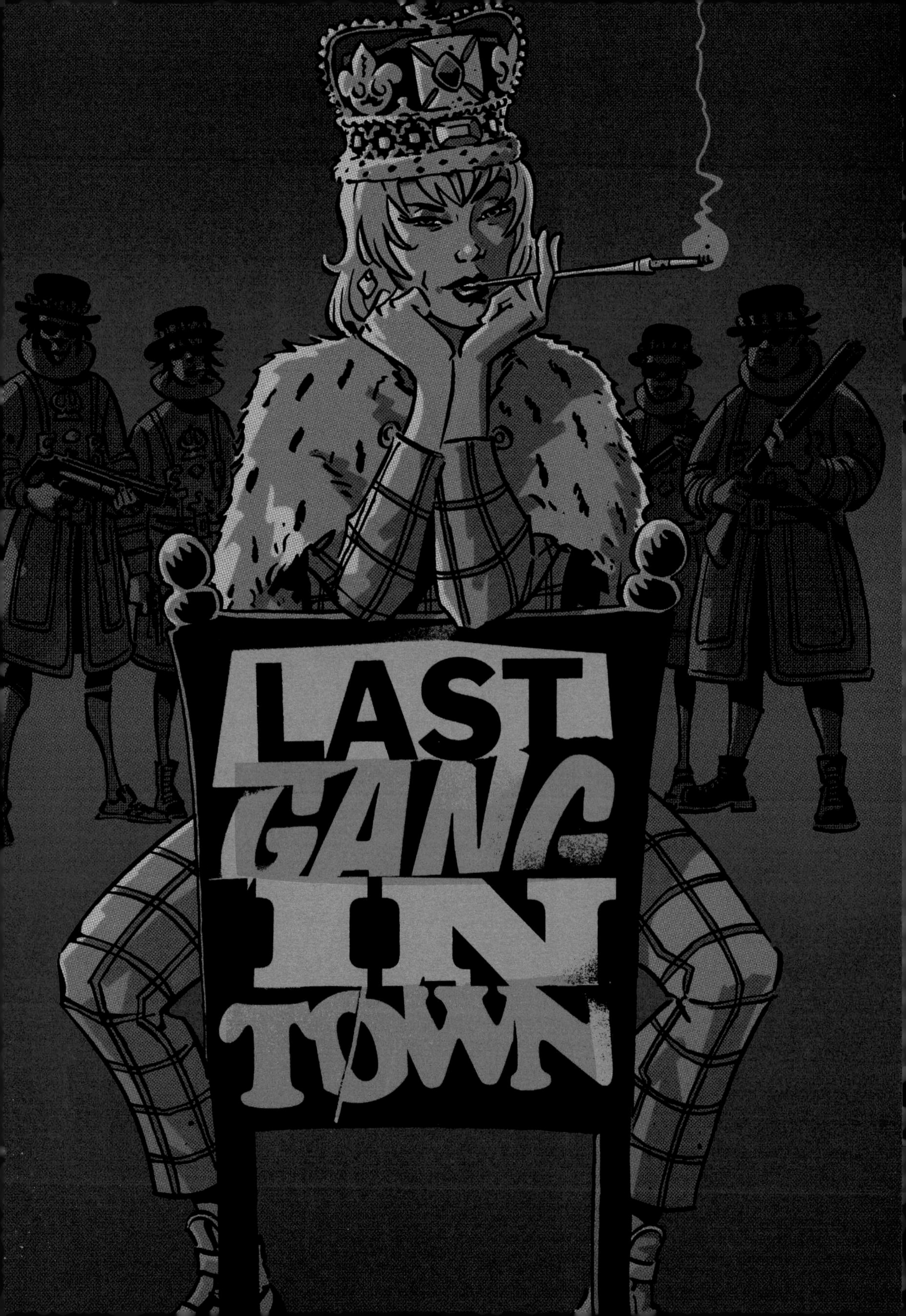
LAST
GANG
IN
TOWN

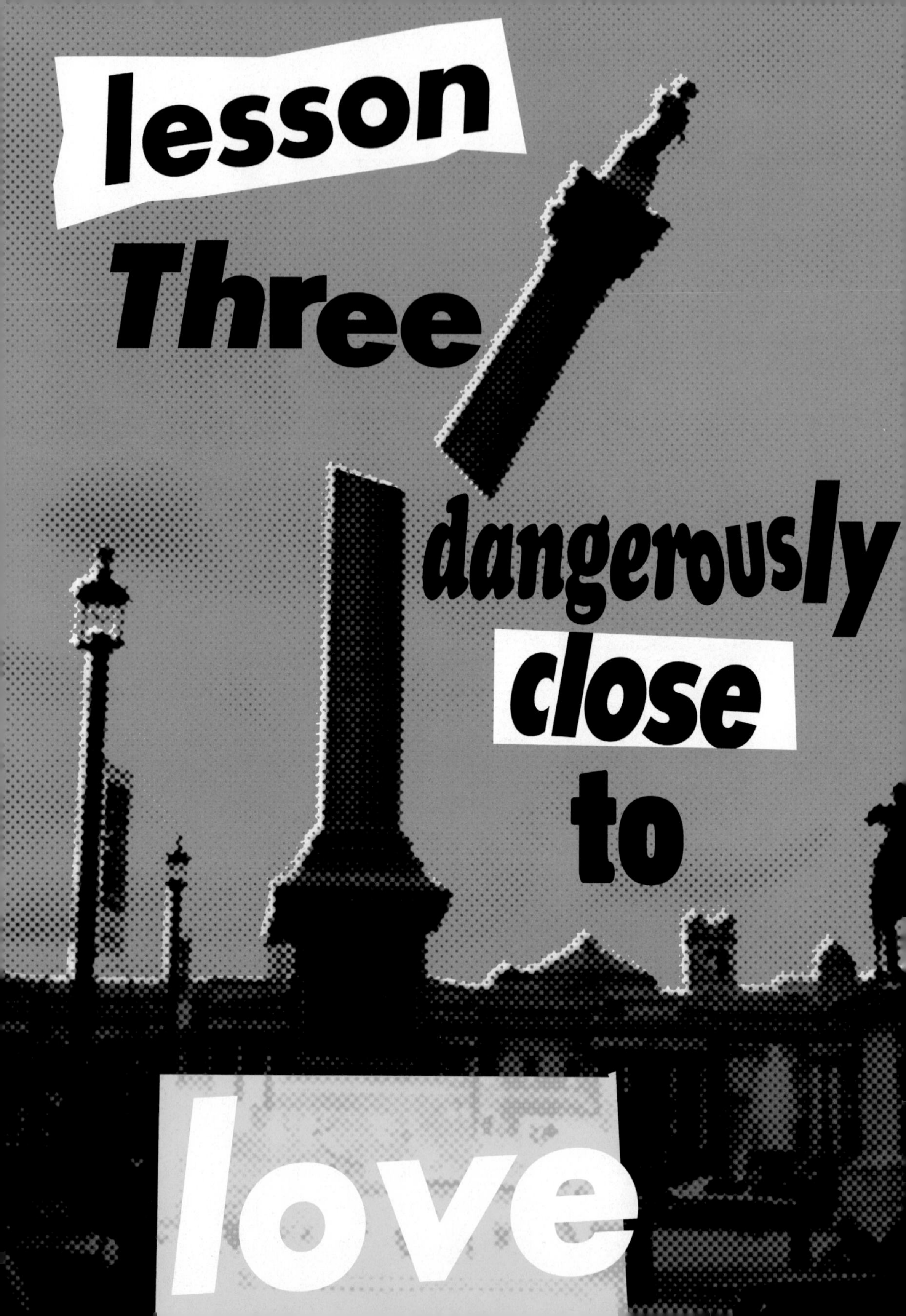
lesson
Three
dangerously
close
to
love

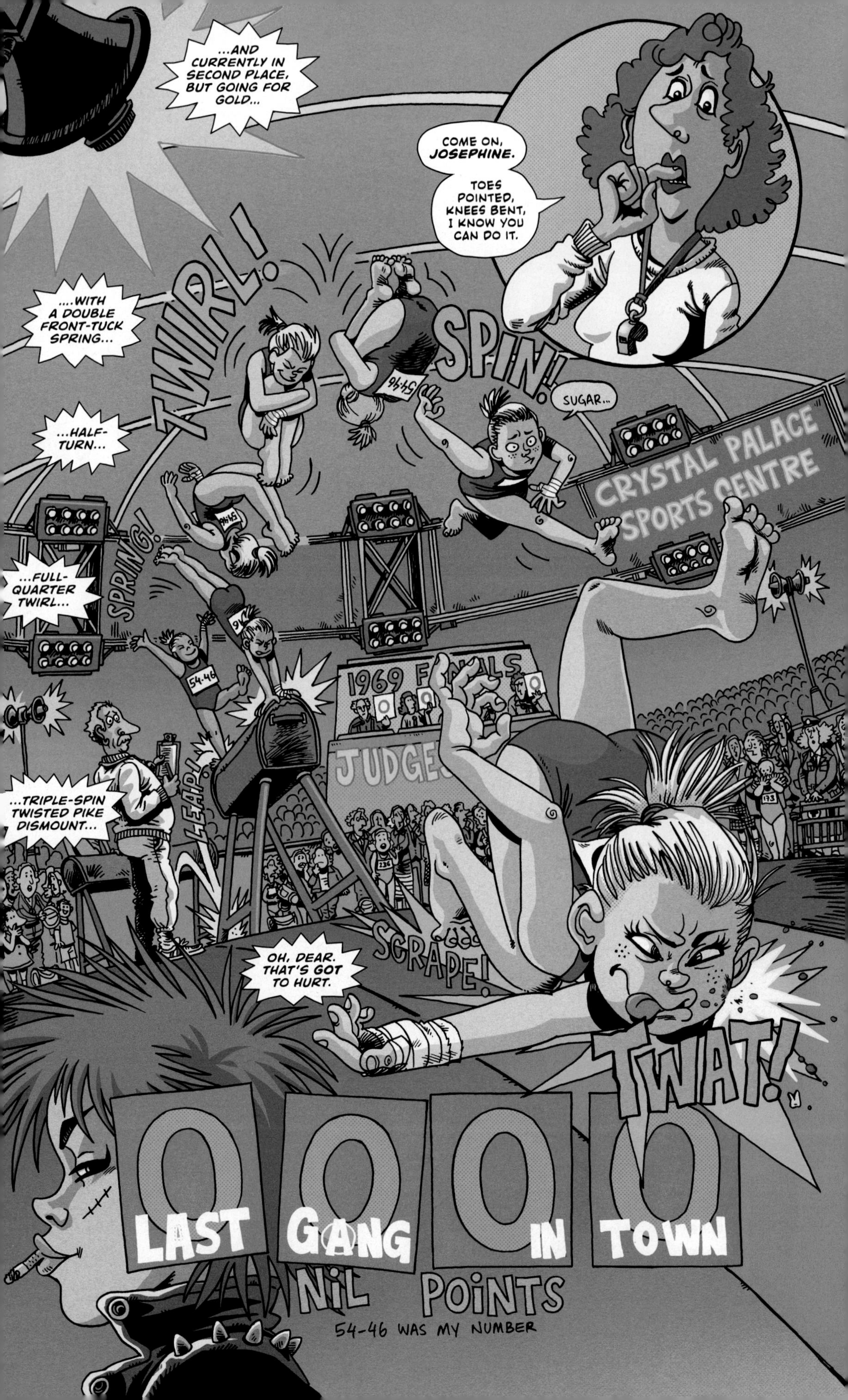
...AND CURRENTLY IN SECOND PLACE, BUT GOING FOR GOLD...
COME ON, JOSEPHINE.
TOES POINTED, KNEES BENT, I KNOW YOU CAN DO IT.
....WITH A DOUBLE FRONT-TUCK SPRING...
TWIRL!
SPIN!
SUGAR...
...HALF-TURN...
CRYSTAL PALACE SPORTS CENTRE
SPRING!
...FULL-QUARTER TWIRL...
1969 FINALS
JUDGES
LEAP!
...TRIPLE-SPIN TWISTED PIKE DISMOUNT...
SCRAPE!
OH, DEAR. THAT'S GOT TO HURT.
TWAT!
LAST GANG IN TOWN
NIL POINTS
54-46 WAS MY NUMBER

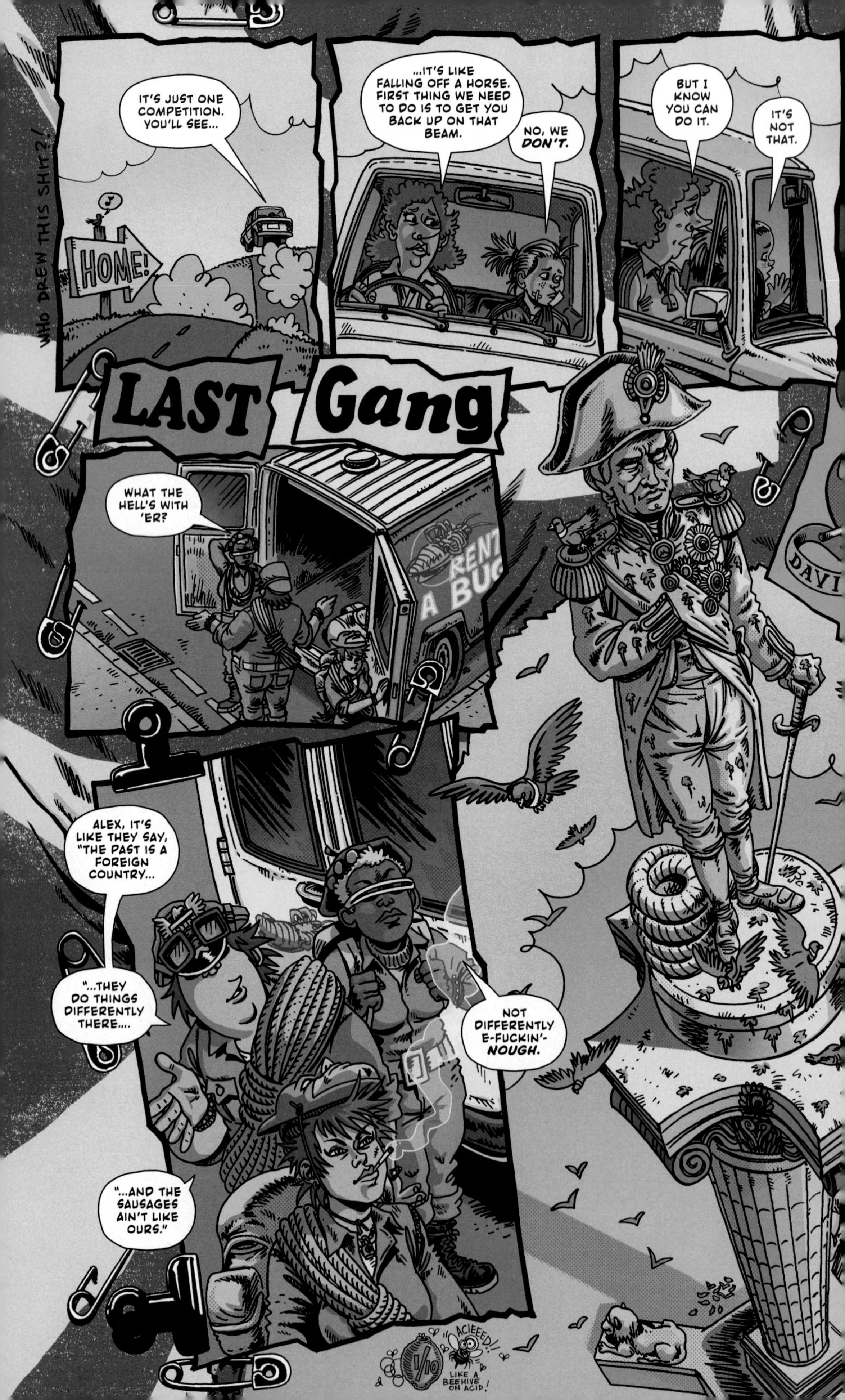
WHO DREW THIS SHIT?!
HOME!
IT'S JUST ONE COMPETITION. YOU'LL SEE...
...IT'S LIKE FALLING OFF A HORSE. FIRST THING WE NEED TO DO IS TO GET YOU BACK UP ON THAT BEAM.
NO, WE DON'T.
BUT I KNOW YOU CAN DO IT.
IT'S NOT THAT.
LAST Gang
WHAT THE HELL'S WITH 'ER?
RENT A BUG
DAVI
ALEX, IT'S LIKE THEY SAY, "THE PAST IS A FOREIGN COUNTRY...
"...THEY DO THINGS DIFFERENTLY THERE....
NOT DIFFERENTLY E-FUCKIN'-NOUGH.
"...AND THE SAUSAGES AIN'T LIKE OURS."
ACIEEED!!
LIKE A BEEHIVE ON ACID!

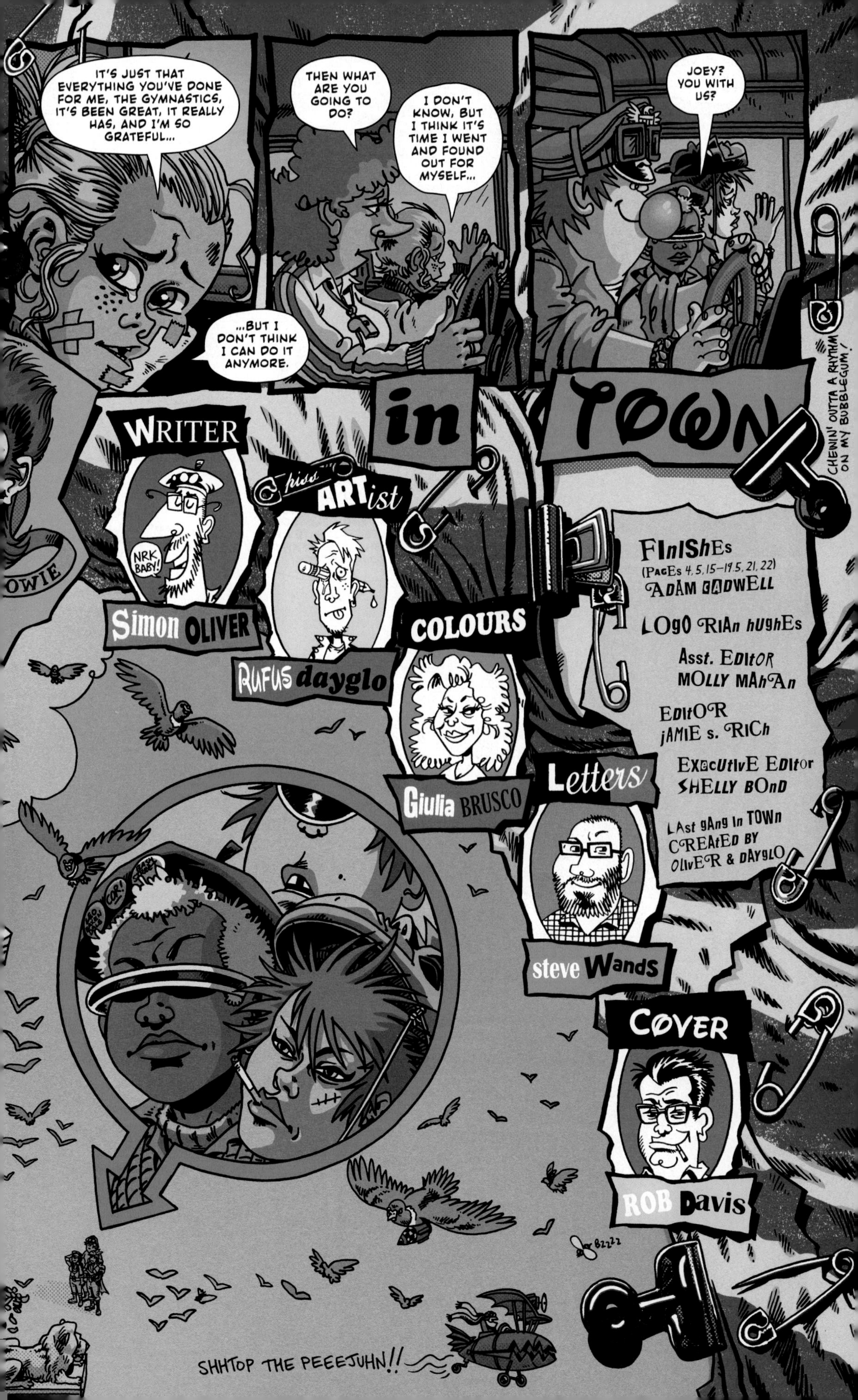

IT'S JUST THAT EVERYTHING YOU'VE DONE FOR ME, THE GYMNASTICS, IT'S BEEN GREAT, IT REALLY HAS, AND I'M SO GRATEFUL...
...BUT I DON'T THINK I CAN DO IT ANYMORE.
THEN WHAT ARE YOU GOING TO DO?
I DON'T KNOW, BUT I THINK IT'S TIME I WENT AND FOUND OUT FOR MYSELF...
JOEY? YOU WITH US?
CHEWIN' OUTTA A RHYTHM ON MY BUBBLEGUM!
in TOWN
WRITER
NRK BABY!
Simon OLIVER
ARTist
RUFUS dayglo
COLOURS
Giulia BRUSCO
Letters
steve Wands
COVER
ROB Davis
FInIShEs
(PAGES 4, 5, 15–19.5, 21, 22)
ADAM CADWELL
LOgO RIAn hUghEs
Asst. EDItOR
MOLLY MAhAn
EDItOR
jAMIE s. RICh
ExECUtIvE EDItOR
SHELLY BOnD
LAst gAng In TOWn
CREAtED BY
OLIvER & DAYgLO
COR!
SHHTOP THE PEEEJUHN!!

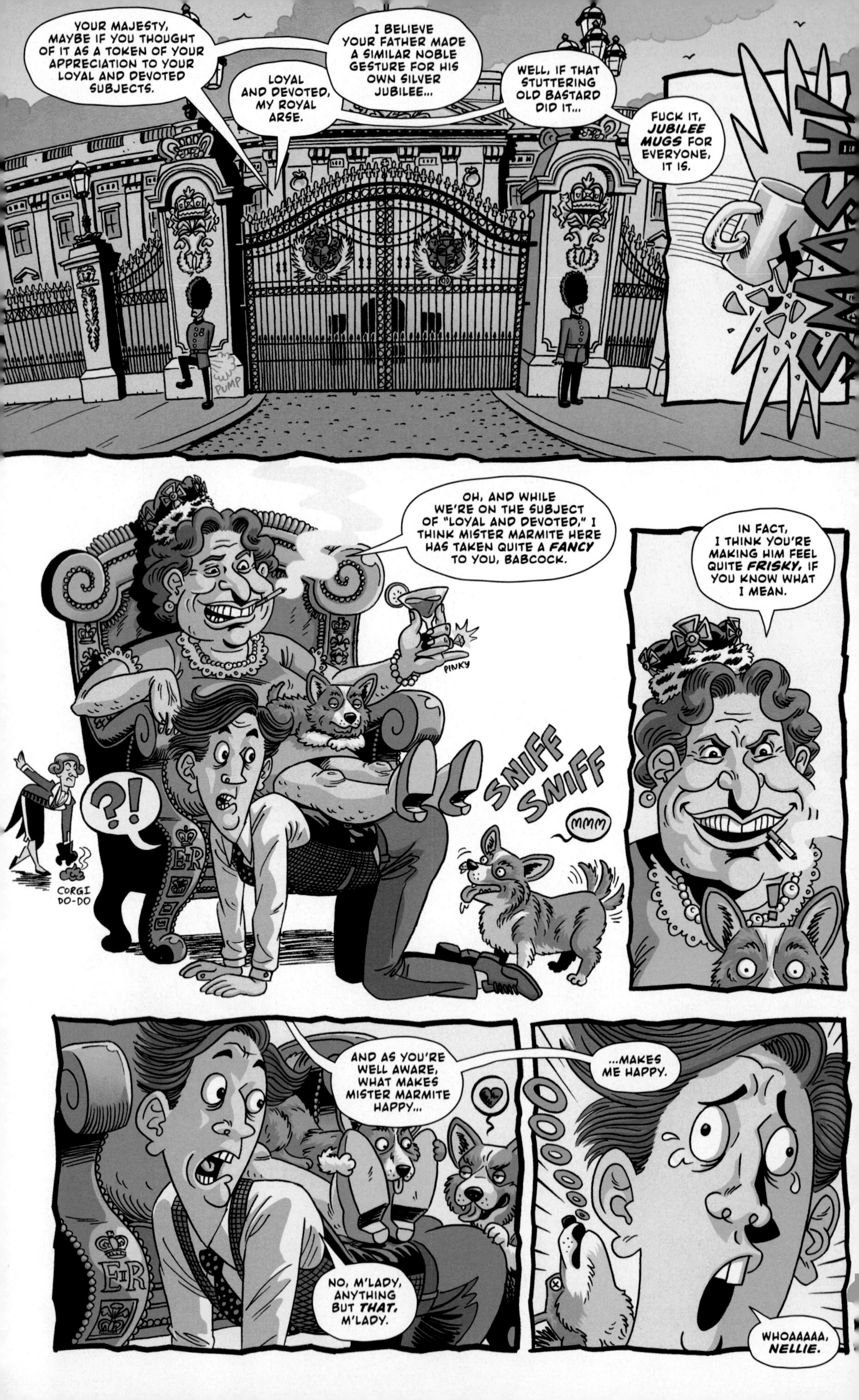
YOUR MAJESTY, MAYBE IF YOU THOUGHT OF IT AS A TOKEN OF YOUR APPRECIATION TO YOUR LOYAL AND DEVOTED SUBJECTS.
LOYAL AND DEVOTED, MY ROYAL ARSE.
I BELIEVE YOUR FATHER MADE A SIMILAR NOBLE GESTURE FOR HIS OWN SILVER JUBILEE...
WELL, IF THAT STUTTERING OLD BASTARD DID IT...
FUCK IT, JUBILEE MUGS FOR EVERYONE, IT IS.
SMASH!
PUMP
OH, AND WHILE WE'RE ON THE SUBJECT OF "LOYAL AND DEVOTED," I THINK MISTER MARMITE HERE HAS TAKEN QUITE A FANCY TO YOU, BABCOCK.
PINKY
?!
CORGI DO-DO
SNIFF SNIFF
MMM
IN FACT, I THINK YOU'RE MAKING HIM FEEL QUITE FRISKY, IF YOU KNOW WHAT I MEAN.
AND AS YOU'RE WELL AWARE, WHAT MAKES MISTER MARMITE HAPPY...
...MAKES ME HAPPY.
NO, M'LADY, ANYTHING BUT THAT, M'LADY.
WHOAAAAA, NELLIE.

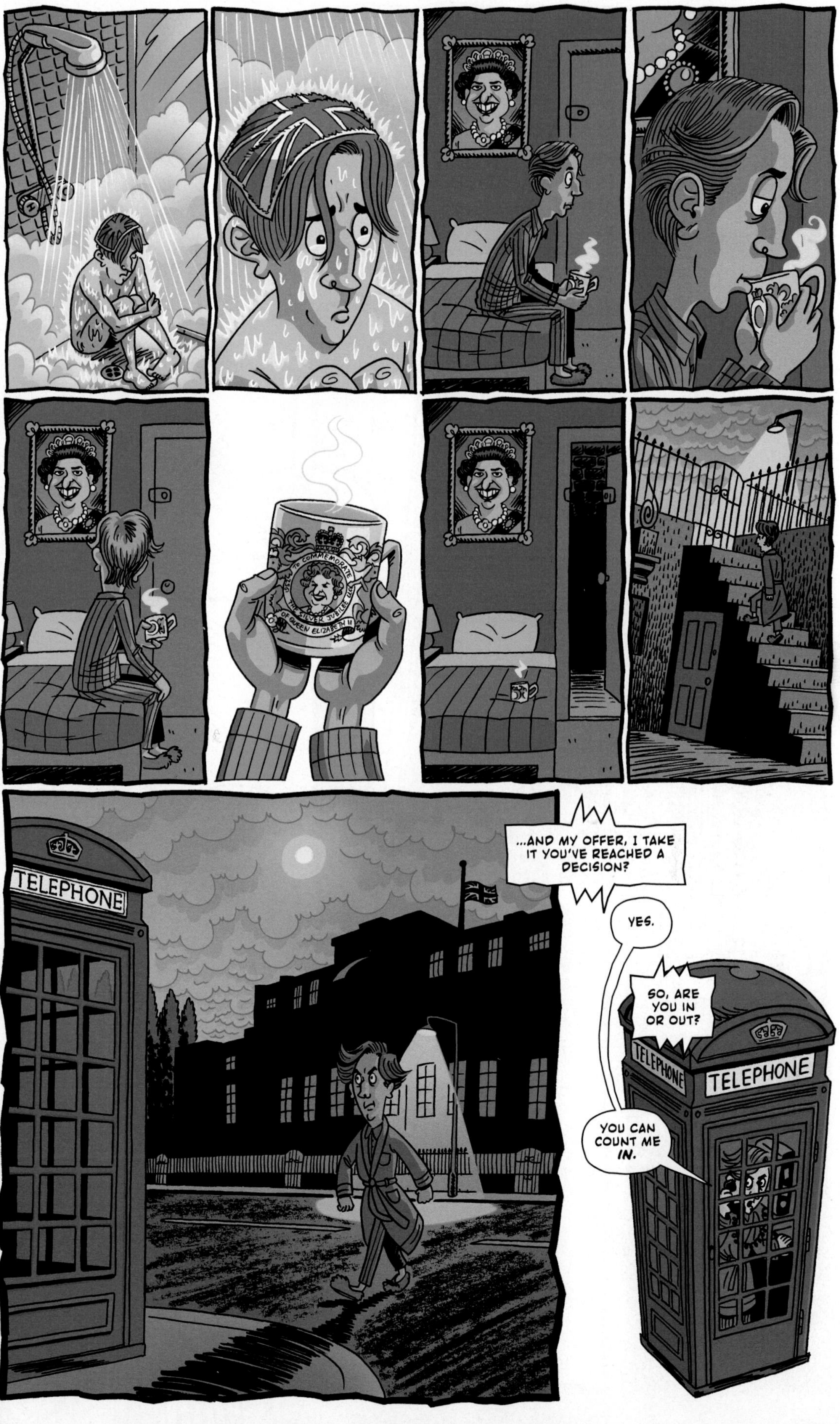
TO COMMEMORATE
THE SILVER JUBILEE
OF QUEEN ELIZABETH II
TELEPHONE
...AND MY OFFER, I TAKE IT YOU'VE REACHED A DECISION?
YES.
SO, ARE YOU IN OR OUT?
TELEPHONE
TELEPHONE
YOU CAN COUNT ME *IN.*

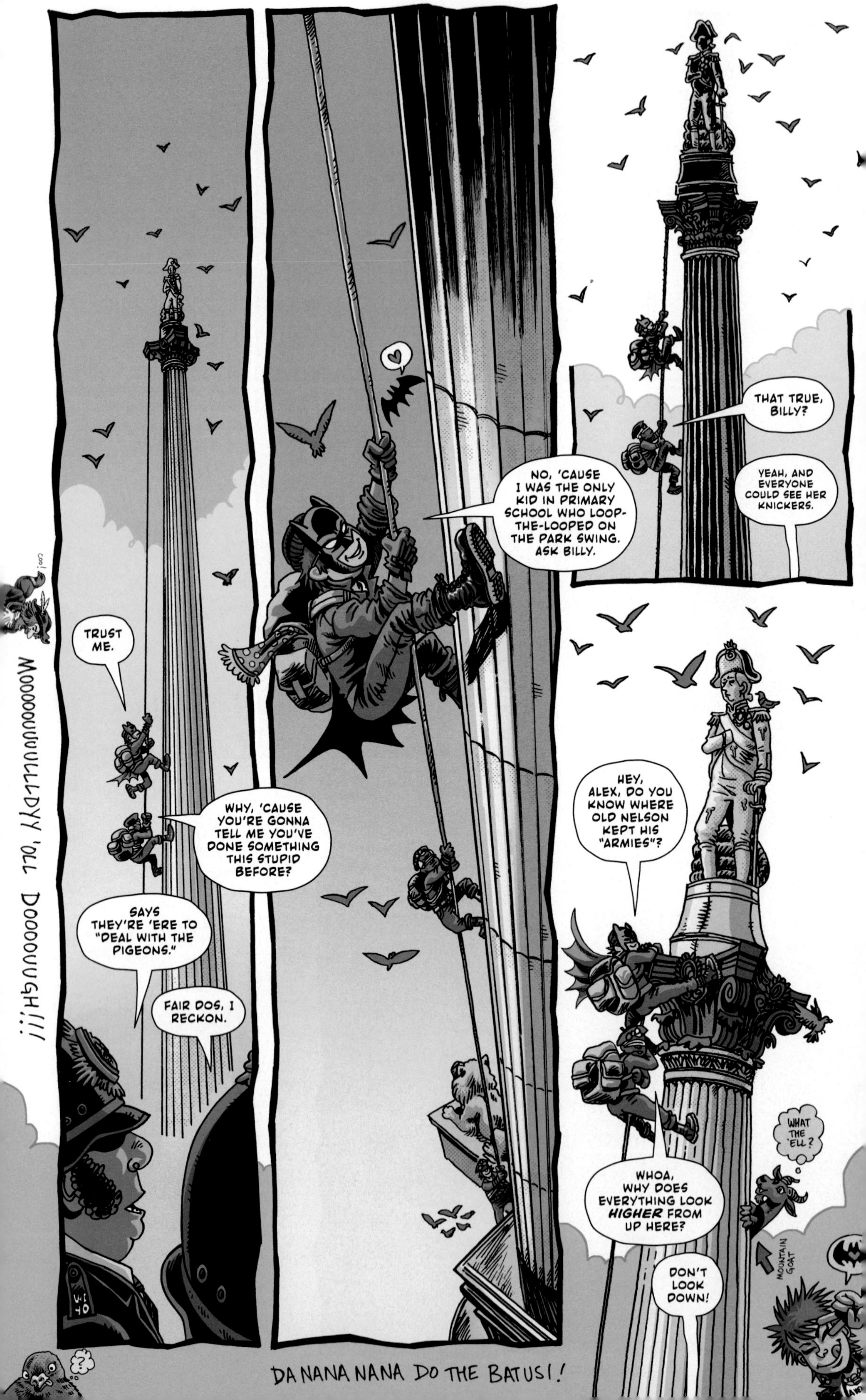
TRUST ME.
WHY, 'CAUSE YOU'RE GONNA TELL ME YOU'VE DONE SOMETHING THIS STUPID BEFORE?
SAYS THEY'RE 'ERE TO "DEAL WITH THE PIGEONS."
FAIR DOS, I RECKON.
NO, 'CAUSE I WAS THE ONLY KID IN PRIMARY SCHOOL WHO LOOP-THE-LOOPED ON THE PARK SWING. ASK BILLY.
THAT TRUE, BILLY?
YEAH, AND EVERYONE COULD SEE HER KNICKERS.
HEY, ALEX, DO YOU KNOW WHERE OLD NELSON KEPT HIS "ARMIES"?
WHOA, WHY DOES EVERYTHING LOOK **HIGHER** FROM UP HERE?
DON'T LOOK DOWN!
WHAT THE 'ELL?
MOUNTAIN GOAT
COO!
MOOOOUUULLLDYY 'OLL DOOOOUGH!!!
DA NANA NANA DO THE BATUSI!

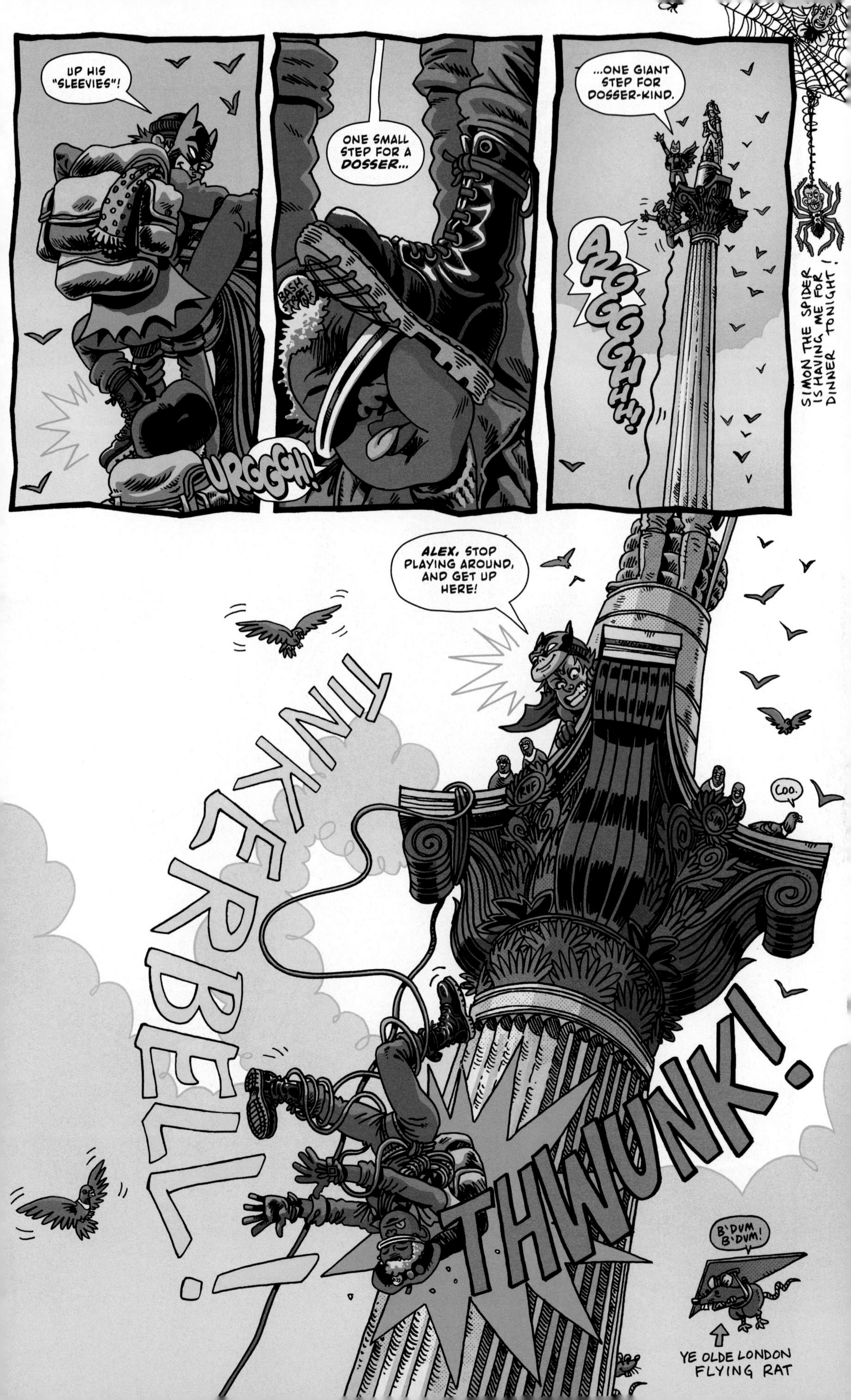

UP HIS "SLEEVIES"!
URGGGH!
ONE SMALL STEP FOR A DOSSER...
...ONE GIANT STEP FOR DOSSER-KIND.
ARGGGGHHH!
SIMON THE SPIDER IS HAVING ME FOR DINNER TONIGHT!
ALEX, STOP PLAYING AROUND, AND GET UP HERE!
TINKERBELL!
COO.
THWUNK!
B'DUM B'DUM!
YE OLDE LONDON FLYING RAT

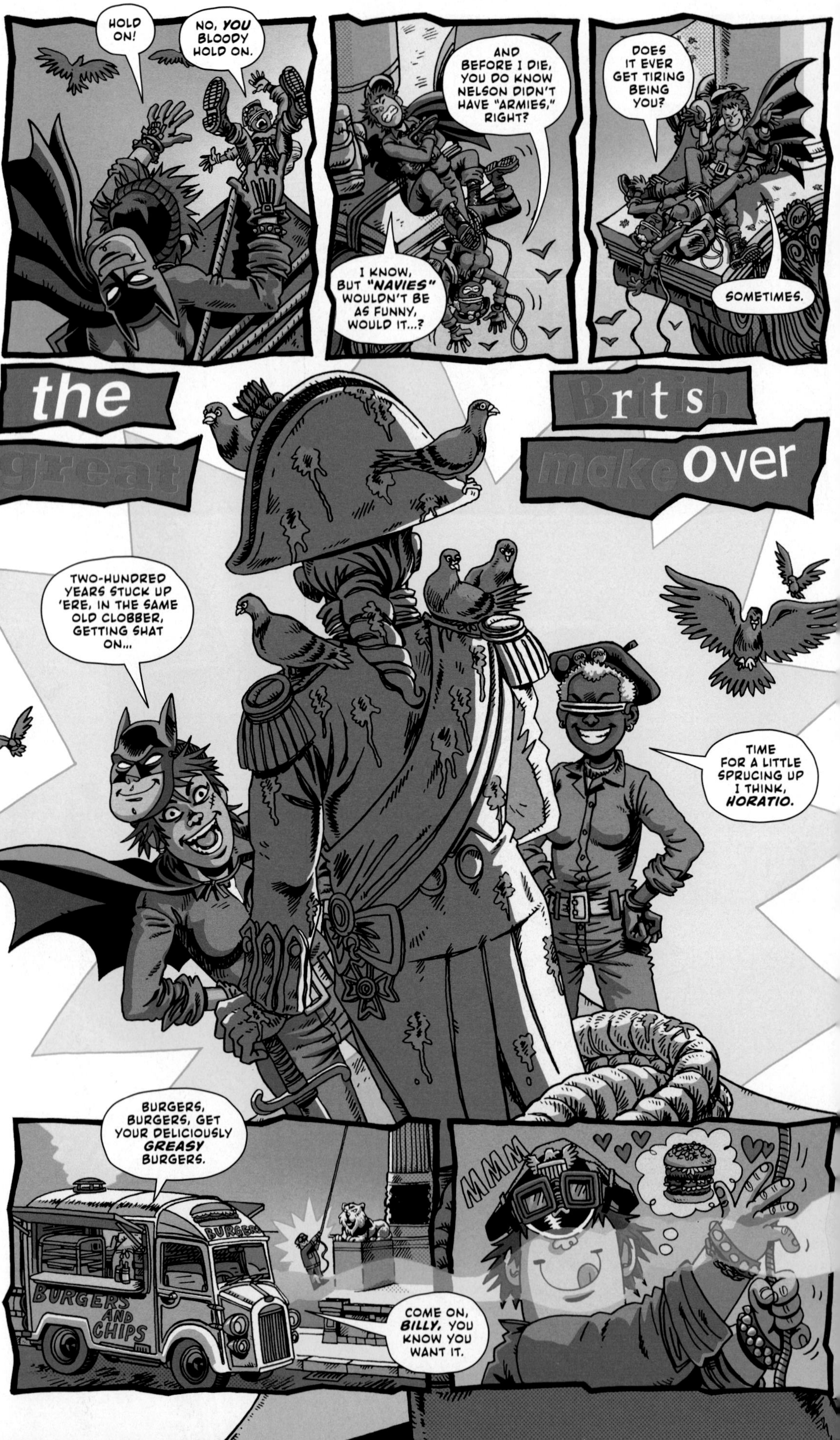
HOLD ON!
NO, YOU BLOODY HOLD ON.
AND BEFORE I DIE, YOU DO KNOW NELSON DIDN'T HAVE "ARMIES," RIGHT?
I KNOW, BUT "NAVIES" WOULDN'T BE AS FUNNY, WOULD IT...?
DOES IT EVER GET TIRING BEING YOU?
SOMETIMES.
the great British makeOver
TWO-HUNDRED YEARS STUCK UP 'ERE, IN THE SAME OLD CLOBBER, GETTING SHAT ON...
TIME FOR A LITTLE SPRUCING UP I THINK, HORATIO.
BURGERS, BURGERS, GET YOUR DELICIOUSLY GREASY BURGERS.
BURGERS
BURGERS AND CHIPS
COME ON, BILLY, YOU KNOW YOU WANT IT.
MMM

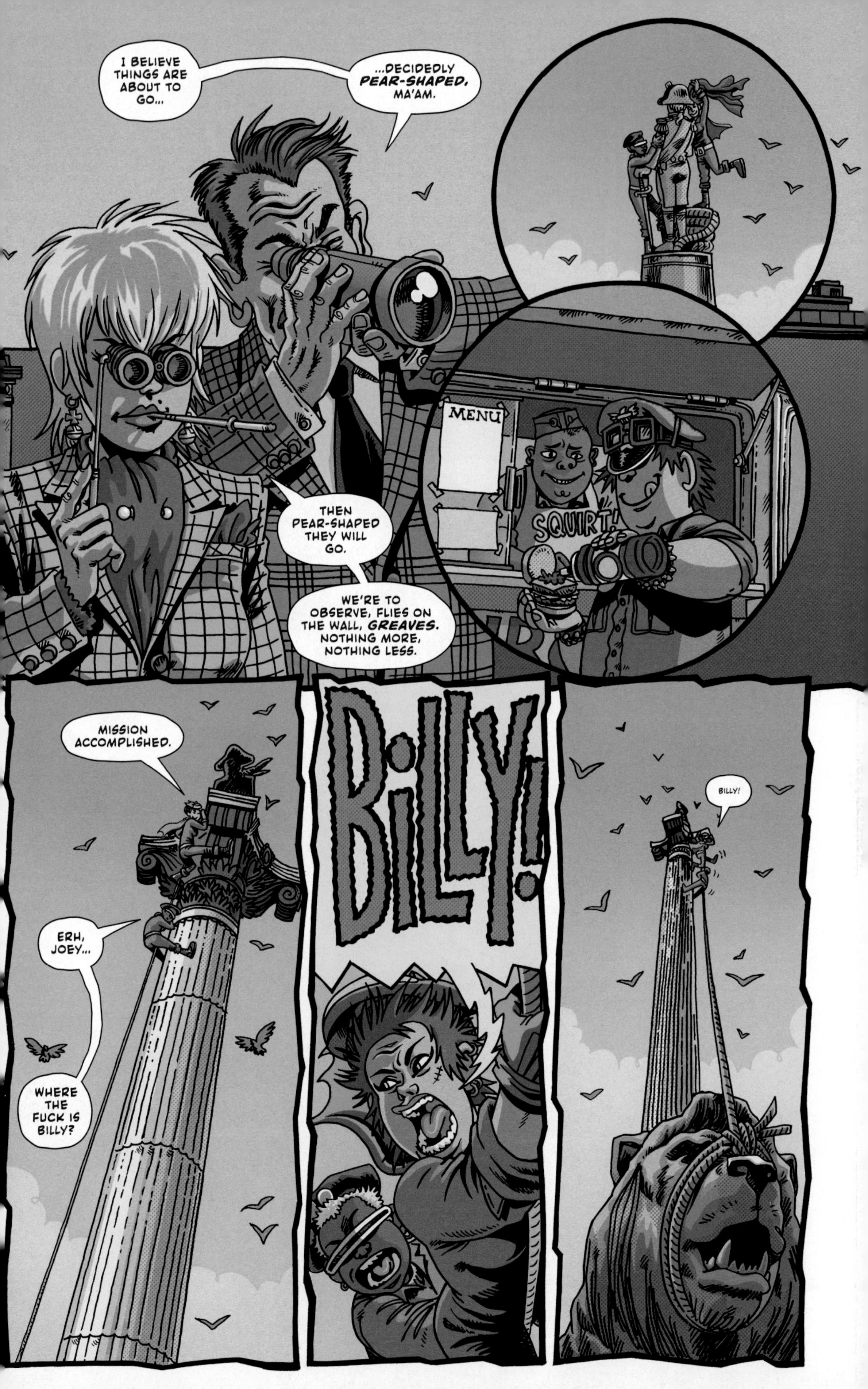
I BELIEVE THINGS ARE ABOUT TO GO...
...DECIDEDLY *PEAR-SHAPED,* MA'AM.
MENU
SQUIRT!
THEN PEAR-SHAPED THEY WILL GO.
WE'RE TO OBSERVE, FLIES ON THE WALL, *GREAVES.* NOTHING MORE, NOTHING LESS.
MISSION ACCOMPLISHED.
ERH, JOEY...
WHERE THE FUCK IS BILLY?
BILLY!
BILLY!

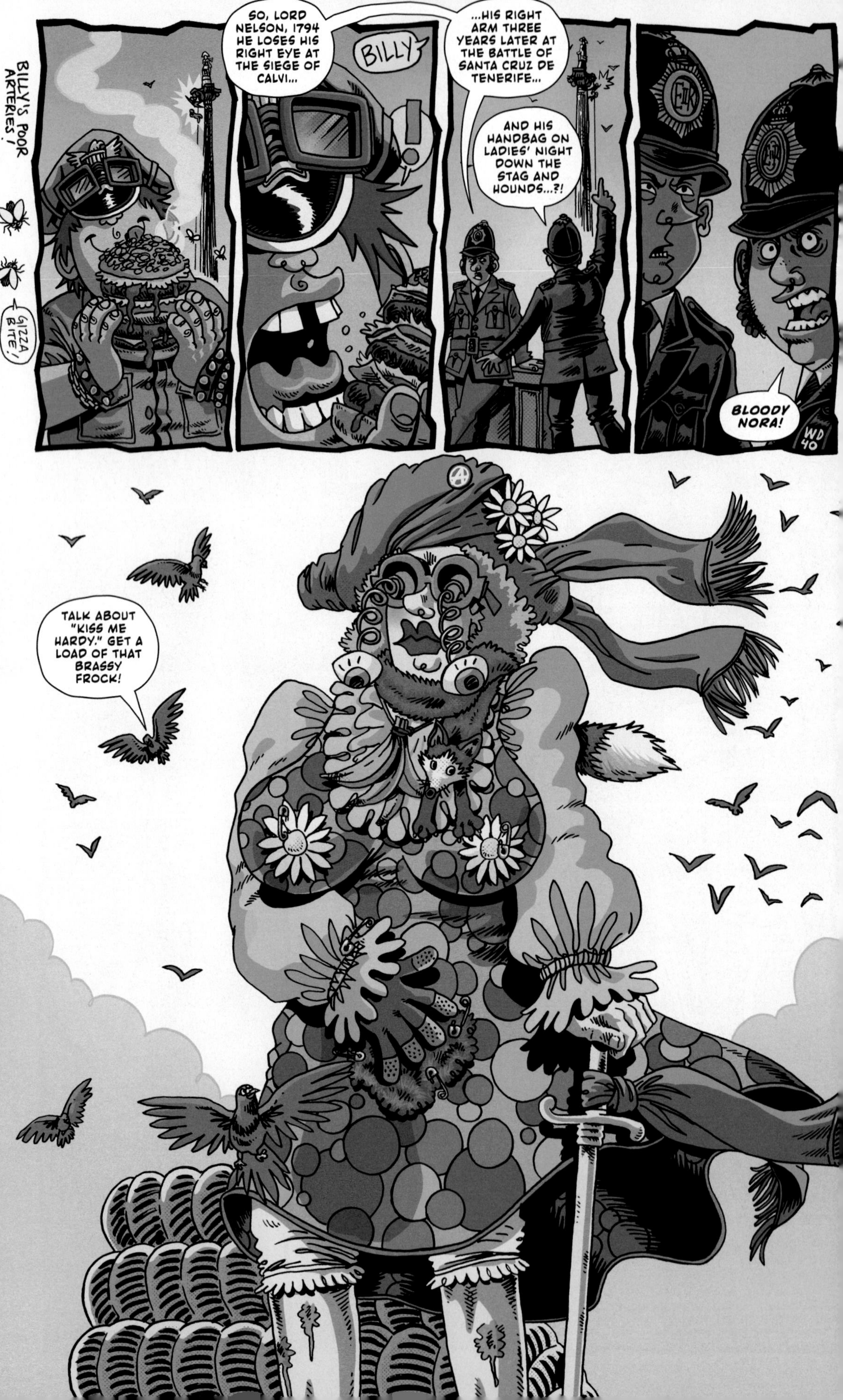
BILLY'S POOR ARTERIES!
GIZZA BITE!
SO, LORD NELSON, 1794 HE LOSES HIS RIGHT EYE AT THE SIEGE OF CALVI...
BILLY
...HIS RIGHT ARM THREE YEARS LATER AT THE BATTLE OF SANTA CRUZ DE TENERIFE...
AND HIS HANDBAG ON LADIES' NIGHT DOWN THE STAG AND HOUNDS...?!
BLOODY NORA!
WD 40
TALK ABOUT "KISS ME HARDY." GET A LOAD OF THAT BRASSY FROCK!

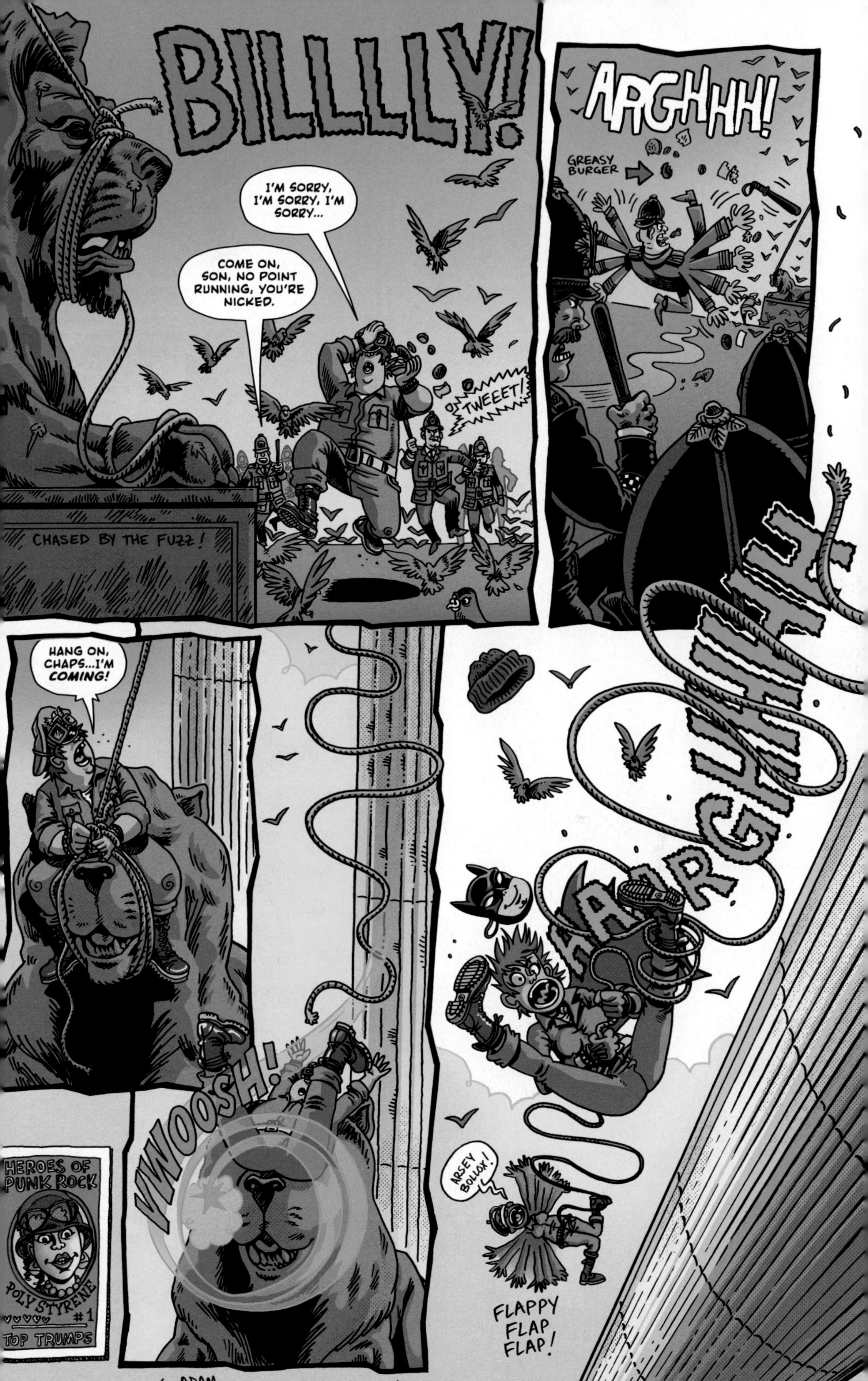
BILLLLY!
I'M SORRY, I'M SORRY, I'M SORRY...
COME ON, SON, NO POINT RUNNING, YOU'RE NICKED.
TWEEET!
CHASED BY THE FUZZ!
ARGHHH!
GREASY BURGER
HANG ON, CHAPS...I'M COMING!
WOOSH!
AARGHHHHH!
ARSEY BOLLOX!
FLAPPY FLAP FLAP!
HEROES OF PUNK ROCK
POLY STYRENE
#1
TOP TRUMPS

ADAM THE ANT SEZ WUT A WAZZOCH!

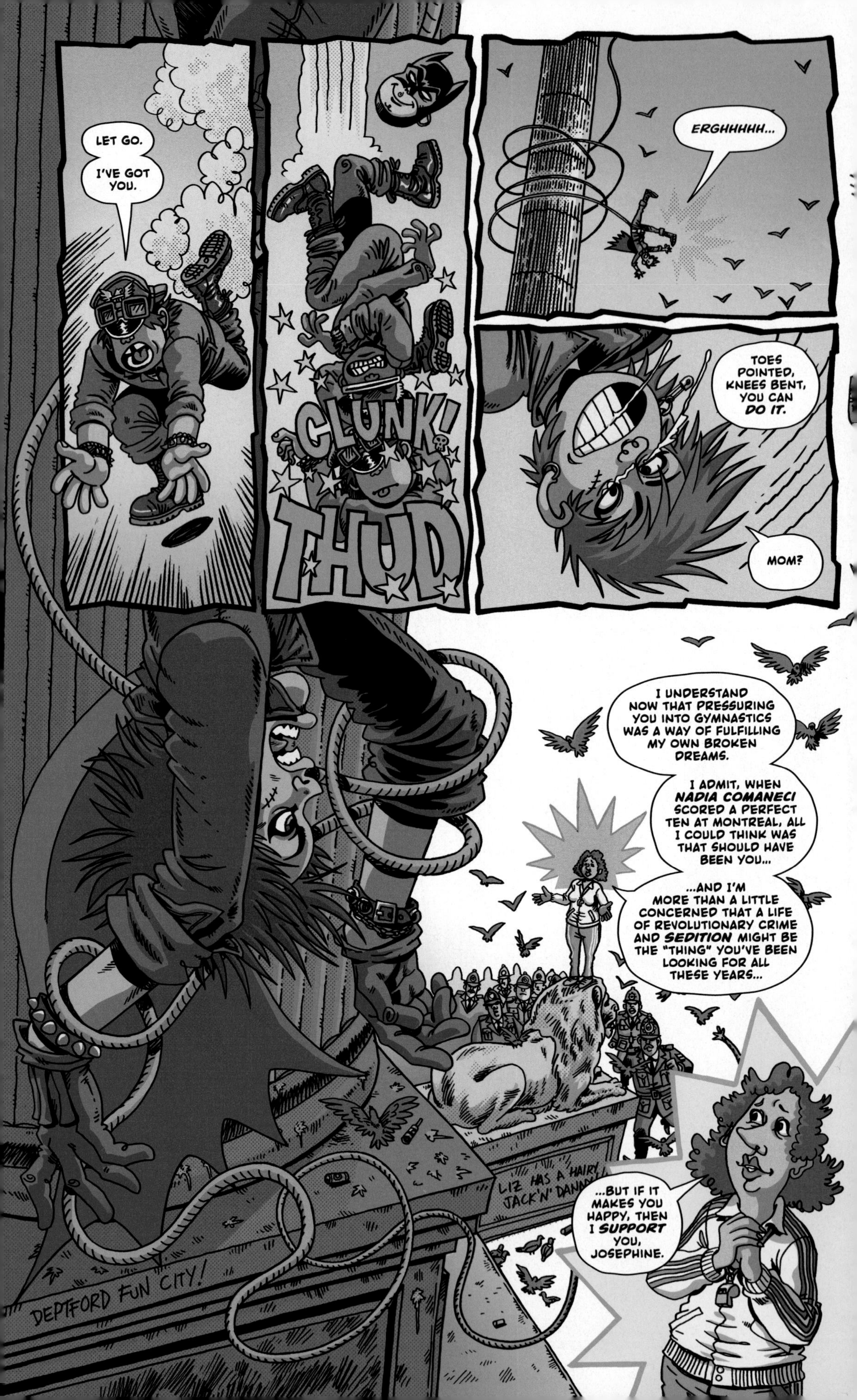
LET GO.
I'VE GOT YOU.
CLUNK!
THUD
ERGHHHHH...
TOES POINTED, KNEES BENT, YOU CAN DO IT.
MOM?
I UNDERSTAND NOW THAT PRESSURING YOU INTO GYMNASTICS WAS A WAY OF FULFILLING MY OWN BROKEN DREAMS.
I ADMIT, WHEN NADIA COMANECI SCORED A PERFECT TEN AT MONTREAL, ALL I COULD THINK WAS THAT SHOULD HAVE BEEN YOU...
...AND I'M MORE THAN A LITTLE CONCERNED THAT A LIFE OF REVOLUTIONARY CRIME AND SEDITION MIGHT BE THE "THING" YOU'VE BEEN LOOKING FOR ALL THESE YEARS...
...BUT IF IT MAKES YOU HAPPY, THEN I SUPPORT YOU, JOSEPHINE.
DEPTFORD FUN CITY!

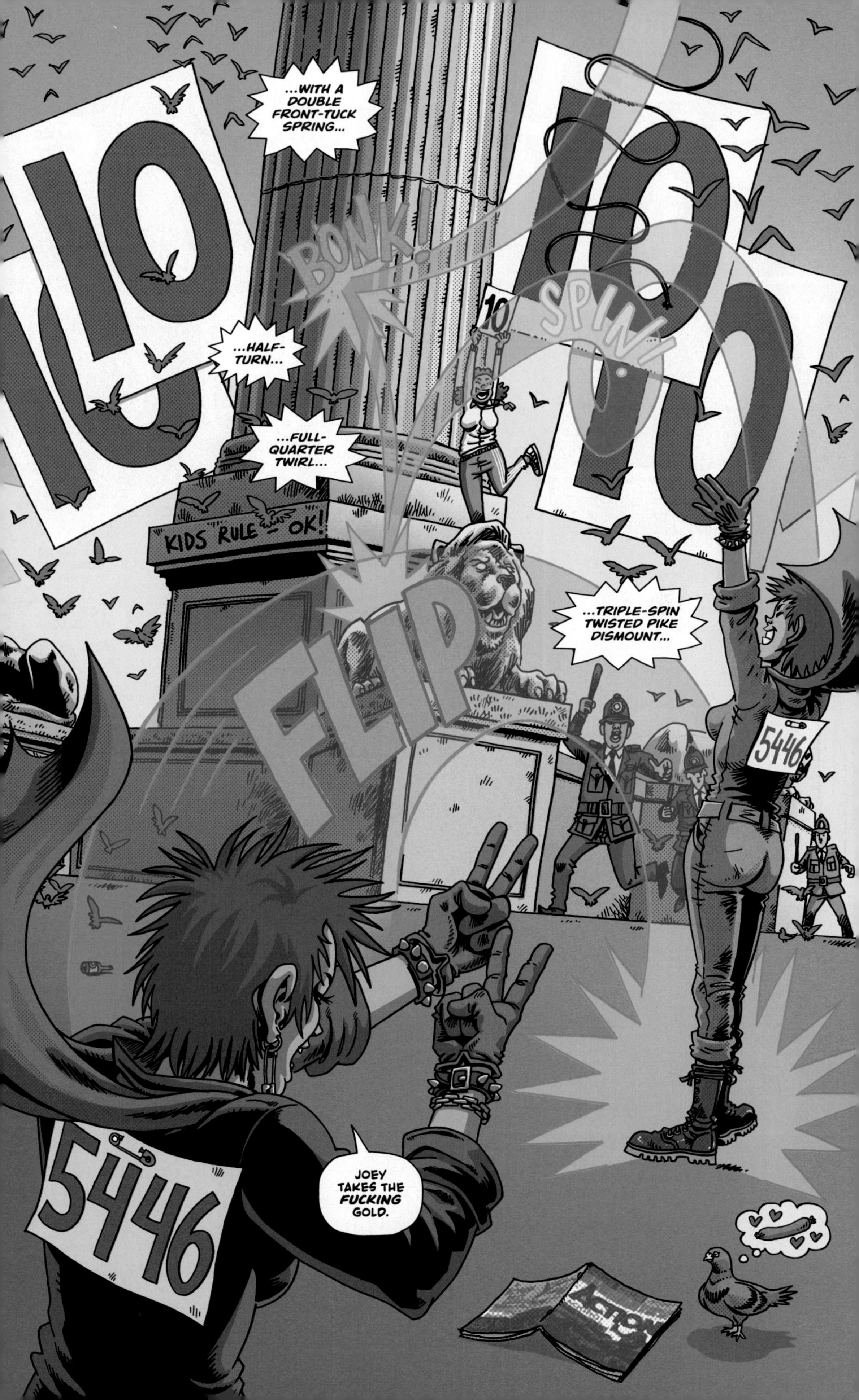

...WITH A DOUBLE FRONT-TUCK SPRING...
BONK!
SPIN!
...HALF-TURN...
...FULL-QUARTER TWIRL...
KIDS RULE - OK!
FLIP
...TRIPLE-SPIN TWISTED PIKE DISMOUNT...
5446
JOEY TAKES THE FUCKING GOLD.

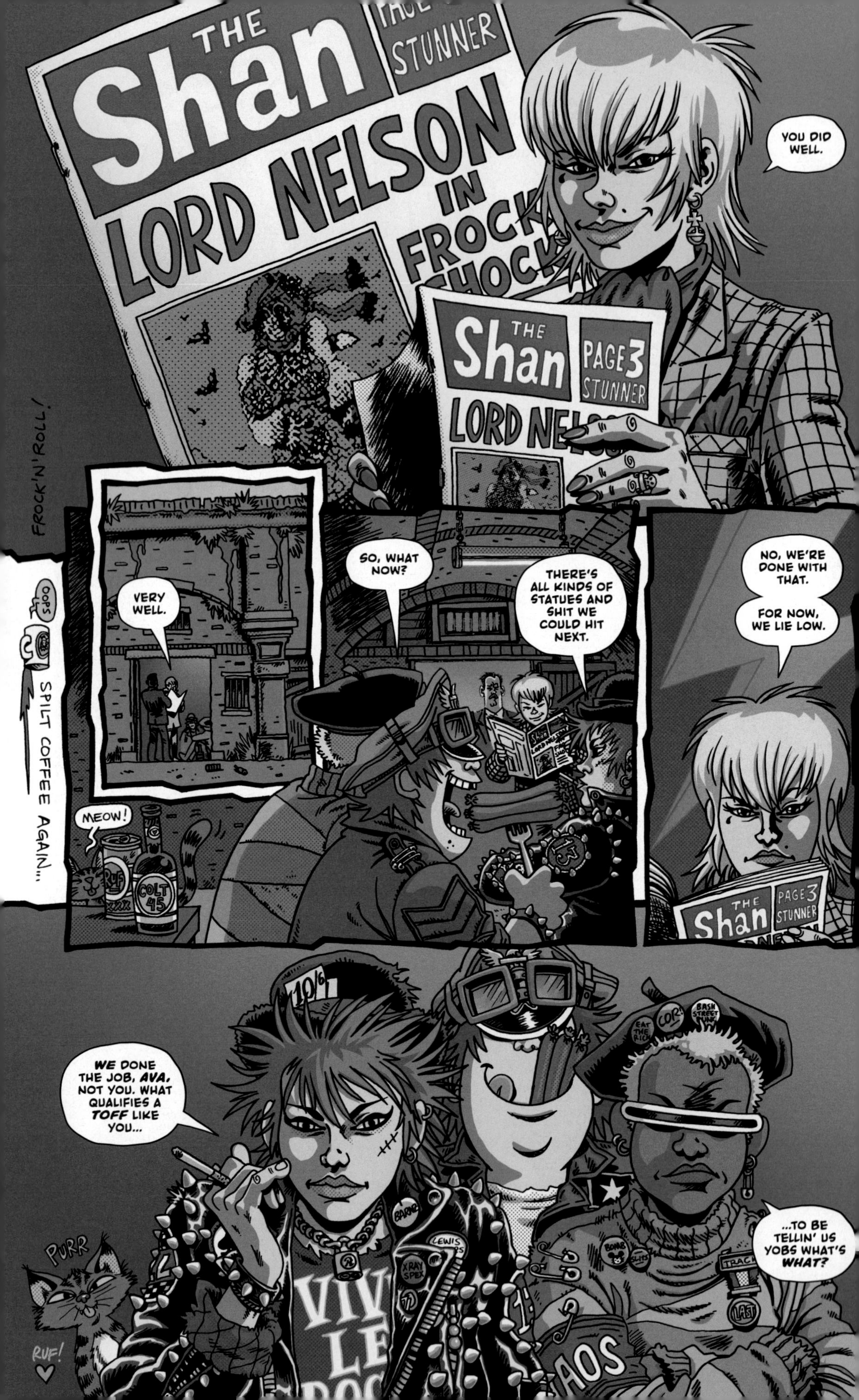
THE Shan
STUNNER
LORD NELSON IN
THE Shan PAGE 3 STUNNER
LORD NE
YOU DID WELL.
FROCK'N'ROLL!
VERY WELL.
SO, WHAT NOW?
THERE'S ALL KINDS OF STATUES AND SHIT WE COULD HIT NEXT.
NO, WE'RE DONE WITH THAT.
FOR NOW, WE LIE LOW.
OOPS
SPILT COFFEE AGAIN...
MEOW!
COLT 45
THE Shan PAGE 3 STUNNER
10/6
EAT THE RICH
COR!
BASH STREET
WE DONE THE JOB, AVA, NOT YOU. WHAT QUALIFIES A TOFF LIKE YOU...
...TO BE TELLIN' US YOBS WHAT'S WHAT?
PURR
X RAY SPEX
RUF!

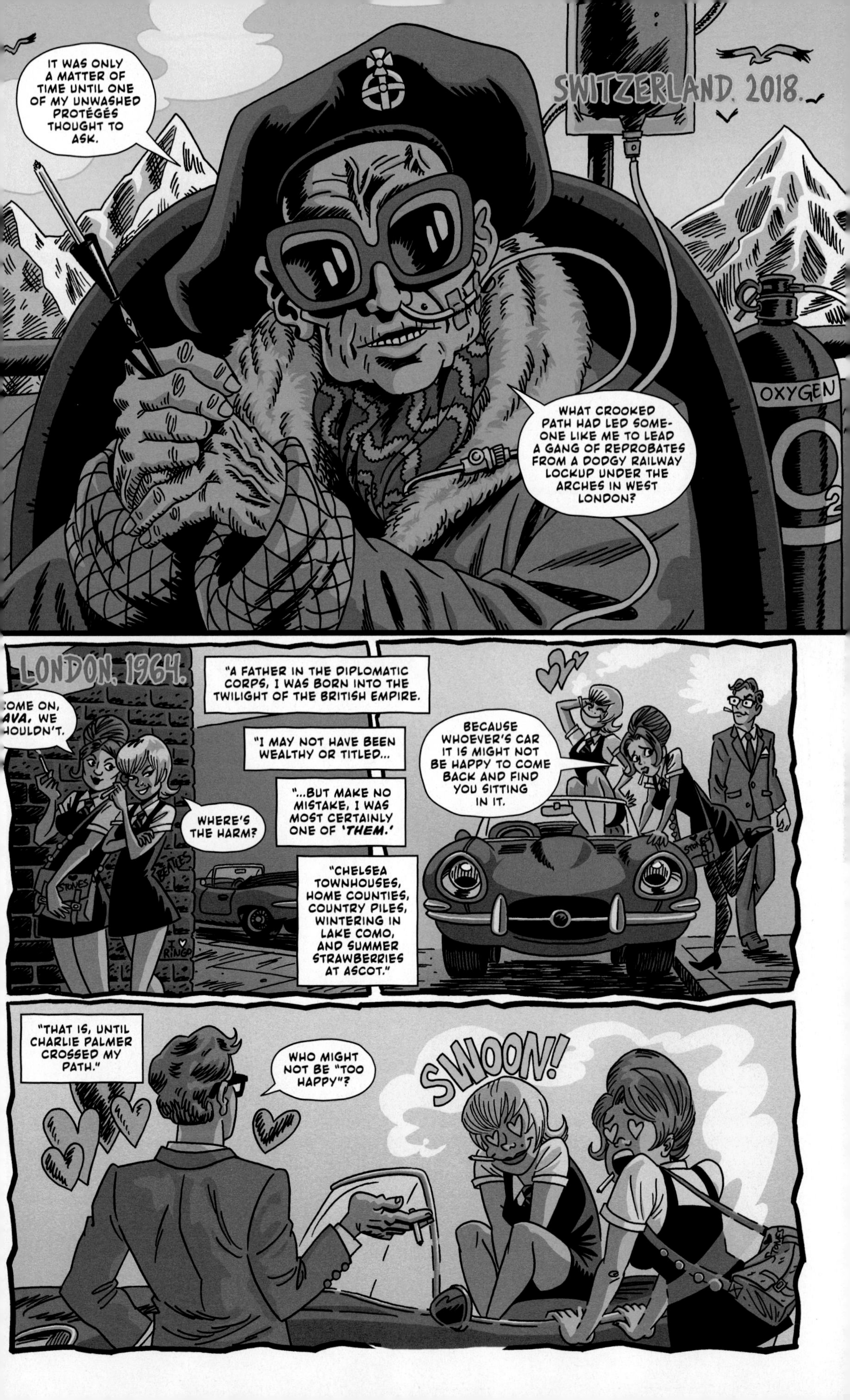
SWITZERLAND, 2018.
IT WAS ONLY A MATTER OF TIME UNTIL ONE OF MY UNWASHED PROTÉGÉS THOUGHT TO ASK.
WHAT CROOKED PATH HAD LED SOMEONE LIKE ME TO LEAD A GANG OF REPROBATES FROM A DODGY RAILWAY LOCKUP UNDER THE ARCHES IN WEST LONDON?
OXYGEN
LONDON, 1964.
"A FATHER IN THE DIPLOMATIC CORPS, I WAS BORN INTO THE TWILIGHT OF THE BRITISH EMPIRE.
"I MAY NOT HAVE BEEN WEALTHY OR TITLED...
"...BUT MAKE NO MISTAKE, I WAS MOST CERTAINLY ONE OF '*THEM*.'
"CHELSEA TOWNHOUSES, HOME COUNTIES, COUNTRY PILES, WINTERING IN LAKE COMO, AND SUMMER STRAWBERRIES AT ASCOT."
OME ON, *AVA*. WE HOULDN'T.
WHERE'S THE HARM?
STONES
BEATLES
I ♥ RINGO
BECAUSE WHOEVER'S CAR IT IS MIGHT NOT BE HAPPY TO COME BACK AND FIND YOU SITTING IN IT.
"THAT IS, UNTIL CHARLIE PALMER CROSSED MY PATH."
WHO MIGHT NOT BE "TOO HAPPY"?
SWOON!

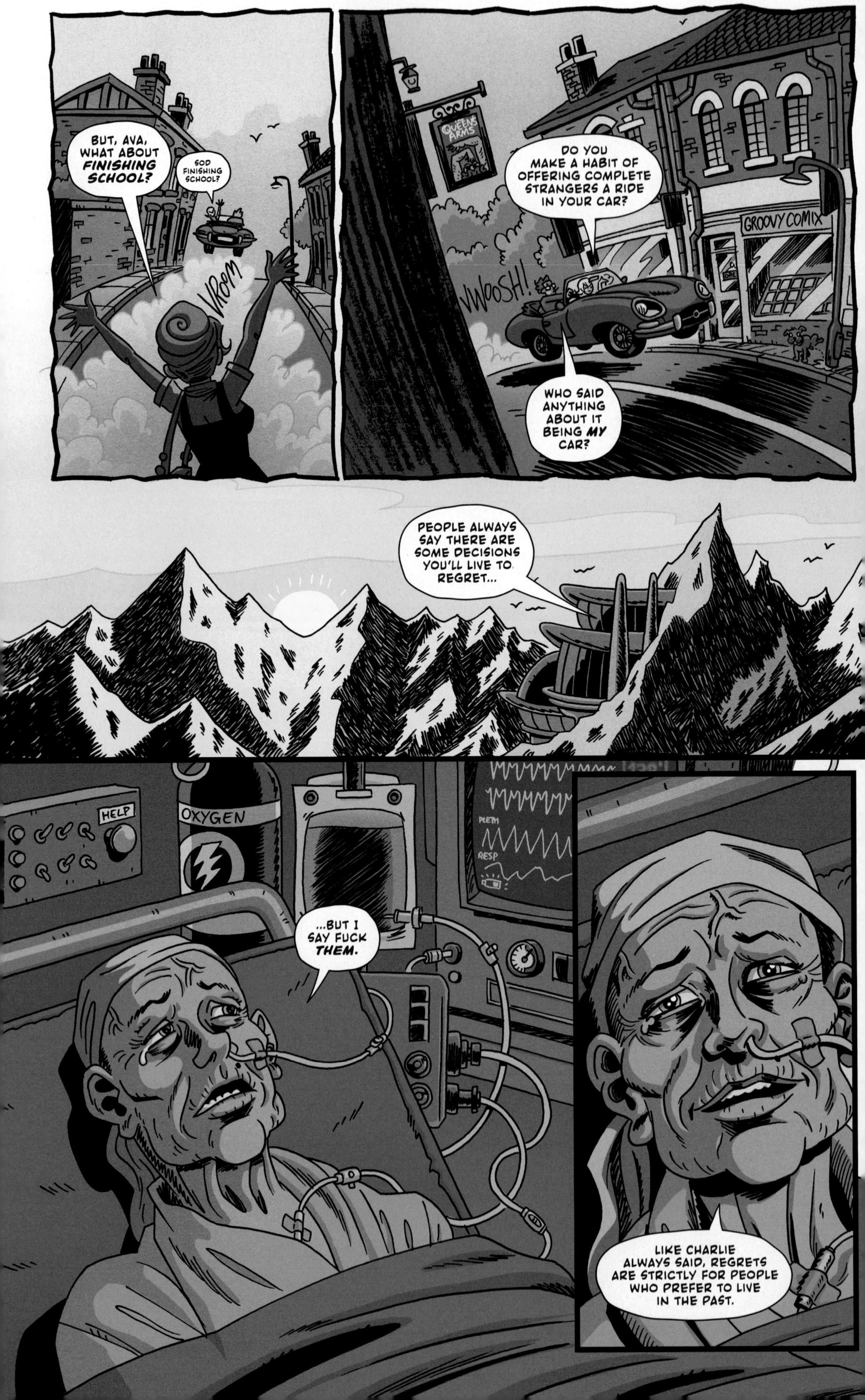
BUT, AVA, WHAT ABOUT FINISHING SCHOOL?
SOD FINISHING SCHOOL!
VROOM
QUEEN'S ARMS
DO YOU MAKE A HABIT OF OFFERING COMPLETE STRANGERS A RIDE IN YOUR CAR?
GROOVY COMIX
VWOOSH!
WHO SAID ANYTHING ABOUT IT BEING MY CAR?
PEOPLE ALWAYS SAY THERE ARE SOME DECISIONS YOU'LL LIVE TO REGRET...
HELP
OXYGEN
PLETH
RESP
...BUT I SAY FUCK THEM.
LIKE CHARLIE ALWAYS SAID, REGRETS ARE STRICTLY FOR PEOPLE WHO PREFER TO LIVE IN THE PAST.

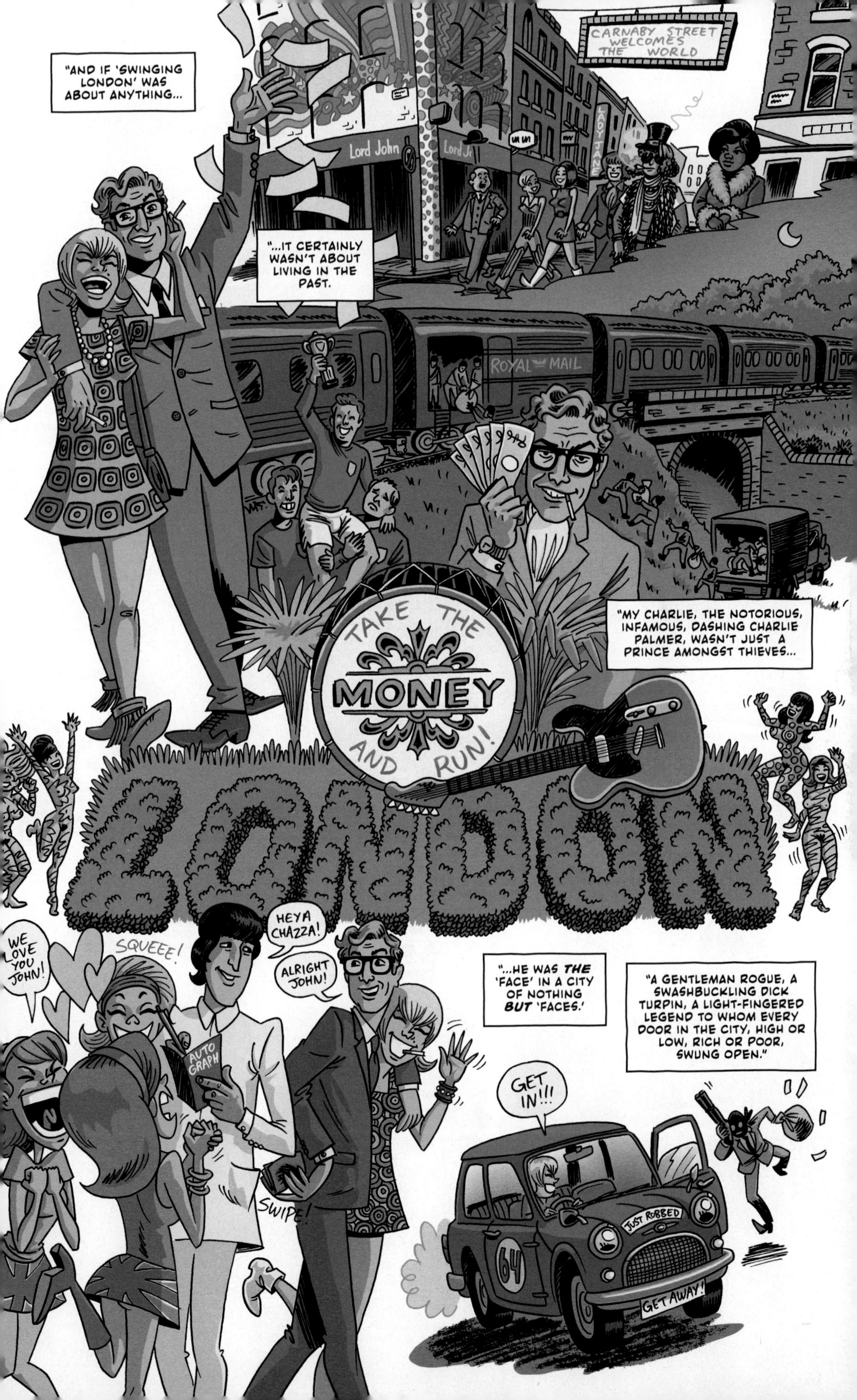
"AND IF 'SWINGING LONDON' WAS ABOUT ANYTHING...
CARNABY STREET WELCOMES THE WORLD
Lord John
LADY JANE
"...IT CERTAINLY WASN'T ABOUT LIVING IN THE PAST.
ROYAL MAIL
TAKE THE MONEY AND RUN!
"MY CHARLIE, THE NOTORIOUS, INFAMOUS, DASHING CHARLIE PALMER, WASN'T JUST A PRINCE AMONGST THIEVES...
LONDON
WE LOVE YOU JOHN!
SQUEEE!
HEYA CHAZZA!
ALRIGHT JOHN!
AUTO GRAPH
SWIPE!
"...HE WAS THE 'FACE' IN A CITY OF NOTHING BUT 'FACES.'
"A GENTLEMAN ROGUE, A SWASHBUCKLING DICK TURPIN, A LIGHT-FINGERED LEGEND TO WHOM EVERY DOOR IN THE CITY, HIGH OR LOW, RICH OR POOR, SWUNG OPEN."
GET IN!!!
JUST ROBBED
64
GETAWAY!

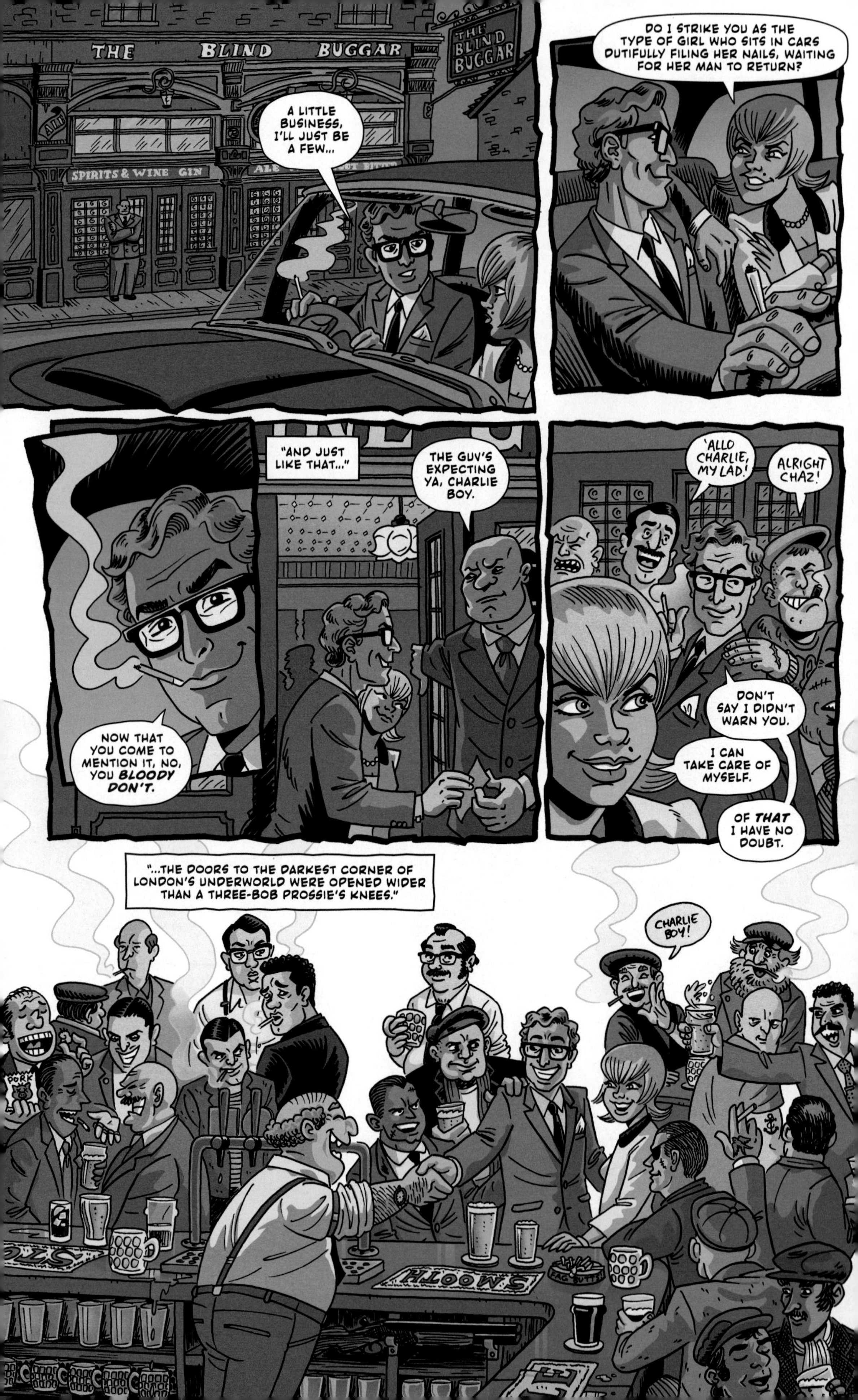
THE BLIND BUGGAR
SPIRITS & WINE GIN
THE BLIND BUGGAR
A LITTLE BUSINESS, I'LL JUST BE A FEW...
DO I STRIKE YOU AS THE TYPE OF GIRL WHO SITS IN CARS DUTIFULLY FILING HER NAILS, WAITING FOR HER MAN TO RETURN?
NOW THAT YOU COME TO MENTION IT, NO, YOU BLOODY DON'T.
"AND JUST LIKE THAT..."
THE GUV'S EXPECTING YA, CHARLIE BOY.
'ALLO CHARLIE, MY LAD!
ALRIGHT CHAZ!
DON'T SAY I DIDN'T WARN YOU.
I CAN TAKE CARE OF MYSELF.
OF THAT I HAVE NO DOUBT.
"...THE DOORS TO THE DARKEST CORNER OF LONDON'S UNDERWORLD WERE OPENED WIDER THAN A THREE-BOB PROSSIE'S KNEES."
CHARLIE BOY!
PORK
SMOOTH
FAG BUTTS

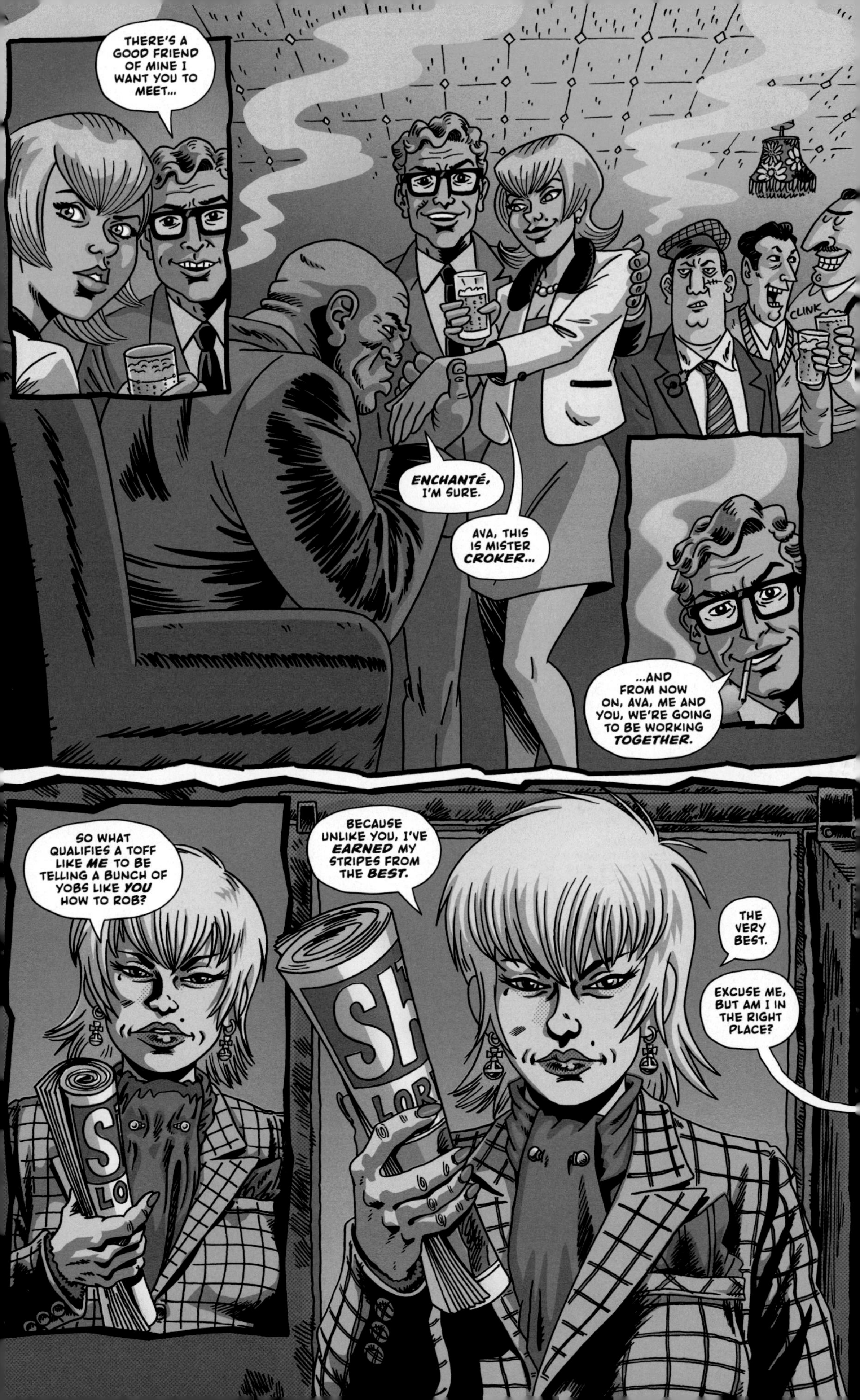
THERE'S A GOOD FRIEND OF MINE I WANT YOU TO MEET...
CLINK
ENCHANTÉ, I'M SURE.
AVA, THIS IS MISTER CROKER...
...AND FROM NOW ON, AVA, ME AND YOU, WE'RE GOING TO BE WORKING TOGETHER.
SO WHAT QUALIFIES A TOFF LIKE ME TO BE TELLING A BUNCH OF YOBS LIKE YOU HOW TO ROB?
BECAUSE UNLIKE YOU, I'VE EARNED MY STRIPES FROM THE BEST.
THE VERY BEST.
EXCUSE ME, BUT AM I IN THE RIGHT PLACE?

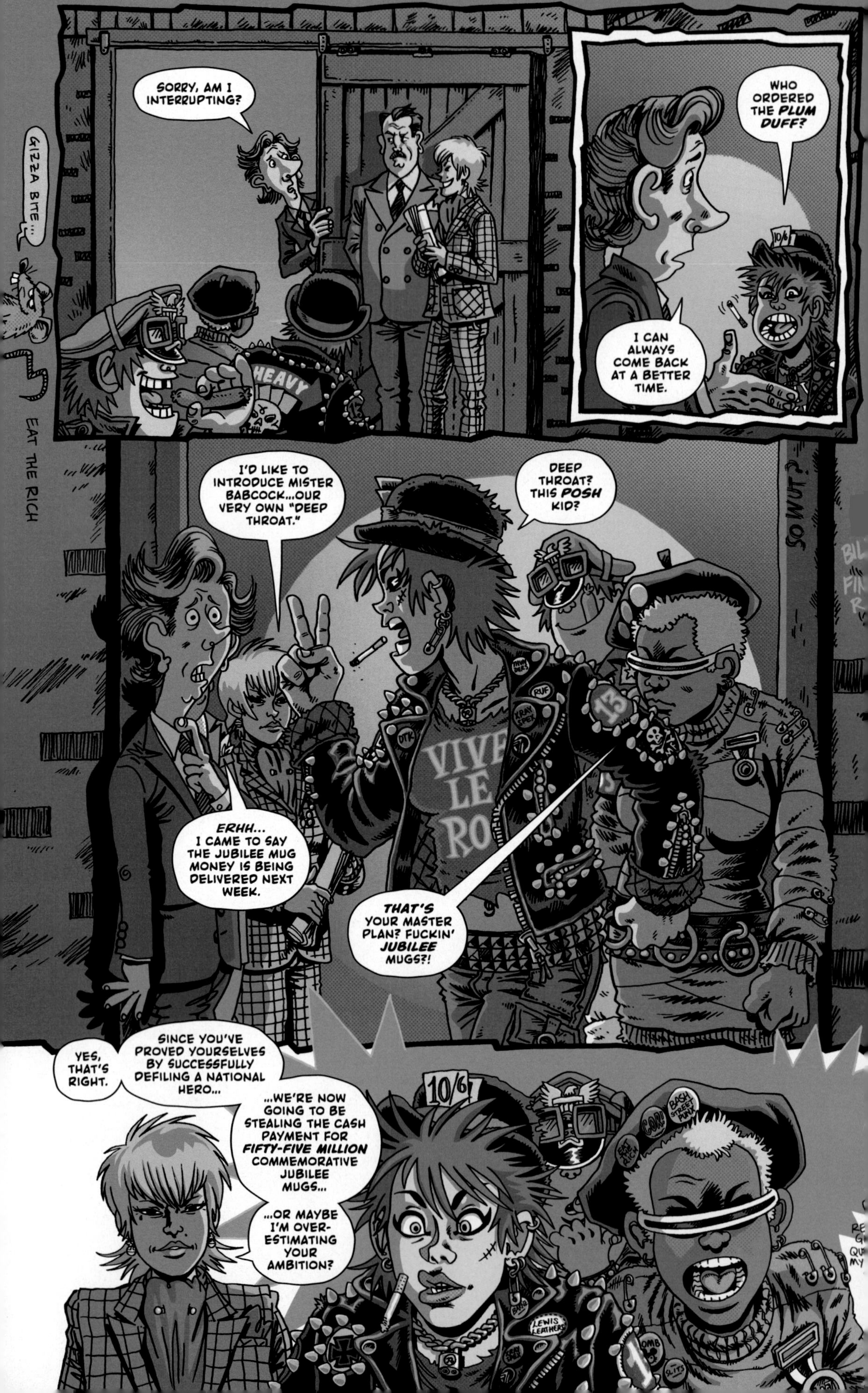
GIZZA BITE...
SORRY, AM I INTERRUPTING?
WHO ORDERED THE PLUM DUFF?
I CAN ALWAYS COME BACK AT A BETTER TIME.
HEAVY
10/6
EAT THE RICH
SO WUT?
I'D LIKE TO INTRODUCE MISTER BABCOCK...OUR VERY OWN "DEEP THROAT."
DEEP THROAT? THIS POSH KID?
ERHH... I CAME TO SAY THE JUBILEE MUG MONEY IS BEING DELIVERED NEXT WEEK.
THAT'S YOUR MASTER PLAN? FUCKIN' JUBILEE MUGS?!
VIVE LE RO
13
YES, THAT'S RIGHT.
SINCE YOU'VE PROVED YOURSELVES BY SUCCESSFULLY DEFILING A NATIONAL HERO...
...WE'RE NOW GOING TO BE STEALING THE CASH PAYMENT FOR FIFTY-FIVE MILLION COMMEMORATIVE JUBILEE MUGS...
...OR MAYBE I'M OVER-ESTIMATING YOUR AMBITION?
10/6
BASH STREET PUNX
LEWIS LEATHERS

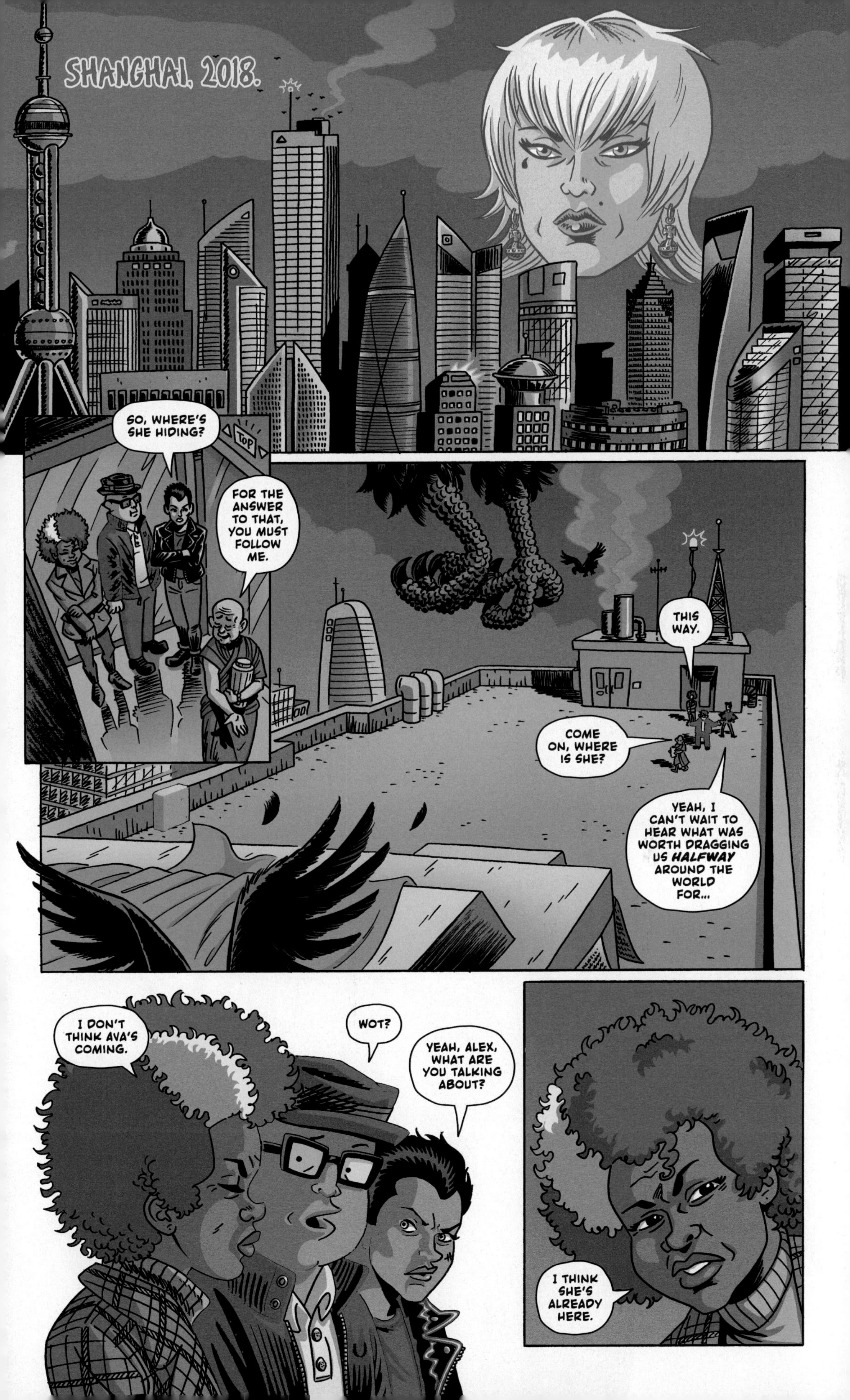
SHANGHAI, 2018.
SO, WHERE'S SHE HIDING?
TOP
FOR THE ANSWER TO THAT, YOU MUST FOLLOW ME.
THIS WAY.
COME ON, WHERE IS SHE?
YEAH, I CAN'T WAIT TO HEAR WHAT WAS WORTH DRAGGING US HALFWAY AROUND THE WORLD FOR...
I DON'T THINK AVA'S COMING.
WOT?
YEAH, ALEX, WHAT ARE YOU TALKING ABOUT?
I THINK SHE'S ALREADY HERE.

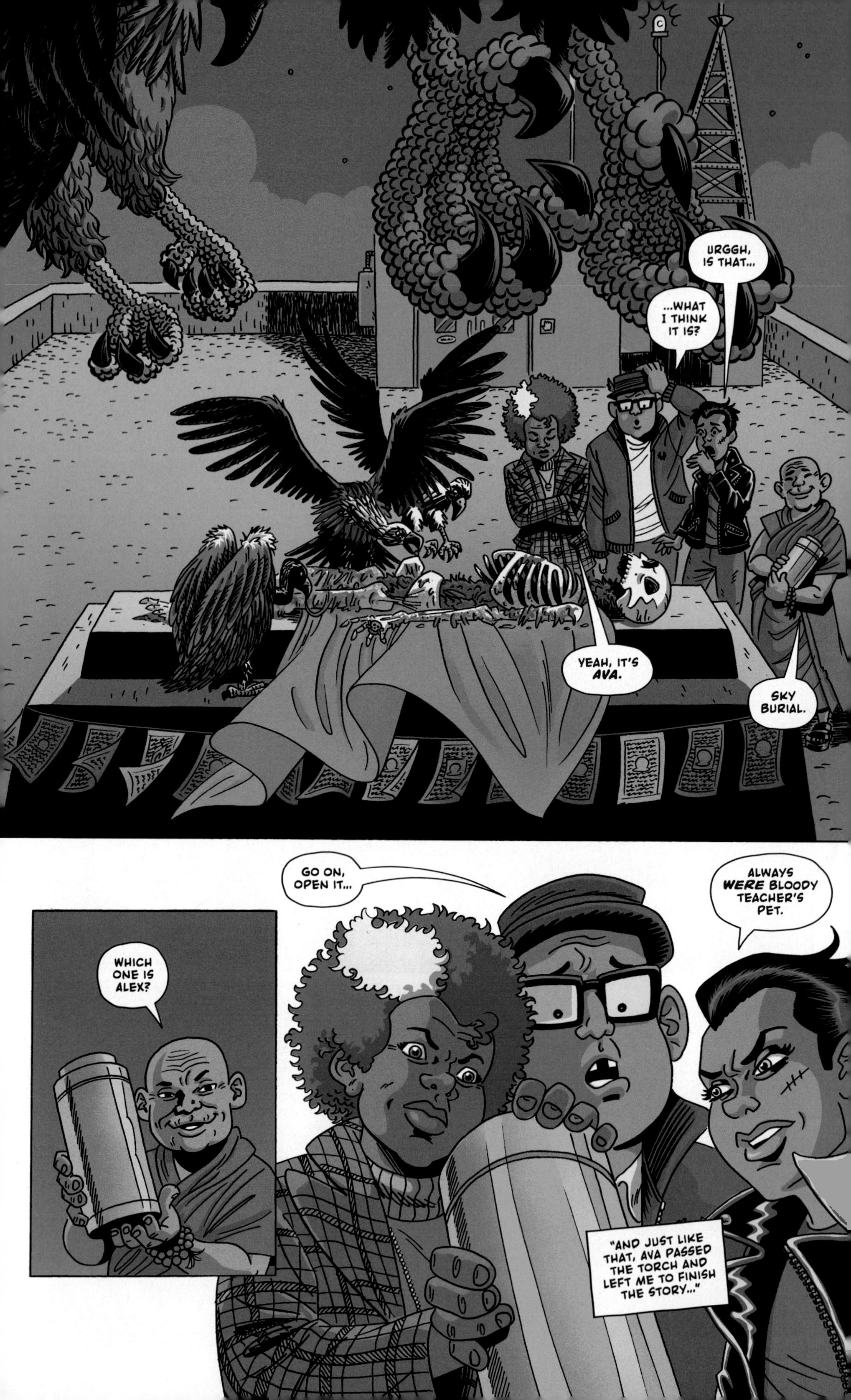
URGGH, IS THAT...
...WHAT I THINK IT IS?
YEAH, IT'S AVA.
SKY BURIAL.
WHICH ONE IS ALEX?
GO ON, OPEN IT...
ALWAYS WERE BLOODY TEACHER'S PET.
"AND JUST LIKE THAT, AVA PASSED THE TORCH AND LEFT ME TO FINISH THE STORY..."

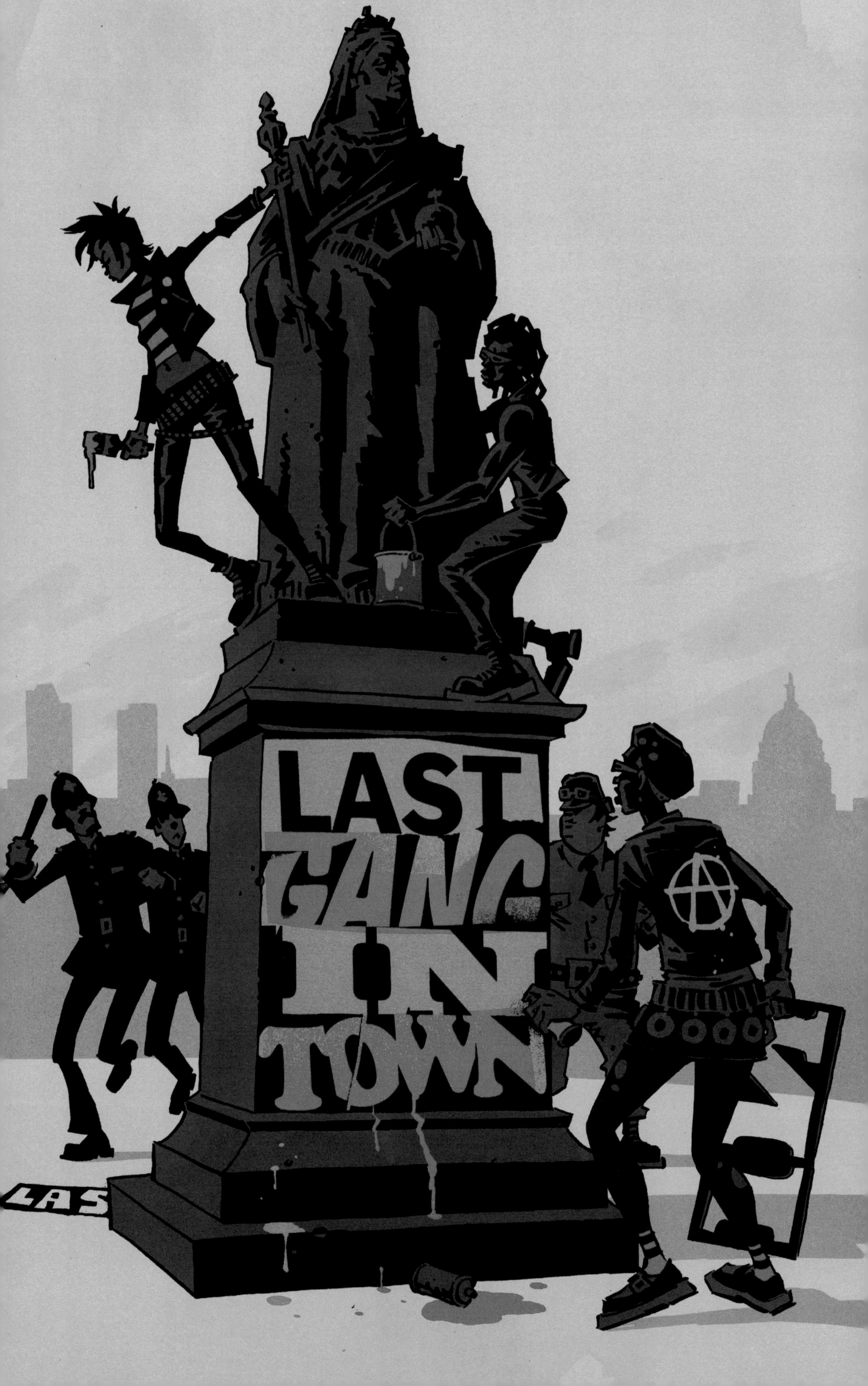
LAST
GANG
IN
TOWN
LAS

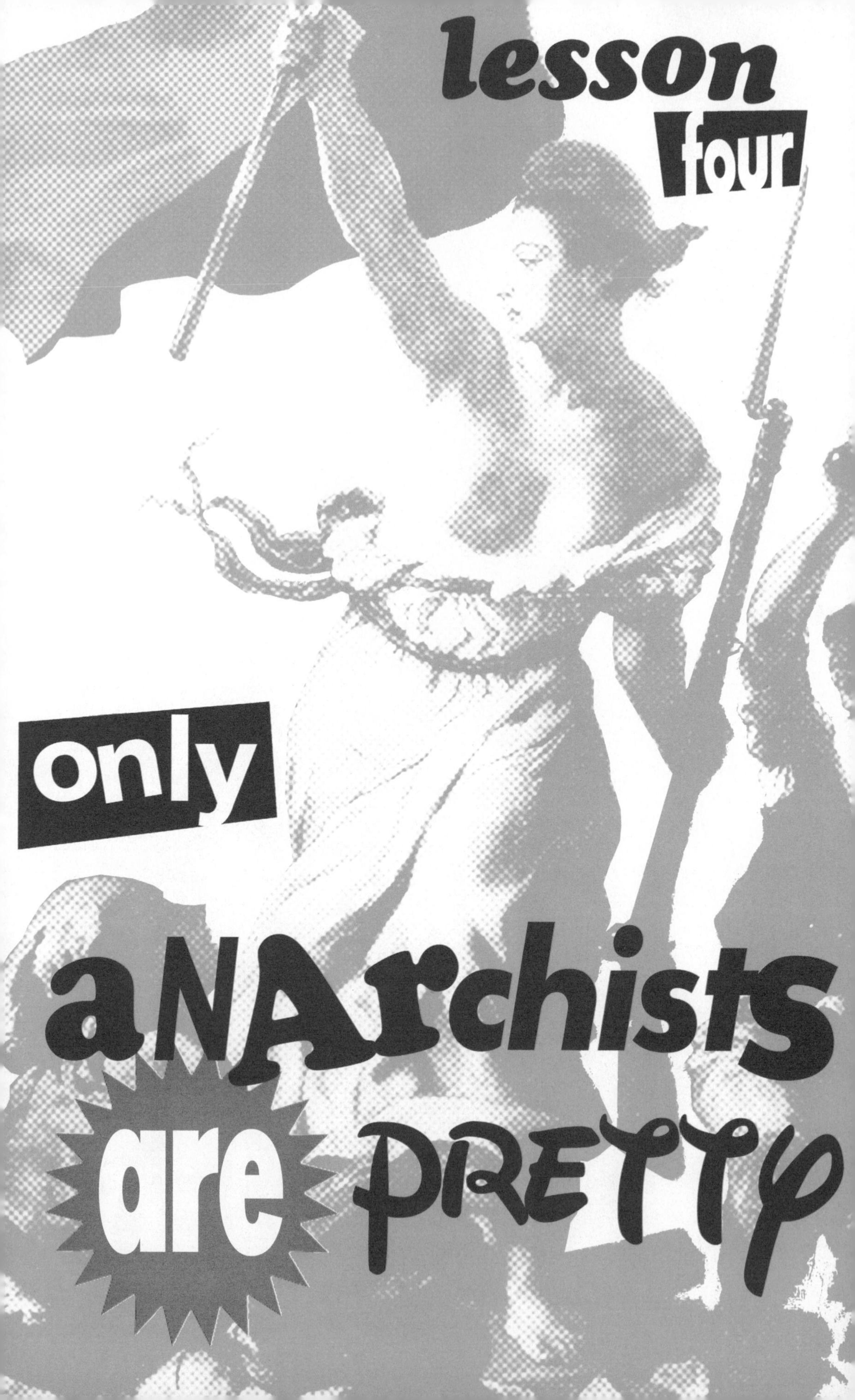
lesson
four
only
anarchists
are
PRETTY

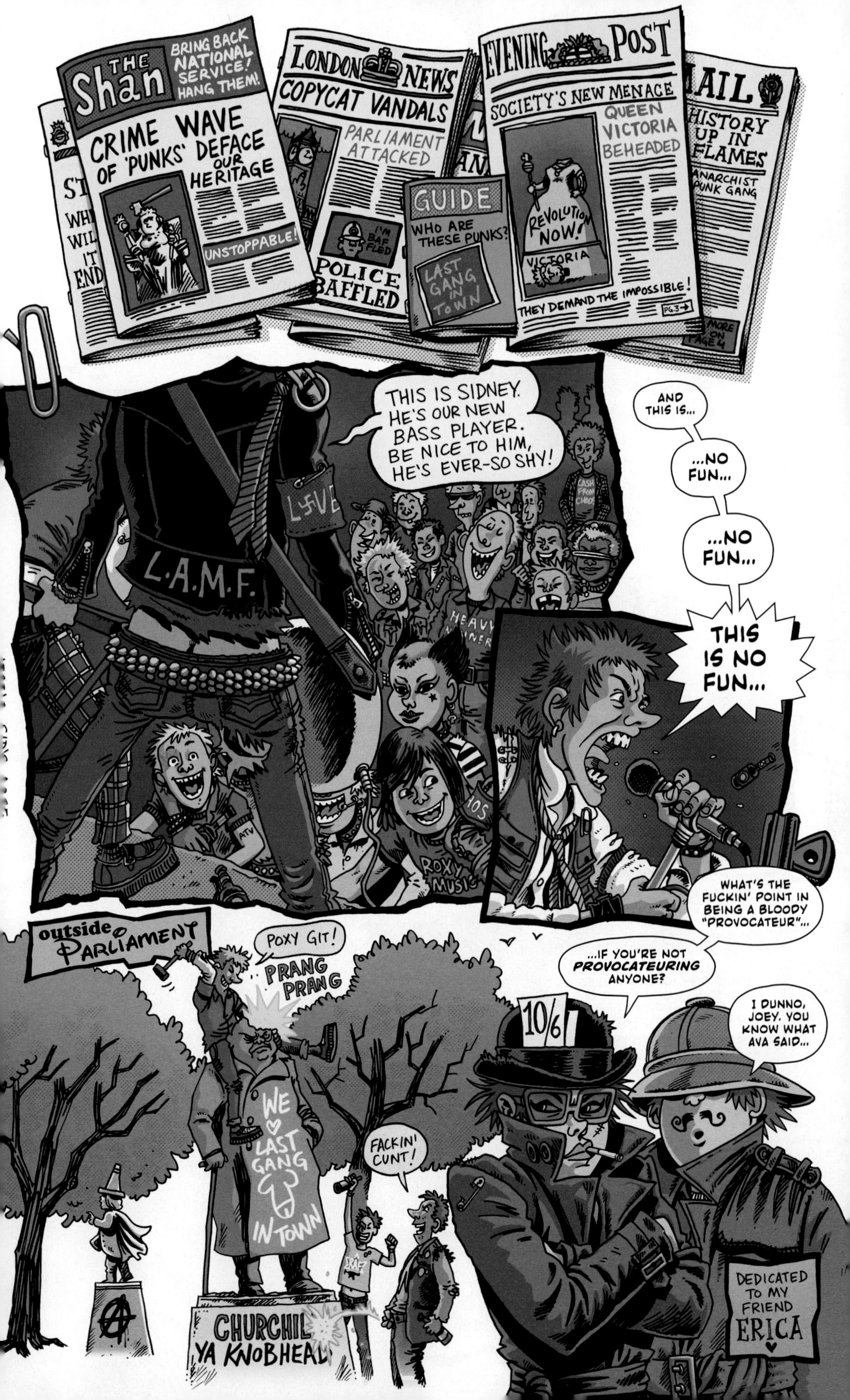
THE Shan
BRING BACK NATIONAL SERVICE! HANG THEM!
CRIME WAVE OF 'PUNKS' DEFACE OUR HERITAGE
UNSTOPPABLE!
LONDON NEWS
COPYCAT VANDALS
PARLIAMENT ATTACKED
I'M BAFFLED
POLICE BAFFLED
GUIDE
WHO ARE THESE PUNKS?
LAST GANG IN TOWN
EVENING POST
SOCIETY'S NEW MENACE
QUEEN VICTORIA BEHEADED
REVOLUTION NOW!
VICTORIA
THEY DEMAND THE IMPOSSIBLE!
PG.3
HISTORY UP IN FLAMES
ANARCHIST PUNK GANG
L.A.M.F.
THIS IS SIDNEY. HE'S OUR NEW BASS PLAYER. BE NICE TO HIM, HE'S EVER-SO SHY!
CASH FROM CHAOS
HEAVY MANNERS
ROXY MUSIC
AND THIS IS...
...NO FUN...
...NO FUN...
THIS IS NO FUN...
WHAT'S THE FUCKIN' POINT IN BEING A BLOODY "PROVOCATEUR"...
...IF YOU'RE NOT PROVOCATEURING ANYONE?
outside PARLIAMENT
POXY GIT!
PRANG PRANG
WE ♥ LAST GANG IN TOWN
FACKIN' CUNT!
CHURCHIL
YA KNOBHEA
10/6
I DUNNO, JOEY. YOU KNOW WHAT AVA SAID...
DEDICATED TO MY FRIEND ERICA

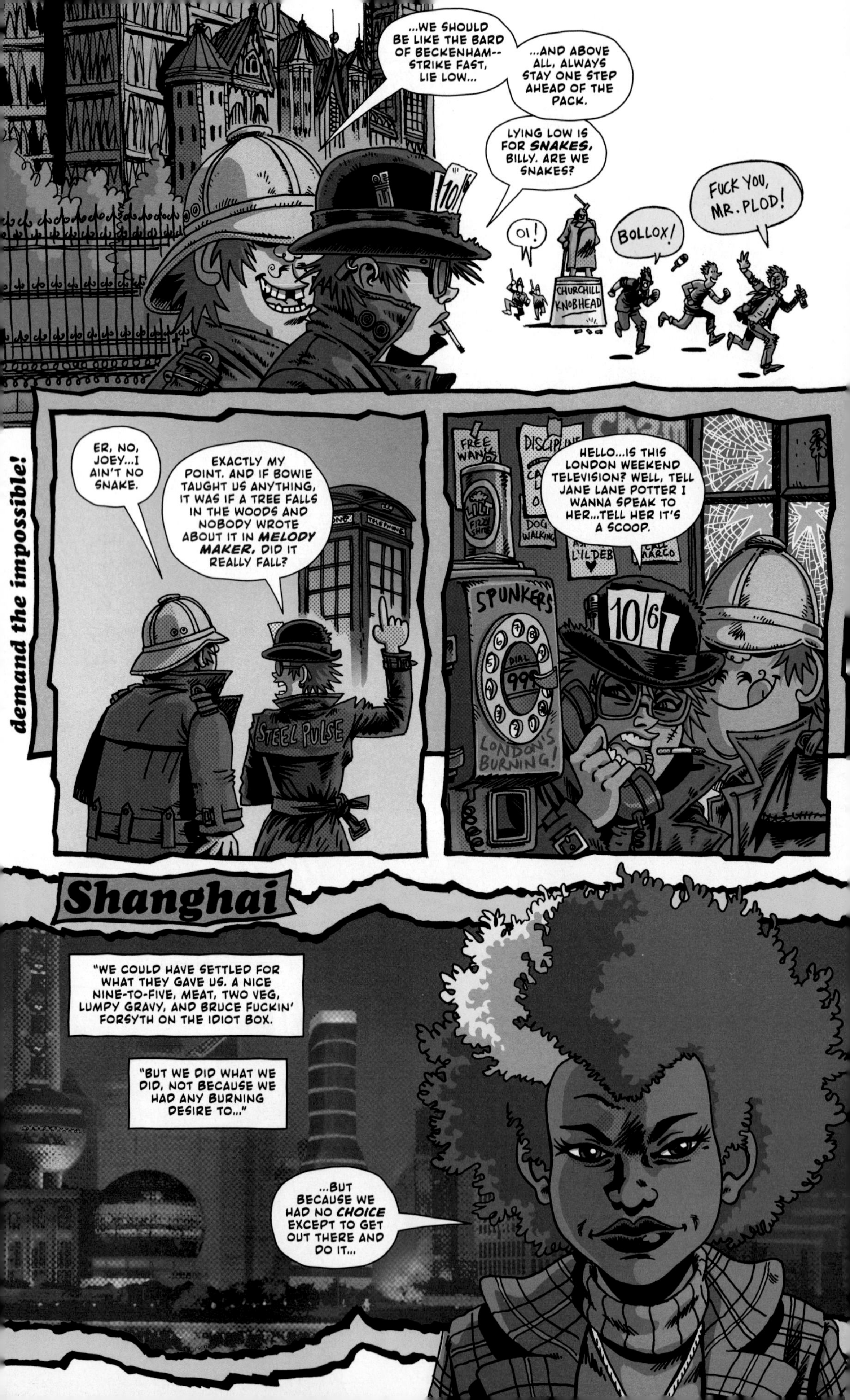
...WE SHOULD BE LIKE THE BARD OF BECKENHAM-- STRIKE FAST, LIE LOW...
...AND ABOVE ALL, ALWAYS STAY ONE STEP AHEAD OF THE PACK.
LYING LOW IS FOR SNAKES, BILLY. ARE WE SNAKES?
OI!
CHURCHILL KNOBHEAD
BOLLOX!
FUCK YOU, MR. PLOD!
demand the impossible!
ER, NO, JOEY...I AIN'T NO SNAKE.
EXACTLY MY POINT. AND IF BOWIE TAUGHT US ANYTHING, IT WAS IF A TREE FALLS IN THE WOODS AND NOBODY WROTE ABOUT IT IN MELODY MAKER, DID IT REALLY FALL?
STEEL PULSE
HELLO...IS THIS LONDON WEEKEND TELEVISION? WELL, TELL JANE LANE POTTER I WANNA SPEAK TO HER...TELL HER IT'S A SCOOP.
SPUNKERS
LONDON'S BURNING!
10/6
Shanghai
"WE COULD HAVE SETTLED FOR WHAT THEY GAVE US. A NICE NINE-TO-FIVE, MEAT, TWO VEG, LUMPY GRAVY, AND BRUCE FUCKIN' FORSYTH ON THE IDIOT BOX.
"BUT WE DID WHAT WE DID, NOT BECAUSE WE HAD ANY BURNING DESIRE TO..."
...BUT BECAUSE WE HAD NO CHOICE EXCEPT TO GET OUT THERE AND DO IT...

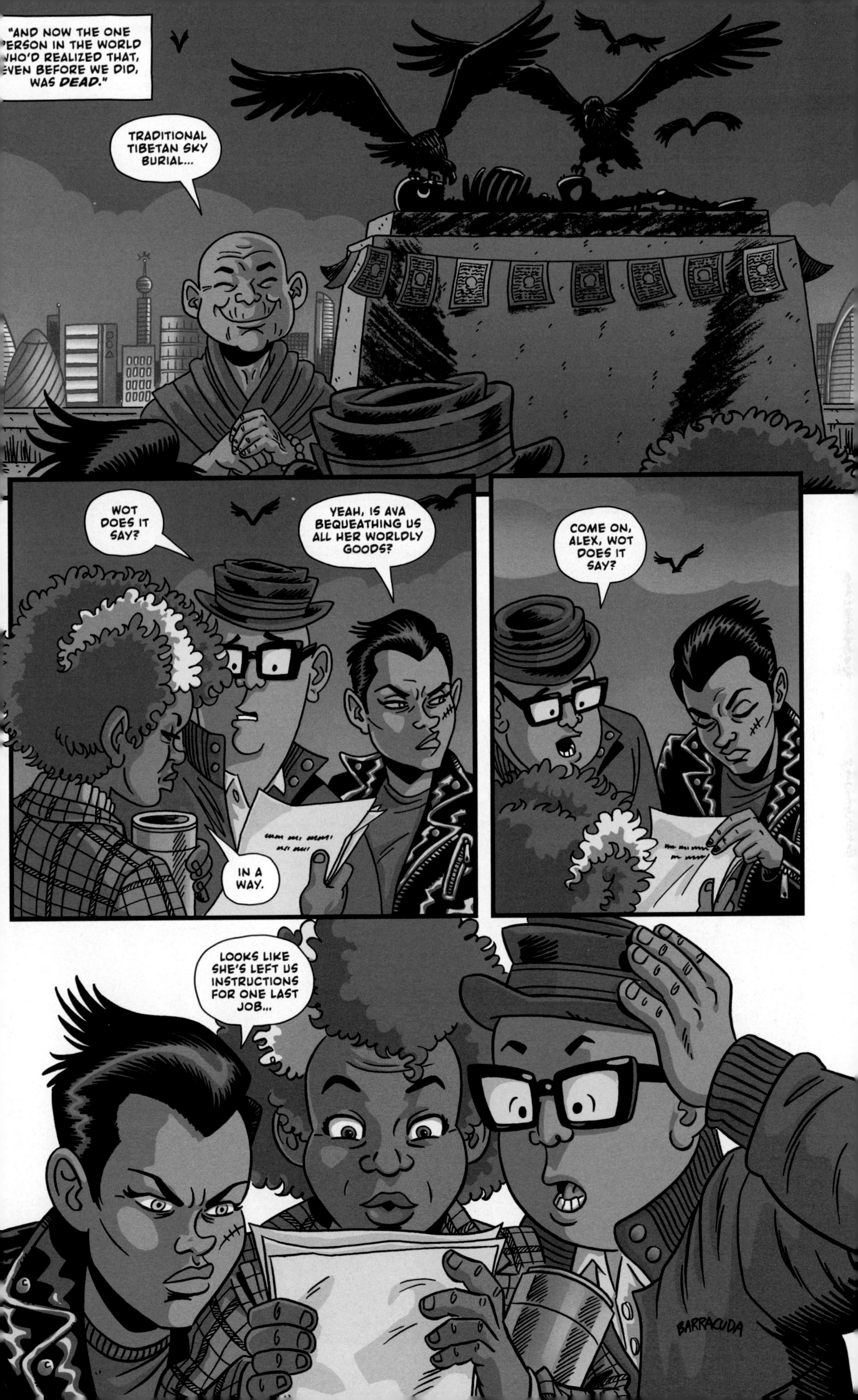
"AND NOW THE ONE PERSON IN THE WORLD WHO'D REALIZED THAT, EVEN BEFORE WE DID, WAS *DEAD*."
TRADITIONAL TIBETAN SKY BURIAL...
WOT DOES IT SAY?
YEAH, IS AVA BEQUEATHING US ALL HER WORLDLY GOODS?
IN A WAY.
COME ON, ALEX, WOT DOES IT SAY?
LOOKS LIKE SHE'S LEFT US INSTRUCTIONS FOR ONE LAST JOB...
BARRACUDA

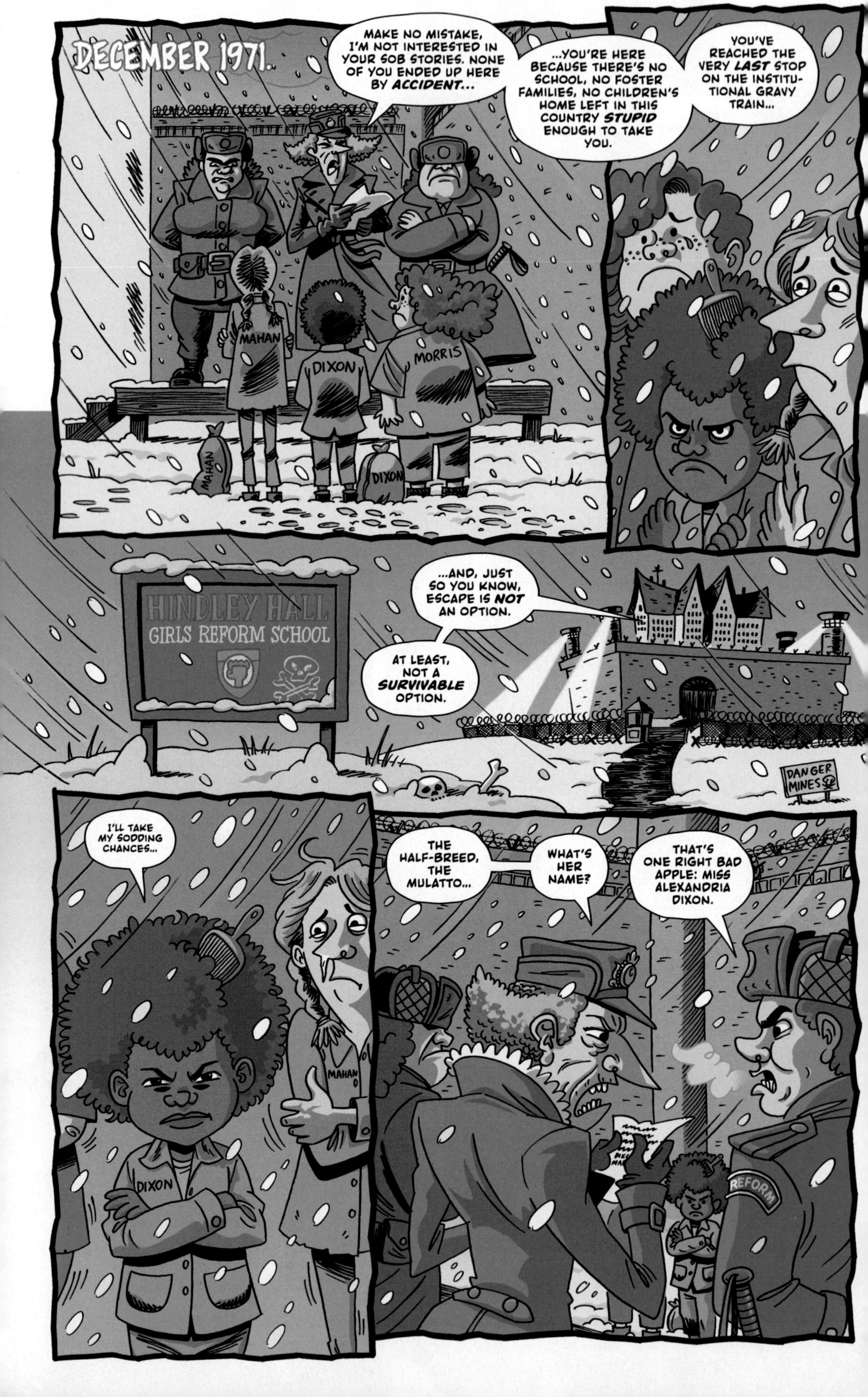
DECEMBER 1971...
MAKE NO MISTAKE, I'M NOT INTERESTED IN YOUR SOB STORIES. NONE OF YOU ENDED UP HERE BY ACCIDENT...
MAHAN
DIXON
MORRIS
MAHAN
DIXON
...YOU'RE HERE BECAUSE THERE'S NO SCHOOL, NO FOSTER FAMILIES, NO CHILDREN'S HOME LEFT IN THIS COUNTRY STUPID ENOUGH TO TAKE YOU.
YOU'VE REACHED THE VERY LAST STOP ON THE INSTITU-TIONAL GRAVY TRAIN...
HINDLEY HALL
GIRLS REFORM SCHOOL
...AND, JUST SO YOU KNOW, ESCAPE IS NOT AN OPTION.
AT LEAST, NOT A SURVIVABLE OPTION.
DANGER MINES
I'LL TAKE MY SODDING CHANCES...
DIXON
MAHAN
THE HALF-BREED, THE MULATTO...
WHAT'S HER NAME?
THAT'S ONE RIGHT BAD APPLE: MISS ALEXANDRIA DIXON.
REFORM

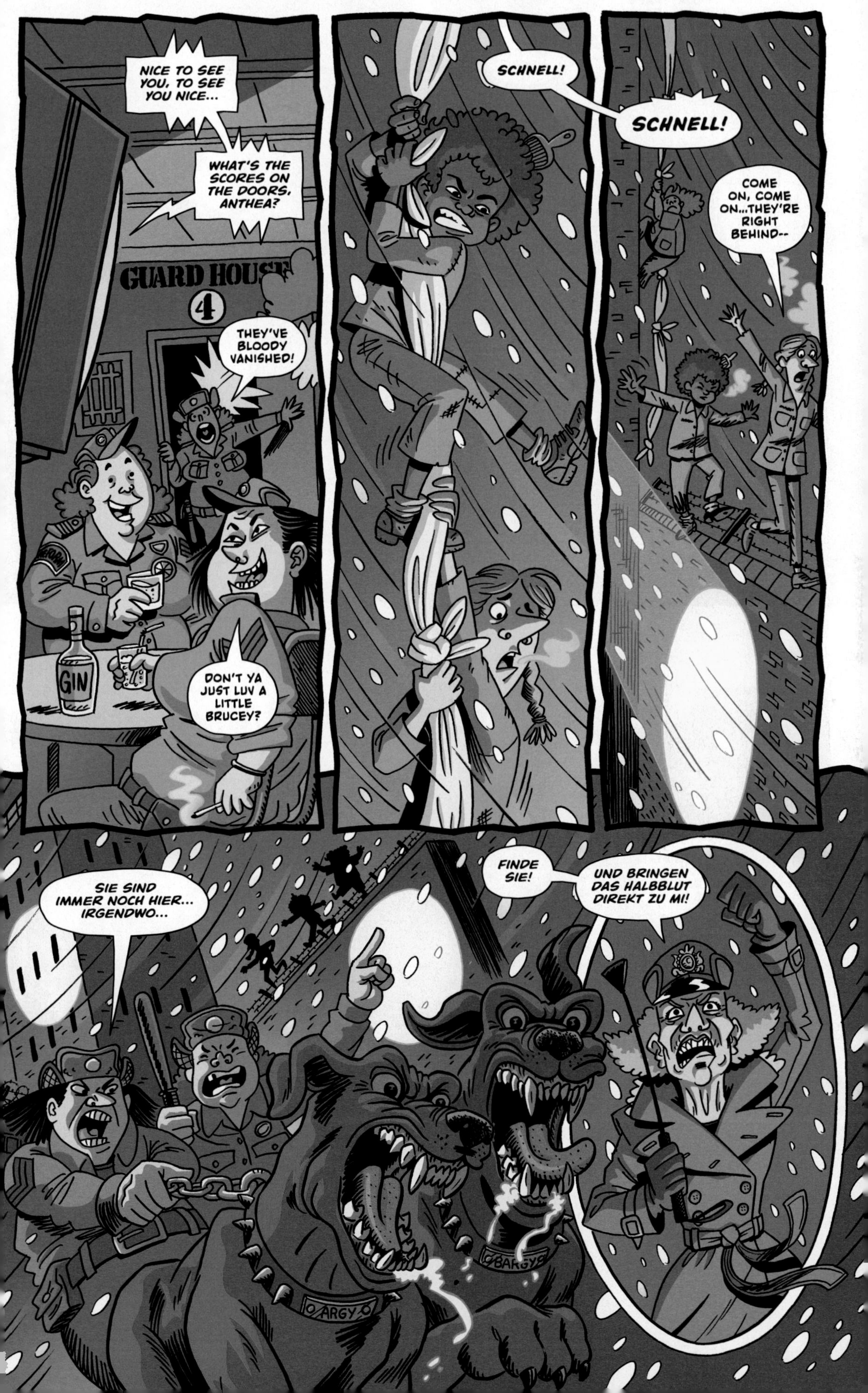
NICE TO SEE YOU, TO SEE YOU NICE...
WHAT'S THE SCORES ON THE DOORS, ANTHEA?
GUARD HOUSE
4
THEY'VE BLOODY VANISHED!
GIN
DON'T YA JUST LUV A LITTLE BRUCEY?
SCHNELL!
SCHNELL!
COME ON, COME ON...THEY'RE RIGHT BEHIND--
SIE SIND IMMER NOCH HIER... IRGENDWO...
FINDE SIE!
UND BRINGEN DAS HALBBLUT DIREKT ZU MI!
ARGY
BARGY

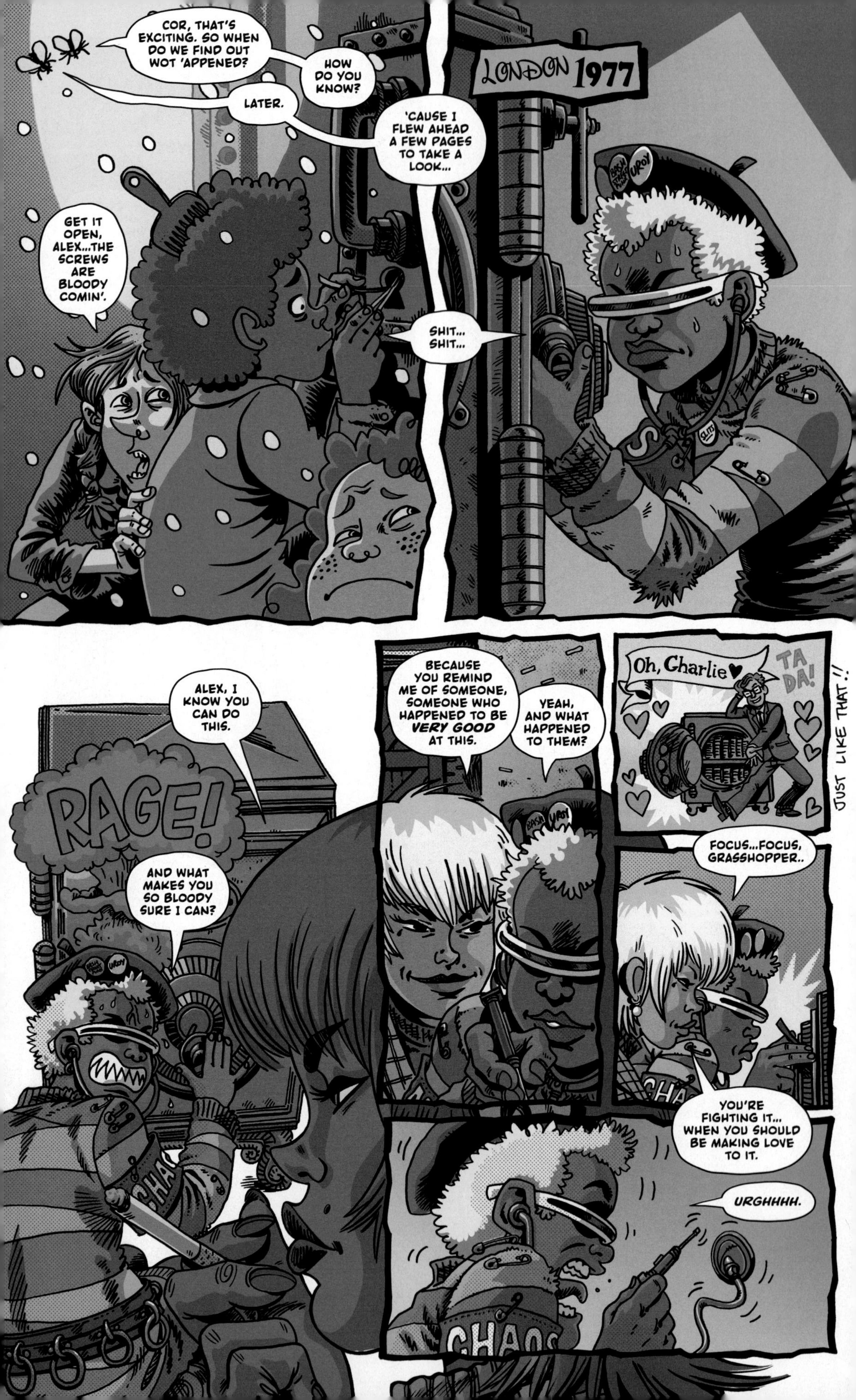
LONDON 1977
COR, THAT'S EXCITING. SO WHEN DO WE FIND OUT WOT 'APPENED?
LATER.
HOW DO YOU KNOW?
'CAUSE I FLEW AHEAD A FEW PAGES TO TAKE A LOOK...
GET IT OPEN, ALEX...THE SCREWS ARE BLOODY COMIN'.
SHIT... SHIT...
ALEX, I KNOW YOU CAN DO THIS.
RAGE!
AND WHAT MAKES YOU SO BLOODY SURE I CAN?
BECAUSE YOU REMIND ME OF SOMEONE, SOMEONE WHO HAPPENED TO BE *VERY GOOD* AT THIS.
YEAH, AND WHAT HAPPENED TO THEM?
Oh, Charlie
TA DA!
JUST LIKE THAT !!
FOCUS...FOCUS, GRASSHOPPER..
YOU'RE FIGHTING IT... WHEN YOU SHOULD BE MAKING LOVE TO IT.
URGHHHH.
CHAOS

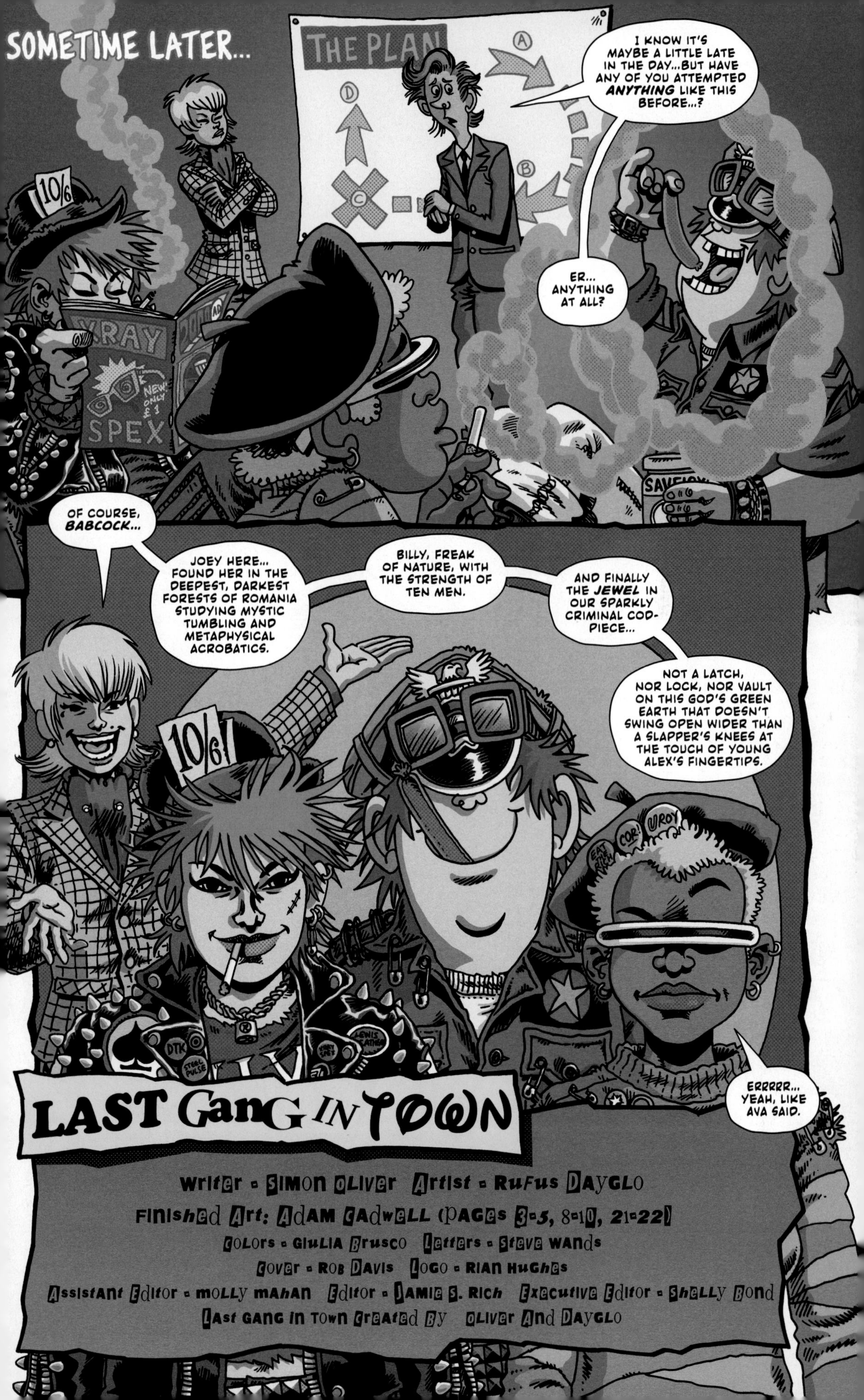
SOMETIME LATER...
THE PLAN
A
B
C
D
I KNOW IT'S MAYBE A LITTLE LATE IN THE DAY...BUT HAVE ANY OF YOU ATTEMPTED ANYTHING LIKE THIS BEFORE...?
ER... ANYTHING AT ALL?
10/6
X-RAY SPEX
2000 AD
NEW! ONLY £1
OF COURSE, BABCOCK...
JOEY HERE... FOUND HER IN THE DEEPEST, DARKEST FORESTS OF ROMANIA STUDYING MYSTIC TUMBLING AND METAPHYSICAL ACROBATICS.
BILLY, FREAK OF NATURE, WITH THE STRENGTH OF TEN MEN.
AND FINALLY THE JEWEL IN OUR SPARKLY CRIMINAL COD-PIECE...
NOT A LATCH, NOR LOCK, NOR VAULT ON THIS GOD'S GREEN EARTH THAT DOESN'T SWING OPEN WIDER THAN A SLAPPER'S KNEES AT THE TOUCH OF YOUNG ALEX'S FINGERTIPS.
10/6
EAT THE RICH
COR!
U ROY
ERRRRR... YEAH, LIKE AVA SAID.
LAST GANG IN TOWN
Writer - Simon Oliver Artist - Rufus Dayglo
Finished Art: Adam Cadwell (pages 3-5, 8-10, 21-22)
Colors - Giulia Brusco Letters - Steve Wands
Cover - Rob Davis Logo - Rian Hughes
Assistant Editor - Molly Mahan Editor - Jamie S. Rich Executive Editor - Shelly Bond
Last Gang in Town created by Oliver and Dayglo

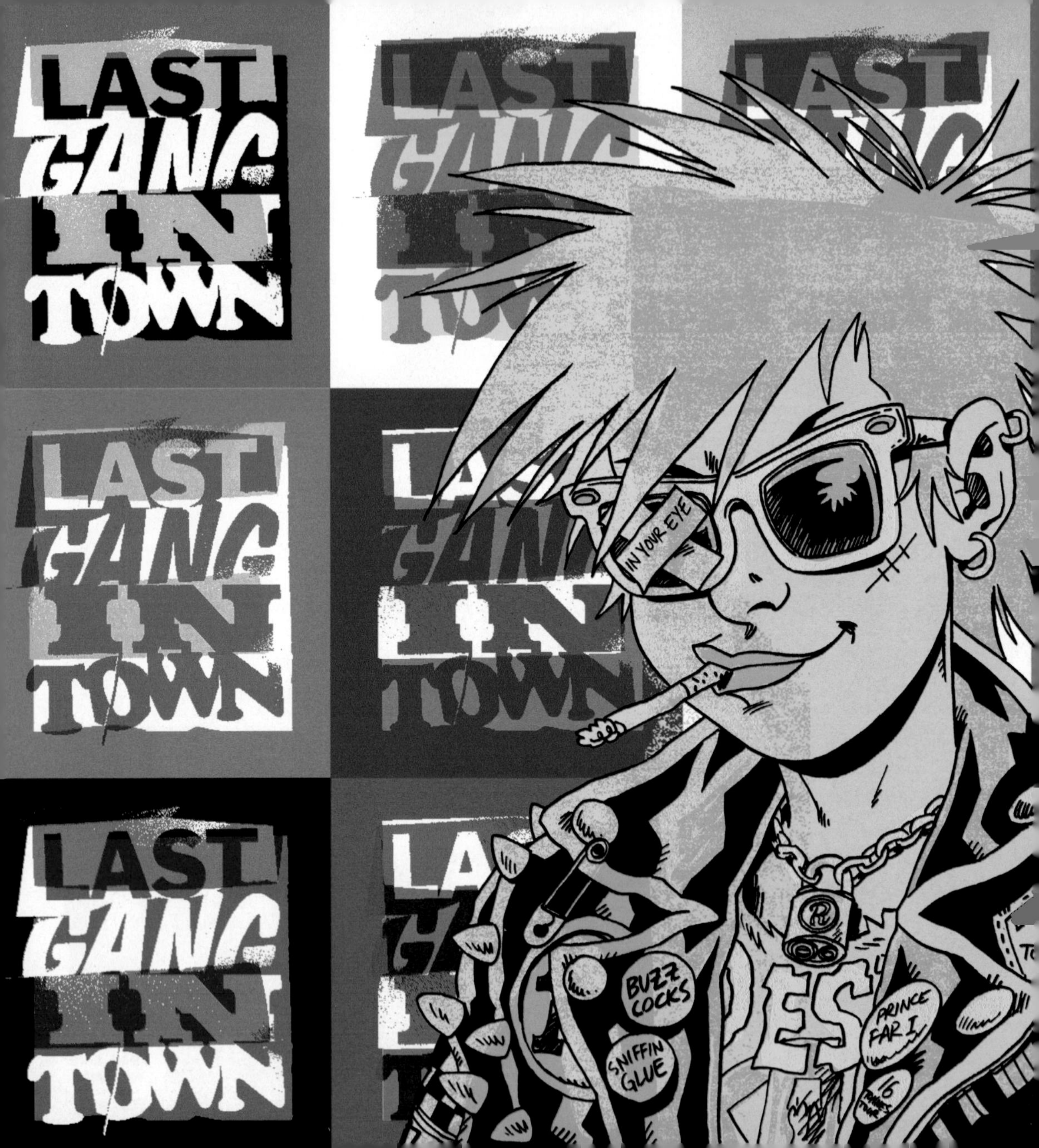

LAST GANG IN TOWN
LAST GANG IN TOWN
LAST GANG IN TOWN
LAST GANG IN TOWN
IN YOUR EYE
BUZZ COCKS
SNIFFIN GLUE
PRINCE FAR I

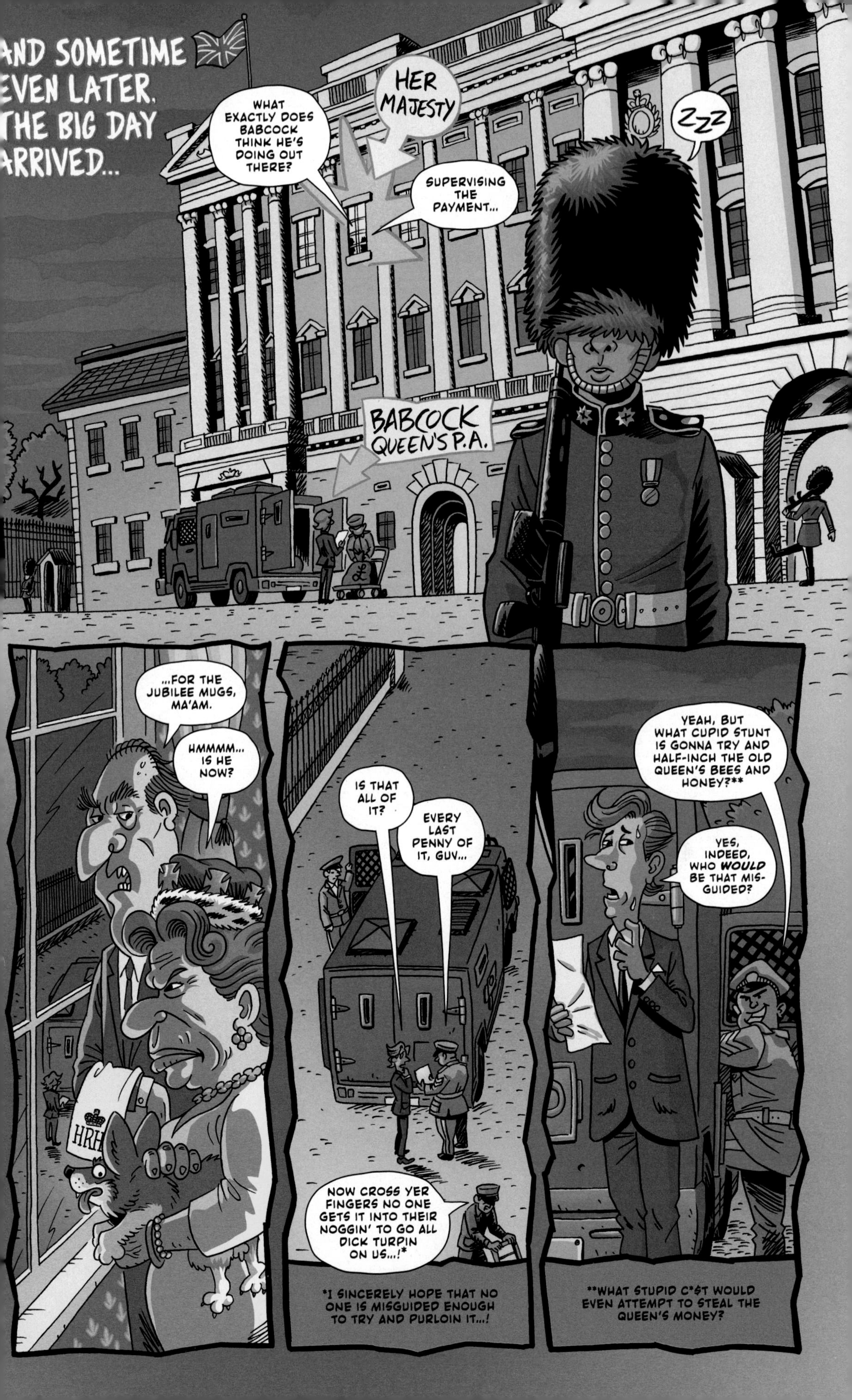
AND SOMETIME EVEN LATER, THE BIG DAY ARRIVED...
WHAT EXACTLY DOES BABCOCK THINK HE'S DOING OUT THERE?
HER MAJESTY
SUPERVISING THE PAYMENT...
ZZZ
BABCOCK QUEEN'S P.A.
...FOR THE JUBILEE MUGS, MA'AM.
HMMMM... IS HE NOW?
HRH
IS THAT ALL OF IT?
EVERY LAST PENNY OF IT, GUV...
NOW CROSS YER FINGERS NO ONE GETS IT INTO THEIR NOGGIN' TO GO ALL DICK TURPIN ON US...!*
*I SINCERELY HOPE THAT NO ONE IS MISGUIDED ENOUGH TO TRY AND PURLOIN IT...!
YEAH, BUT WHAT CUPID STUNT IS GONNA TRY AND HALF-INCH THE OLD QUEEN'S BEES AND HONEY?**
YES, INDEED, WHO WOULD BE THAT MIS-GUIDED?
**WHAT STUPID C*$T WOULD EVEN ATTEMPT TO STEAL THE QUEEN'S MONEY?

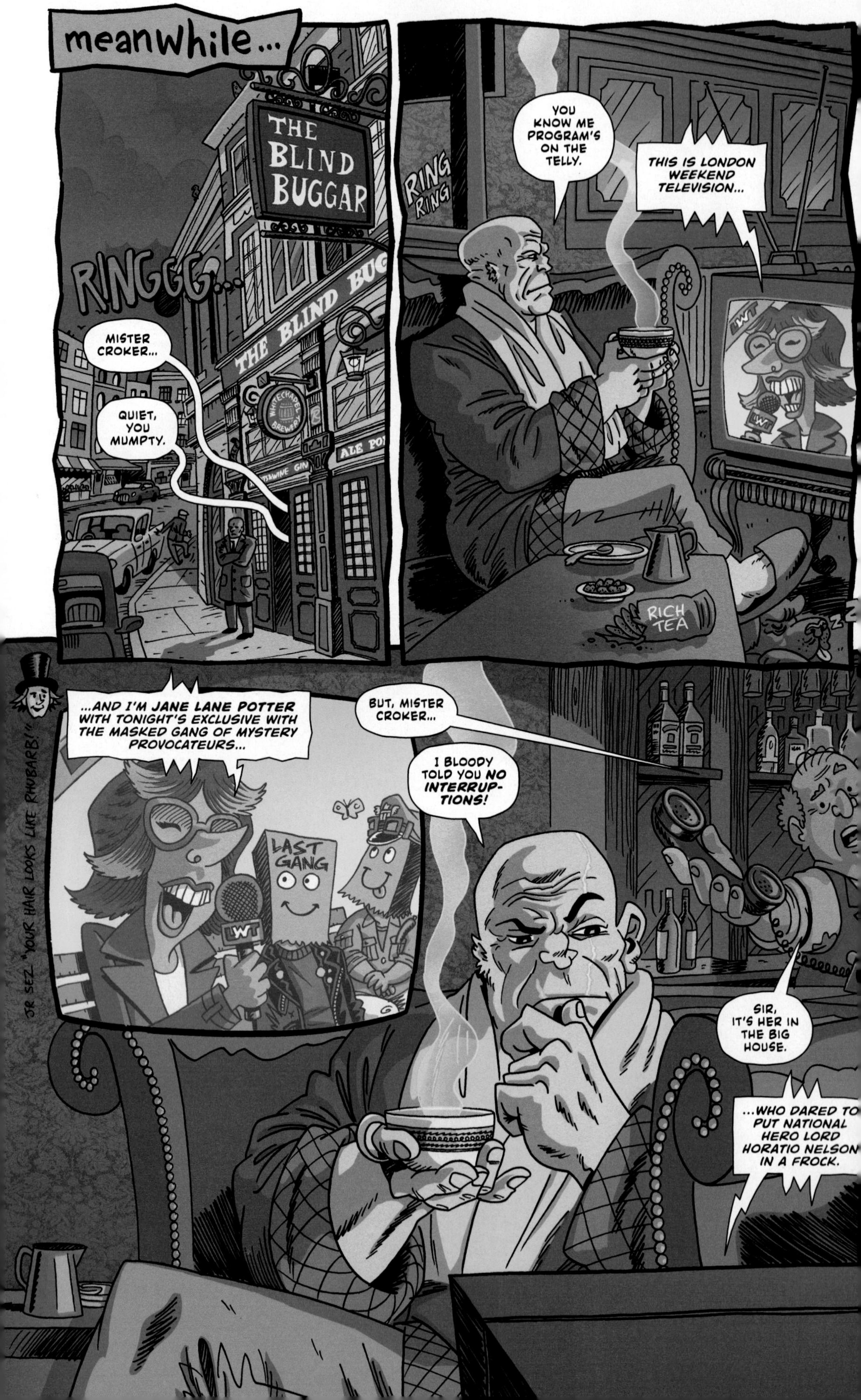
meanwhile...
THE BLIND BUGGAR
RINGGG...
THE BLIND BUG
WHITECHAPEL BREWERY
ALE PO
MISTER CROKER...
QUIET, YOU MUMPTY.
RING RING
YOU KNOW ME PROGRAM'S ON THE TELLY.
THIS IS LONDON WEEKEND TELEVISION...
LWT
RICH TEA
...AND I'M JANE LANE POTTER WITH TONIGHT'S EXCLUSIVE WITH THE MASKED GANG OF MYSTERY PROVOCATEURS...
LAST GANG
BUT, MISTER CROKER...
I BLOODY TOLD YOU NO INTERRUP-TIONS!
SIR, IT'S HER IN THE BIG HOUSE.
...WHO DARED TO PUT NATIONAL HERO LORD HORATIO NELSON IN A FROCK.
JR SEZ "YOUR HAIR LOOKS LIKE RHUBARB!"

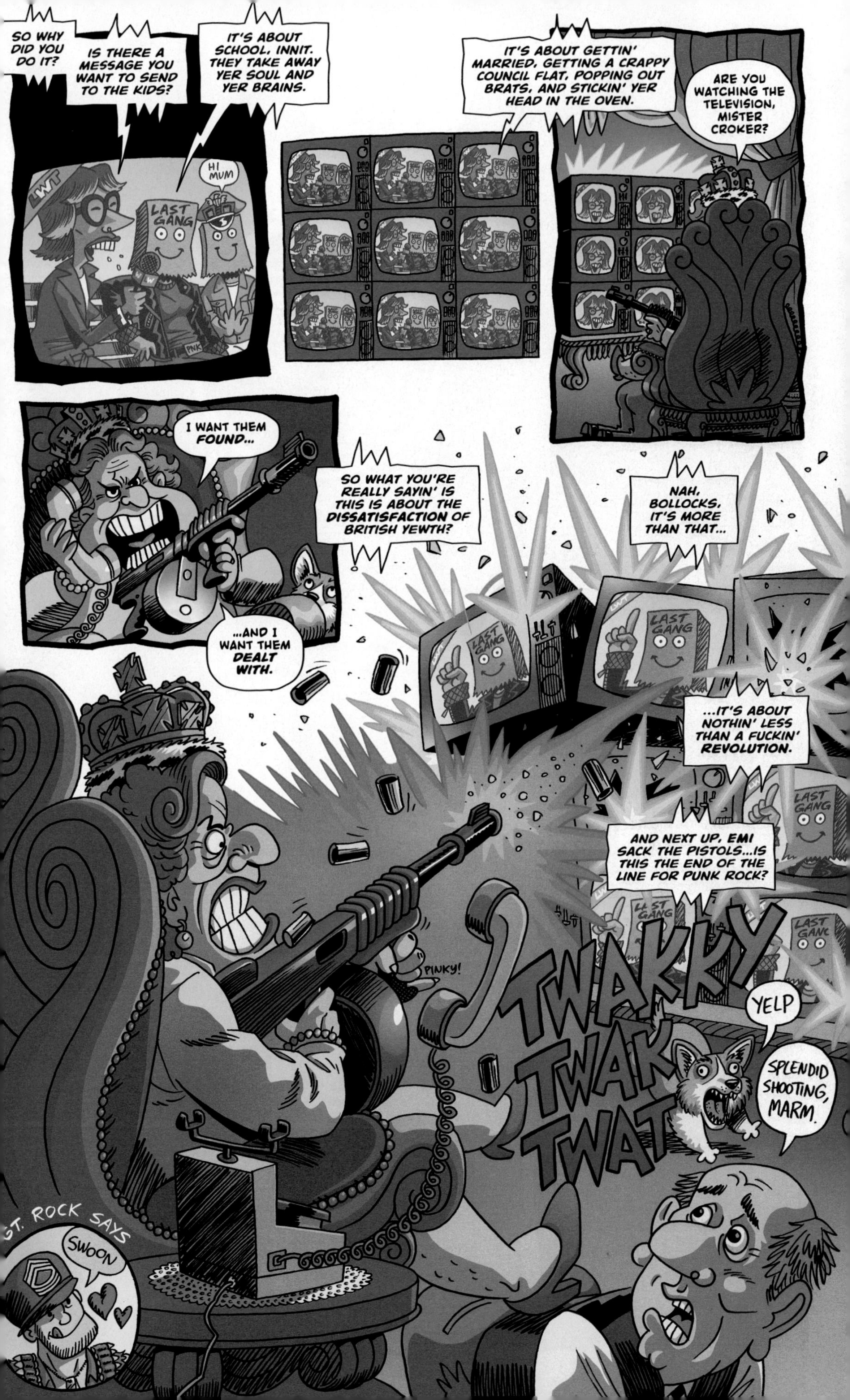
SO WHY DID YOU DO IT?
IS THERE A MESSAGE YOU WANT TO SEND TO THE KIDS?
IT'S ABOUT SCHOOL, INNIT. THEY TAKE AWAY YER SOUL AND YER BRAINS.
HI MUM
LWT
LAST GANG
PNK
IT'S ABOUT GETTIN' MARRIED, GETTING A CRAPPY COUNCIL FLAT, POPPING OUT BRATS, AND STICKIN' YER HEAD IN THE OVEN.
ARE YOU WATCHING THE TELEVISION, MISTER CROKER?
I WANT THEM FOUND...
...AND I WANT THEM DEALT WITH.
SO WHAT YOU'RE REALLY SAYIN' IS THIS IS ABOUT THE DISSATISFACTION OF BRITISH YEWTH?
NAH, BOLLOCKS, IT'S MORE THAN THAT...
LAST GANG
...IT'S ABOUT NOTHIN' LESS THAN A FUCKIN' REVOLUTION.
AND NEXT UP, EMI SACK THE PISTOLS...IS THIS THE END OF THE LINE FOR PUNK ROCK?
PINKY!
TWAKKY TWAK TWAT
YELP
SPLENDID SHOOTING, MARM.
SGT. ROCK SAYS
SWOON

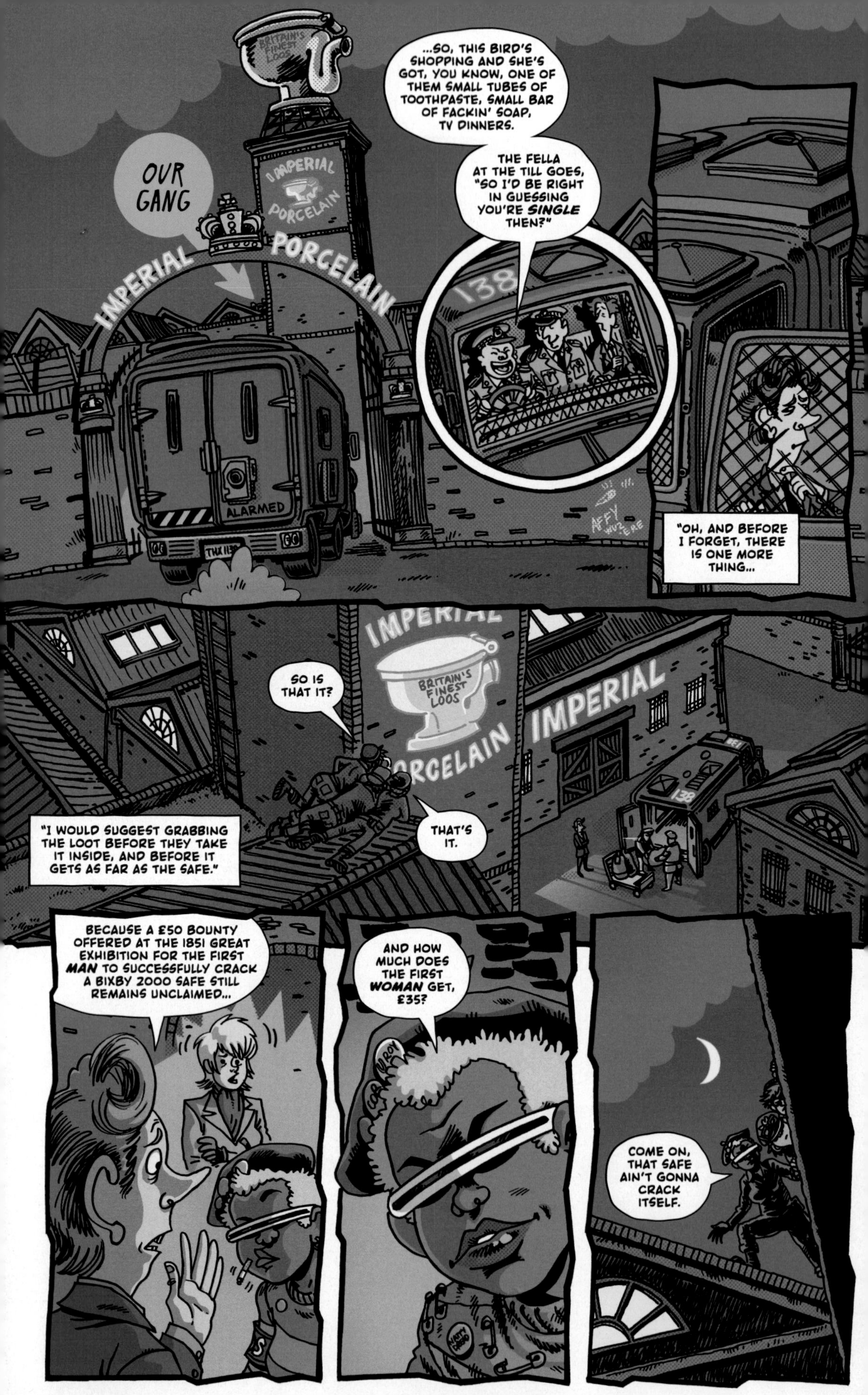
BRITAIN'S FINEST LOOS
IMPERIAL PORCELAIN
OUR GANG
IMPERIAL PORCELAIN
ALARMED
...SO, THIS BIRD'S SHOPPING AND SHE'S GOT, YOU KNOW, ONE OF THEM SMALL TUBES OF TOOTHPASTE, SMALL BAR OF FACKIN' SOAP, TV DINNERS.
THE FELLA AT THE TILL GOES, "SO I'D BE RIGHT IN GUESSING YOU'RE SINGLE THEN?"
138
AFFY WUZ 'ERE
"OH, AND BEFORE I FORGET, THERE IS ONE MORE THING...
IMPERIAL
BRITAIN'S FINEST LOOS
PORCELAIN
IMPERIAL
SO IS THAT IT?
THAT'S IT.
"I WOULD SUGGEST GRABBING THE LOOT BEFORE THEY TAKE IT INSIDE, AND BEFORE IT GETS AS FAR AS THE SAFE."
138
BECAUSE A £50 BOUNTY OFFERED AT THE 1851 GREAT EXHIBITION FOR THE FIRST MAN TO SUCCESSFULLY CRACK A BIXBY 2000 SAFE STILL REMAINS UNCLAIMED...
AND HOW MUCH DOES THE FIRST WOMAN GET, £35?
COME ON, THAT SAFE AIN'T GONNA CRACK ITSELF.

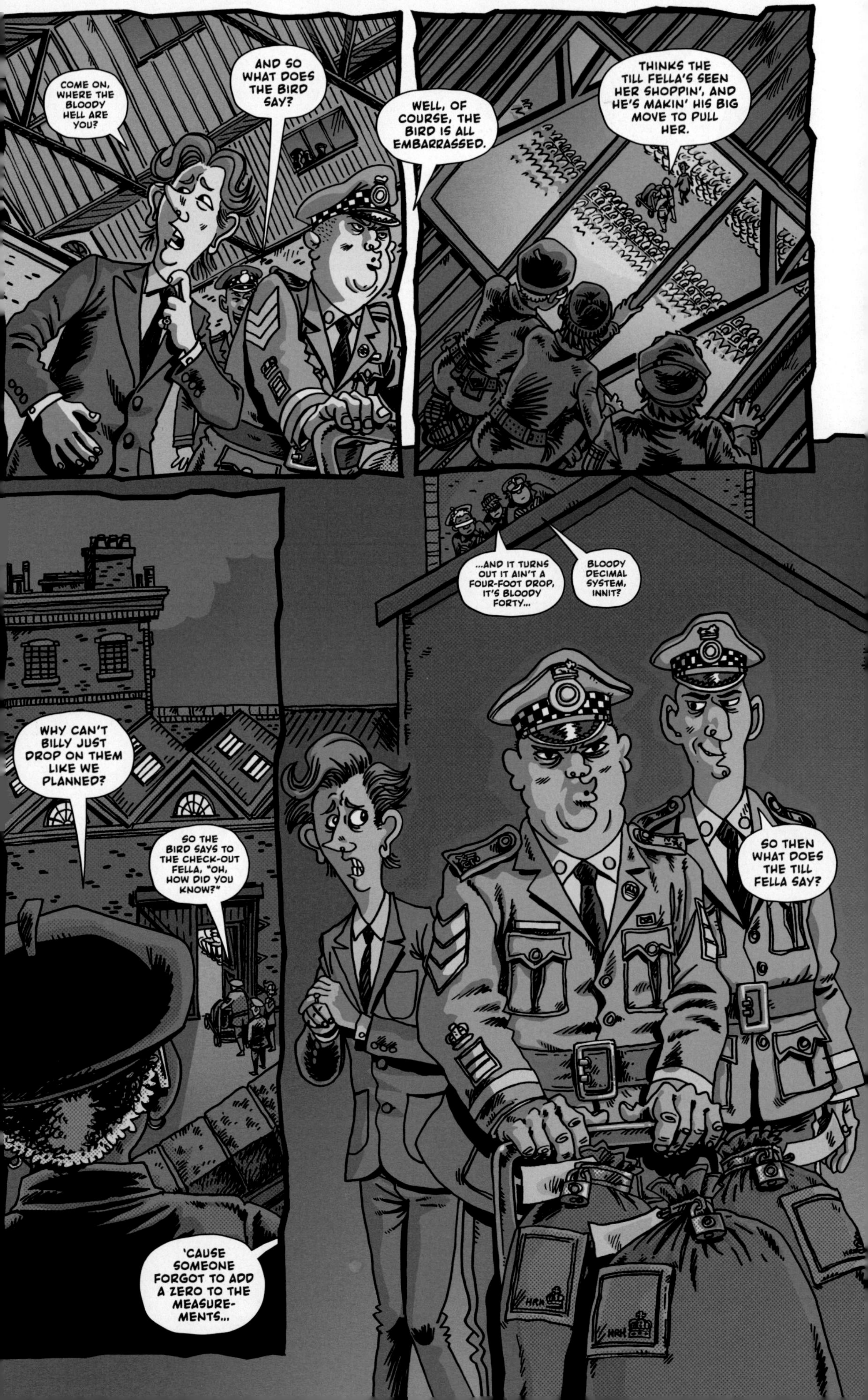
COME ON, WHERE THE BLOODY HELL ARE YOU?
AND SO WHAT DOES THE BIRD SAY?
WELL, OF COURSE, THE BIRD IS ALL EMBARRASSED.
THINKS THE TILL FELLA'S SEEN HER SHOPPIN', AND HE'S MAKIN' HIS BIG MOVE TO PULL HER.
...AND IT TURNS OUT IT AIN'T A FOUR-FOOT DROP, IT'S BLOODY FORTY...
BLOODY DECIMAL SYSTEM, INNIT?
WHY CAN'T BILLY JUST DROP ON THEM LIKE WE PLANNED?
SO THE BIRD SAYS TO THE CHECK-OUT FELLA, "OH, HOW DID YOU KNOW?"
SO THEN WHAT DOES THE TILL FELLA SAY?
'CAUSE SOMEONE FORGOT TO ADD A ZERO TO THE MEASURE-MENTS...

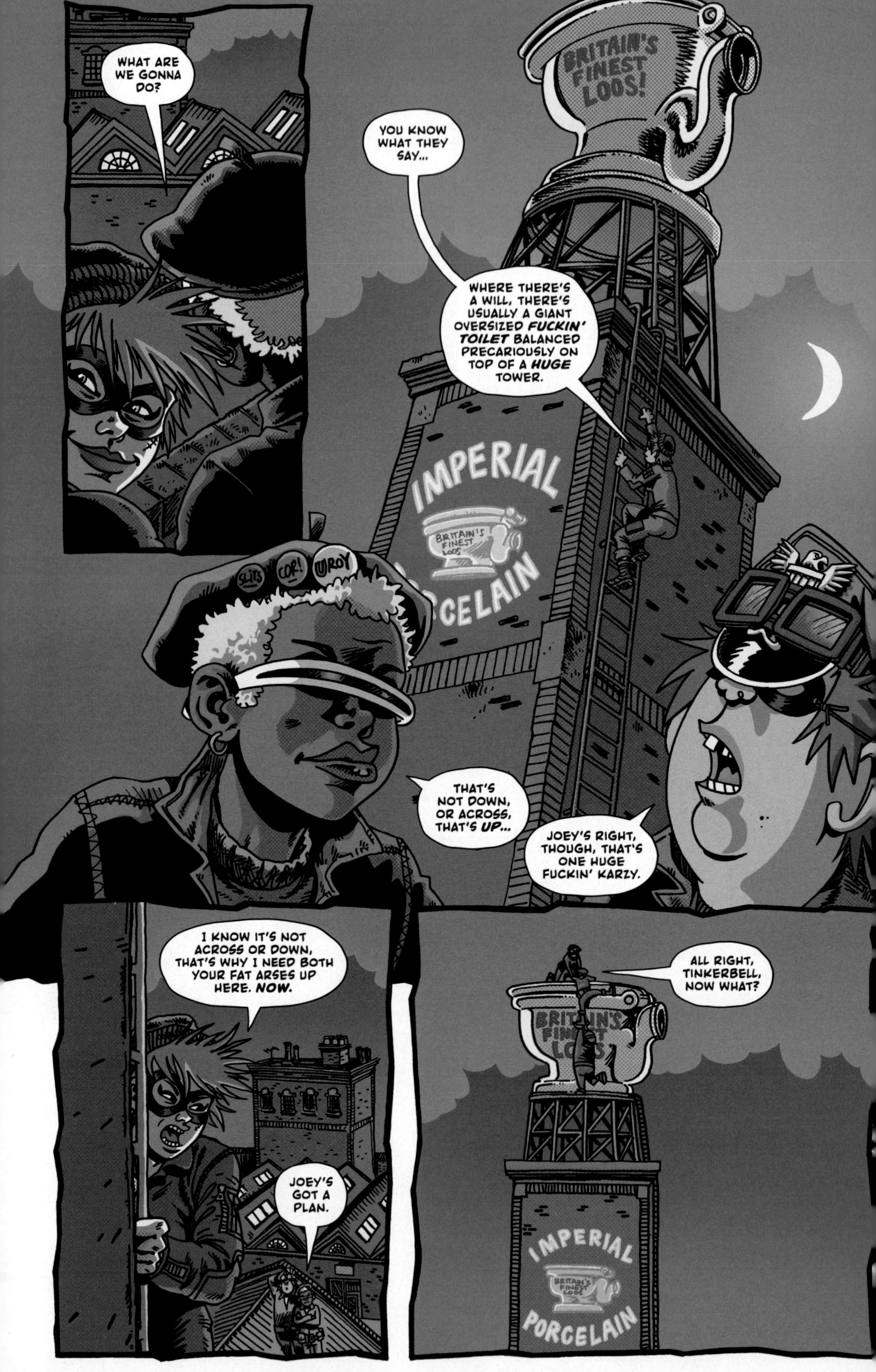
WHAT ARE WE GONNA DO?
BRITAIN'S FINEST LOOS!
YOU KNOW WHAT THEY SAY...
WHERE THERE'S A WILL, THERE'S USUALLY A GIANT OVERSIZED FUCKIN' TOILET BALANCED PRECARIOUSLY ON TOP OF A HUGE TOWER.
IMPERIAL
BRITAIN'S FINEST LOOS
CELAIN
SLITS
COR!
UROY
THAT'S NOT DOWN, OR ACROSS, THAT'S UP...
JOEY'S RIGHT, THOUGH, THAT'S ONE HUGE FUCKIN' KARZY.
I KNOW IT'S NOT ACROSS OR DOWN, THAT'S WHY I NEED BOTH YOUR FAT ARSES UP HERE. NOW.
JOEY'S GOT A PLAN.
ALL RIGHT, TINKERBELL, NOW WHAT?
BRITAIN'S FINEST LOOS
IMPERIAL
BRITAIN'S FINEST LOOS
PORCELAIN

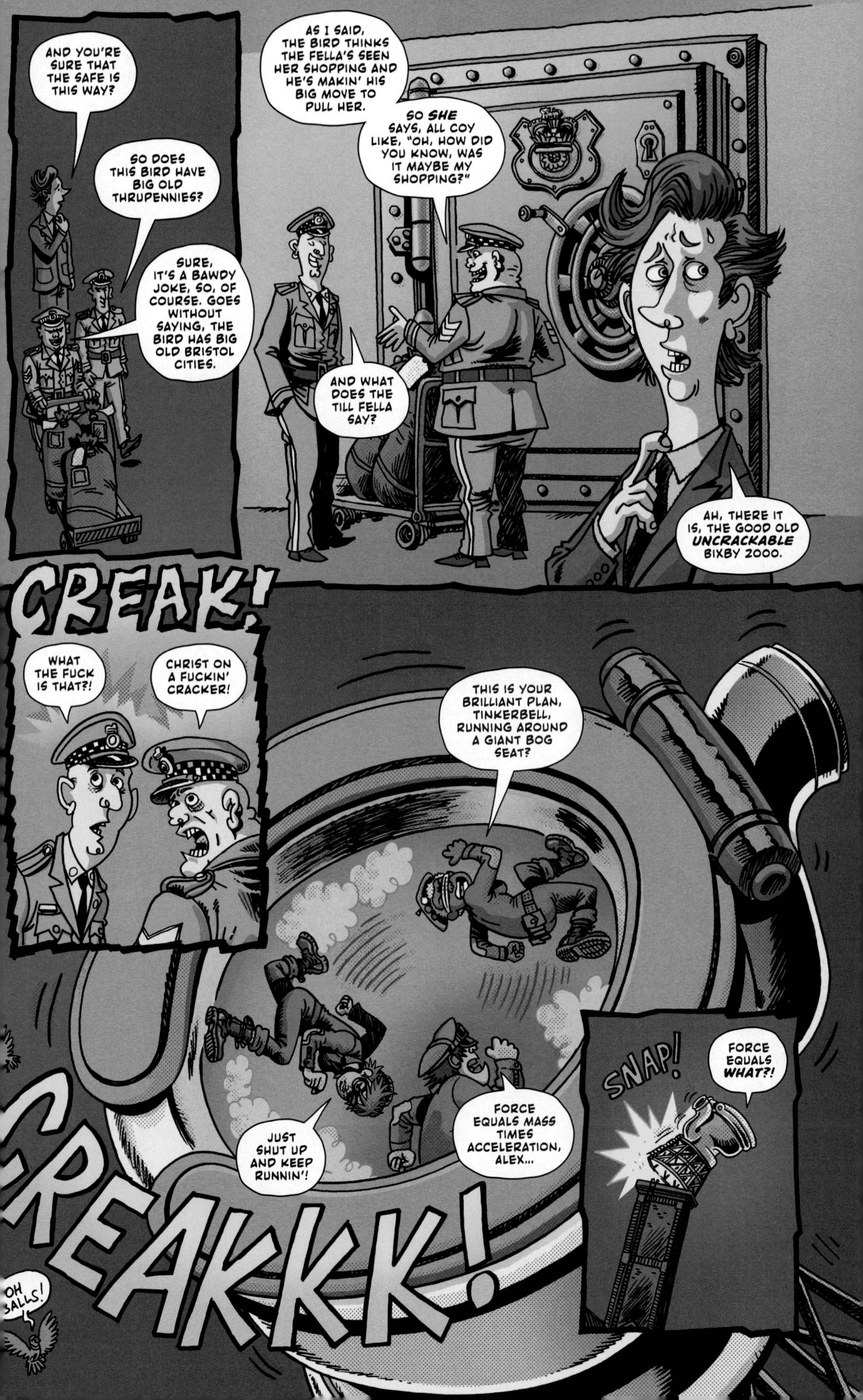
AND YOU'RE SURE THAT THE SAFE IS THIS WAY?
SO DOES THIS BIRD HAVE BIG OLD THRUPENNIES?
SURE, IT'S A BAWDY JOKE, SO, OF COURSE. GOES WITHOUT SAYING, THE BIRD HAS BIG OLD BRISTOL CITIES.
AS I SAID, THE BIRD THINKS THE FELLA'S SEEN HER SHOPPING AND HE'S MAKIN' HIS BIG MOVE TO PULL HER.
SO SHE SAYS, ALL COY LIKE, "OH, HOW DID YOU KNOW, WAS IT MAYBE MY SHOPPING?"
AND WHAT DOES THE TILL FELLA SAY?
AH, THERE IT IS, THE GOOD OLD UNCRACKABLE BIXBY 2000.
CREAK!
WHAT THE FUCK IS THAT?!
CHRIST ON A FUCKIN' CRACKER!
THIS IS YOUR BRILLIANT PLAN, TINKERBELL, RUNNING AROUND A GIANT BOG SEAT?
JUST SHUT UP AND KEEP RUNNIN'!
FORCE EQUALS MASS TIMES ACCELERATION, ALEX...
SNAP!
FORCE EQUALS WHAT?!
CREAKKK!
OH BALLS!

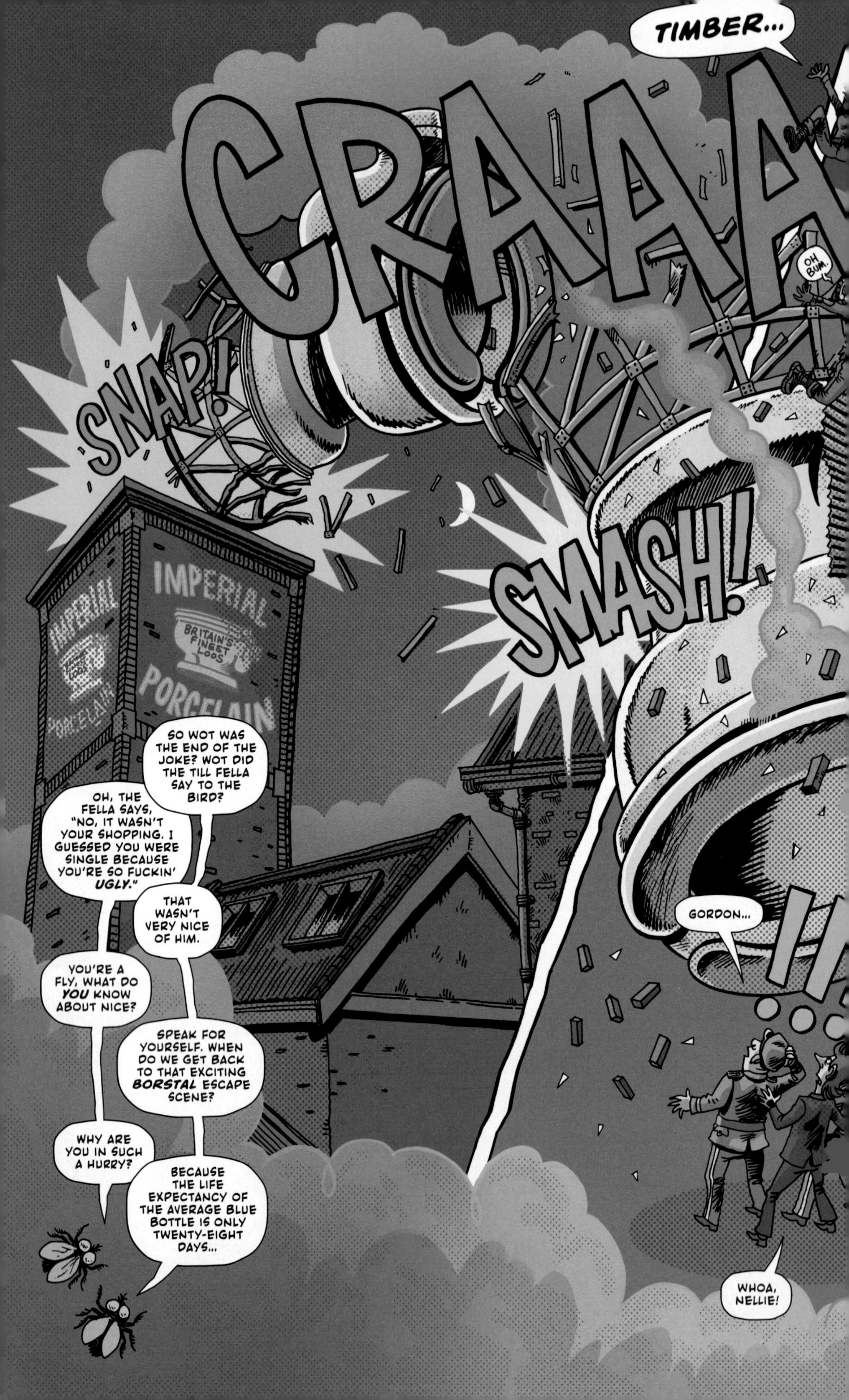
TIMBER...
CRAAA
OH BUM.
SNAP!
IMPERIAL
BRITAIN'S FINEST LOOS
PORCELAIN
SMASH!
SO WOT WAS THE END OF THE JOKE? WOT DID THE TILL FELLA SAY TO THE BIRD?
OH, THE FELLA SAYS, "NO, IT WASN'T YOUR SHOPPING. I GUESSED YOU WERE SINGLE BECAUSE YOU'RE SO FUCKIN' UGLY."
THAT WASN'T VERY NICE OF HIM.
YOU'RE A FLY, WHAT DO YOU KNOW ABOUT NICE?
SPEAK FOR YOURSELF. WHEN DO WE GET BACK TO THAT EXCITING BORSTAL ESCAPE SCENE?
WHY ARE YOU IN SUCH A HURRY?
BECAUSE THE LIFE EXPECTANCY OF THE AVERAGE BLUE BOTTLE IS ONLY TWENTY-EIGHT DAYS...
GORDON...
WHOA, NELLIE!

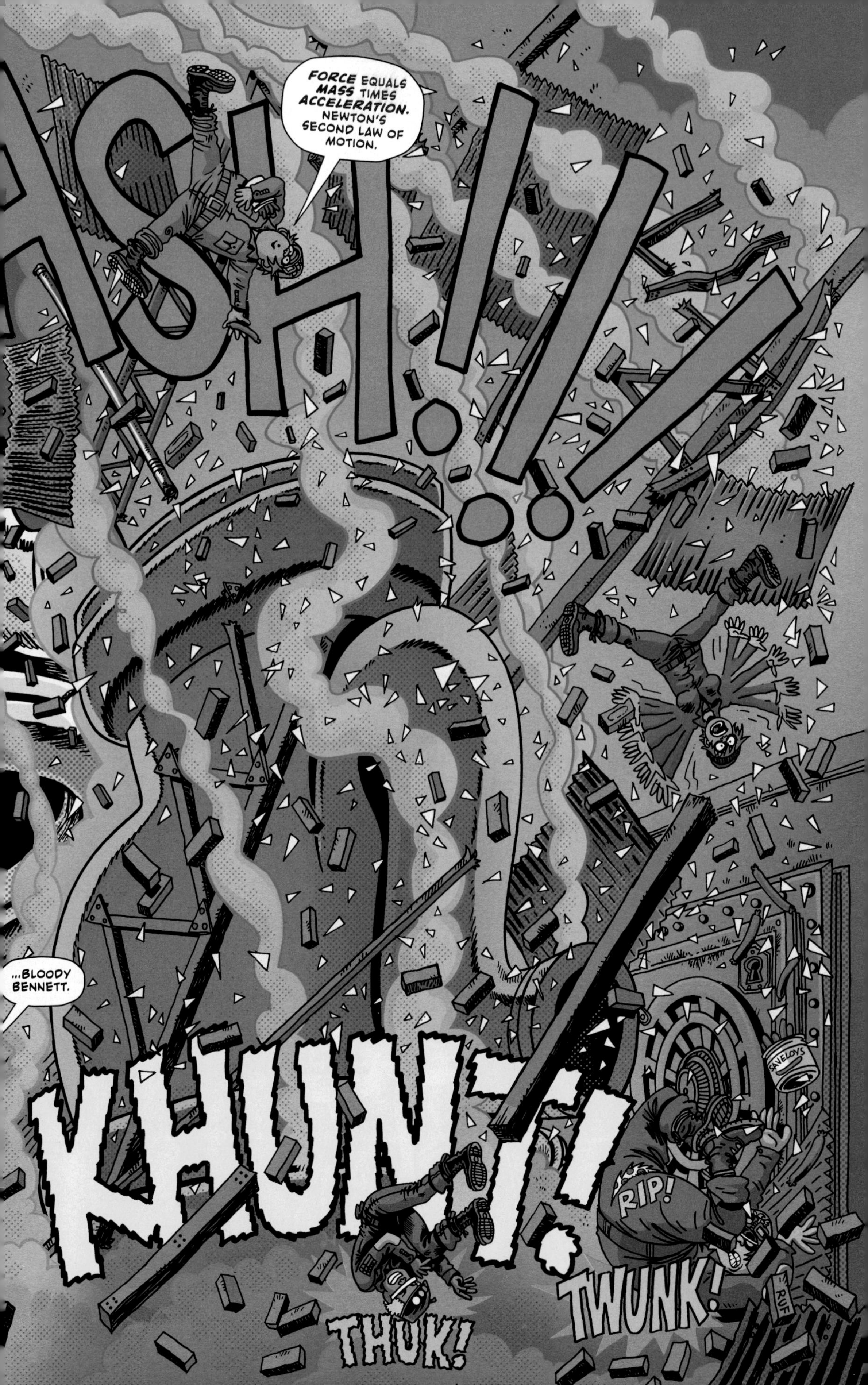
SH!!!
FORCE EQUALS MASS TIMES ACCELERATION. NEWTON'S SECOND LAW OF MOTION.
...BLOODY BENNETT.
KHUNT!
RIP!
SAVELOYS
TWUNK!
THUK!

I LOVE THE SOUND OF BREAKING GLASS!

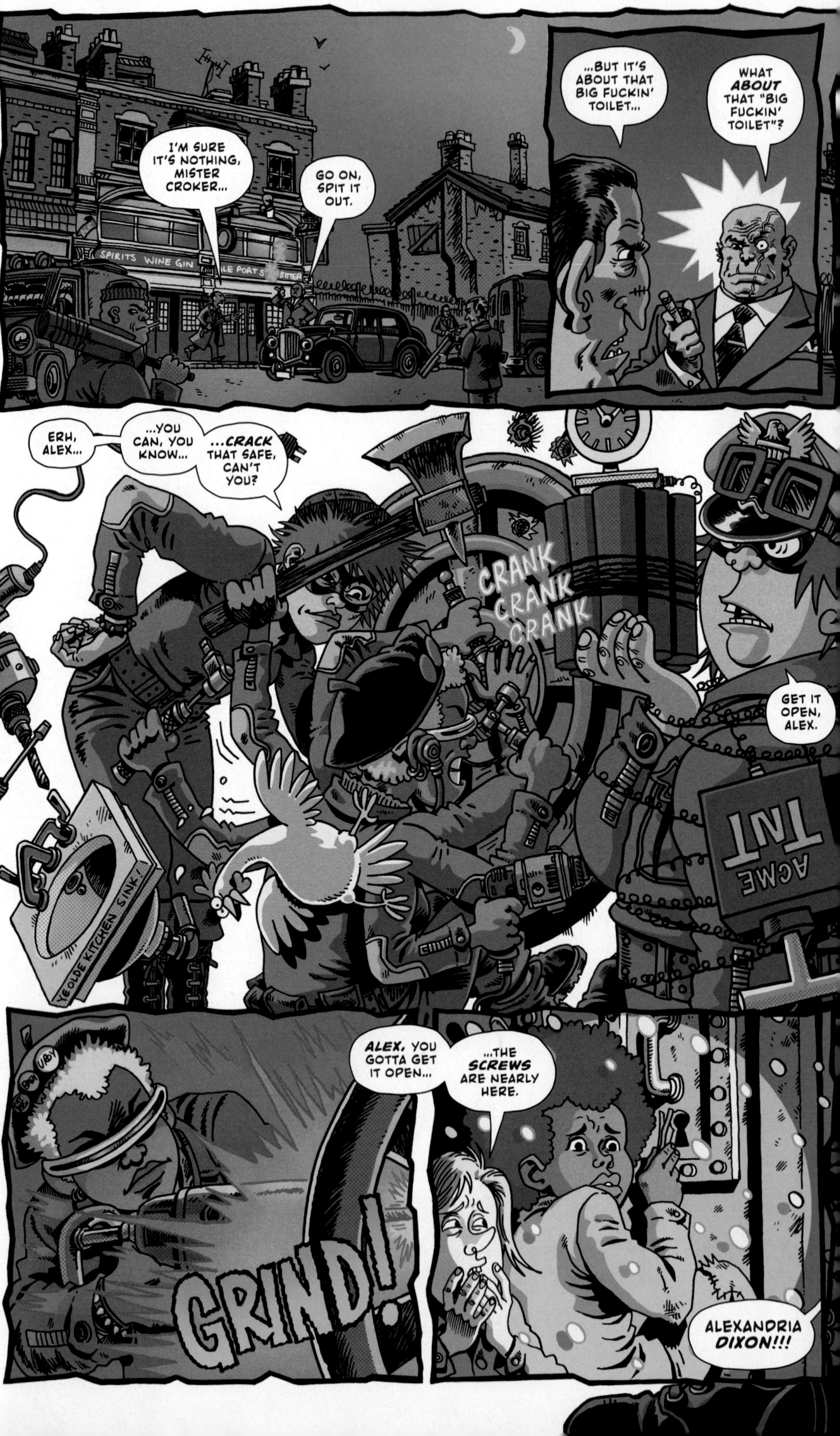
SPIRITS WINE GIN
I'M SURE IT'S NOTHING, MISTER CROKER...
GO ON, SPIT IT OUT.
...BUT IT'S ABOUT THAT BIG FUCKIN' TOILET...
WHAT **ABOUT** THAT "BIG FUCKIN' TOILET"?
ERH, ALEX...
...YOU CAN, YOU KNOW...
...**CRACK** THAT SAFE, CAN'T YOU?
CRANK CRANK CRANK
GET IT OPEN, ALEX.
YE OLDE KITCHEN SINK!
ACME TNT
GRIND!
ALEX, YOU GOTTA GET IT OPEN...
...THE **SCREWS** ARE NEARLY HERE.
ALEXANDRIA **DIXON!!!**

DIRTY DEEDS DONE DIRT CHEAP!

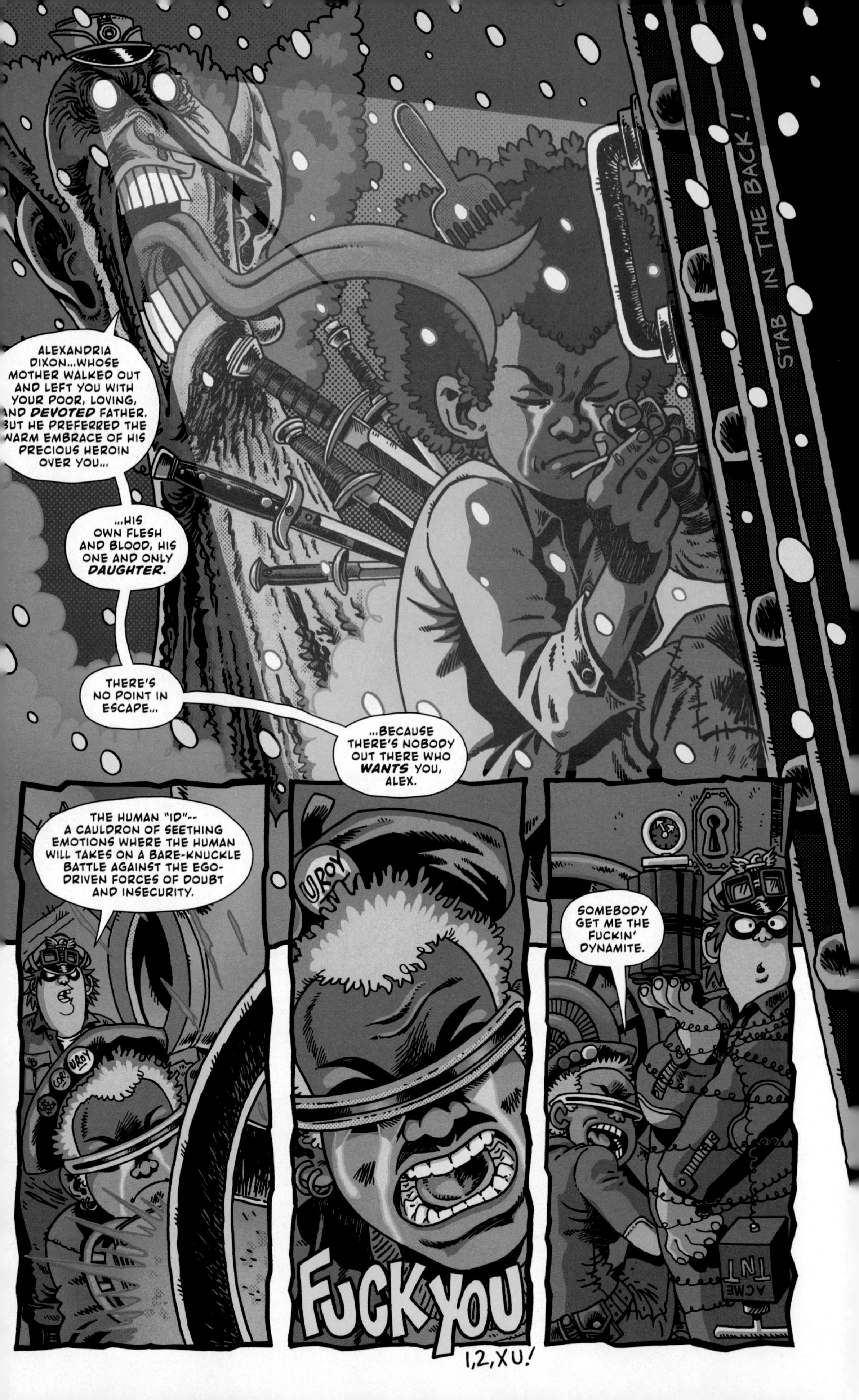
STAB IN THE BACK!
ALEXANDRIA DIXON...WHOSE MOTHER WALKED OUT AND LEFT YOU WITH YOUR POOR, LOVING, AND DEVOTED FATHER. BUT HE PREFERRED THE WARM EMBRACE OF HIS PRECIOUS HEROIN OVER YOU...
...HIS OWN FLESH AND BLOOD, HIS ONE AND ONLY DAUGHTER.
THERE'S NO POINT IN ESCAPE...
...BECAUSE THERE'S NOBODY OUT THERE WHO WANTS YOU, ALEX.
THE HUMAN "ID"-- A CAULDRON OF SEETHING EMOTIONS WHERE THE HUMAN WILL TAKES ON A BARE-KNUCKLE BATTLE AGAINST THE EGO-DRIVEN FORCES OF DOUBT AND INSECURITY.
U ROY
FUCK YOU
SOMEBODY GET ME THE FUCKIN' DYNAMITE.
ACME TNT
1,2,XU!

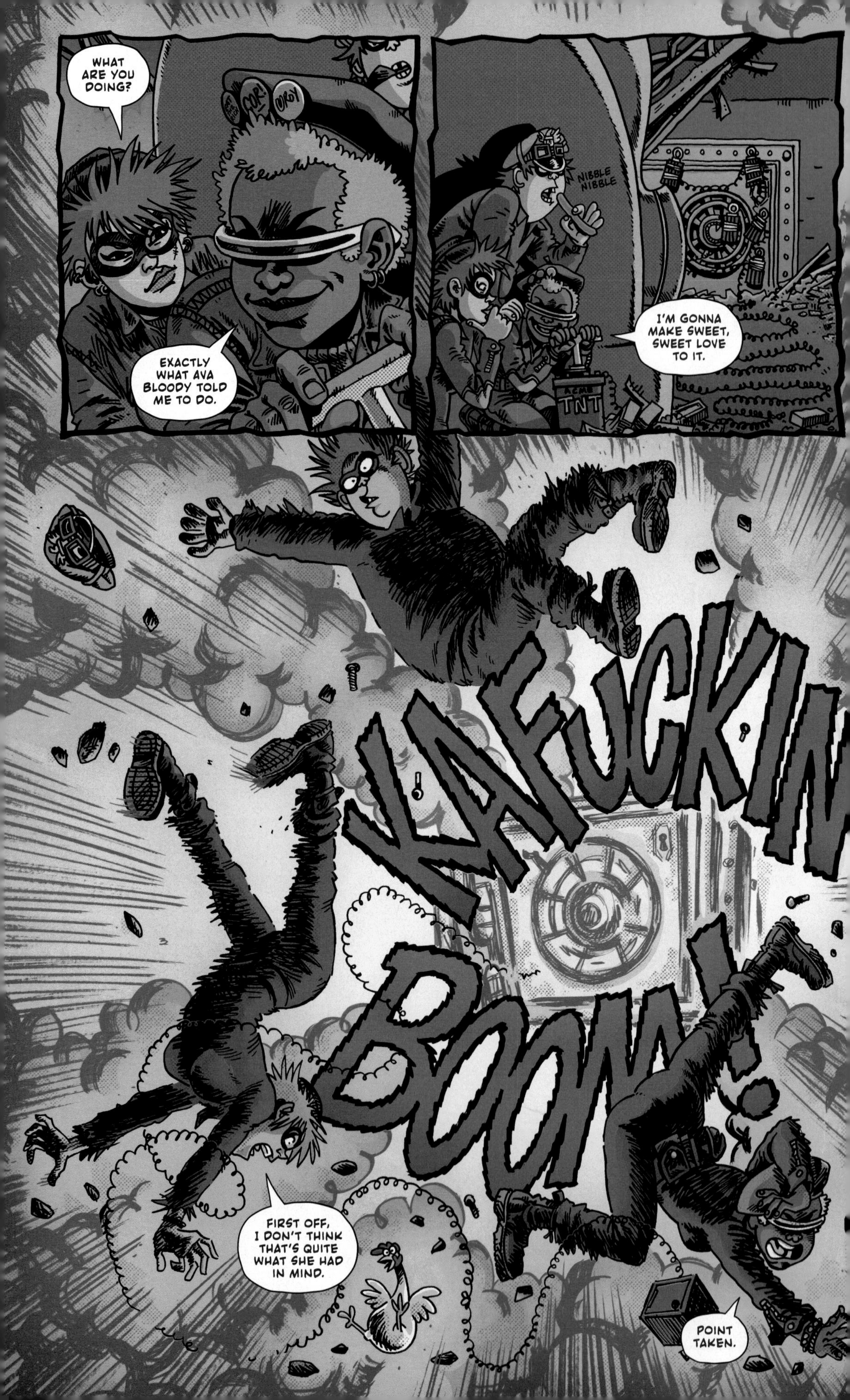
WHAT ARE YOU DOING?
EXACTLY WHAT AVA BLOODY TOLD ME TO DO.
NIBBLE NIBBLE
I'M GONNA MAKE SWEET, SWEET LOVE TO IT.
ACME TNT
KAFUCKIN BOOM!
FIRST OFF, I DON'T THINK THAT'S QUITE WHAT SHE HAD IN MIND.
POINT TAKEN.

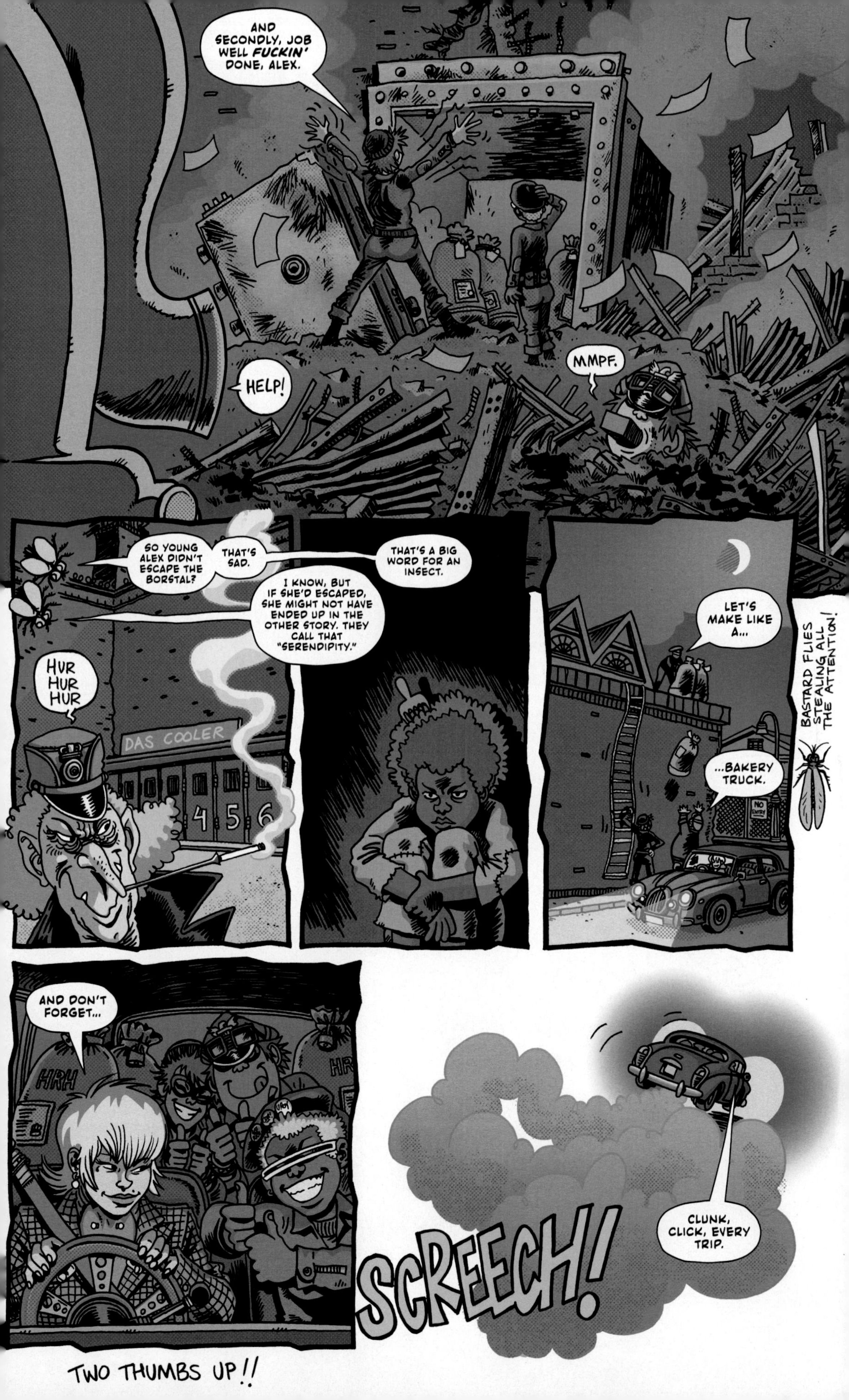
AND SECONDLY, JOB WELL FUCKIN' DONE, ALEX.
HELP!
MMPF.
SO YOUNG ALEX DIDN'T ESCAPE THE BORSTAL?
THAT'S SAD.
THAT'S A BIG WORD FOR AN INSECT.
I KNOW, BUT IF SHE'D ESCAPED, SHE MIGHT NOT HAVE ENDED UP IN THE OTHER STORY. THEY CALL THAT "SERENDIPITY."
HUR HUR HUR
DAS COOLER
4 5 6
LET'S MAKE LIKE A...
...BAKERY TRUCK.
NO ENTRY
BASTARD FLIES STEALING ALL THE ATTENTION!
AND DON'T FORGET...
HRH
SCREECH!
CLUNK, CLICK, EVERY TRIP.
TWO THUMBS UP!!

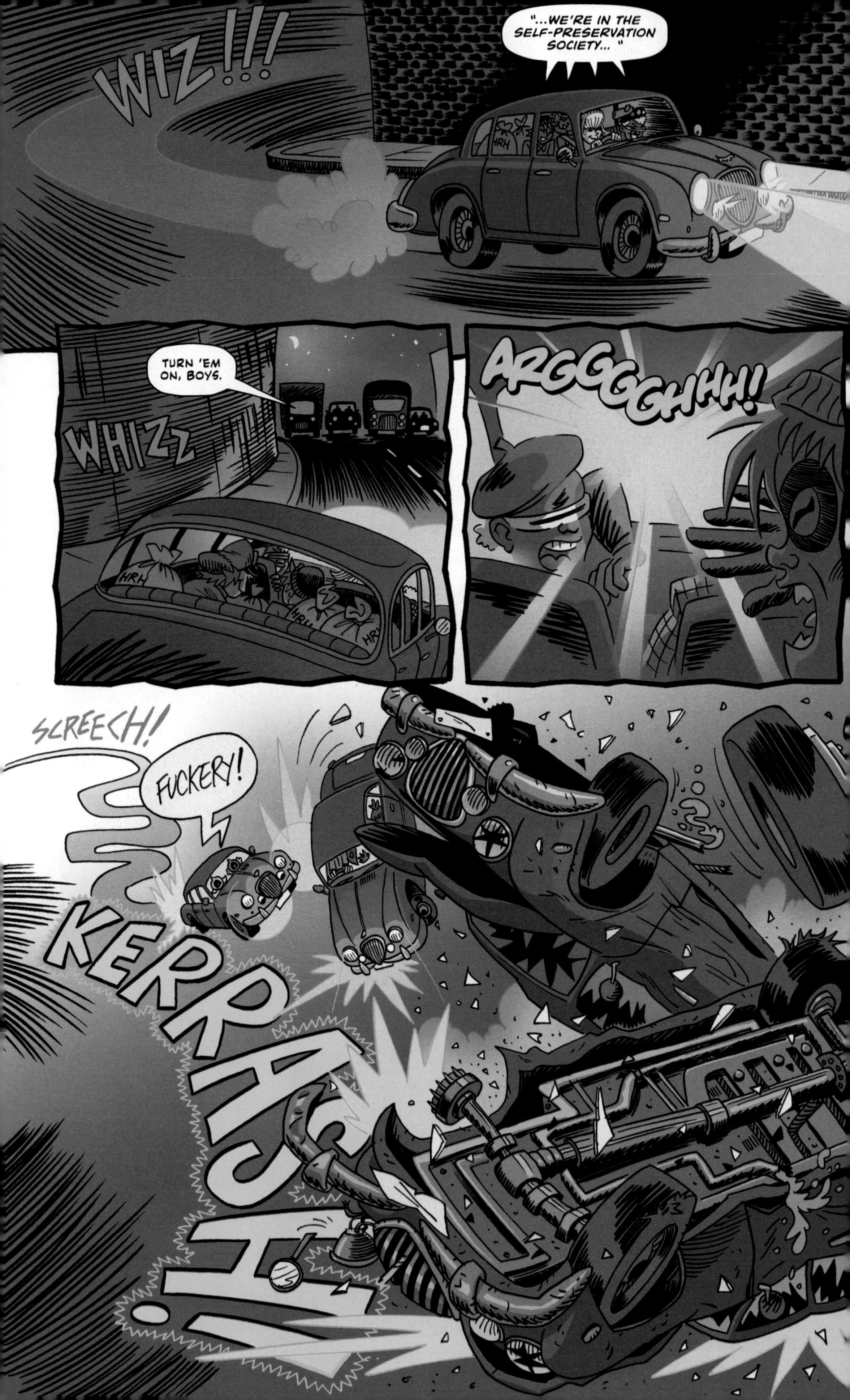
WIZ!!!
"...WE'RE IN THE SELF-PRESERVATION SOCIETY..."
TURN 'EM ON, BOYS.
WHIZZ
ARGGGGGHHH!
SCREECH!
FUCKERY!
KERRASH!

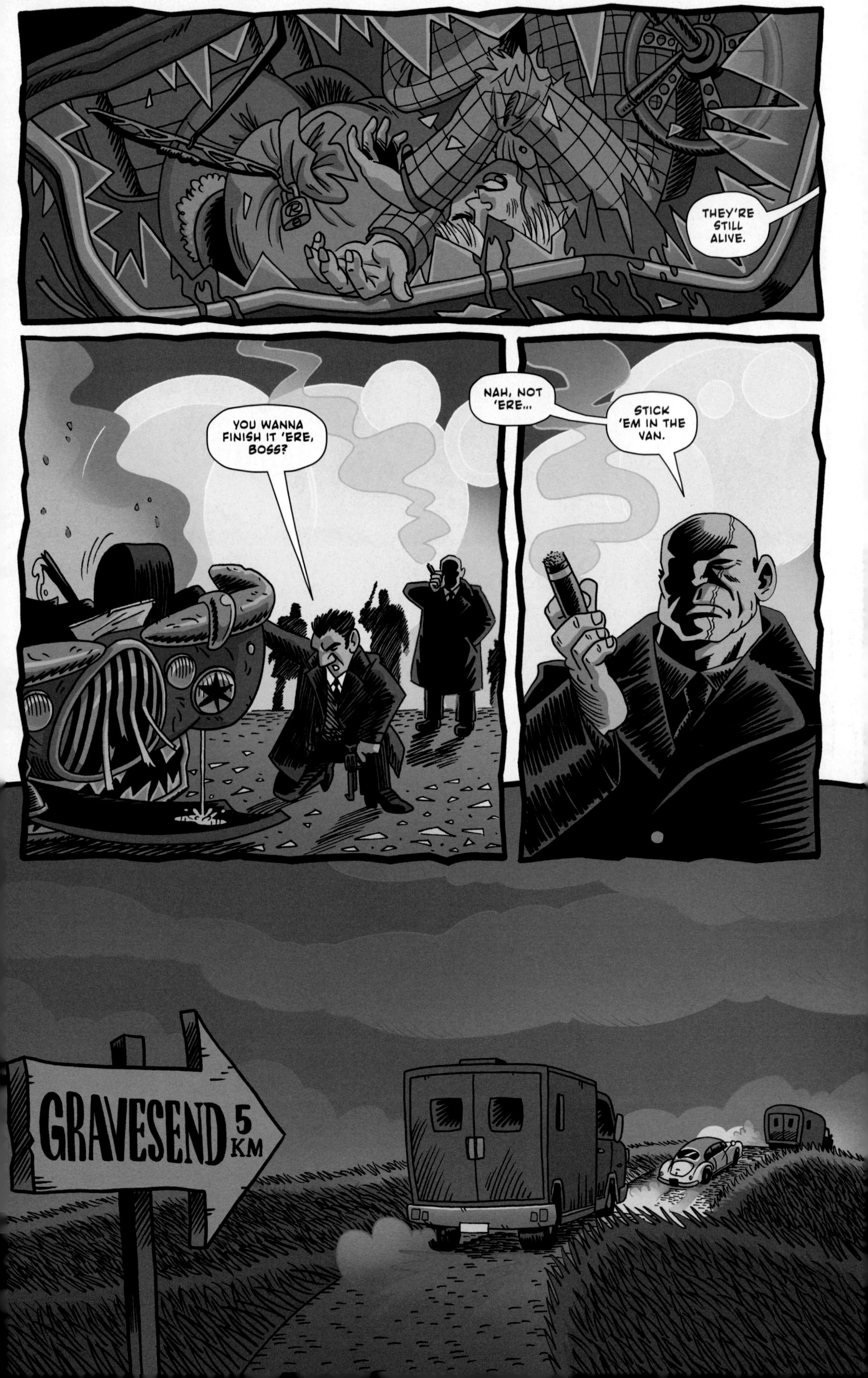
THEY'RE STILL ALIVE.
YOU WANNA FINISH IT 'ERE, BOSS?
NAH, NOT 'ERE...
STICK 'EM IN THE VAN.
GRAVESEND 5 KM

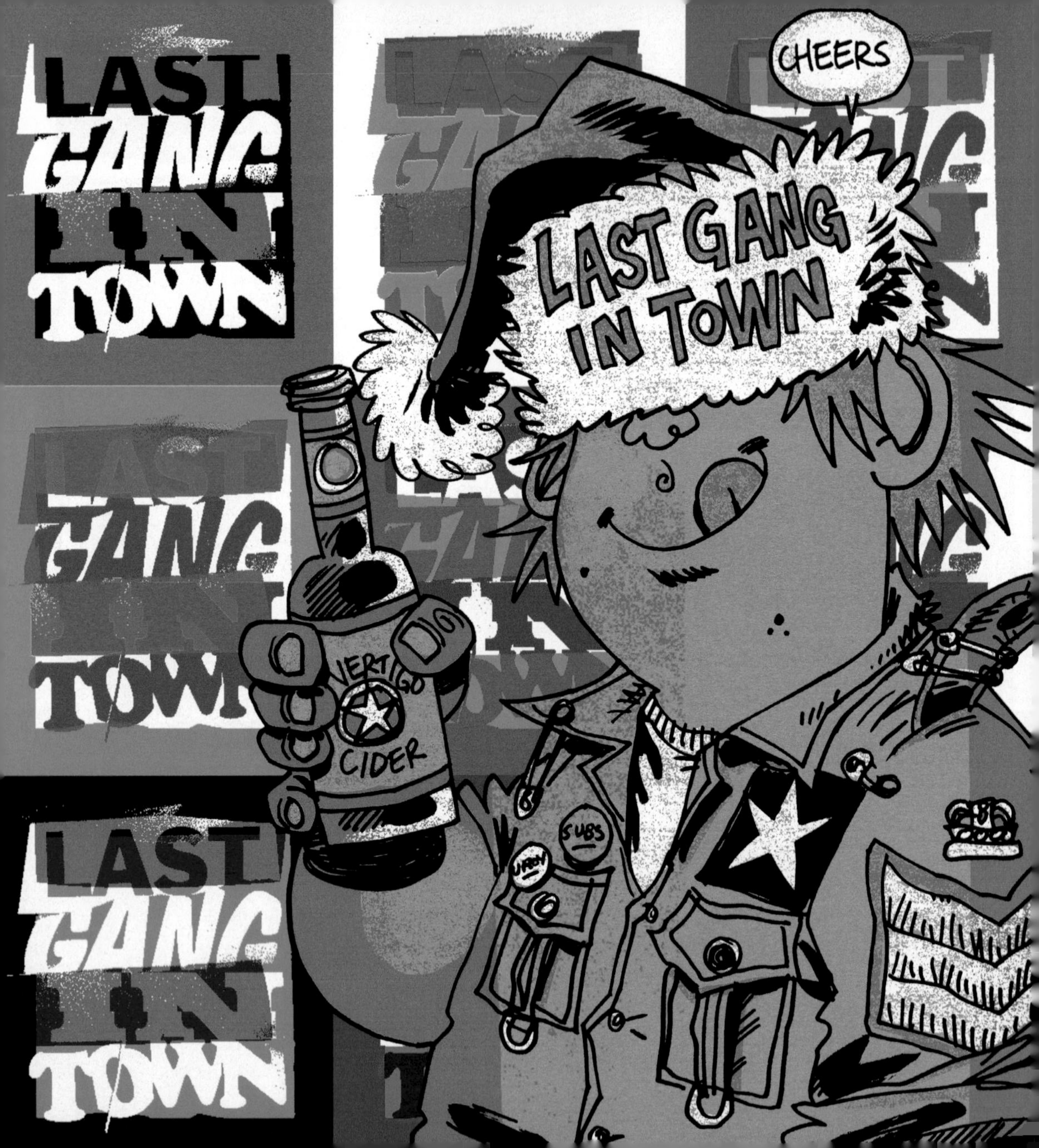

LAST GANG IN TOWN
LAST GANG IN TOWN
LAST GANG IN TOWN
CHEERS
LAST GANG IN TOWN
VERTIGO CIDER
SUBS

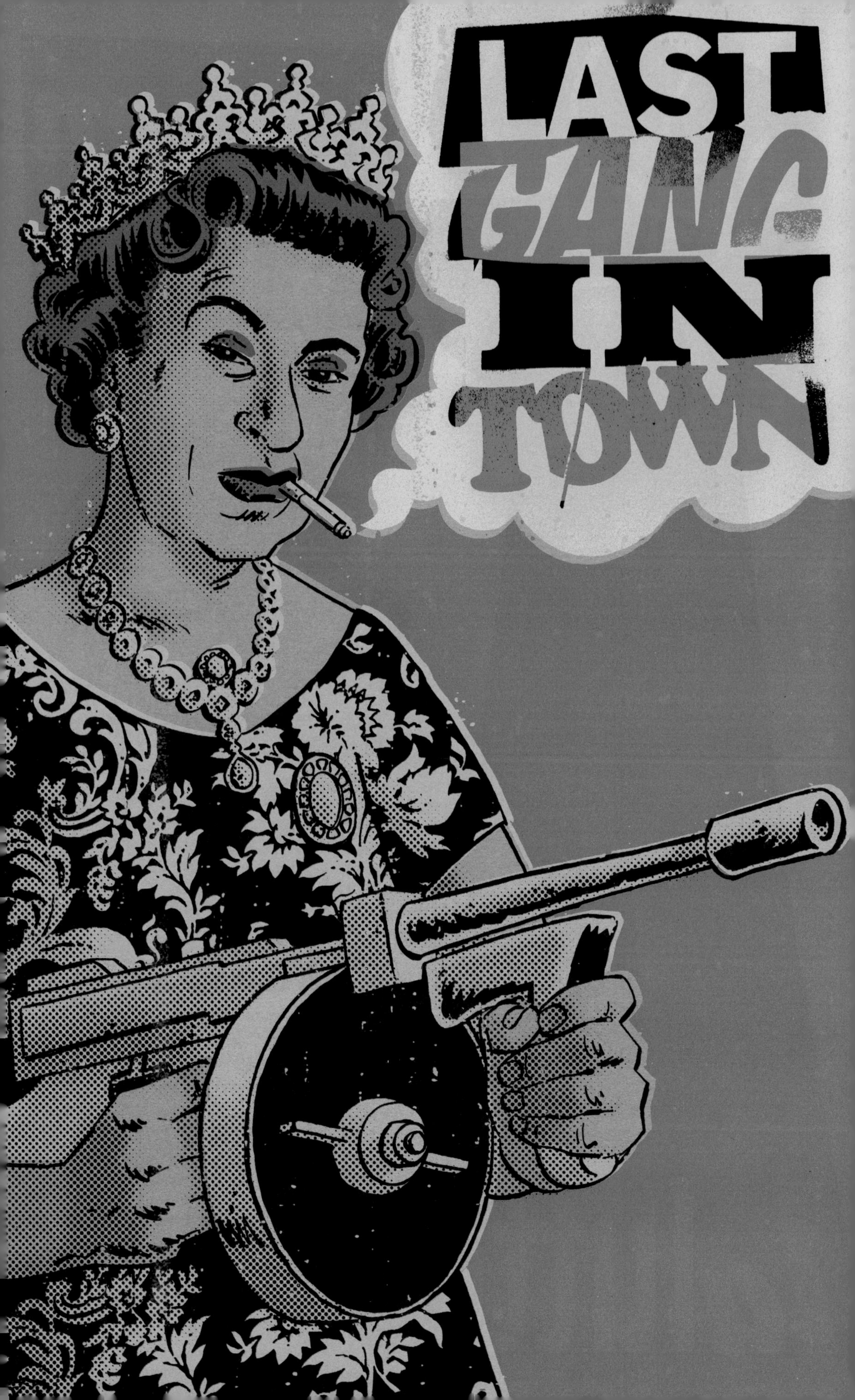
LAST
GANG
IN
TOWN

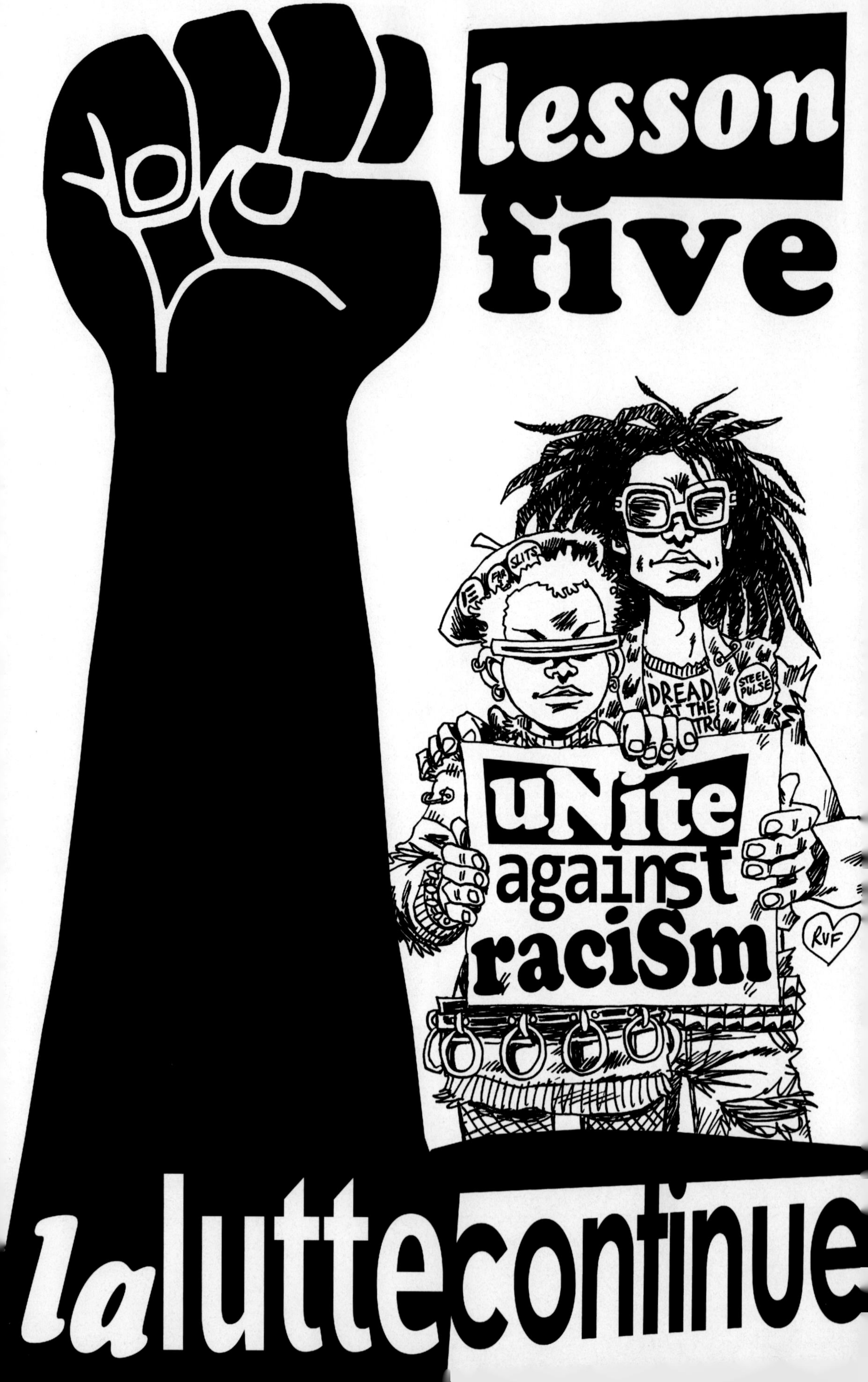
lesson
five
SLITS
DREAD AT THE
STEEL PULSE
uNite against raciSm
RVF
la lutte continue

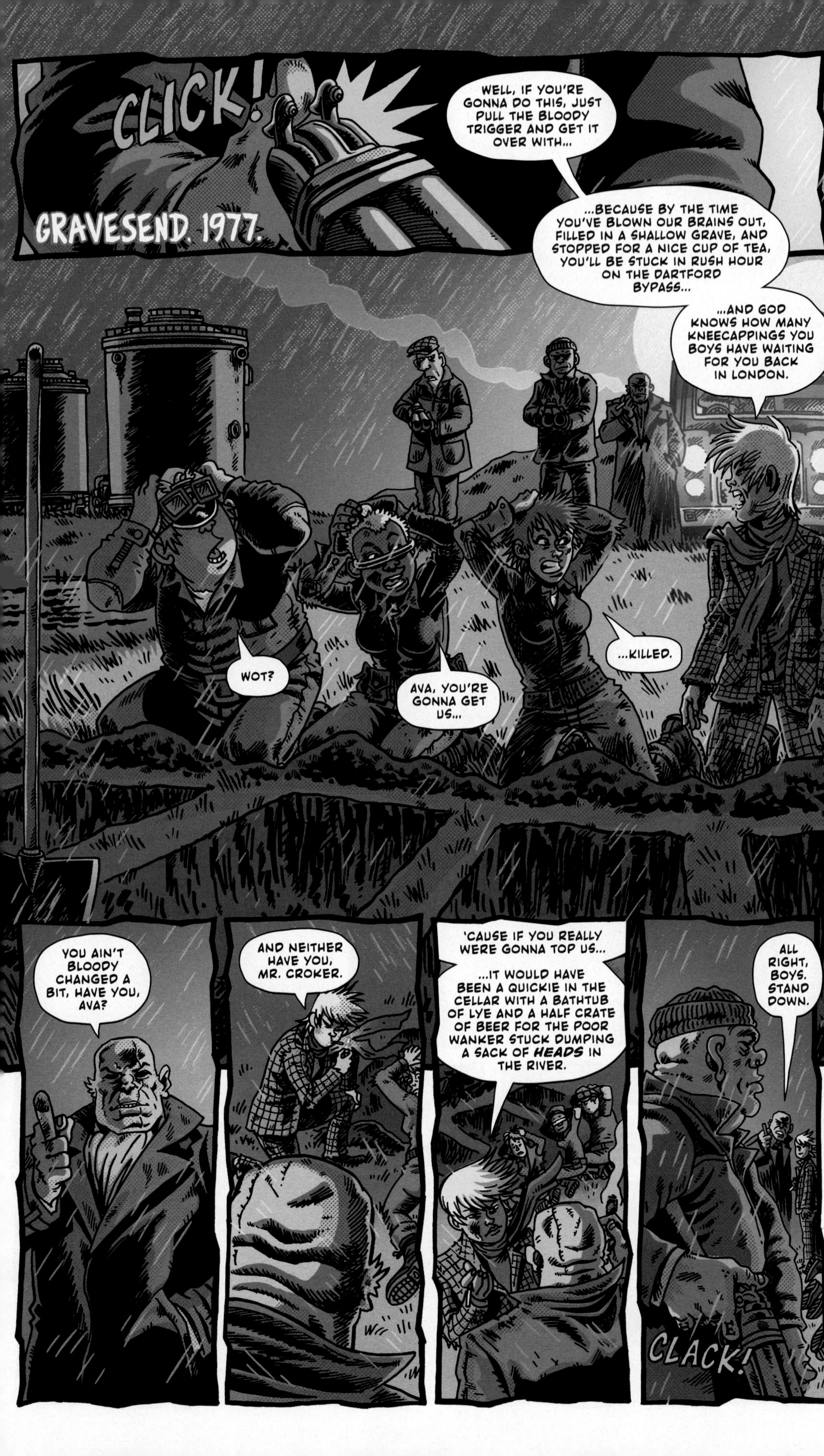
CLICK!
GRAVESEND, 1977.
WELL, IF YOU'RE GONNA DO THIS, JUST PULL THE BLOODY TRIGGER AND GET IT OVER WITH...
...BECAUSE BY THE TIME YOU'VE BLOWN OUR BRAINS OUT, FILLED IN A SHALLOW GRAVE, AND STOPPED FOR A NICE CUP OF TEA, YOU'LL BE STUCK IN RUSH HOUR ON THE DARTFORD BYPASS...
...AND GOD KNOWS HOW MANY KNEECAPPINGS YOU BOYS HAVE WAITING FOR YOU BACK IN LONDON.
WOT?
AVA, YOU'RE GONNA GET US...
...KILLED.
YOU AIN'T BLOODY CHANGED A BIT, HAVE YOU, AVA?
AND NEITHER HAVE YOU, MR. CROKER.
'CAUSE IF YOU REALLY WERE GONNA TOP US...
...IT WOULD HAVE BEEN A QUICKIE IN THE CELLAR WITH A BATHTUB OF LYE AND A HALF CRATE OF BEER FOR THE POOR WANKER STUCK DUMPING A SACK OF HEADS IN THE RIVER.
ALL RIGHT, BOYS. STAND DOWN.
CLACK!

DEAD AND BURIED! THE LIVING AIN'T EASY, LIVIN' AIN'T CLEAN!

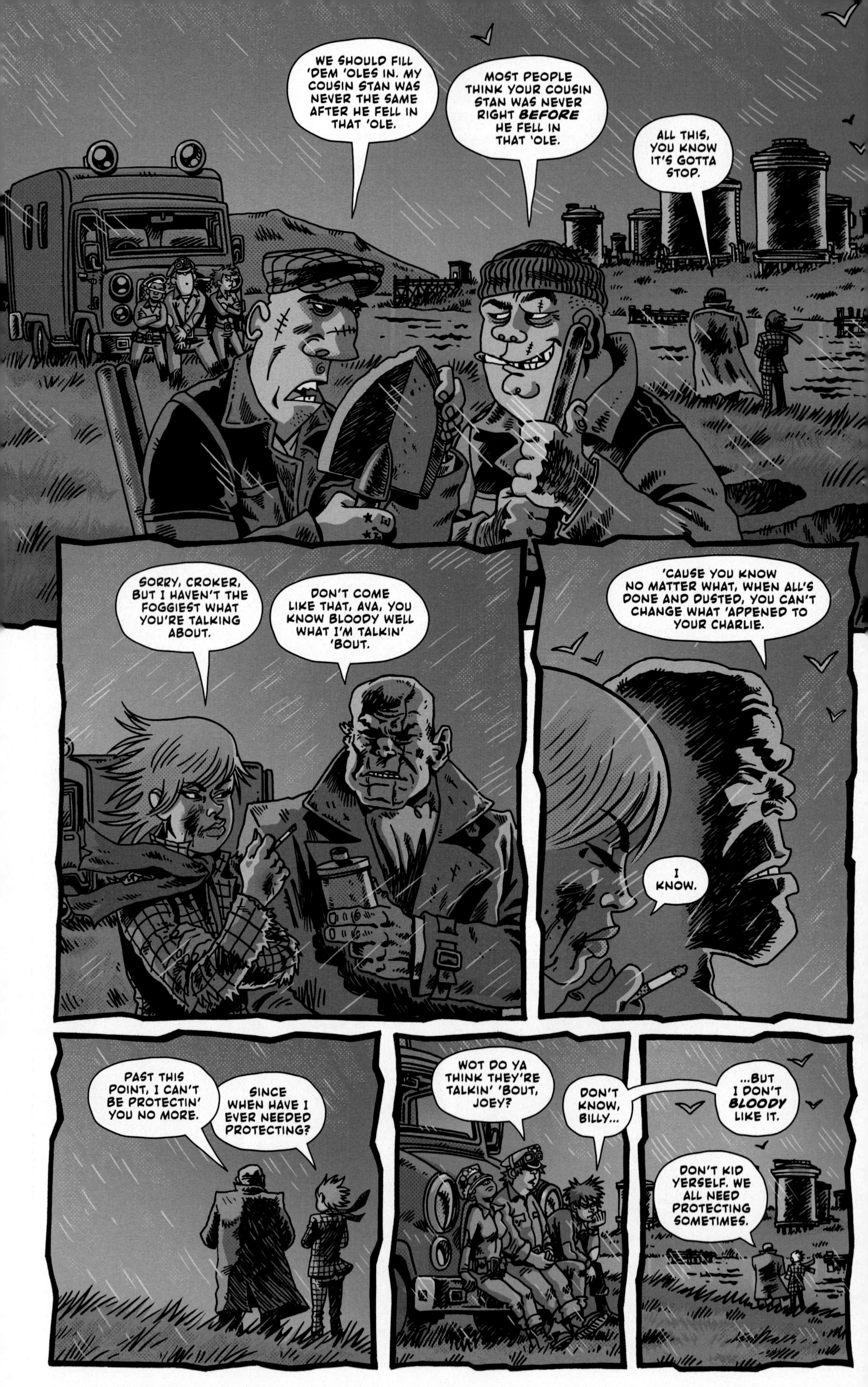
WE SHOULD FILL 'DEM 'OLES IN. MY COUSIN STAN WAS NEVER THE SAME AFTER HE FELL IN THAT 'OLE.
MOST PEOPLE THINK YOUR COUSIN STAN WAS NEVER RIGHT BEFORE HE FELL IN THAT 'OLE.
ALL THIS, YOU KNOW IT'S GOTTA STOP.
SORRY, CROKER, BUT I HAVEN'T THE FOGGIEST WHAT YOU'RE TALKING ABOUT.
DON'T COME LIKE THAT, AVA, YOU KNOW BLOODY WELL WHAT I'M TALKIN' 'BOUT.
'CAUSE YOU KNOW NO MATTER WHAT, WHEN ALL'S DONE AND DUSTED, YOU CAN'T CHANGE WHAT 'APPENED TO YOUR CHARLIE.
I KNOW.
PAST THIS POINT, I CAN'T BE PROTECTIN' YOU NO MORE.
SINCE WHEN HAVE I EVER NEEDED PROTECTING?
WOT DO YA THINK THEY'RE TALKIN' 'BOUT, JOEY?
DON'T KNOW, BILLY...
...BUT I DON'T BLOODY LIKE IT.
DON'T KID YERSELF. WE ALL NEED PROTECTING SOMETIMES.

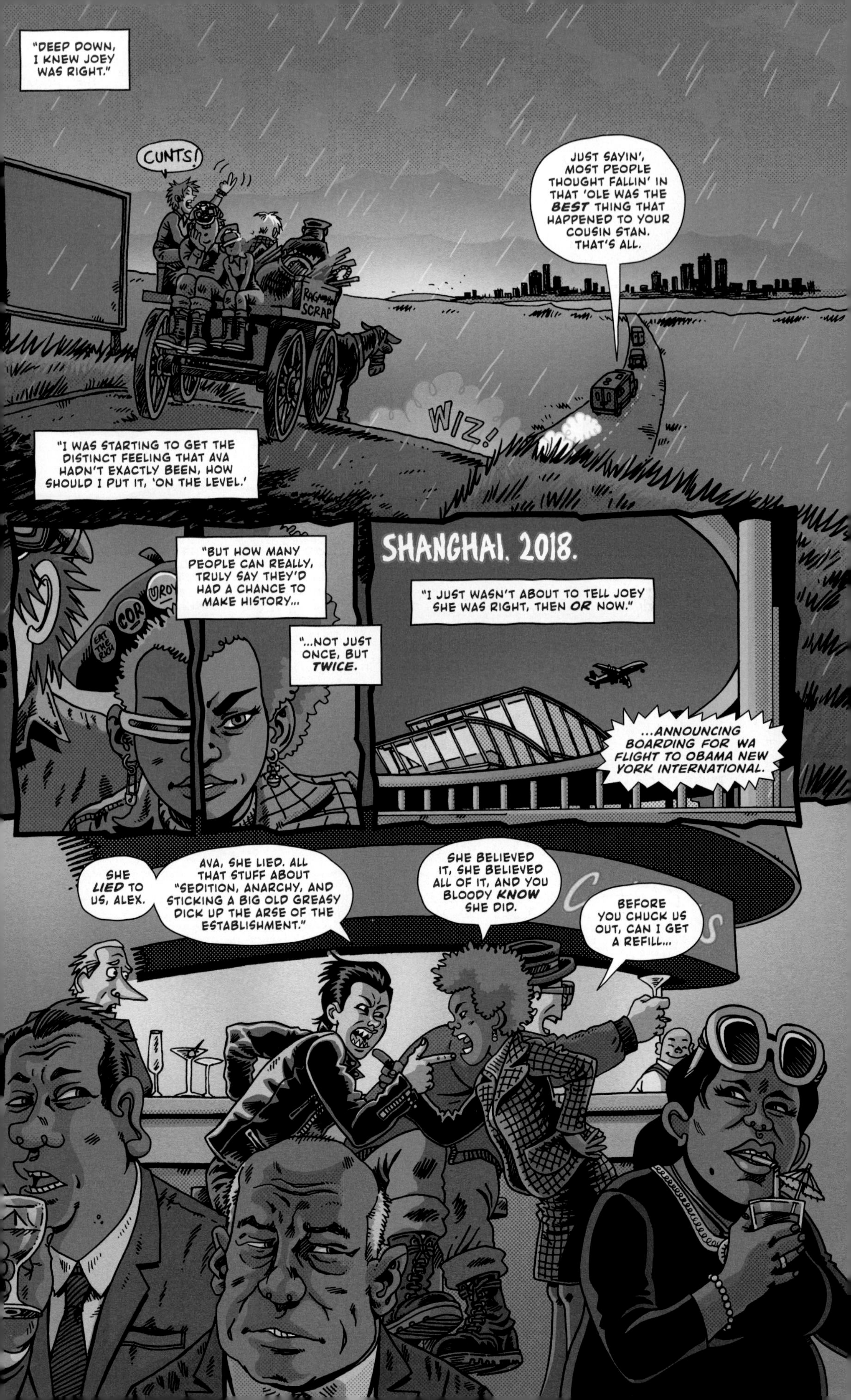
"DEEP DOWN, I KNEW JOEY WAS RIGHT."
CUNTS!
JUST SAYIN', MOST PEOPLE THOUGHT FALLIN' IN THAT 'OLE WAS THE BEST THING THAT HAPPENED TO YOUR COUSIN STAN. THAT'S ALL.
RAG SCRAP
WIZ!
"I WAS STARTING TO GET THE DISTINCT FEELING THAT AVA HADN'T EXACTLY BEEN, HOW SHOULD I PUT IT, 'ON THE LEVEL.'
"BUT HOW MANY PEOPLE CAN REALLY, TRULY SAY THEY'D HAD A CHANCE TO MAKE HISTORY...
"...NOT JUST ONCE, BUT TWICE.
SHANGHAI. 2018.
"I JUST WASN'T ABOUT TO TELL JOEY SHE WAS RIGHT, THEN OR NOW."
...ANNOUNCING BOARDING FOR WA FLIGHT TO OBAMA NEW YORK INTERNATIONAL.
SHE LIED TO US, ALEX.
AVA, SHE LIED. ALL THAT STUFF ABOUT "SEDITION, ANARCHY, AND STICKING A BIG OLD GREASY DICK UP THE ARSE OF THE ESTABLISHMENT."
SHE BELIEVED IT, SHE BELIEVED ALL OF IT, AND YOU BLOODY KNOW SHE DID.
BEFORE YOU CHUCK US OUT, CAN I GET A REFILL...

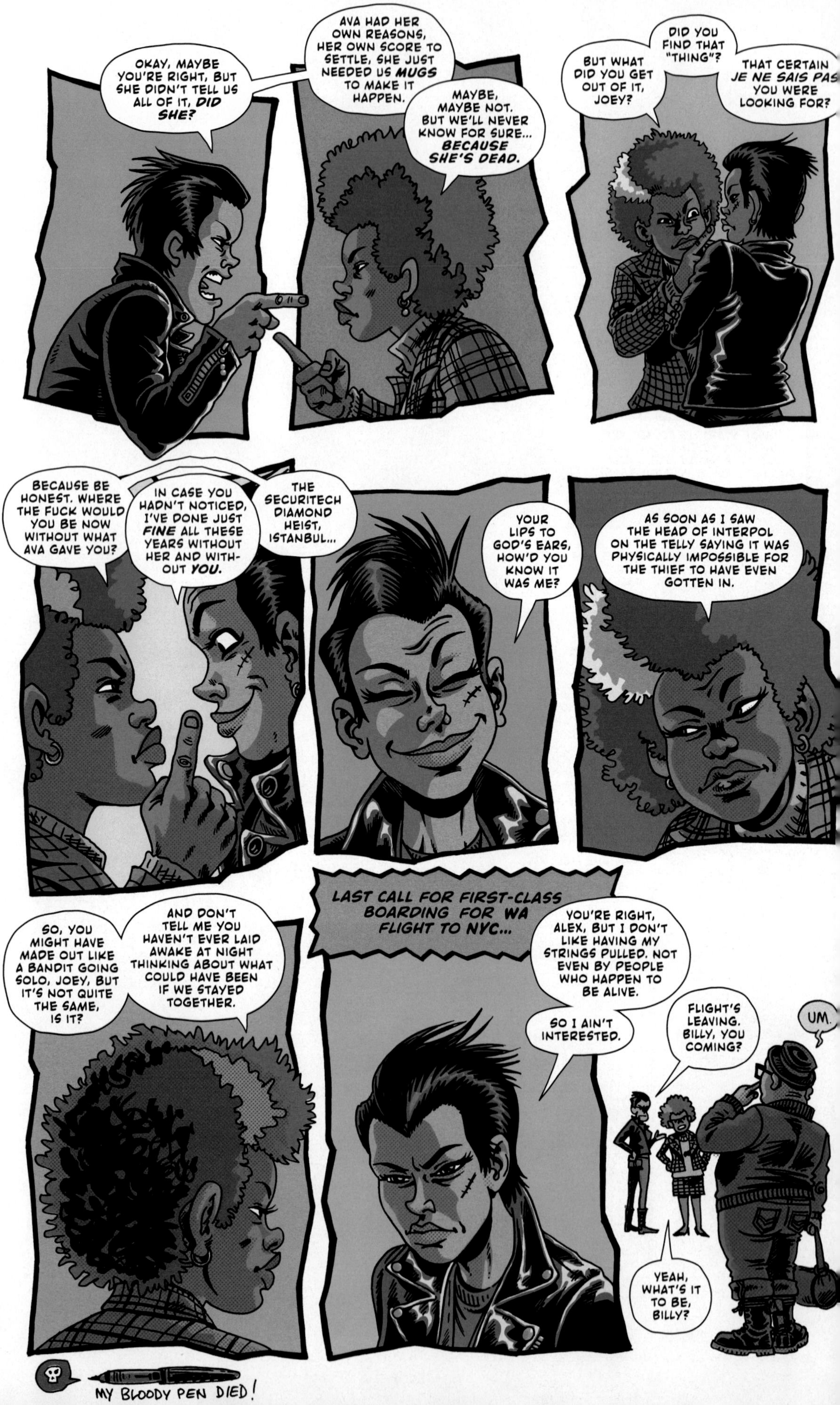
OKAY, MAYBE YOU'RE RIGHT, BUT SHE DIDN'T TELL US ALL OF IT, *DID SHE?*
AVA HAD HER OWN REASONS, HER OWN SCORE TO SETTLE, SHE JUST NEEDED US *MUGS* TO MAKE IT HAPPEN.
MAYBE, MAYBE NOT. BUT WE'LL NEVER KNOW FOR SURE... *BECAUSE SHE'S DEAD.*
BUT WHAT DID YOU GET OUT OF IT, JOEY?
DID YOU FIND THAT "THING"?
THAT CERTAIN *JE NE SAIS PAS* YOU WERE LOOKING FOR?
BECAUSE BE HONEST. WHERE THE FUCK WOULD YOU BE NOW WITHOUT WHAT AVA GAVE YOU?
IN CASE YOU HADN'T NOTICED, I'VE DONE JUST *FINE* ALL THESE YEARS WITHOUT HER AND WITH-OUT *YOU.*
THE SECURITECH DIAMOND HEIST, ISTANBUL...
YOUR LIPS TO GOD'S EARS, HOW'D YOU KNOW IT WAS ME?
AS SOON AS I SAW THE HEAD OF INTERPOL ON THE TELLY SAYING IT WAS PHYSICALLY IMPOSSIBLE FOR THE THIEF TO HAVE EVEN GOTTEN IN.
SO, YOU MIGHT HAVE MADE OUT LIKE A BANDIT GOING SOLO, JOEY, BUT IT'S NOT QUITE THE SAME, IS IT?
AND DON'T TELL ME YOU HAVEN'T EVER LAID AWAKE AT NIGHT THINKING ABOUT WHAT COULD HAVE BEEN IF WE STAYED TOGETHER.
LAST CALL FOR FIRST-CLASS BOARDING FOR WA FLIGHT TO NYC...
YOU'RE RIGHT, ALEX, BUT I DON'T LIKE HAVING MY STRINGS PULLED. NOT EVEN BY PEOPLE WHO HAPPEN TO BE ALIVE.
SO I AIN'T INTERESTED.
FLIGHT'S LEAVING. BILLY, YOU COMING?
UM.
YEAH, WHAT'S IT TO BE, BILLY?
MY BLOODY PEN DIED!

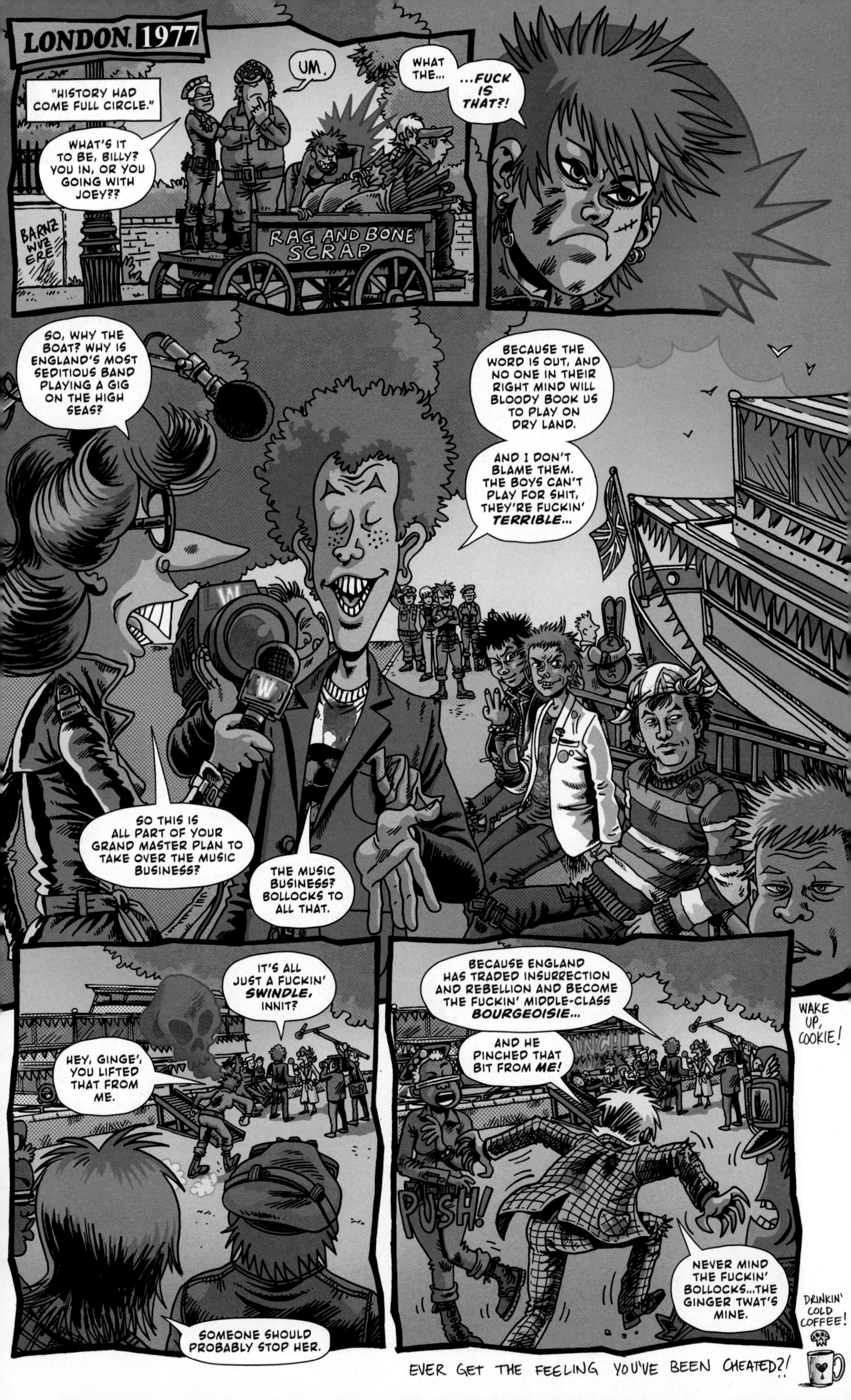
LONDON. 1977
"HISTORY HAD COME FULL CIRCLE."
WHAT'S IT TO BE, BILLY? YOU IN, OR YOU GOING WITH JOEY??
UM.
RAG AND BONE SCRAP
BARNZ WUZ ERE
WHAT THE...
...FUCK IS THAT?!
SO, WHY THE BOAT? WHY IS ENGLAND'S MOST SEDITIOUS BAND PLAYING A GIG ON THE HIGH SEAS?
BECAUSE THE WORD IS OUT, AND NO ONE IN THEIR RIGHT MIND WILL BLOODY BOOK US TO PLAY ON DRY LAND.
AND I DON'T BLAME THEM. THE BOYS CAN'T PLAY FOR SHIT, THEY'RE FUCKIN' TERRIBLE...
SO THIS IS ALL PART OF YOUR GRAND MASTER PLAN TO TAKE OVER THE MUSIC BUSINESS?
THE MUSIC BUSINESS? BOLLOCKS TO ALL THAT.
IT'S ALL JUST A FUCKIN' SWINDLE, INNIT?
HEY, GINGE', YOU LIFTED THAT FROM ME.
SOMEONE SHOULD PROBABLY STOP HER.
BECAUSE ENGLAND HAS TRADED INSURRECTION AND REBELLION AND BECOME THE FUCKIN' MIDDLE-CLASS BOURGEOISIE...
AND HE PINCHED THAT BIT FROM ME!
PUSH!
NEVER MIND THE FUCKIN' BOLLOCKS...THE GINGER TWAT'S MINE.
WAKE UP, COOKIE!
DRINKIN' COLD COFFEE!
EVER GET THE FEELING YOU'VE BEEN CHEATED?!

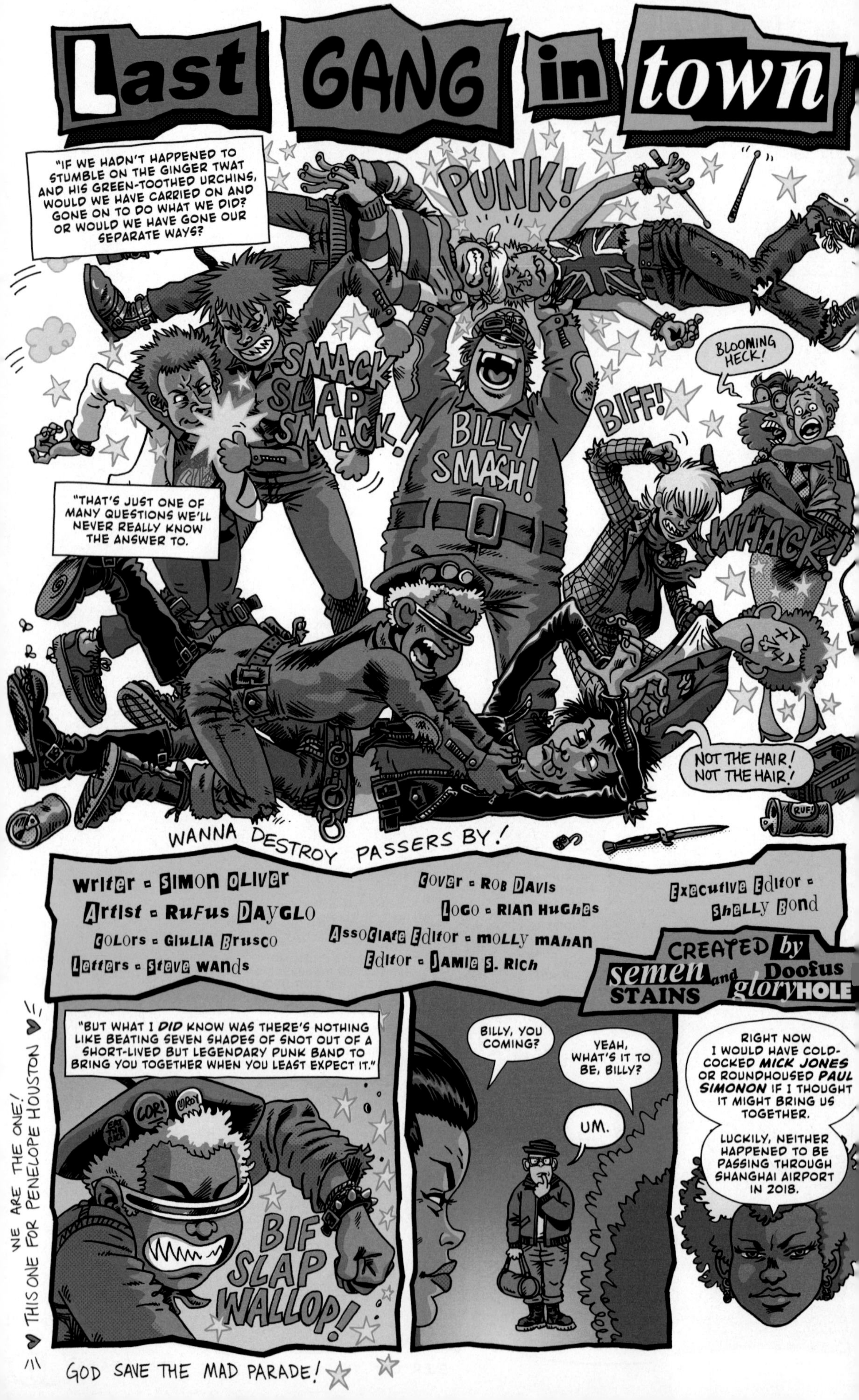

Last GANG in town
"IF WE HADN'T HAPPENED TO STUMBLE ON THE GINGER TWAT AND HIS GREEN-TOOTHED URCHINS, WOULD WE HAVE CARRIED ON AND GONE ON TO DO WHAT WE DID? OR WOULD WE HAVE GONE OUR SEPARATE WAYS?
PUNK!
SMACK SLAP SMACK!
BILLY SMASH!
BIFF!
BLOOMING HECK!
"THAT'S JUST ONE OF MANY QUESTIONS WE'LL NEVER REALLY KNOW THE ANSWER TO.
WHACK!
NOT THE HAIR! NOT THE HAIR!
RUF!
WANNA DESTROY PASSERS BY!
Writer - SIMON OLIVER
Artist - RUFUS DAYGLO
COLORS - GIULIA BRUSCO
Letters - STEVE WANDS
Cover - ROB DAVIS
LOGO - RIAN HUGHES
Associate Editor - MOLLY MAHAN
Editor - JAMIE S. RICH
Executive Editor - SHELLY BOND
CREATED by semen STAINS and Doofus gloryHOLE
"BUT WHAT I DID KNOW WAS THERE'S NOTHING LIKE BEATING SEVEN SHADES OF SNOT OUT OF A SHORT-LIVED BUT LEGENDARY PUNK BAND TO BRING YOU TOGETHER WHEN YOU LEAST EXPECT IT."
COR!
EAT THE RICH
BIF SLAP WALLOP!
BILLY, YOU COMING?
YEAH, WHAT'S IT TO BE, BILLY?
UM.
RIGHT NOW I WOULD HAVE COLD-COCKED MICK JONES OR ROUNDHOUSED PAUL SIMONON IF I THOUGHT IT MIGHT BRING US TOGETHER.
LUCKILY, NEITHER HAPPENED TO BE PASSING THROUGH SHANGHAI AIRPORT IN 2018.
WE ARE THE ONE! THIS ONE FOR PENELOPE HOUSTON
GOD SAVE THE MAD PARADE!

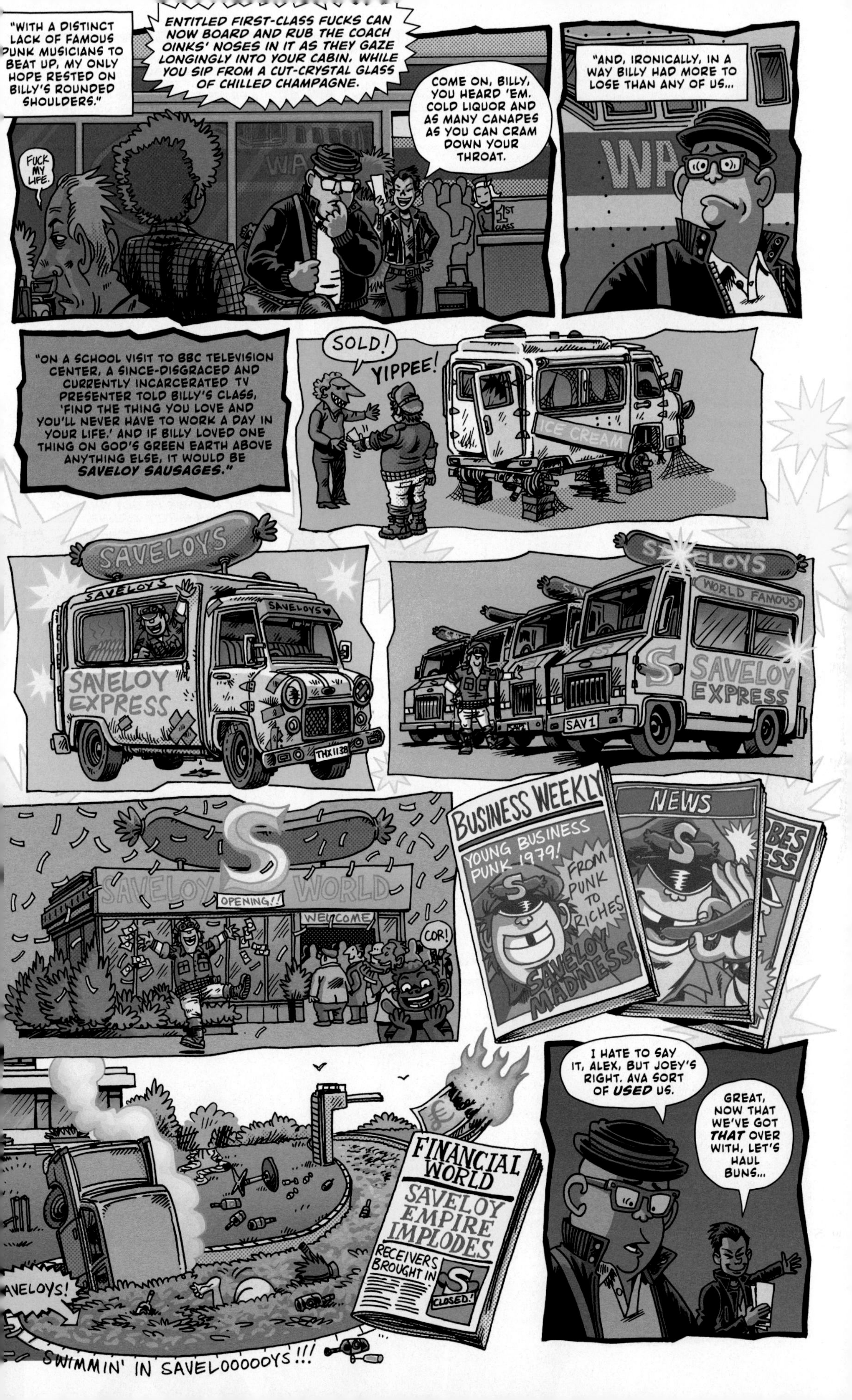
"WITH A DISTINCT LACK OF FAMOUS PUNK MUSICIANS TO BEAT UP, MY ONLY HOPE RESTED ON BILLY'S ROUNDED SHOULDERS."
ENTITLED FIRST-CLASS FUCKS CAN NOW BOARD AND RUB THE COACH OINKS' NOSES IN IT AS THEY GAZE LONGINGLY INTO YOUR CABIN, WHILE YOU SIP FROM A CUT-CRYSTAL GLASS OF CHILLED CHAMPAGNE.
FUCK MY LIFE.
COME ON, BILLY, YOU HEARD 'EM. COLD LIQUOR AND AS MANY CANAPES AS YOU CAN CRAM DOWN YOUR THROAT.
1ST CLASS
"AND, IRONICALLY, IN A WAY BILLY HAD MORE TO LOSE THAN ANY OF US...
"ON A SCHOOL VISIT TO BBC TELEVISION CENTER, A SINCE-DISGRACED AND CURRENTLY INCARCERATED TV PRESENTER TOLD BILLY'S CLASS, 'FIND THE THING YOU LOVE AND YOU'LL NEVER HAVE TO WORK A DAY IN YOUR LIFE.' AND IF BILLY LOVED ONE THING ON GOD'S GREEN EARTH ABOVE ANYTHING ELSE, IT WOULD BE *SAVELOY SAUSAGES.*"
SOLD!
YIPPEE!
ICE CREAM
SAVELOYS
SAVELOYS
SAVELOYS
SAVELOY EXPRESS
THX1138
SAVELOYS
WORLD FAMOUS
SAVELOY EXPRESS
SAV1
SAVELOY WORLD
OPENING!!
WELCOME
COR!
BUSINESS WEEKLY
YOUNG BUSINESS PUNK 1979!
FROM PUNK TO RICHES
SAVELOY MADNESS!
NEWS
FINANCIAL WORLD
SAVELOY EMPIRE IMPLODES
RECEIVERS BROUGHT IN
CLOSED!
AVELOYS!
SWIMMIN' IN SAVELOOOOOYS!!!
I HATE TO SAY IT, ALEX, BUT JOEY'S RIGHT. AVA SORT OF *USED* US.
GREAT, NOW THAT WE'VE GOT *THAT* OVER WITH, LET'S HAUL BUNS...

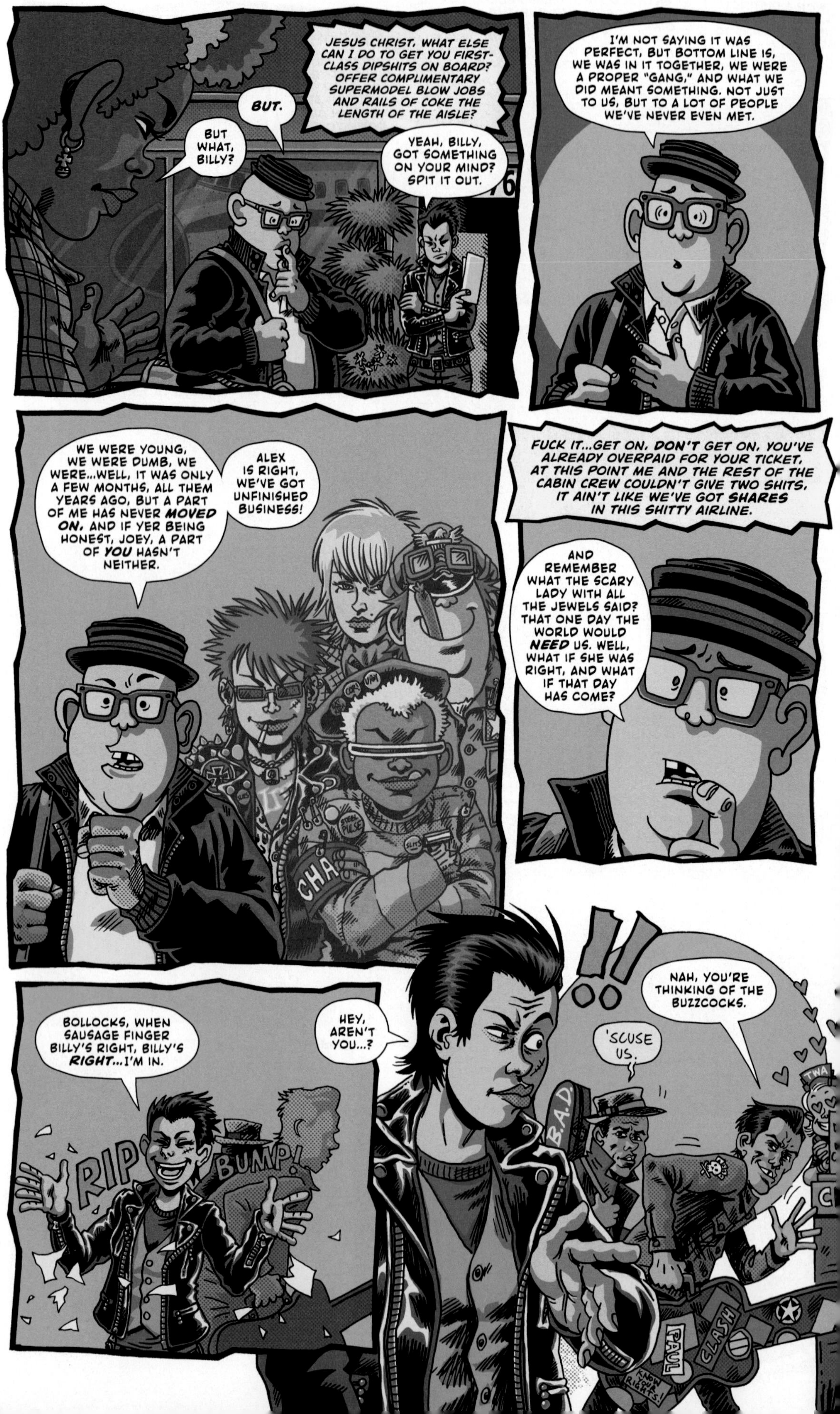
JESUS CHRIST. WHAT ELSE CAN I DO TO GET YOU FIRST-CLASS DIPSHITS ON BOARD? OFFER COMPLIMENTARY SUPERMODEL BLOW JOBS AND RAILS OF COKE THE LENGTH OF THE AISLE?
BUT.
BUT WHAT, BILLY?
YEAH, BILLY, GOT SOMETHING ON YOUR MIND? SPIT IT OUT.
I'M NOT SAYING IT WAS PERFECT, BUT BOTTOM LINE IS, WE WAS IN IT TOGETHER, WE WERE A PROPER "GANG," AND WHAT WE DID MEANT SOMETHING. NOT JUST TO US, BUT TO A LOT OF PEOPLE WE'VE NEVER EVEN MET.
WE WERE YOUNG, WE WERE DUMB, WE WERE...WELL, IT WAS ONLY A FEW MONTHS, ALL THEM YEARS AGO, BUT A PART OF ME HAS NEVER MOVED ON. AND IF YER BEING HONEST, JOEY, A PART OF YOU HASN'T NEITHER.
ALEX IS RIGHT, WE'VE GOT UNFINISHED BUSINESS!
FUCK IT...GET ON. DON'T GET ON. YOU'VE ALREADY OVERPAID FOR YOUR TICKET. AT THIS POINT ME AND THE REST OF THE CABIN CREW COULDN'T GIVE TWO SHITS. IT AIN'T LIKE WE'VE GOT SHARES IN THIS SHITTY AIRLINE.
AND REMEMBER WHAT THE SCARY LADY WITH ALL THE JEWELS SAID? THAT ONE DAY THE WORLD WOULD NEED US. WELL, WHAT IF SHE WAS RIGHT, AND WHAT IF THAT DAY HAS COME?
BOLLOCKS, WHEN SAUSAGE FINGER BILLY'S RIGHT, BILLY'S RIGHT...I'M IN.
RIP
BUMP!
HEY, AREN'T YOU...?
'SCUSE US.
NAH, YOU'RE THINKING OF THE BUZZCOCKS.
B.A.D.
CLASH
PAUL
KNOW YOUR RIGHTS!

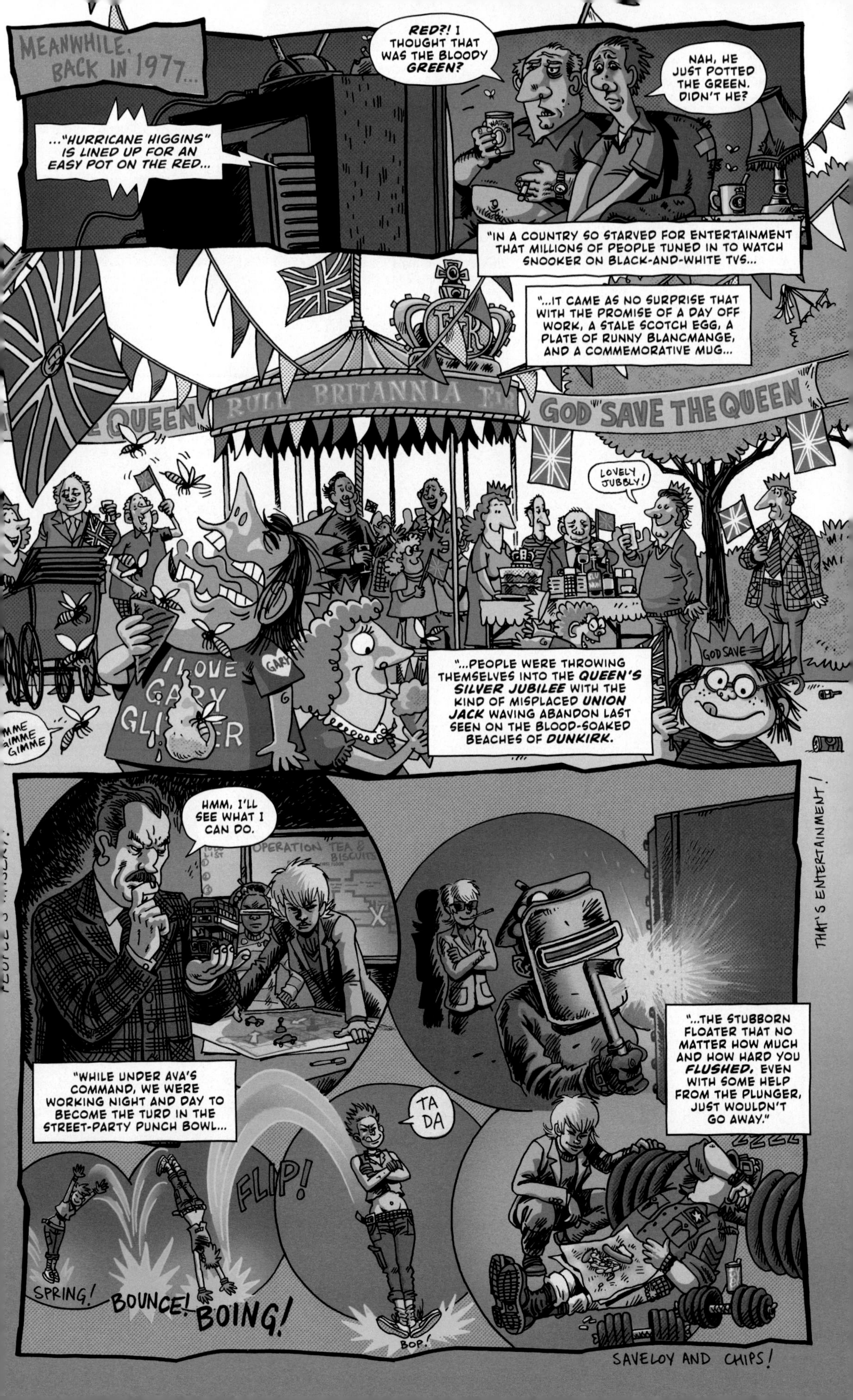
MEANWHILE, BACK IN 1977...
RED?! I THOUGHT THAT WAS THE BLOODY GREEN?
NAH, HE JUST POTTED THE GREEN. DIDN'T HE?
..."HURRICANE HIGGINS" IS LINED UP FOR AN EASY POT ON THE RED...
"IN A COUNTRY SO STARVED FOR ENTERTAINMENT THAT MILLIONS OF PEOPLE TUNED IN TO WATCH SNOOKER ON BLACK-AND-WHITE TVS...
"...IT CAME AS NO SURPRISE THAT WITH THE PROMISE OF A DAY OFF WORK, A STALE SCOTCH EGG, A PLATE OF RUNNY BLANCMANGE, AND A COMMEMORATIVE MUG...
RULE BRITANNIA
QUEEN
GOD SAVE THE QUEEN
LOVELY JUBBLY!
I LOVE GARY GLITTER
GARY
GOD SAVE
MME GIMME GIMME
"...PEOPLE WERE THROWING THEMSELVES INTO THE QUEEN'S SILVER JUBILEE WITH THE KIND OF MISPLACED UNION JACK WAVING ABANDON LAST SEEN ON THE BLOOD-SOAKED BEACHES OF DUNKIRK.
HMM, I'LL SEE WHAT I CAN DO.
OPERATION TEA & BISCUITS
THAT'S ENTERTAINMENT!
"WHILE UNDER AVA'S COMMAND, WE WERE WORKING NIGHT AND DAY TO BECOME THE TURD IN THE STREET-PARTY PUNCH BOWL...
"...THE STUBBORN FLOATER THAT NO MATTER HOW MUCH AND HOW HARD YOU FLUSHED, EVEN WITH SOME HELP FROM THE PLUNGER, JUST WOULDN'T GO AWAY."
TA DA
FLIP!
SPRING!
BOUNCE!
BOING!
BOP!
SAVELOY AND CHIPS!

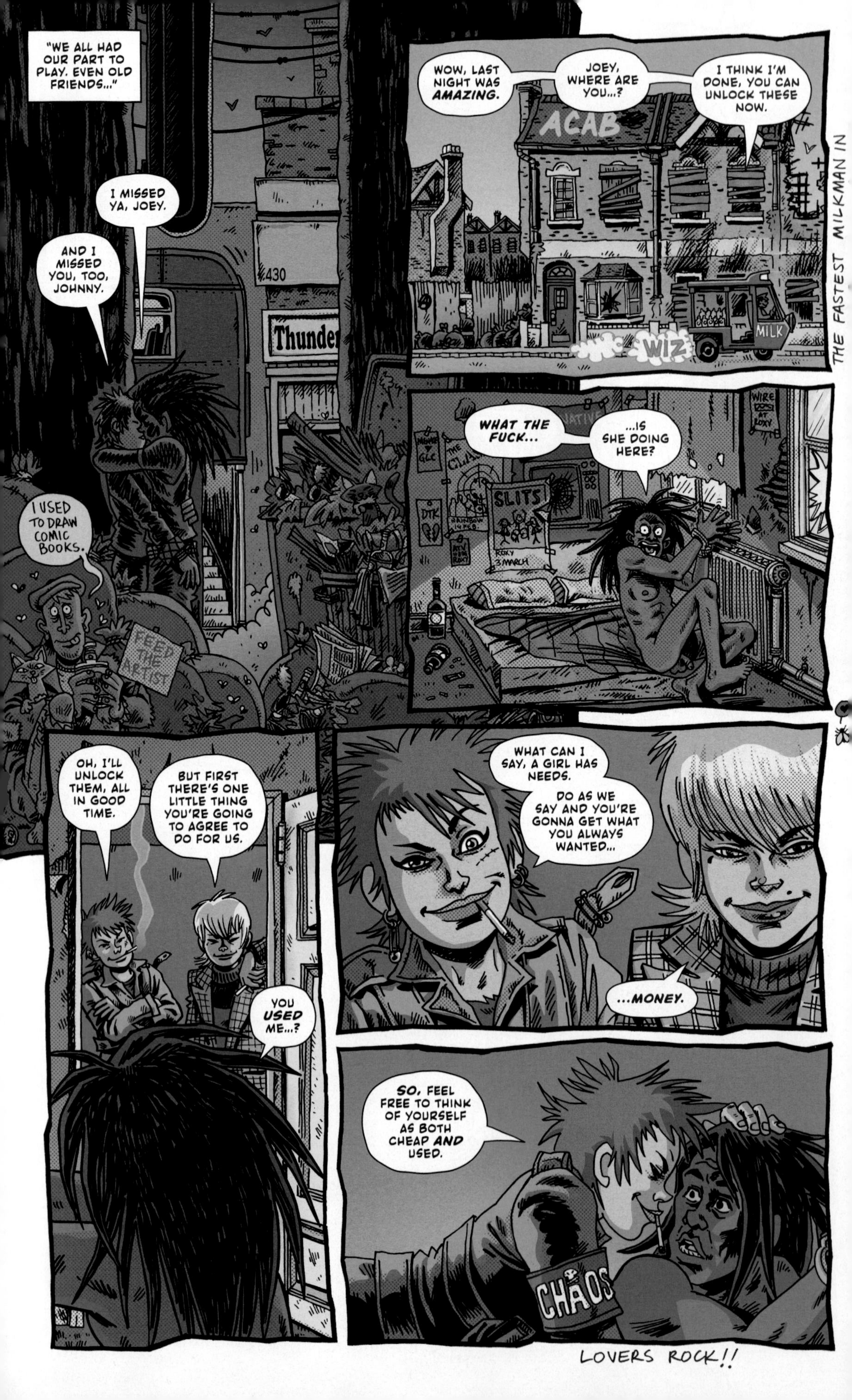
"WE ALL HAD OUR PART TO PLAY. EVEN OLD FRIENDS..."
I MISSED YA, JOEY.
AND I MISSED YOU, TOO, JOHNNY.
I USED TO DRAW COMIC BOOKS.
FEED THE ARTIST
430
Thunder
WOW, LAST NIGHT WAS AMAZING.
JOEY, WHERE ARE YOU...?
I THINK I'M DONE, YOU CAN UNLOCK THESE NOW.
ACAB
WIZ
MILK
THE FASTEST MILKMAN IN
WHAT THE FUCK...
...IS SHE DOING HERE?
SLITS
ROXY 3 MARCH
OH, I'LL UNLOCK THEM, ALL IN GOOD TIME.
BUT FIRST THERE'S ONE LITTLE THING YOU'RE GOING TO AGREE TO DO FOR US.
YOU USED ME...?
WHAT CAN I SAY, A GIRL HAS NEEDS.
DO AS WE SAY AND YOU'RE GONNA GET WHAT YOU ALWAYS WANTED...
...MONEY.
SO, FEEL FREE TO THINK OF YOURSELF AS BOTH CHEAP AND USED.
CHAOS
LOVERS ROCK!!

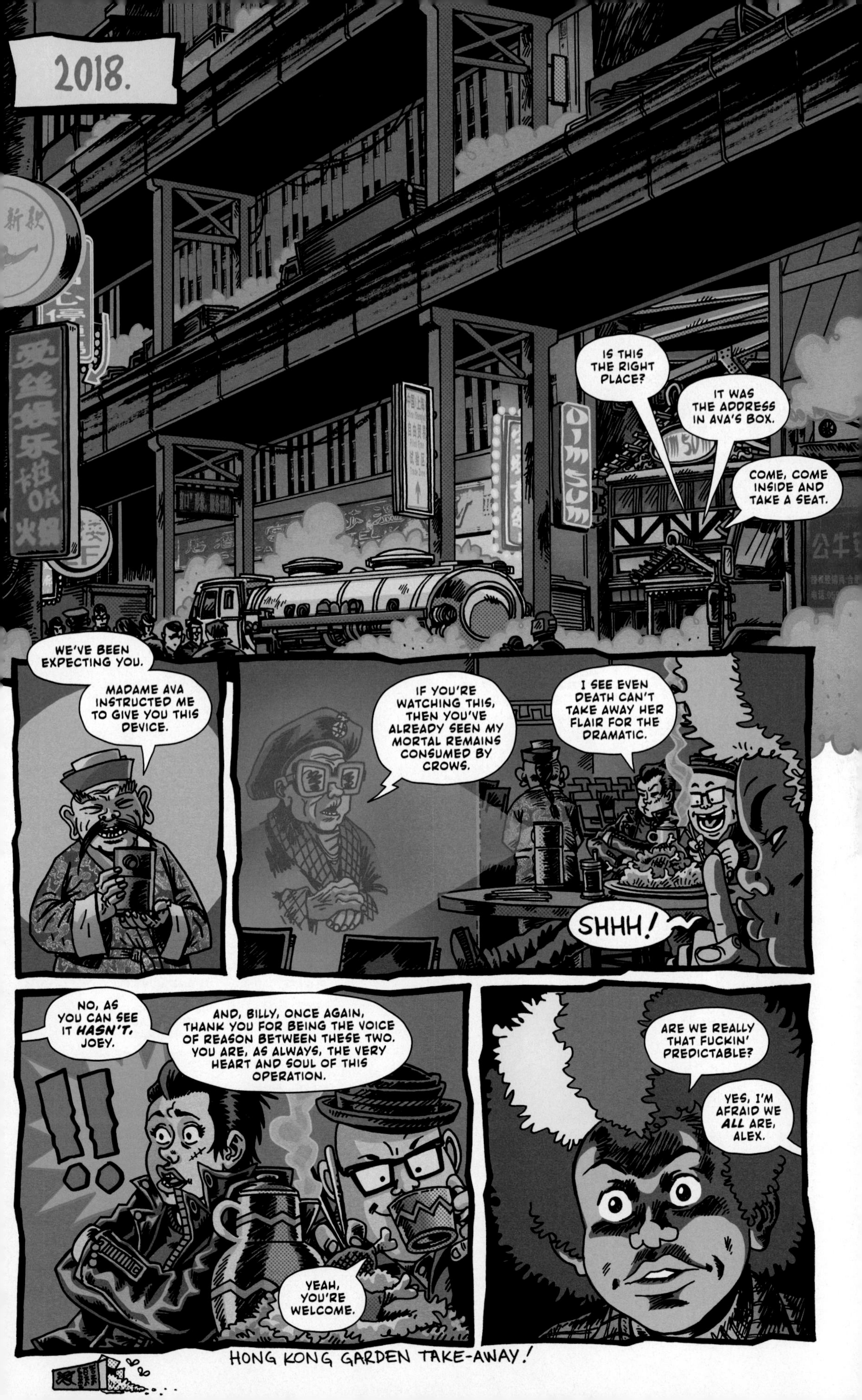
2018.
IS THIS THE RIGHT PLACE?
IT WAS THE ADDRESS IN AVA'S BOX.
COME, COME INSIDE AND TAKE A SEAT.
WE'VE BEEN EXPECTING YOU.
MADAME AVA INSTRUCTED ME TO GIVE YOU THIS DEVICE.
IF YOU'RE WATCHING THIS, THEN YOU'VE ALREADY SEEN MY MORTAL REMAINS CONSUMED BY CROWS.
I SEE EVEN DEATH CAN'T TAKE AWAY HER FLAIR FOR THE DRAMATIC.
SHHH!
NO, AS YOU CAN SEE IT ***HASN'T,*** JOEY.
AND, BILLY, ONCE AGAIN, THANK YOU FOR BEING THE VOICE OF REASON BETWEEN THESE TWO. YOU ARE, AS ALWAYS, THE VERY HEART AND SOUL OF THIS OPERATION.
!!
YEAH, YOU'RE WELCOME.
ARE WE REALLY THAT FUCKIN' PREDICTABLE?
YES, I'M AFRAID WE ***ALL*** ARE, ALEX.
HONG KONG GARDEN TAKE-AWAY!

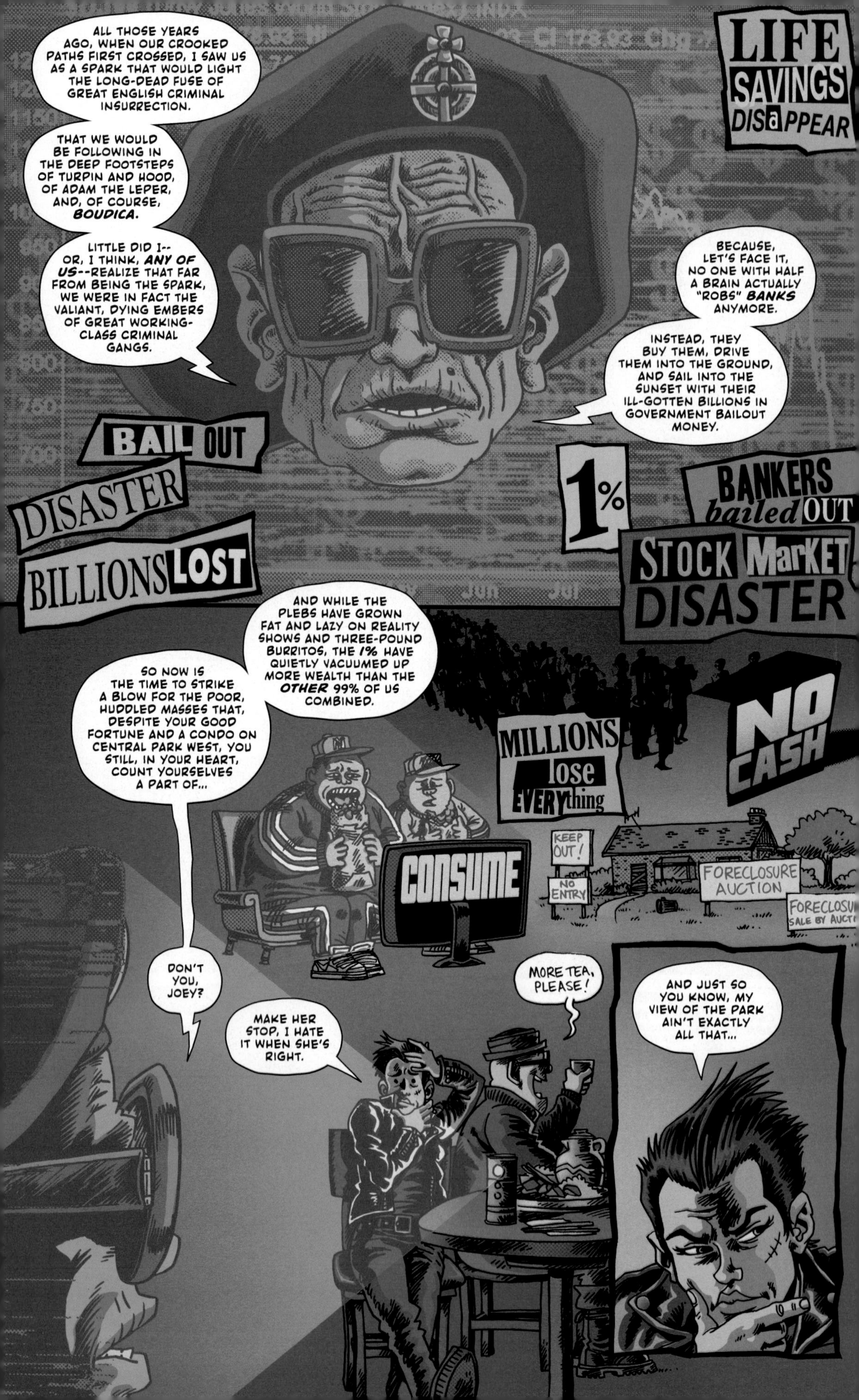
ALL THOSE YEARS AGO, WHEN OUR CROOKED PATHS FIRST CROSSED, I SAW US AS A SPARK THAT WOULD LIGHT THE LONG-DEAD FUSE OF GREAT ENGLISH CRIMINAL INSURRECTION.
THAT WE WOULD BE FOLLOWING IN THE DEEP FOOTSTEPS OF TURPIN AND HOOD, OF ADAM THE LEPER, AND, OF COURSE, BOUDICA.
LITTLE DID I--OR, I THINK, ANY OF US--REALIZE THAT FAR FROM BEING THE SPARK, WE WERE IN FACT THE VALIANT, DYING EMBERS OF GREAT WORKING-CLASS CRIMINAL GANGS.
LIFE SAVINGS DISAPPEAR
BECAUSE, LET'S FACE IT, NO ONE WITH HALF A BRAIN ACTUALLY "ROBS" BANKS ANYMORE.
INSTEAD, THEY BUY THEM, DRIVE THEM INTO THE GROUND, AND SAIL INTO THE SUNSET WITH THEIR ILL-GOTTEN BILLIONS IN GOVERNMENT BAILOUT MONEY.
BAIL OUT
DISASTER
BILLIONS LOST
1%
BANKERS bailed OUT
STOCK MarKET DISASTER
AND WHILE THE PLEBS HAVE GROWN FAT AND LAZY ON REALITY SHOWS AND THREE-POUND BURRITOS, THE 1% HAVE QUIETLY VACUUMED UP MORE WEALTH THAN THE OTHER 99% OF US COMBINED.
SO NOW IS THE TIME TO STRIKE A BLOW FOR THE POOR, HUDDLED MASSES THAT, DESPITE YOUR GOOD FORTUNE AND A CONDO ON CENTRAL PARK WEST, YOU STILL, IN YOUR HEART, COUNT YOURSELVES A PART OF...
MILLIONS lose EVERYthing
NO CASH
CONSUME
KEEP OUT!
NO ENTRY
FORECLOSURE AUCTION
DON'T YOU, JOEY?
MORE TEA, PLEASE!
MAKE HER STOP, I HATE IT WHEN SHE'S RIGHT.
AND JUST SO YOU KNOW, MY VIEW OF THE PARK AIN'T EXACTLY ALL THAT...

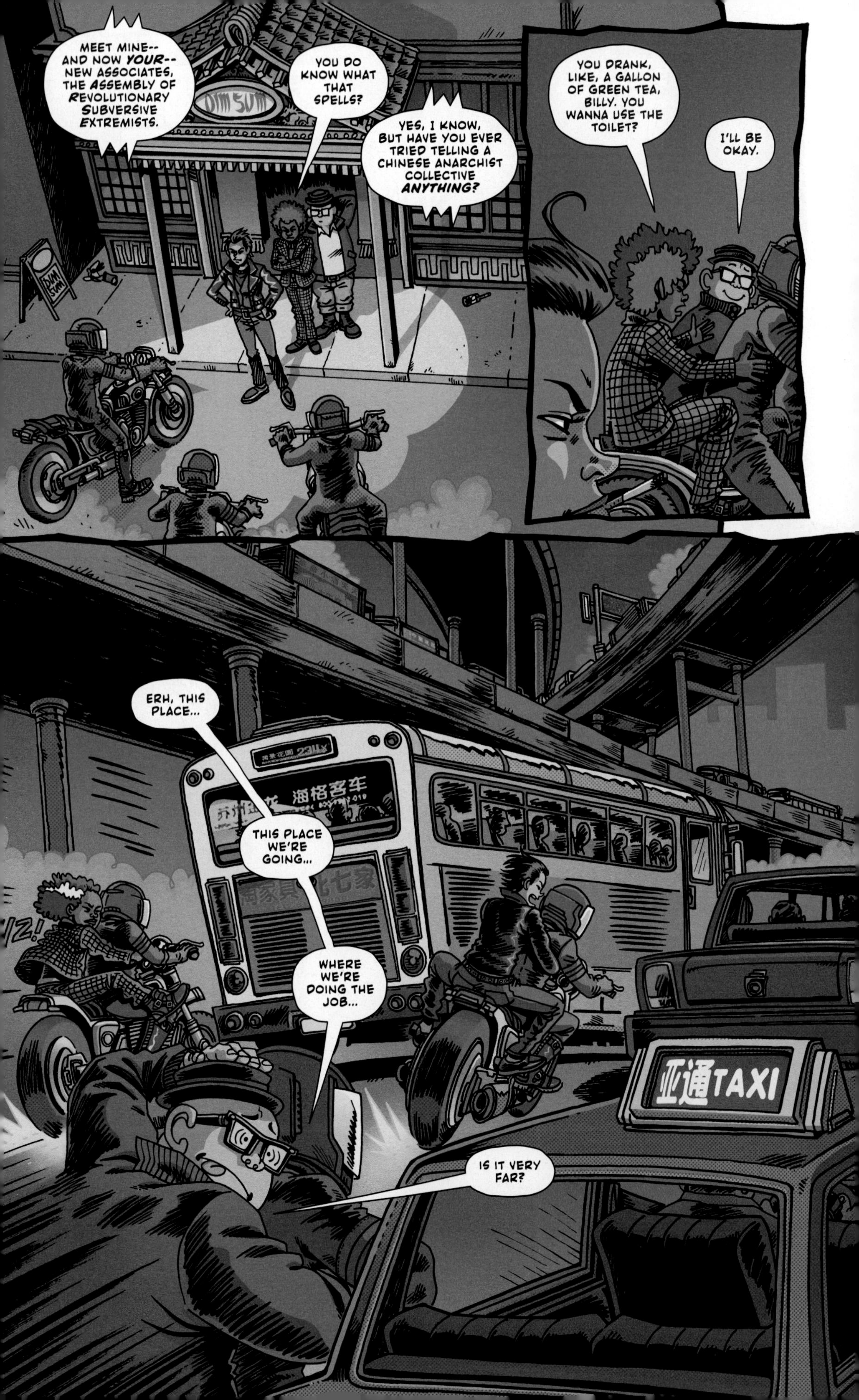
DIM SUM
MEET MINE-- AND NOW YOUR-- NEW ASSOCIATES, THE ASSEMBLY OF REVOLUTIONARY SUBVERSIVE EXTREMISTS.
YOU DO KNOW WHAT THAT SPELLS?
YES, I KNOW, BUT HAVE YOU EVER TRIED TELLING A CHINESE ANARCHIST COLLECTIVE ANYTHING?
YOU DRANK, LIKE, A GALLON OF GREEN TEA, BILLY. YOU WANNA USE THE TOILET?
I'LL BE OKAY.
ERH, THIS PLACE...
海格客车
THIS PLACE WE'RE GOING...
WHERE WE'RE DOING THE JOB...
亚通TAXI
IS IT VERY FAR?

ACTION, TIME AND VISION!

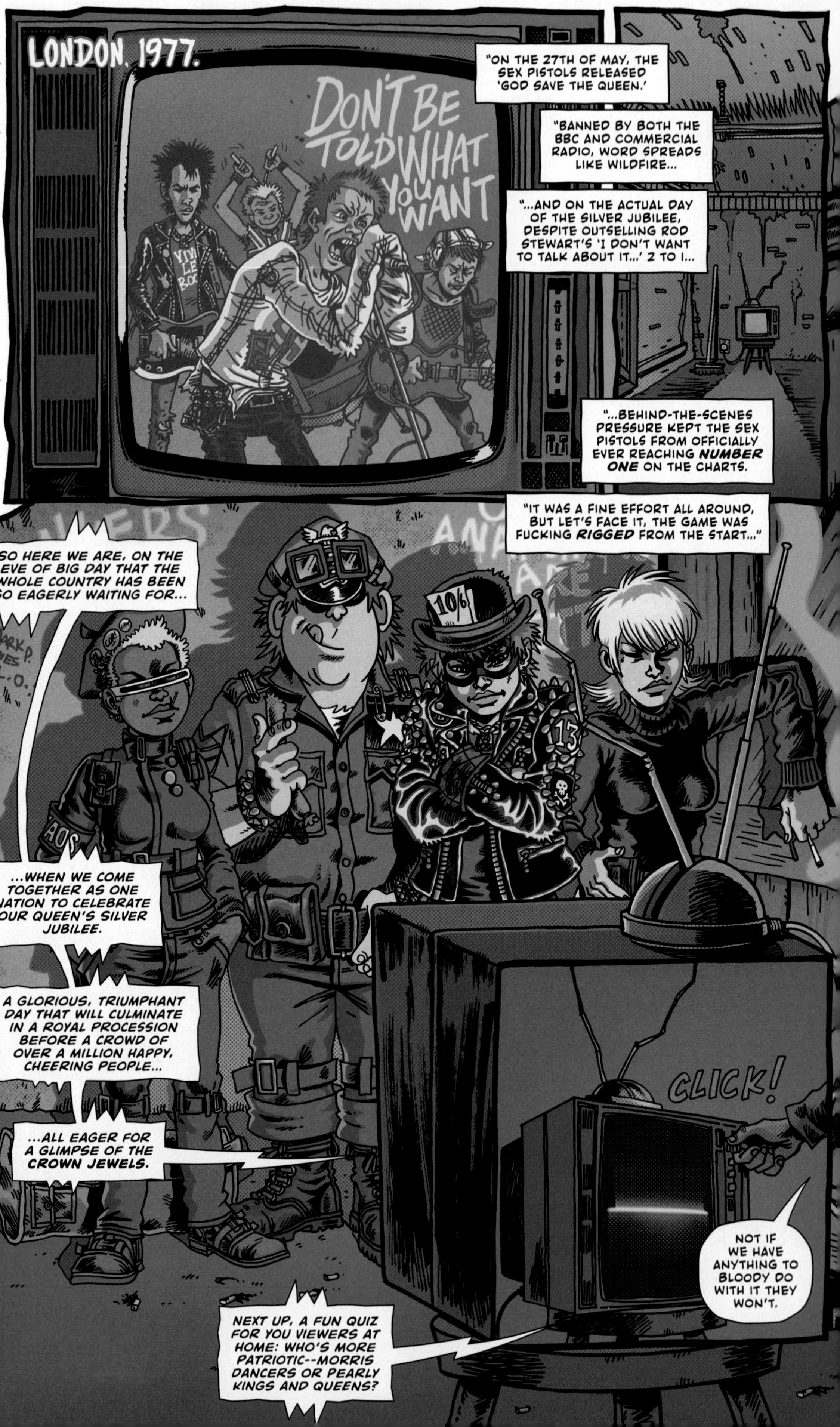

LONDON, 1977.
"ON THE 27TH OF MAY, THE SEX PISTOLS RELEASED 'GOD SAVE THE QUEEN.'
"BANNED BY BOTH THE BBC AND COMMERCIAL RADIO, WORD SPREADS LIKE WILDFIRE...
"...AND ON THE ACTUAL DAY OF THE SILVER JUBILEE, DESPITE OUTSELLING ROD STEWART'S 'I DON'T WANT TO TALK ABOUT IT...' 2 TO 1...
DON'T BE TOLD WHAT YOU WANT
"...BEHIND-THE-SCENES PRESSURE KEPT THE SEX PISTOLS FROM OFFICIALLY EVER REACHING NUMBER ONE ON THE CHARTS.
"IT WAS A FINE EFFORT ALL AROUND, BUT LET'S FACE IT, THE GAME WAS FUCKING RIGGED FROM THE START..."
SO HERE WE ARE, ON THE EVE OF BIG DAY THAT THE WHOLE COUNTRY HAS BEEN SO EAGERLY WAITING FOR...
MARK P. LOVES E.L.O.
10/6
...WHEN WE COME TOGETHER AS ONE NATION TO CELEBRATE OUR QUEEN'S SILVER JUBILEE.
A GLORIOUS, TRIUMPHANT DAY THAT WILL CULMINATE IN A ROYAL PROCESSION BEFORE A CROWD OF OVER A MILLION HAPPY, CHEERING PEOPLE...
...ALL EAGER FOR A GLIMPSE OF THE CROWN JEWELS.
CLICK!
NOT IF WE HAVE ANYTHING TO BLOODY DO WITH IT THEY WON'T.
NEXT UP, A FUN QUIZ FOR YOU VIEWERS AT HOME: WHO'S MORE PATRIOTIC--MORRIS DANCERS OR PEARLY KINGS AND QUEENS?

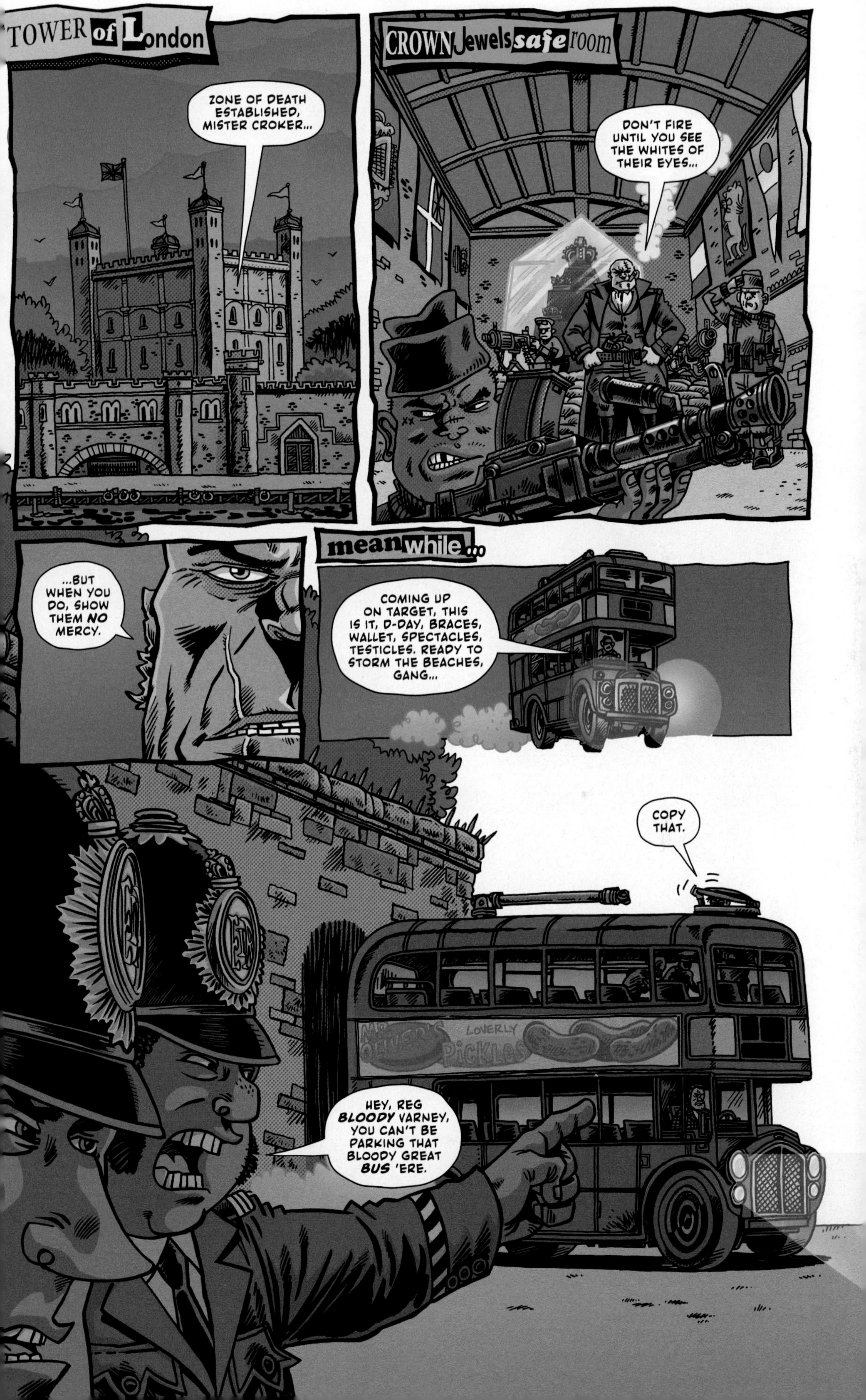
TOWER of London
ZONE OF DEATH ESTABLISHED, MISTER CROKER...
CROWN Jewels safe room
DON'T FIRE UNTIL YOU SEE THE WHITES OF THEIR EYES...
...BUT WHEN YOU DO, SHOW THEM NO MERCY.
meanwhile...
COMING UP ON TARGET, THIS IS IT, D-DAY, BRACES, WALLET, SPECTACLES, TESTICLES. READY TO STORM THE BEACHES, GANG...
COPY THAT.
MR OLIVER'S LOVERLY PICKLES
HEY, REG BLOODY VARNEY, YOU CAN'T BE PARKING THAT BLOODY GREAT BUS 'ERE.

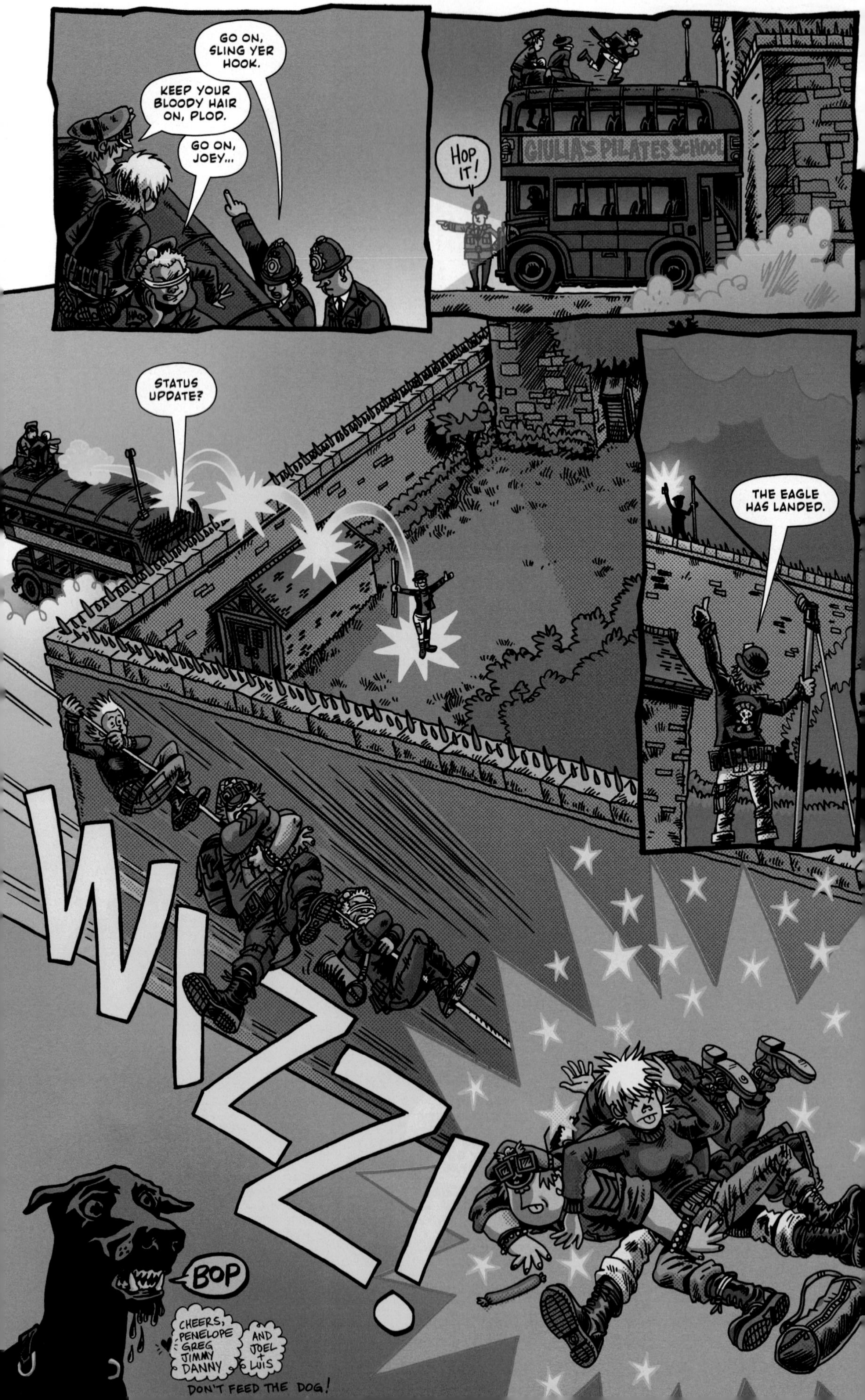
GO ON, SLING YER HOOK.
KEEP YOUR BLOODY HAIR ON, PLOD.
GO ON, JOEY...
HOP IT!
GIULIA'S PILATES SCHOOL
STATUS UPDATE?
THE EAGLE HAS LANDED.
WIZZ!
BOP
CHEERS, PENELOPE GREG JIMMY DANNY
AND JOEL + LUIS
DON'T FEED THE DOG!

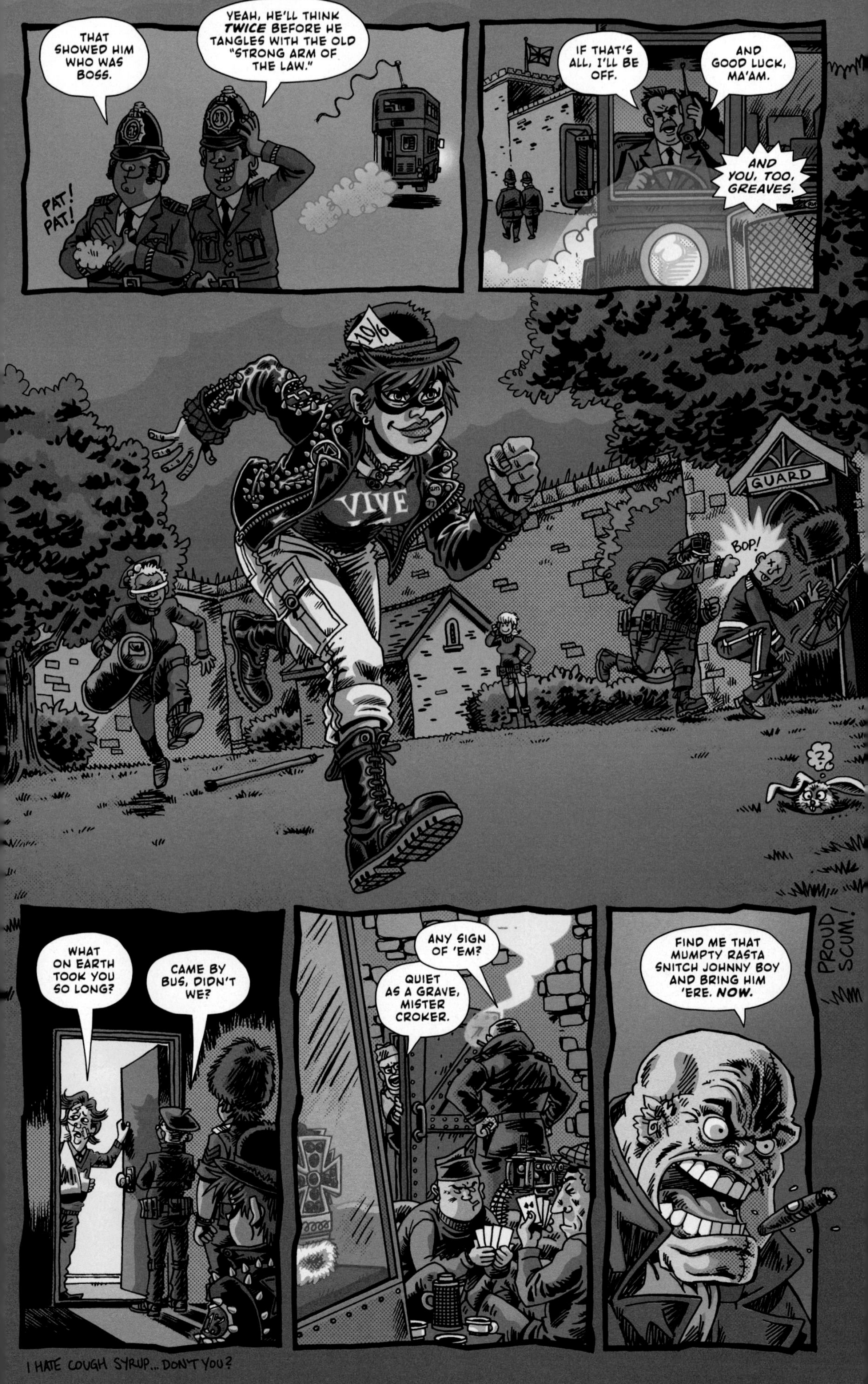
THAT SHOWED HIM WHO WAS BOSS.
YEAH, HE'LL THINK TWICE BEFORE HE TANGLES WITH THE OLD "STRONG ARM OF THE LAW."
PAT! PAT!
IF THAT'S ALL, I'LL BE OFF.
AND GOOD LUCK, MA'AM.
AND YOU, TOO, GREAVES.
10/6
VIVE
GUARD
BOP!
?
WHAT ON EARTH TOOK YOU SO LONG?
CAME BY BUS, DIDN'T WE?
ANY SIGN OF 'EM?
QUIET AS A GRAVE, MISTER CROKER.
FIND ME THAT MUMPTY RASTA SNITCH JOHNNY BOY AND BRING HIM 'ERE. NOW.
PROUD SCUM!
I HATE COUGH SYRUP... DON'T YOU?

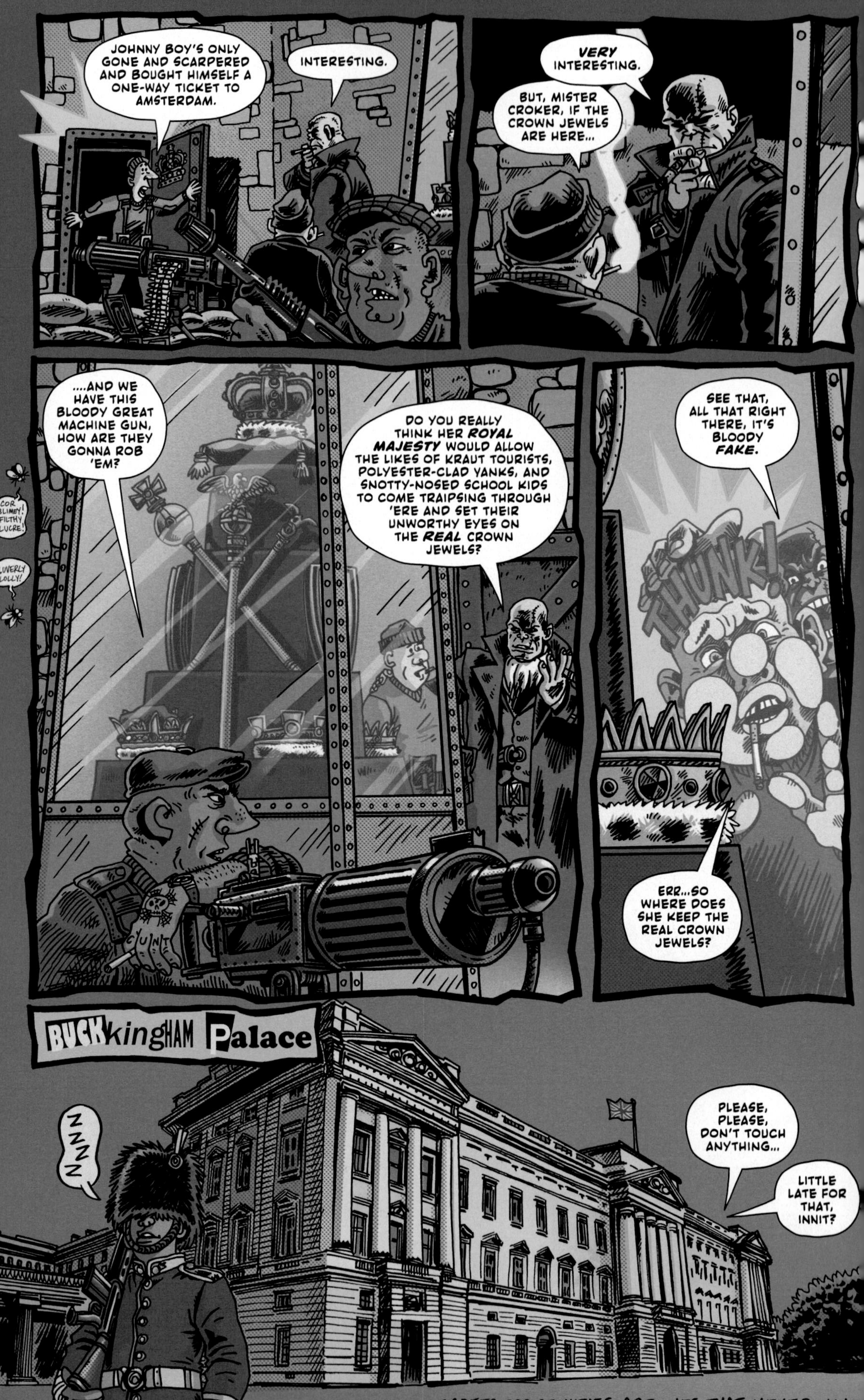
JOHNNY BOY'S ONLY GONE AND SCARPERED AND BOUGHT HIMSELF A ONE-WAY TICKET TO AMSTERDAM.
INTERESTING.
VERY INTERESTING.
BUT, MISTER CROKER, IF THE CROWN JEWELS ARE HERE...
....AND WE HAVE THIS BLOODY GREAT MACHINE GUN, HOW ARE THEY GONNA ROB 'EM?
COR BLIMEY! FILTHY LUCRE!
LUVERLY LOLLY!
DO YOU REALLY THINK HER ROYAL MAJESTY WOULD ALLOW THE LIKES OF KRAUT TOURISTS, POLYESTER-CLAD YANKS, AND SNOTTY-NOSED SCHOOL KIDS TO COME TRAIPSING THROUGH 'ERE AND SET THEIR UNWORTHY EYES ON THE REAL CROWN JEWELS?
SEE THAT, ALL THAT RIGHT THERE, IT'S BLOODY FAKE.
THUNK!
ERR...SO WHERE DOES SHE KEEP THE REAL CROWN JEWELS?
BUCKkingHAM Palace
ZZZ
PLEASE, PLEASE, DON'T TOUCH ANYTHING...
LITTLE LATE FOR THAT, INNIT?

CAREER OPPORTUNITIES ARE ONES THAT NEVER KNO

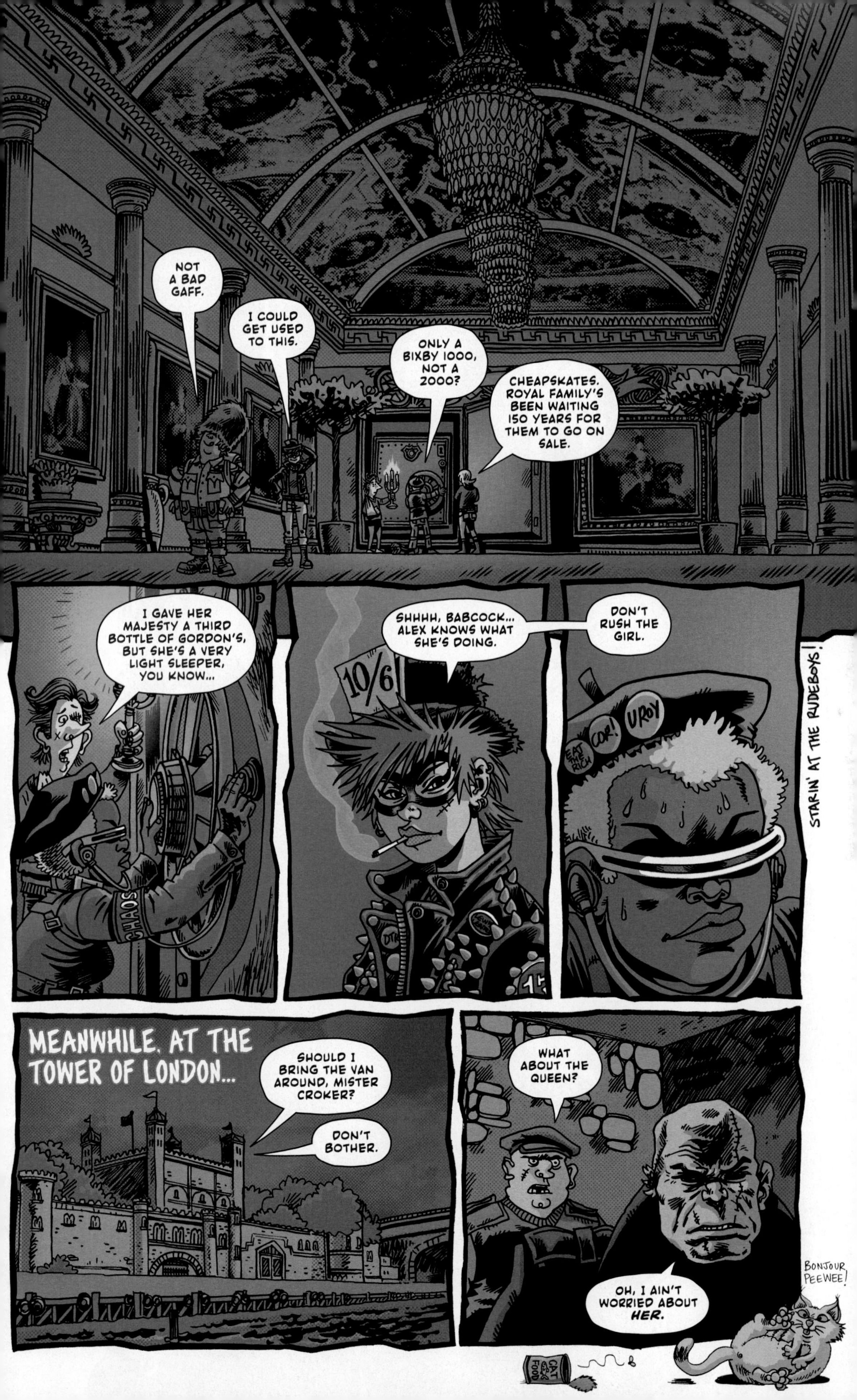
NOT A BAD GAFF.
I COULD GET USED TO THIS.
ONLY A BIXBY 1000, NOT A 2000?
CHEAPSKATES. ROYAL FAMILY'S BEEN WAITING 150 YEARS FOR THEM TO GO ON SALE.
I GAVE HER MAJESTY A THIRD BOTTLE OF GORDON'S, BUT SHE'S A VERY LIGHT SLEEPER, YOU KNOW...
CHAOS
SHHHH, BABCOCK... ALEX KNOWS WHAT SHE'S DOING.
10/6
DON'T RUSH THE GIRL.
EAT THE RICH
COR!
UROY
STARIN' AT THE RUDEBOYS!
MEANWHILE, AT THE TOWER OF LONDON...
SHOULD I BRING THE VAN AROUND, MISTER CROKER?
DON'T BOTHER.
WHAT ABOUT THE QUEEN?
OH, I AIN'T WORRIED ABOUT *HER*.
BONJOUR PEEWEE!
CAT FOOD

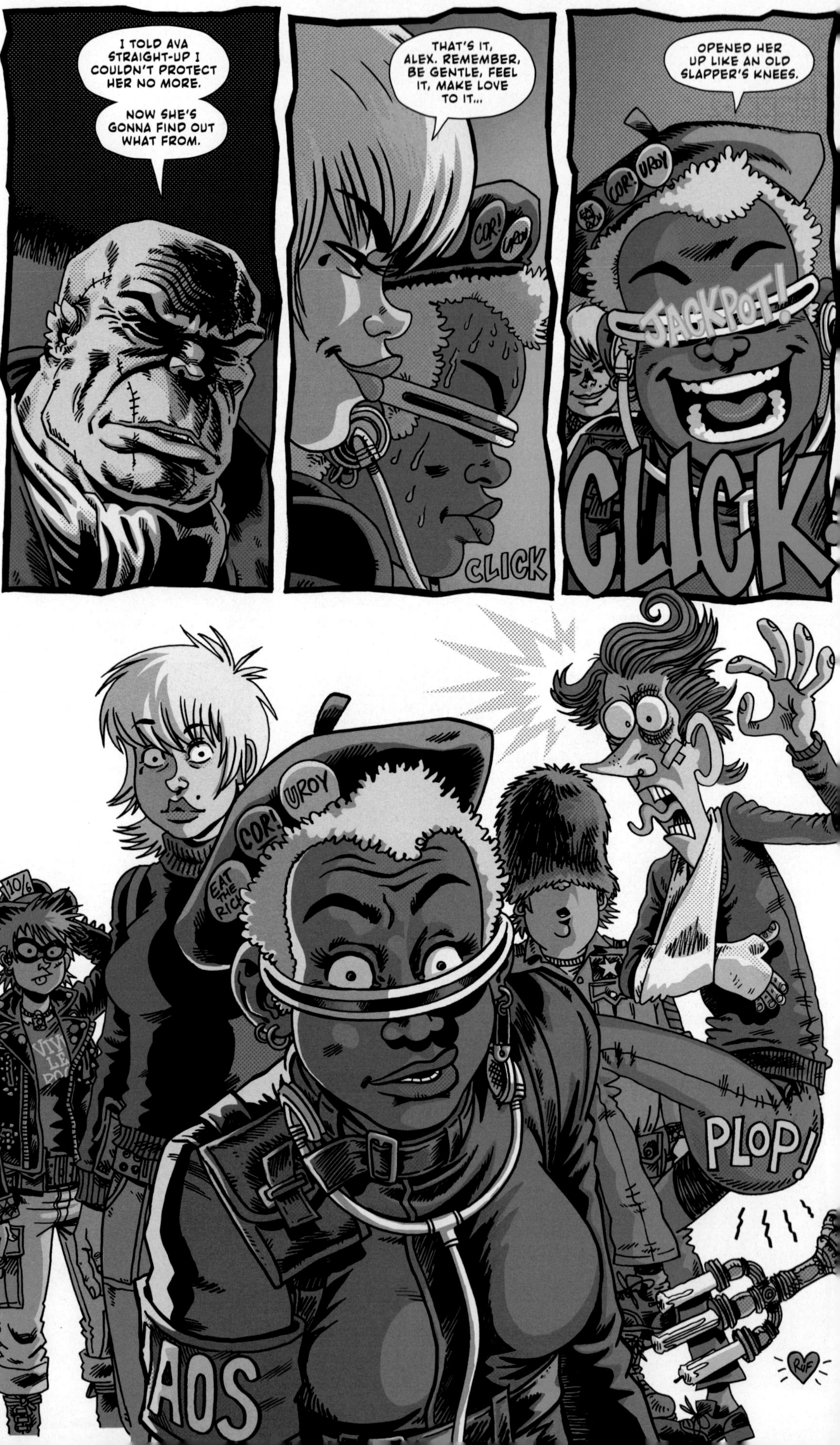

I TOLD AVA STRAIGHT-UP I COULDN'T PROTECT HER NO MORE.
NOW SHE'S GONNA FIND OUT WHAT FROM.
THAT'S IT, ALEX. REMEMBER, BE GENTLE, FEEL IT, MAKE LOVE TO IT...
COR!
UROY
CLICK
OPENED HER UP LIKE AN OLD SLAPPER'S KNEES.
JACKPOT!
CLICK!
UROY
COR!
EAT THE RICH
10/6
AOS
PLOP!

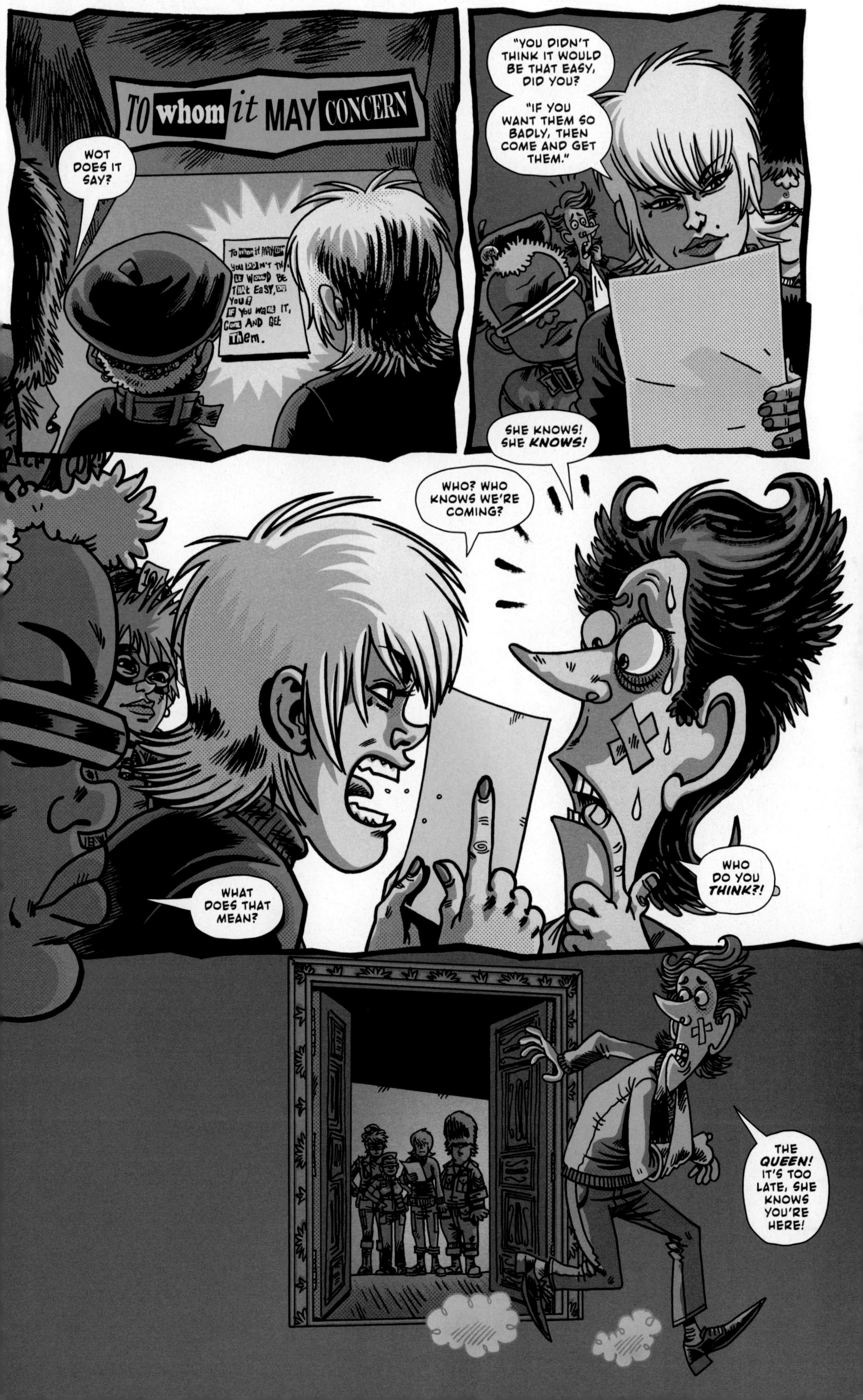
TO whom it MAY CONCERN
WOT DOES IT SAY?
TO whom it MAY CON YOU DIDN'T TH IT WOULD BE THAT EASY, DID YOU? IF YOU WANT IT, COME AND GET Them.
"YOU DIDN'T THINK IT WOULD BE THAT EASY, DID YOU?
"IF YOU WANT THEM SO BADLY, THEN COME AND GET THEM."
SHE KNOWS! SHE *KNOWS!*
WHO? WHO KNOWS WE'RE COMING?
WHO DO YOU *THINK?!*
WHAT DOES THAT MEAN?
THE *QUEEN!* IT'S TOO LATE, SHE KNOWS YOU'RE HERE!

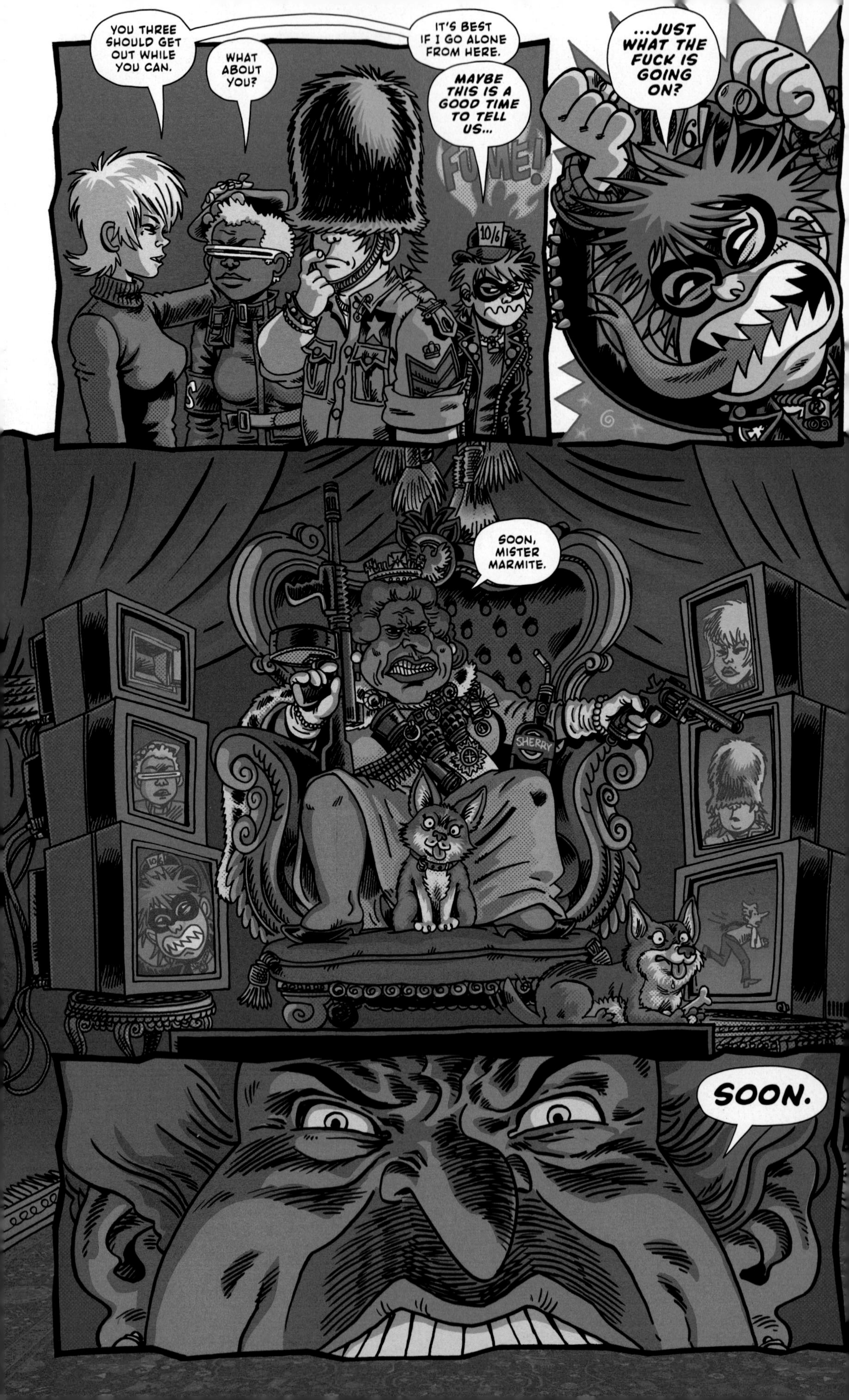
YOU THREE SHOULD GET OUT WHILE YOU CAN.
WHAT ABOUT YOU?
IT'S BEST IF I GO ALONE FROM HERE.
MAYBE THIS IS A GOOD TIME TO TELL US...
FUME!
...JUST WHAT THE FUCK IS GOING ON?
SOON, MISTER MARMITE.
SHERRY
SOON.

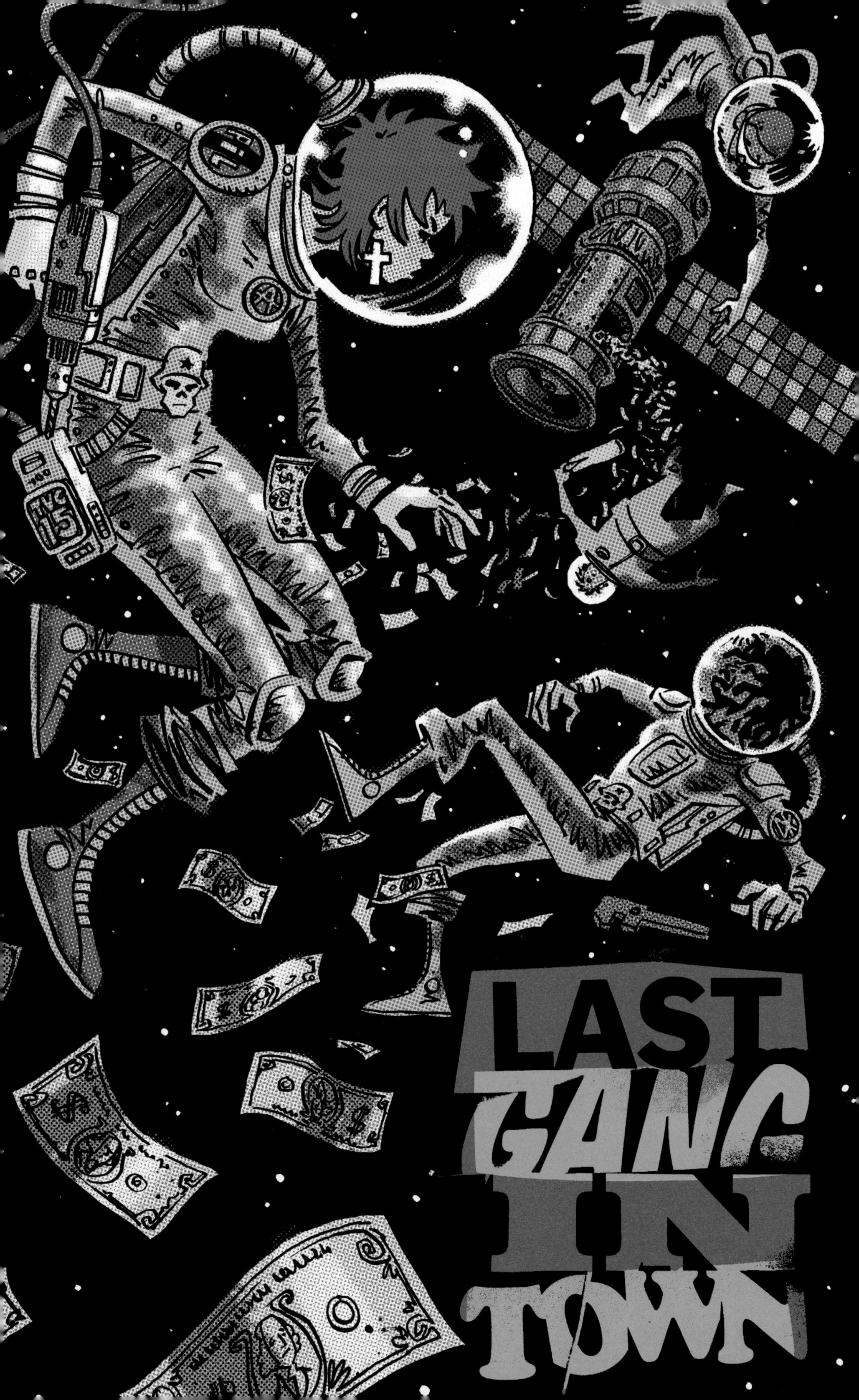
LAST
GANG
IN
TOWN

lesson six

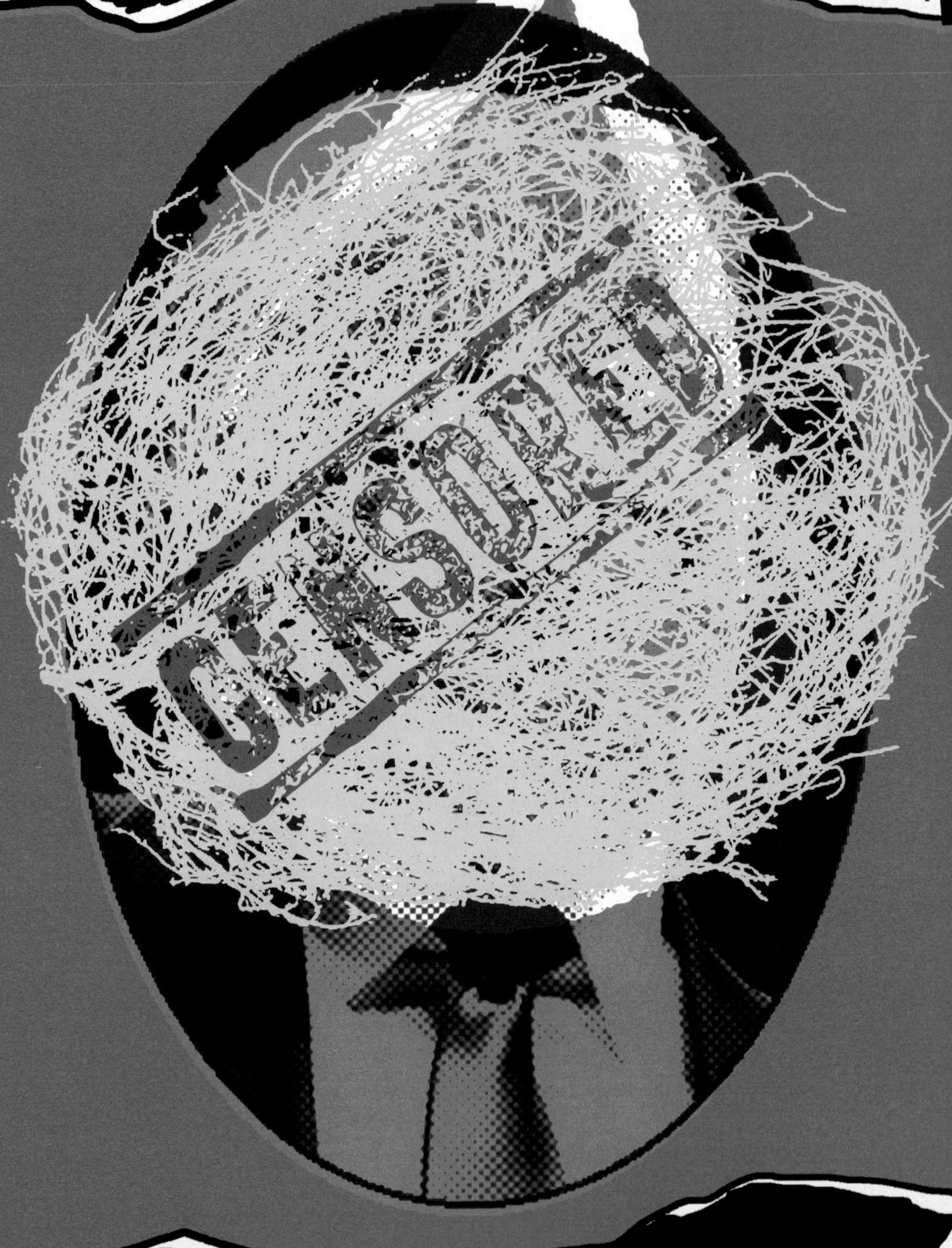
CENSORED

à bas le Capitalisme

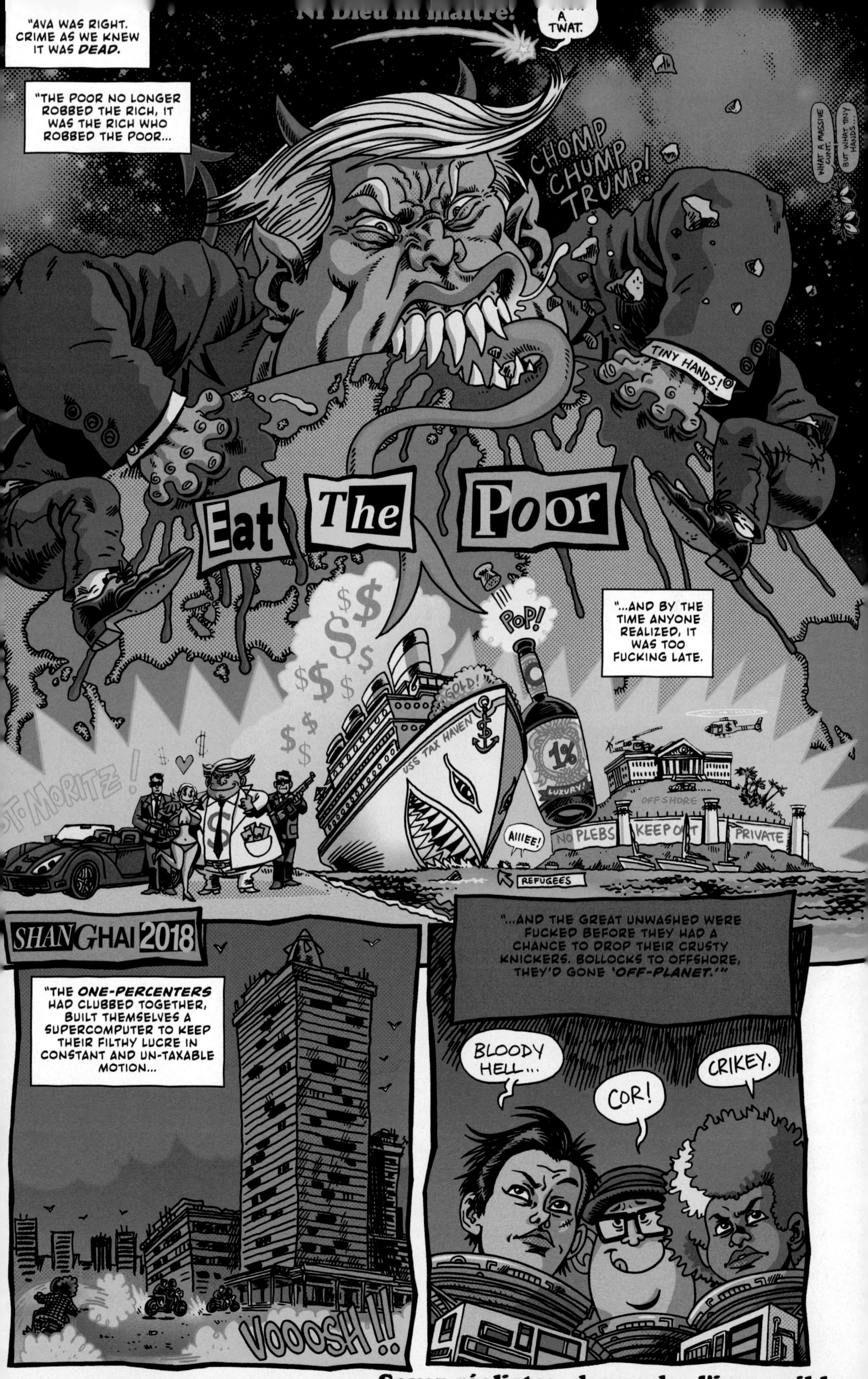
Ni Dieu ni maître!
"AVA WAS RIGHT. CRIME AS WE KNEW IT WAS *DEAD.*
A TWAT.
"THE POOR NO LONGER ROBBED THE RICH, IT WAS THE RICH WHO ROBBED THE POOR...
CHOMP CHUMP TRUMP!
WHAT A MASSIVE CUNT.
BUT WHAT TINY HANDS...
TINY HANDS!
Eat The Poor
POP!
"...AND BY THE TIME ANYONE REALIZED, IT WAS TOO FUCKING LATE.
GOLD!
USS TAX HAVEN
1%
LUXURY!
ST. MORITZ!
OFFSHORE
AIIIEE!
NO PLEBS
KEEP OUT
PRIVATE
REFUGEES
SHANGHAI 2018
"THE *ONE-PERCENTERS* HAD CLUBBED TOGETHER, BUILT THEMSELVES A SUPERCOMPUTER TO KEEP THEIR FILTHY LUCRE IN CONSTANT AND UN-TAXABLE MOTION...
VOOOSH!!
"...AND THE GREAT UNWASHED WERE FUCKED BEFORE THEY HAD A CHANCE TO DROP THEIR CRUSTY KNICKERS. BOLLOCKS TO OFFSHORE, THEY'D GONE *'OFF-PLANET.'*"
BLOODY HELL...
COR!
CRIKEY.

Soyez réalistes, demandez l'impossible

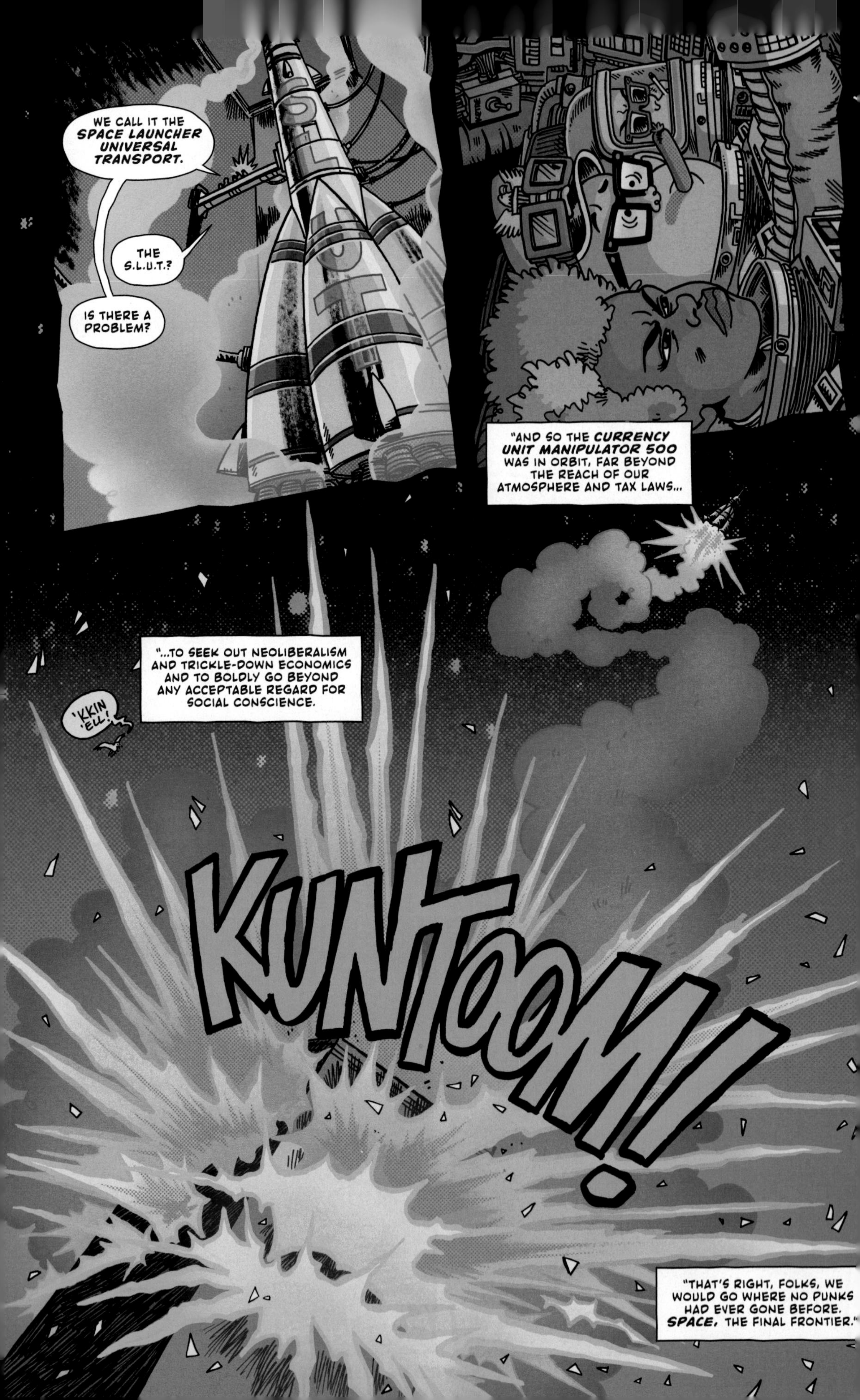

WE CALL IT THE SPACE LAUNCHER UNIVERSAL TRANSPORT.
THE S.L.U.T.?
IS THERE A PROBLEM?
"AND SO THE CURRENCY UNIT MANIPULATOR 500 WAS IN ORBIT, FAR BEYOND THE REACH OF OUR ATMOSPHERE AND TAX LAWS...
"...TO SEEK OUT NEOLIBERALISM AND TRICKLE-DOWN ECONOMICS AND TO BOLDLY GO BEYOND ANY ACCEPTABLE REGARD FOR SOCIAL CONSCIENCE.
'KKIN 'ELL!
KUNTOOM!
"THAT'S RIGHT, FOLKS, WE WOULD GO WHERE NO PUNKS HAD EVER GONE BEFORE. SPACE, THE FINAL FRONTIER."

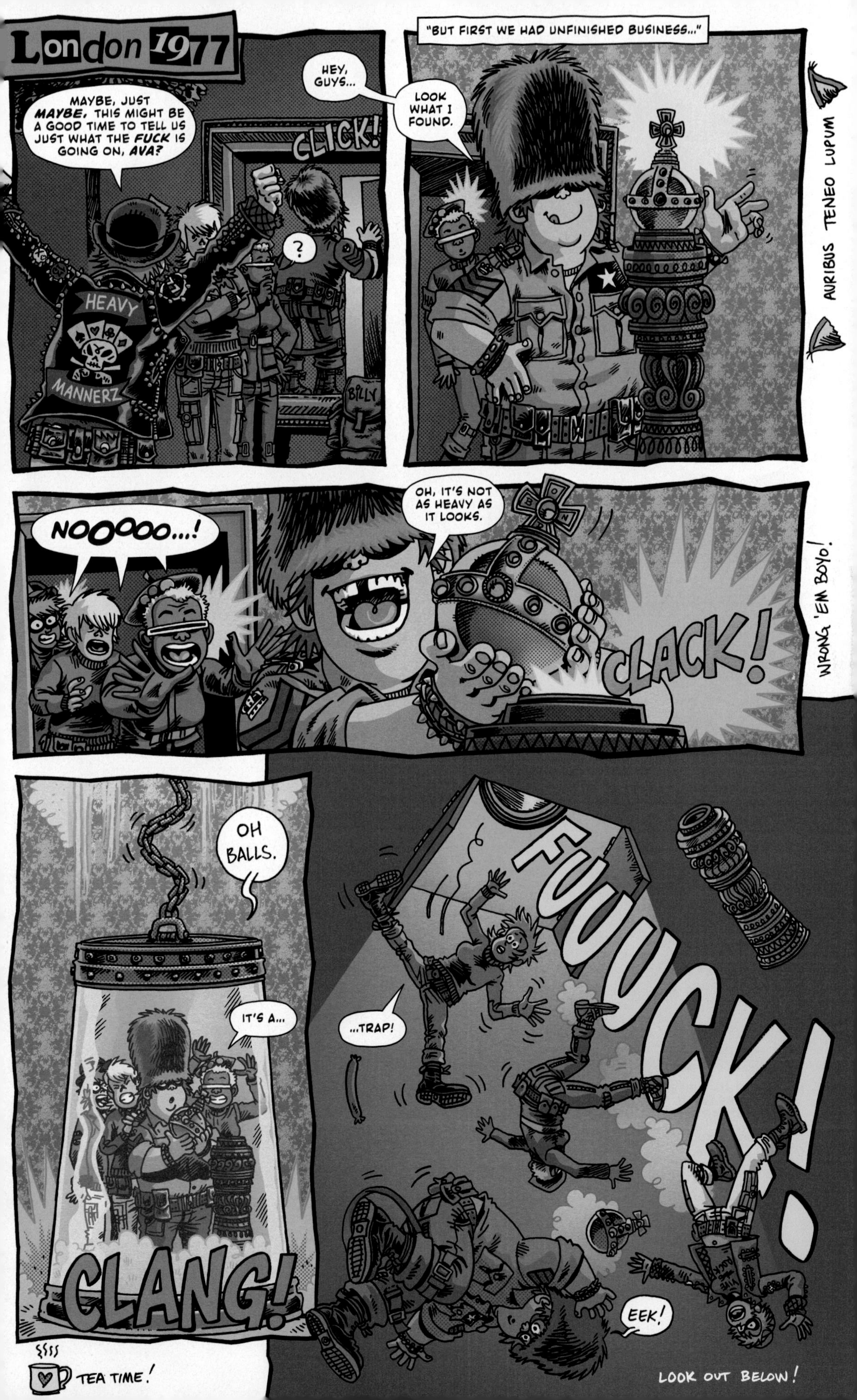
London 1977
MAYBE, JUST MAYBE, THIS MIGHT BE A GOOD TIME TO TELL US JUST WHAT THE FUCK IS GOING ON, AVA?
CLICK!
?
HEAVY
MANNERZ
BILLY
HEY, GUYS...
"BUT FIRST WE HAD UNFINISHED BUSINESS..."
LOOK WHAT I FOUND.
AURIBUS TENEO LUPUM
NOOOOO...!
OH, IT'S NOT AS HEAVY AS IT LOOKS.
CLACK!
WRONG 'EM BOYO!
OH BALLS.
IT'S A...
CLANG!
...TRAP!
FUUUCK!
EEK!
TEA TIME!
LOOK OUT BELOW!

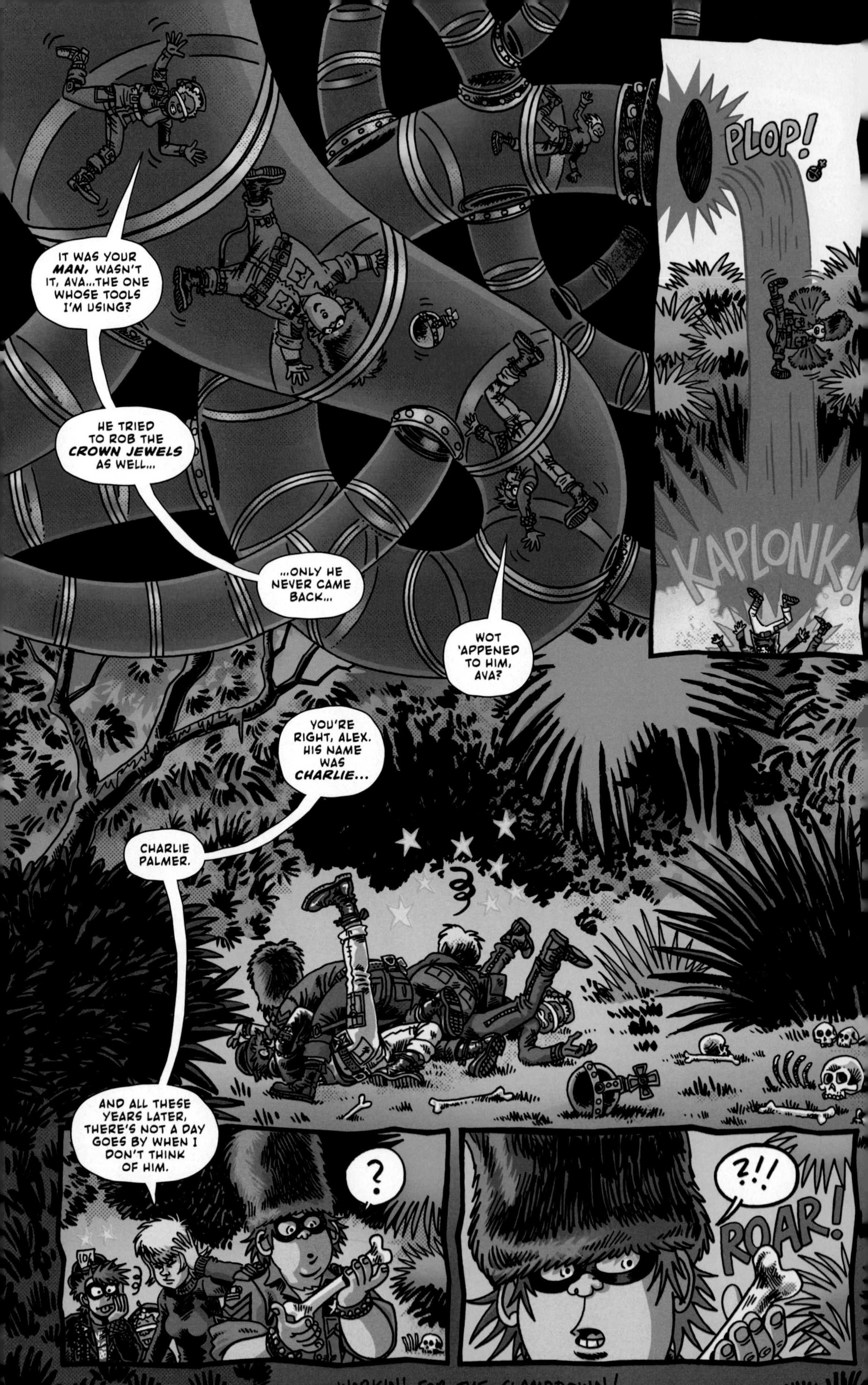
IT WAS YOUR MAN, WASN'T IT, AVA...THE ONE WHOSE TOOLS I'M USING?
HE TRIED TO ROB THE CROWN JEWELS AS WELL...
...ONLY HE NEVER CAME BACK...
WOT 'APPENED TO HIM, AVA?
PLOP!
KAPLONK!
YOU'RE RIGHT, ALEX. HIS NAME WAS CHARLIE...
CHARLIE PALMER.
AND ALL THESE YEARS LATER, THERE'S NOT A DAY GOES BY WHEN I DON'T THINK OF HIM.
?
?!!
ROAR!

WORKIN' FOR THE CLAMPDOWN!

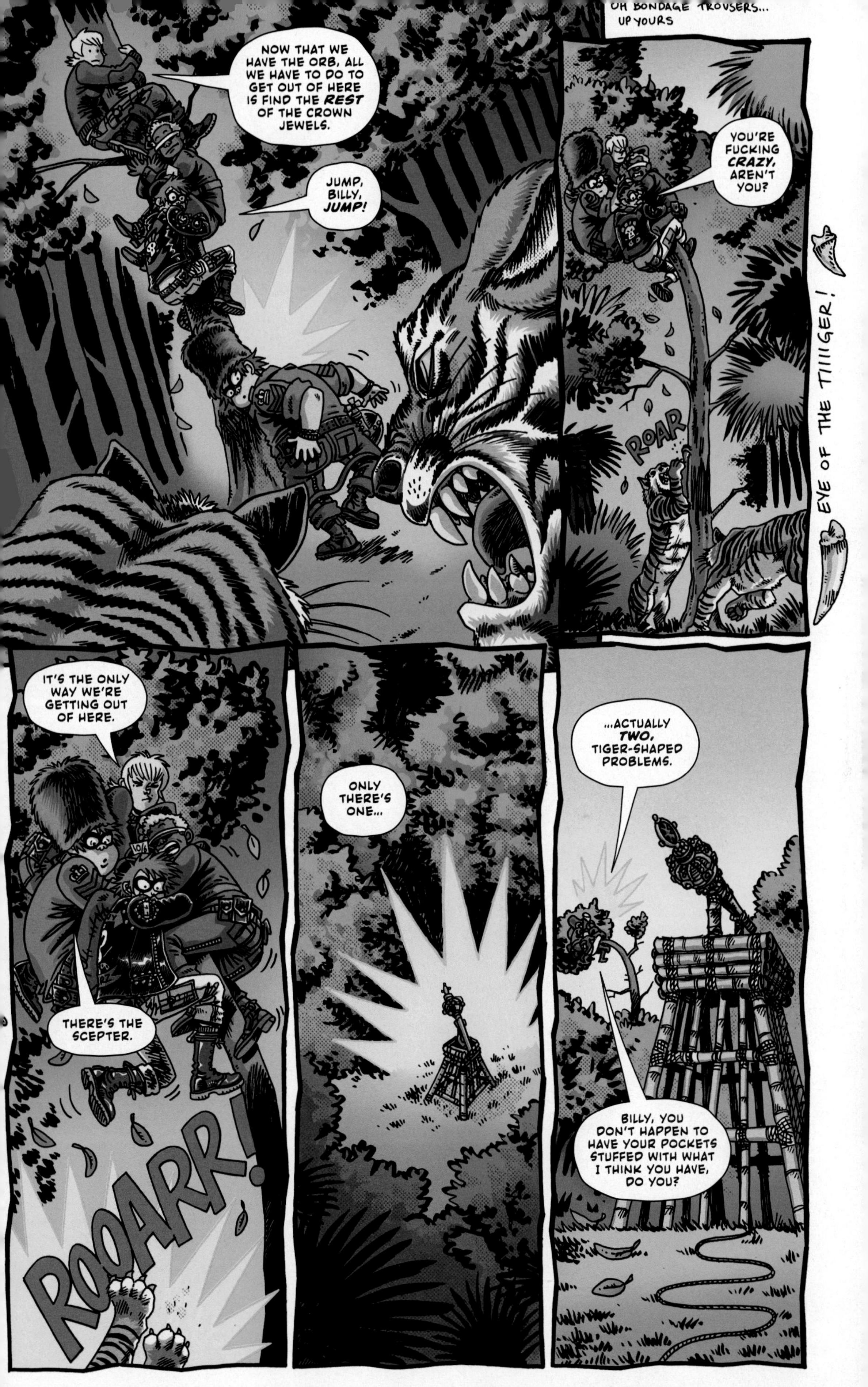
OH BONDAGE TROUSERS...
UP YOURS
NOW THAT WE HAVE THE ORB, ALL WE HAVE TO DO TO GET OUT OF HERE IS FIND THE REST OF THE CROWN JEWELS.
JUMP, BILLY, JUMP!
YOU'RE FUCKING CRAZY, AREN'T YOU?
ROAR
EYE OF THE TIIIIGER!
IT'S THE ONLY WAY WE'RE GETTING OUT OF HERE.
THERE'S THE SCEPTER.
ROOARR!
ONLY THERE'S ONE...
...ACTUALLY TWO, TIGER-SHAPED PROBLEMS.
BILLY, YOU DON'T HAPPEN TO HAVE YOUR POCKETS STUFFED WITH WHAT I THINK YOU HAVE, DO YOU?

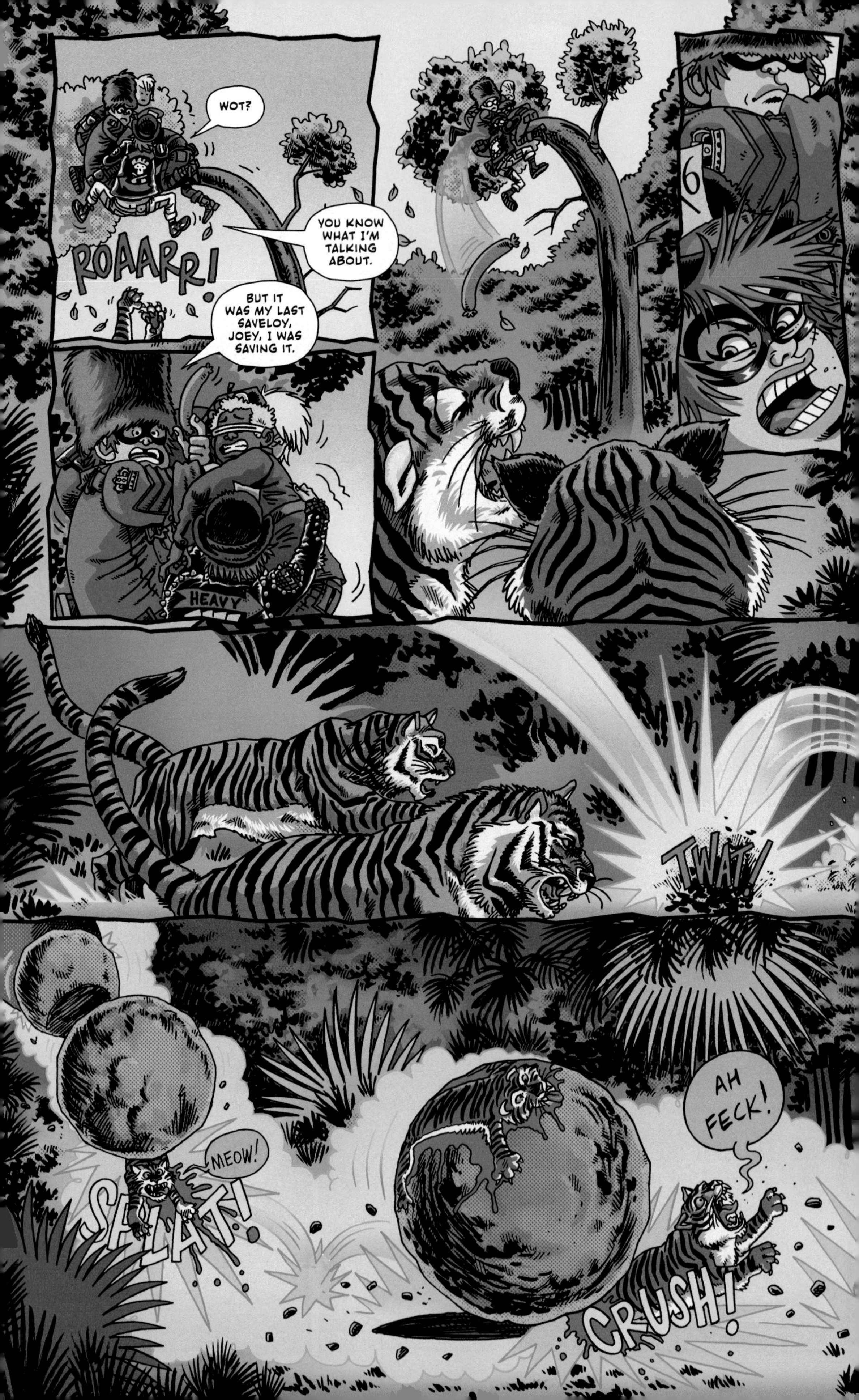
WOT?
ROAARR!
YOU KNOW WHAT I'M TALKING ABOUT.
BUT IT WAS MY LAST SAVELOY, JOEY, I WAS SAVING IT.
HEAVY
TWAT!
MEOW!
SPLAT!
AH FECK!
CRUSH!

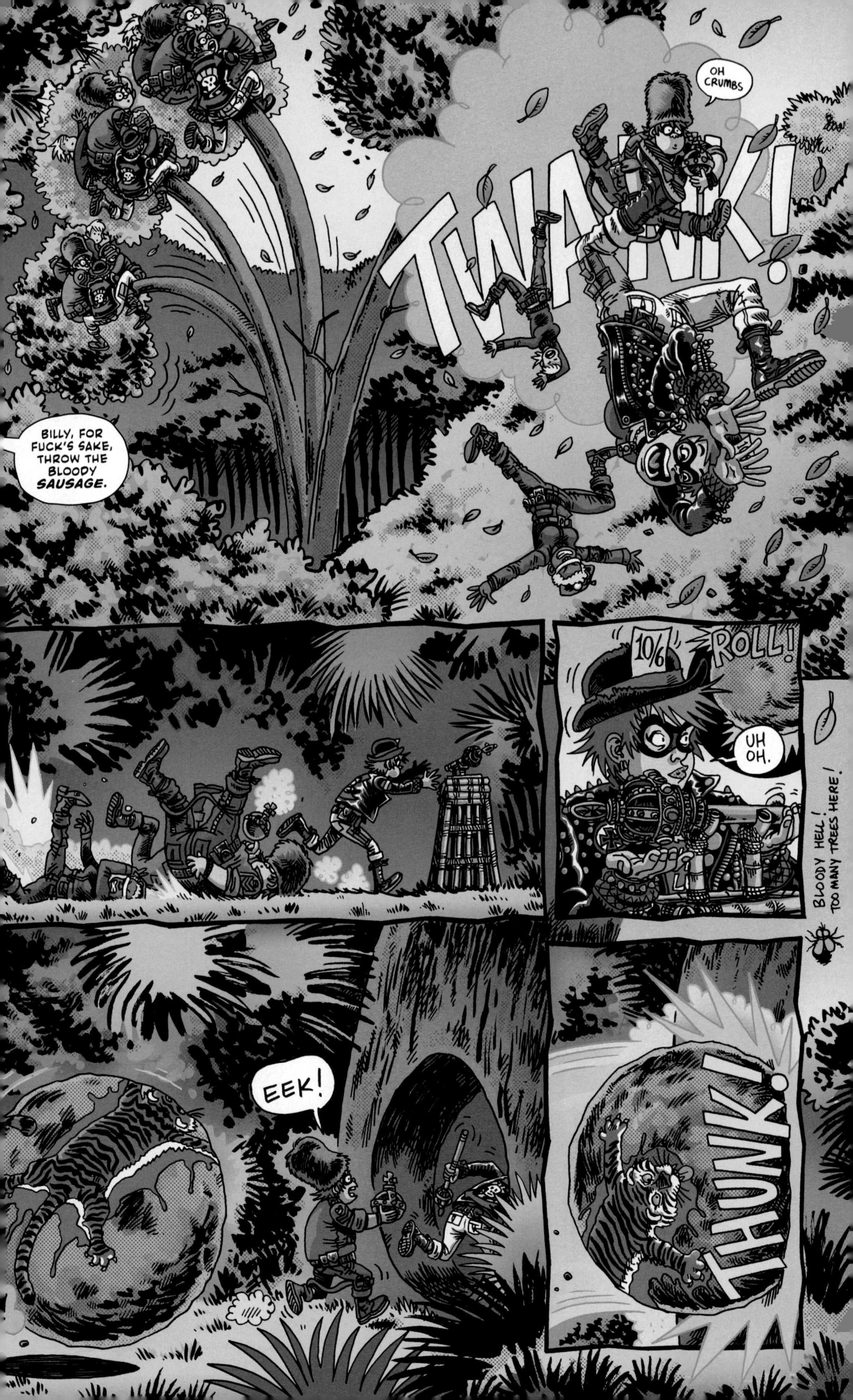

OH CRUMBS
TWANK!
BILLY, FOR FUCK'S SAKE, THROW THE BLOODY SAUSAGE.
10/6
ROLL!
UH OH.
BLOODY HELL! TOO MANY TREES HERE!
EEK!
THUNK!

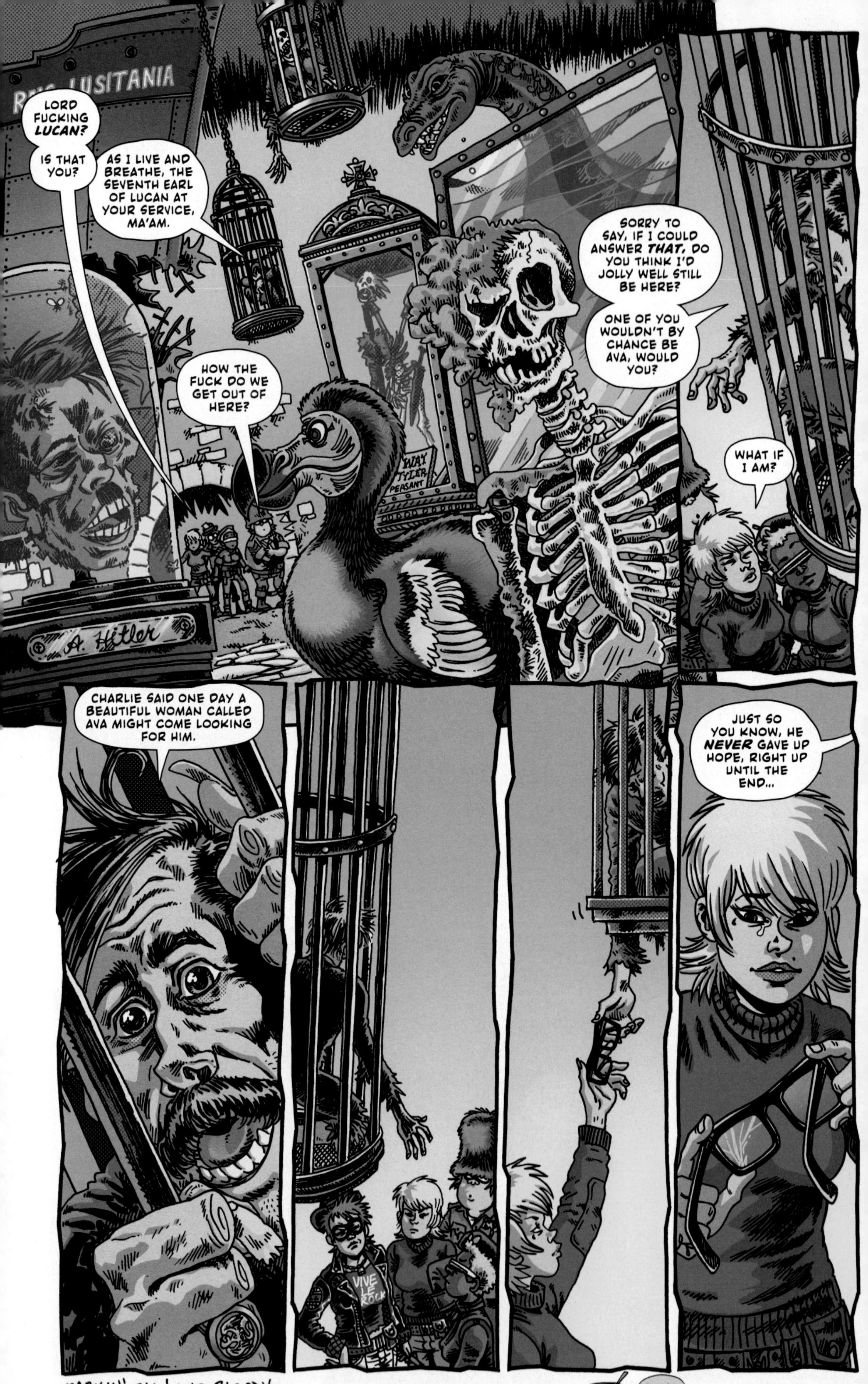
LORD FUCKING *LUCAN?*
IS THAT YOU?
AS I LIVE AND BREATHE, THE SEVENTH EARL OF LUCAN AT YOUR SERVICE, MA'AM.
HOW THE FUCK DO WE GET OUT OF HERE?
SORRY TO SAY, IF I COULD ANSWER *THAT*, DO YOU THINK I'D JOLLY WELL STILL BE HERE?
ONE OF YOU WOULDN'T BY CHANCE BE AVA, WOULD YOU?
WHAT IF I AM?
A. Hitler
CHARLIE SAID ONE DAY A BEAUTIFUL WOMAN CALLED AVA MIGHT COME LOOKING FOR HIM.
VIVE LE ROCK
JUST SO YOU KNOW, HE *NEVER* GAVE UP HOPE, RIGHT UP UNTIL THE END...

FARKIN' ELL! IT'S BLOODY LORD LUCAN!

STONE FUCKIN' COLD!

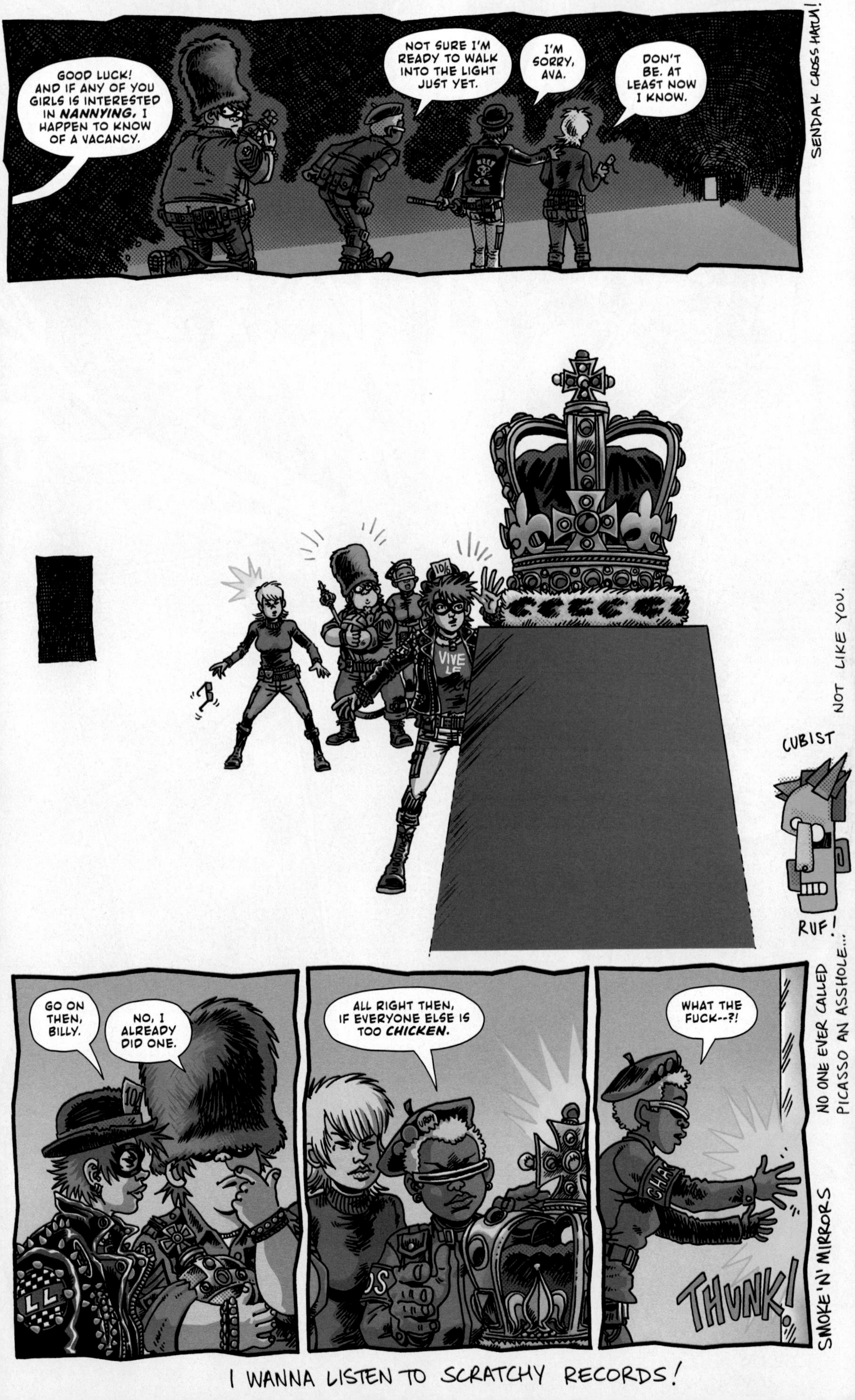
GOOD LUCK! AND IF ANY OF YOU GIRLS IS INTERESTED IN NANNYING, I HAPPEN TO KNOW OF A VACANCY.
NOT SURE I'M READY TO WALK INTO THE LIGHT JUST YET.
I'M SORRY, AVA.
DON'T BE. AT LEAST NOW I KNOW.
SENDAK CROSS HATCH!
NOT LIKE YOU.
CUBIST
RUF!
GO ON THEN, BILLY.
NO, I ALREADY DID ONE.
ALL RIGHT THEN, IF EVERYONE ELSE IS TOO CHICKEN.
WHAT THE FUCK--?!
THUNK!
NO ONE EVER CALLED PICASSO AN ASSHOLE...
SMOKE 'N' MIRRORS
I WANNA LISTEN TO SCRATCHY RECORDS!

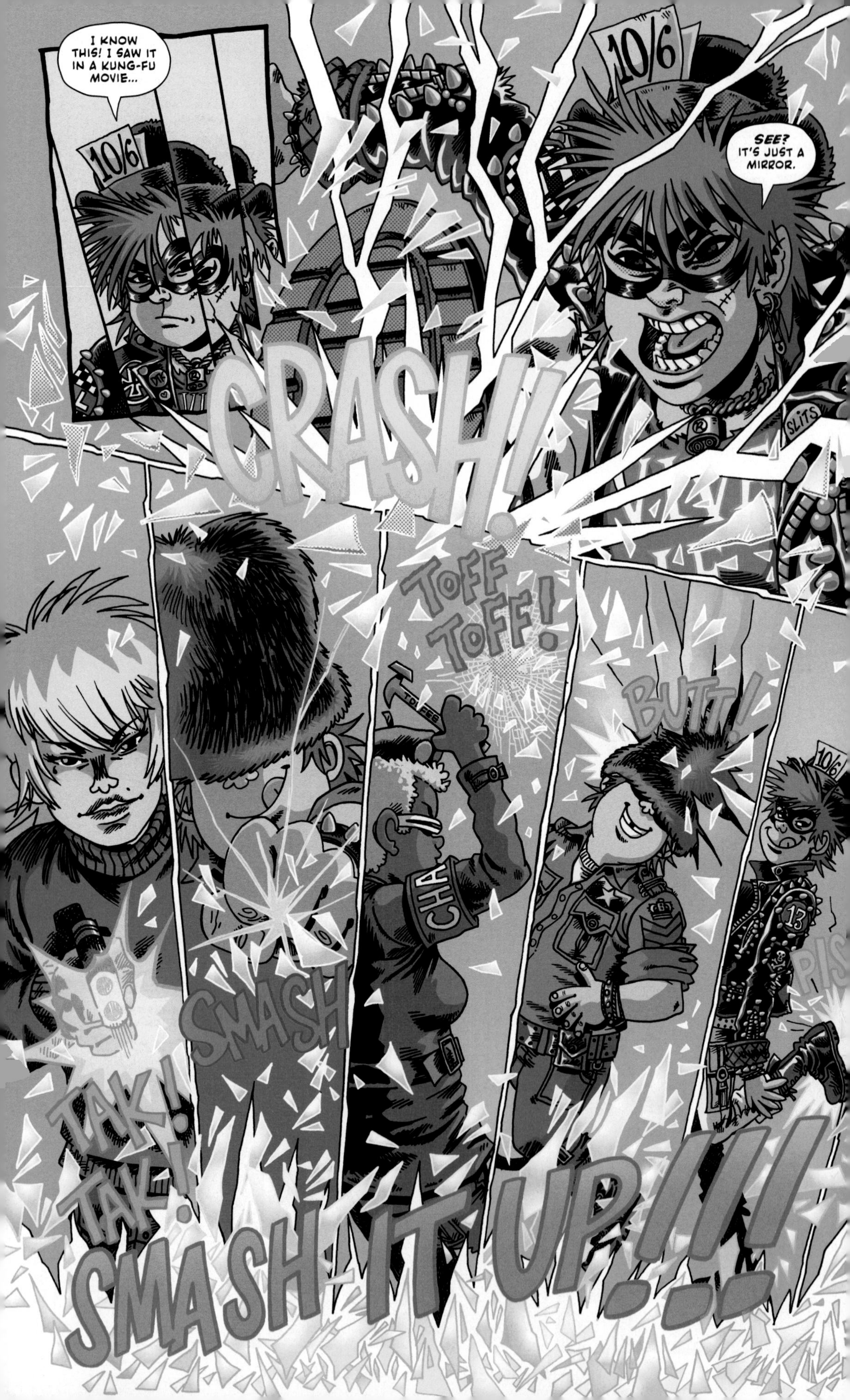
I KNOW THIS! I SAW IT IN A KUNG-FU MOVIE...
10/6
SEE? IT'S JUST A MIRROR.
CRASH!
TOFF TOFF!
BUTT!
SMASH
TAK! TAK!
SMASH IT UP!!!!

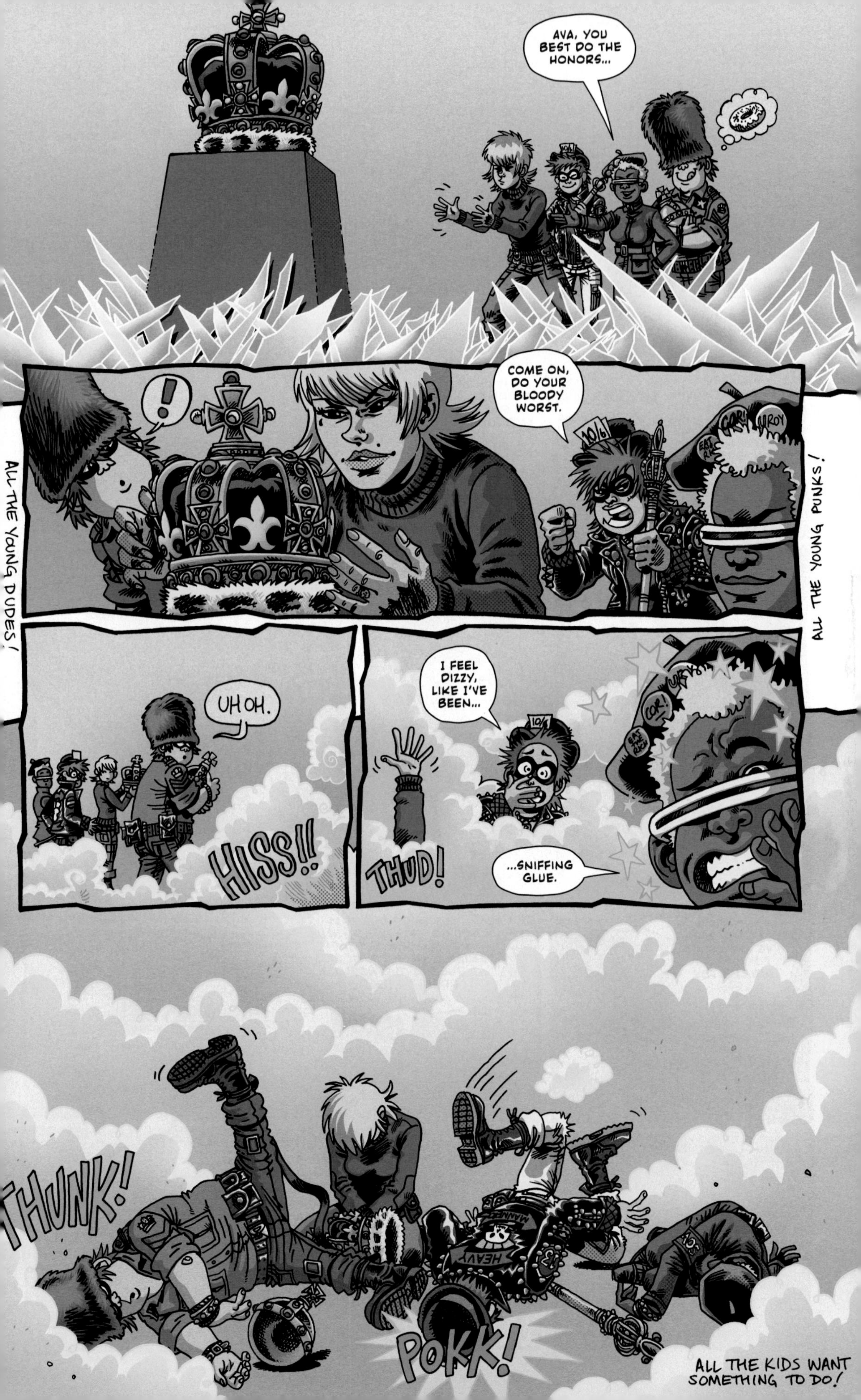
AVA, YOU BEST DO THE HONORS...
!
COME ON, DO YOUR BLOODY WORST.
ALL THE YOUNG DUDES!
ALL THE YOUNG PUNKS!
UH OH.
HISS!!
I FEEL DIZZY, LIKE I'VE BEEN...
THUD!
...SNIFFING GLUE.
THUNK!
POKK!
ALL THE KIDS WANT SOMETHING TO DO!

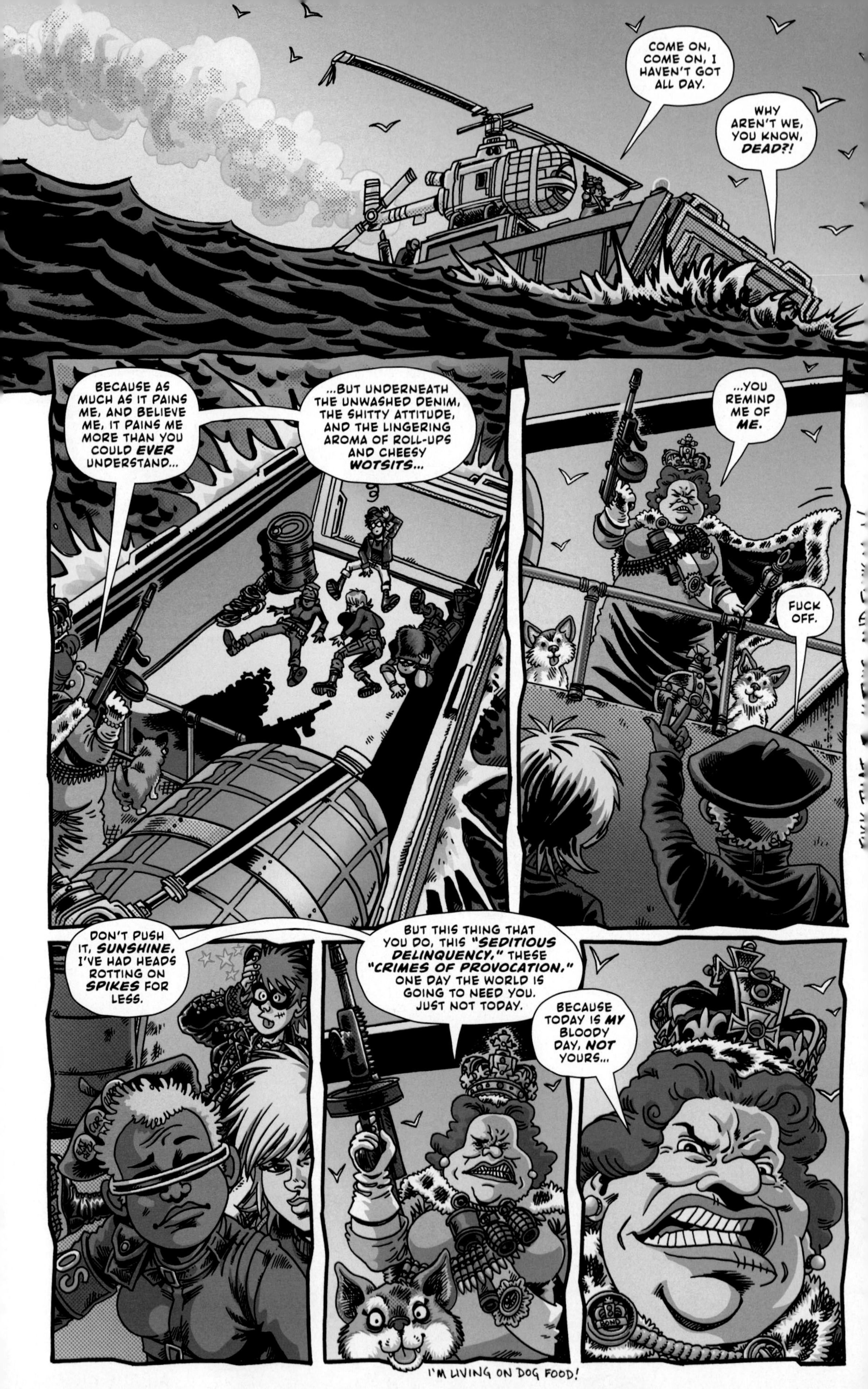
COME ON, COME ON, I HAVEN'T GOT ALL DAY.
WHY AREN'T WE, YOU KNOW, DEAD?!
BECAUSE AS MUCH AS IT PAINS ME, AND BELIEVE ME, IT PAINS ME MORE THAN YOU COULD EVER UNDERSTAND...
...BUT UNDERNEATH THE UNWASHED DENIM, THE SHITTY ATTITUDE, AND THE LINGERING AROMA OF ROLL-UPS AND CHEESY WOTSITS...
...YOU REMIND ME OF ME.
FUCK OFF.
DON'T PUSH IT, SUNSHINE. I'VE HAD HEADS ROTTING ON SPIKES FOR LESS.
BUT THIS THING THAT YOU DO, THIS "SEDITIOUS DELINQUENCY," THESE "CRIMES OF PROVOCATION." ONE DAY THE WORLD IS GOING TO NEED YOU. JUST NOT TODAY.
BECAUSE TODAY IS MY BLOODY DAY, NOT YOURS...
I'M LIVING ON DOG FOOD!

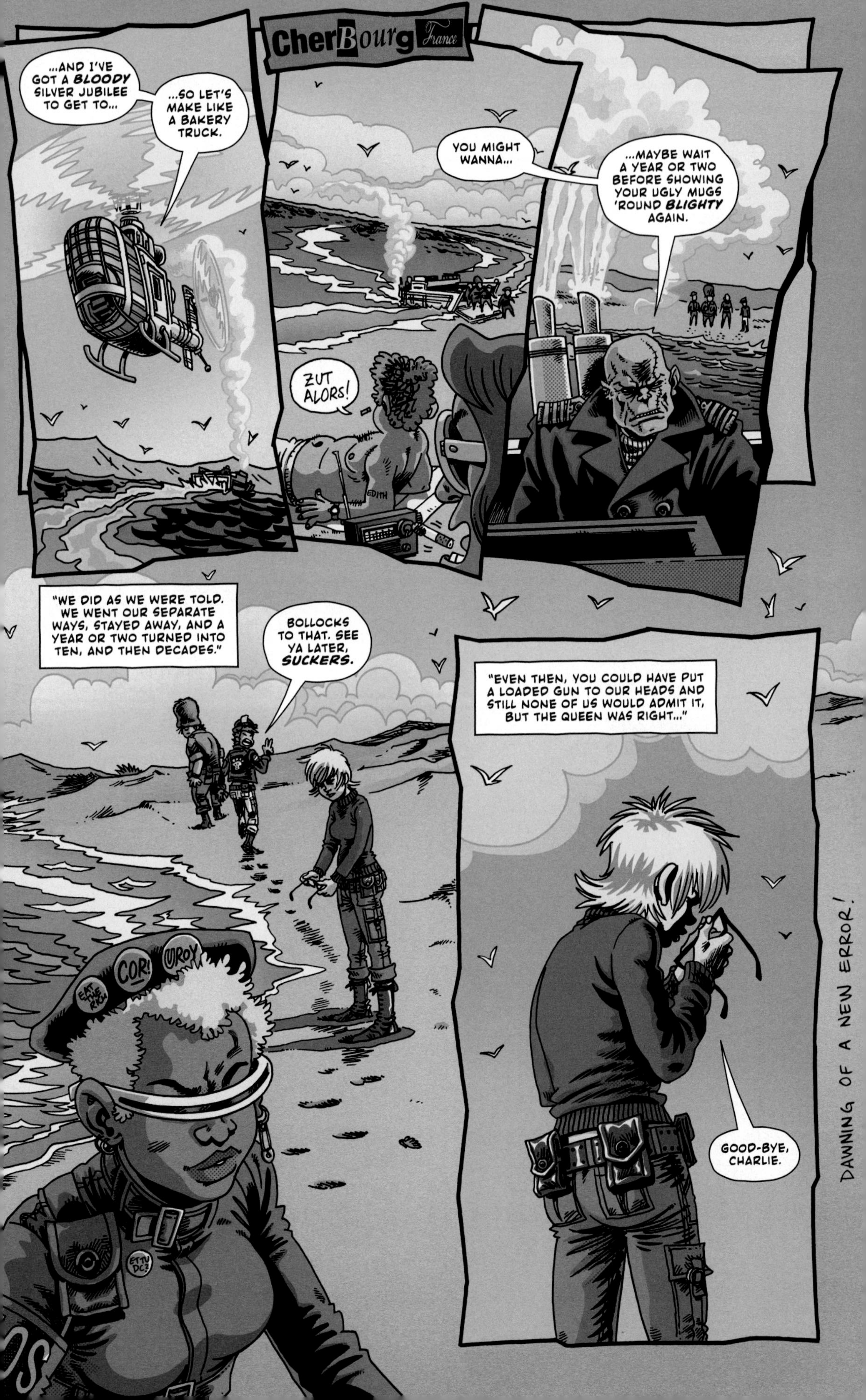
CherBourg France
...AND I'VE GOT A BLOODY SILVER JUBILEE TO GET TO...
...SO LET'S MAKE LIKE A BAKERY TRUCK.
YOU MIGHT WANNA...
...MAYBE WAIT A YEAR OR TWO BEFORE SHOWING YOUR UGLY MUGS 'ROUND BLIGHTY AGAIN.
ZUT ALORS!
EDITH
"WE DID AS WE WERE TOLD. WE WENT OUR SEPARATE WAYS, STAYED AWAY, AND A YEAR OR TWO TURNED INTO TEN, AND THEN DECADES."
BOLLOCKS TO THAT. SEE YA LATER, SUCKERS.
"EVEN THEN, YOU COULD HAVE PUT A LOADED GUN TO OUR HEADS AND STILL NONE OF US WOULD ADMIT IT, BUT THE QUEEN WAS RIGHT..."
COR!
EAT THE RICH
GOOD-BYE, CHARLIE.
DAWNING OF A NEW ERROR!

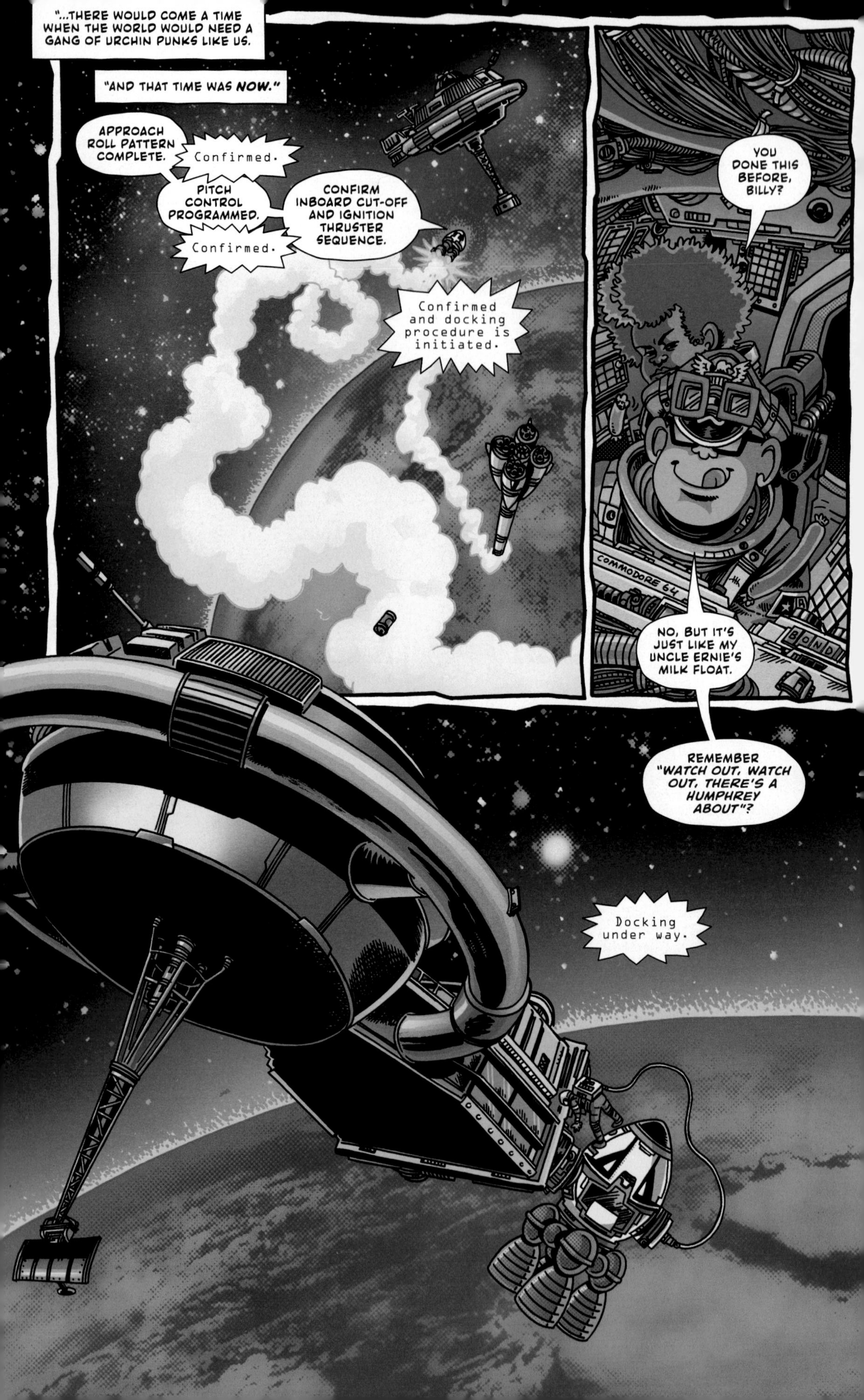
"...THERE WOULD COME A TIME WHEN THE WORLD WOULD NEED A GANG OF URCHIN PUNKS LIKE US.
"AND THAT TIME WAS NOW."
APPROACH ROLL PATTERN COMPLETE.
Confirmed.
PITCH CONTROL PROGRAMMED.
Confirmed.
CONFIRM INBOARD CUT-OFF AND IGNITION THRUSTER SEQUENCE.
Confirmed and docking procedure is initiated.
YOU DONE THIS BEFORE, BILLY?
COMMODORE 64
NO, BUT IT'S JUST LIKE MY UNCLE ERNIE'S MILK FLOAT.
REMEMBER "WATCH OUT, WATCH OUT, THERE'S A HUMPHREY ABOUT"?
Docking under way.

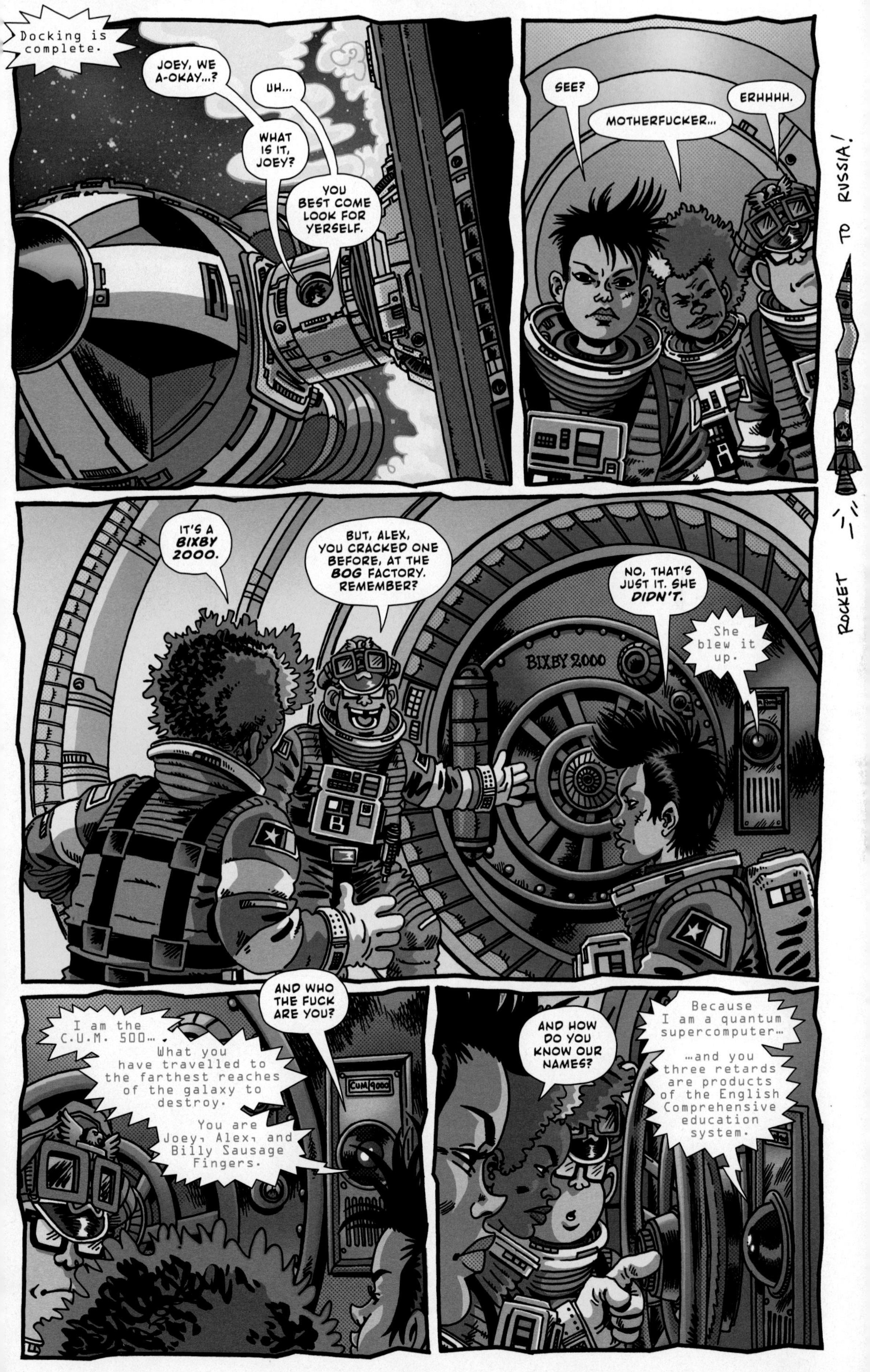
Docking is complete.
JOEY, WE A-OKAY...?
UH...
WHAT IS IT, JOEY?
YOU BEST COME LOOK FOR YERSELF.
SEE?
MOTHERFUCKER...
ERHHHH.
ROCKET TO RUSSIA!
IT'S A BIXBY 2000.
BUT, ALEX, YOU CRACKED ONE BEFORE, AT THE BOG FACTORY. REMEMBER?
NO, THAT'S JUST IT. SHE DIDN'T.
BIXBY 2000
She blew it up.
I am the C.U.M. 500...
What you have travelled to the farthest reaches of the galaxy to destroy.
You are Joey, Alex, and Billy Sausage Fingers.
AND WHO THE FUCK ARE YOU?
CUM 9000
AND HOW DO YOU KNOW OUR NAMES?
Because I am a quantum supercomputer...
...and you three retards are products of the English Comprehensive education system.

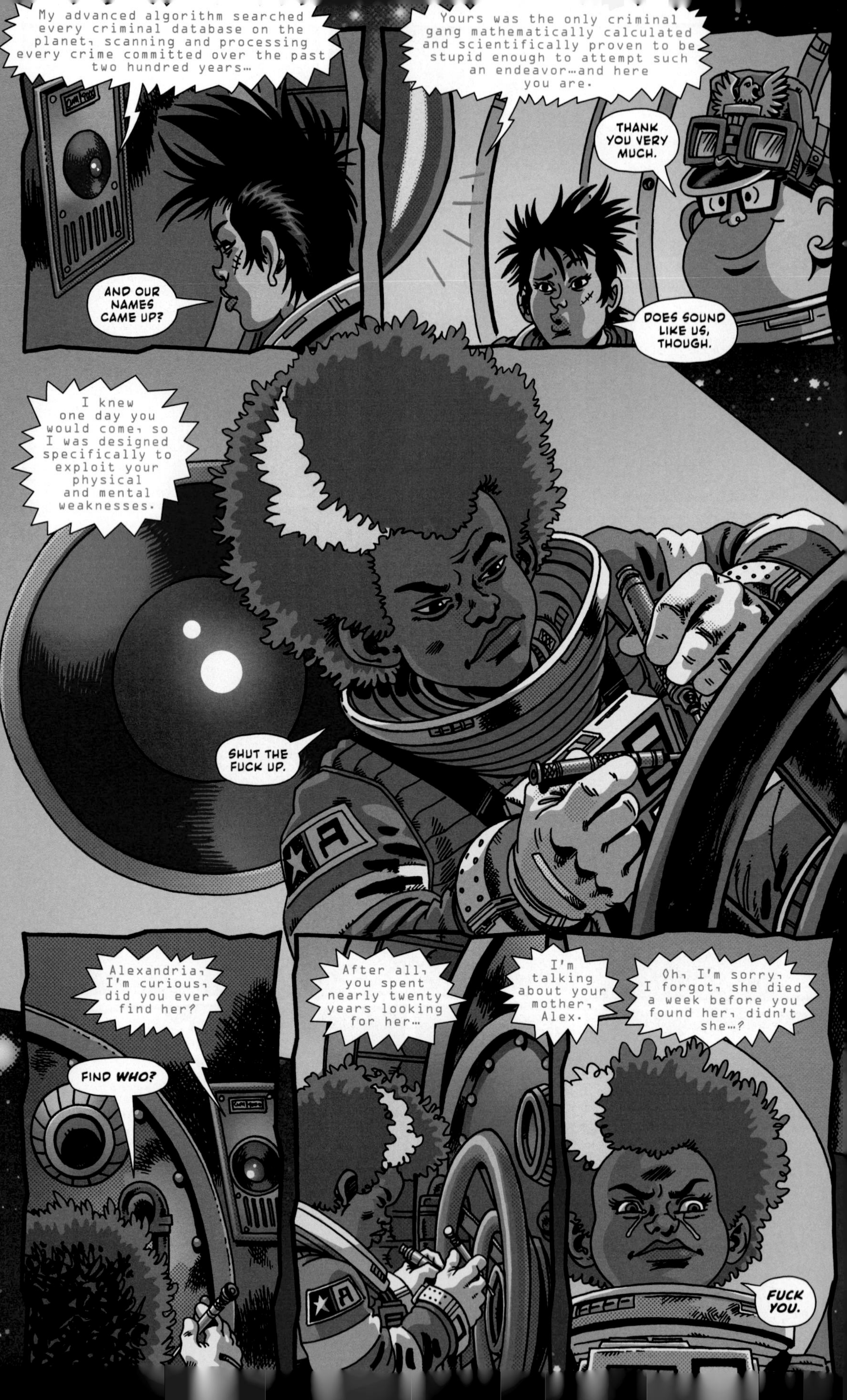
My advanced algorithm searched every criminal database on the planet, scanning and processing every crime committed over the past two hundred years…
AND OUR NAMES CAME UP?
Yours was the only criminal gang mathematically calculated and scientifically proven to be stupid enough to attempt such an endeavor…and here you are.
THANK YOU VERY MUCH.
DOES SOUND LIKE US, THOUGH.
I knew one day you would come, so I was designed specifically to exploit your physical and mental weaknesses.
SHUT THE FUCK UP.
Alexandria, I'm curious, did you ever find her?
FIND WHO?
After all, you spent nearly twenty years looking for her…
I'm talking about your mother, Alex.
Oh, I'm sorry, I forgot, she died a week before you found her, didn't she…?
FUCK YOU.

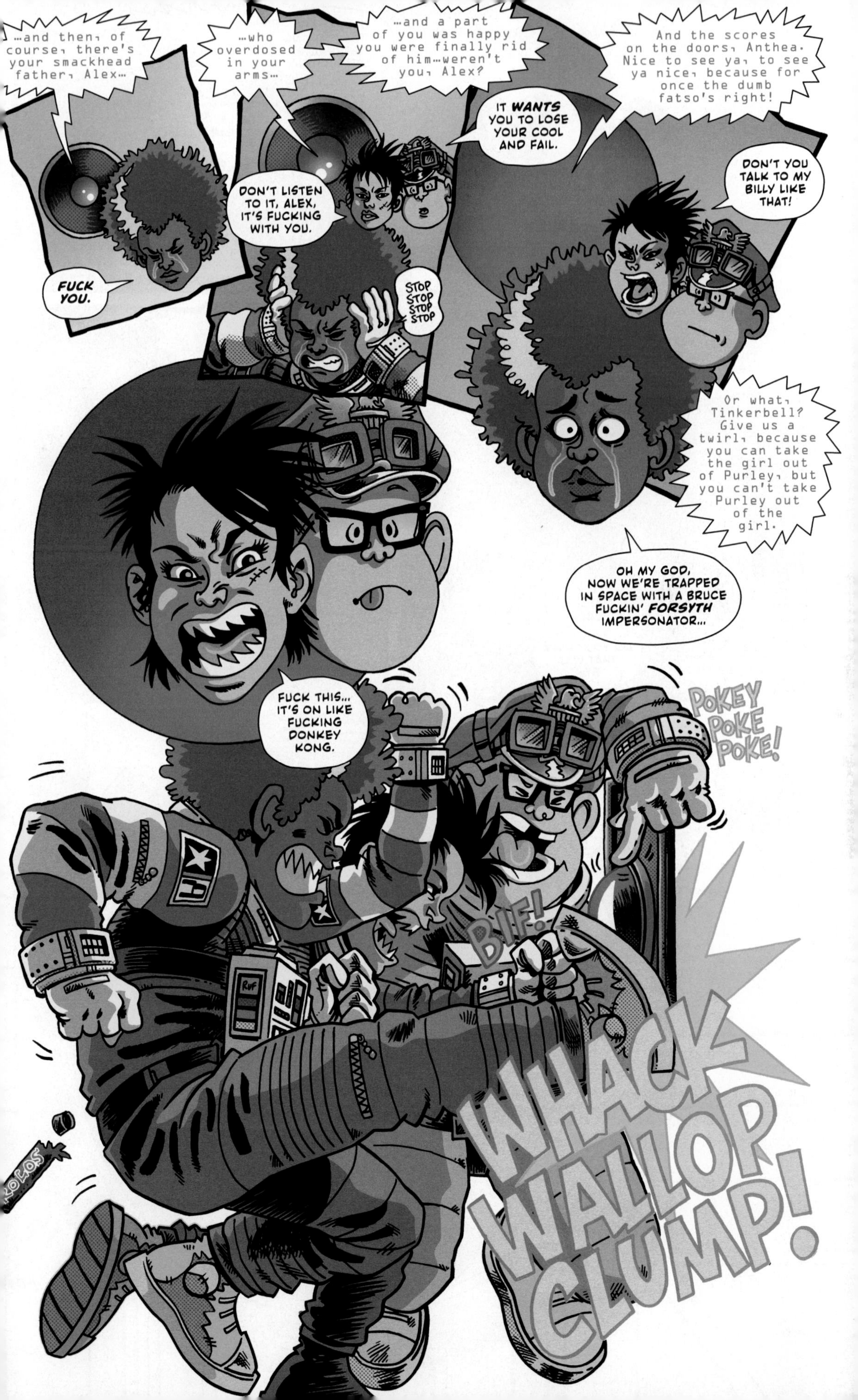
…and then, of course, there's your smackhead father, Alex…
FUCK YOU.
…who overdosed in your arms…
DON'T LISTEN TO IT, ALEX, IT'S FUCKING WITH YOU.
STOP STOP STOP STOP
…and a part of you was happy you were finally rid of him…weren't you, Alex?
IT WANTS YOU TO LOSE YOUR COOL AND FAIL.
And the scores on the doors, Anthea. Nice to see ya, to see ya nice, because for once the dumb fatso's right!
DON'T YOU TALK TO MY BILLY LIKE THAT!
Or what, Tinkerbell? Give us a twirl, because you can take the girl out of Purley, but you can't take Purley out of the girl.
OH MY GOD, NOW WE'RE TRAPPED IN SPACE WITH A BRUCE FUCKIN' FORSYTH IMPERSONATOR…
FUCK THIS… IT'S ON LIKE FUCKING DONKEY KONG.
POKEY POKE POKE!
BIF!
WHACK WALLOP CLUMP!

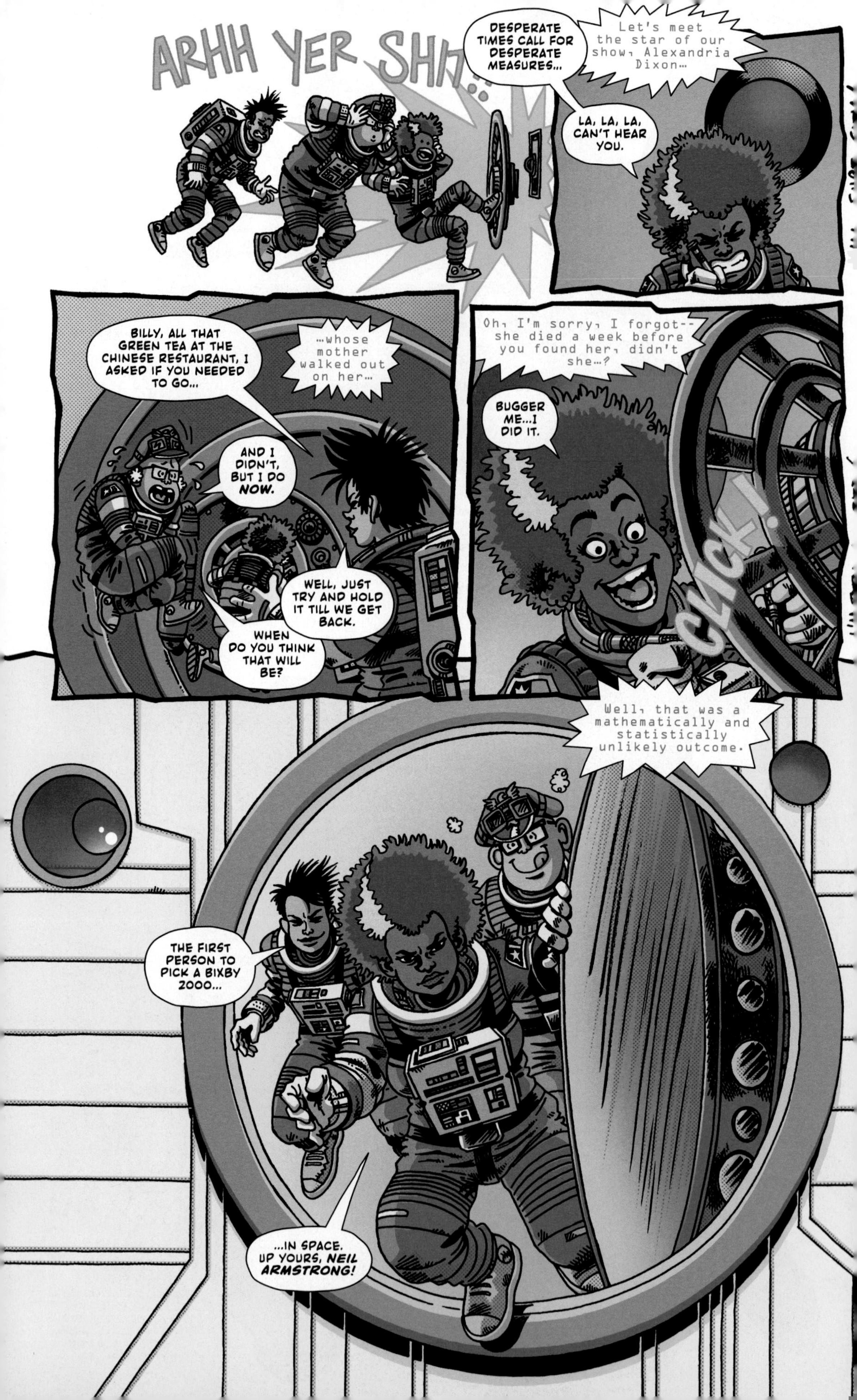
ARHH YER SHIT..!!
DESPERATE TIMES CALL FOR DESPERATE MEASURES...
Let's meet the star of our show, Alexandria Dixon...
LA, LA, LA, CAN'T HEAR YOU.
BILLY, ALL THAT GREEN TEA AT THE CHINESE RESTAURANT, I ASKED IF YOU NEEDED TO GO...
...whose mother walked out on her...
AND I DIDN'T, BUT I DO NOW.
WELL, JUST TRY AND HOLD IT TILL WE GET BACK.
WHEN DO YOU THINK THAT WILL BE?
Oh, I'm sorry, I forgot--she died a week before you found her, didn't she...?
BUGGER ME...I DID IT.
CLICK!
Well, that was a mathematically and statistically unlikely outcome.
THE FIRST PERSON TO PICK A BIXBY 2000...
...IN SPACE. UP YOURS, NEIL ARMSTRONG!

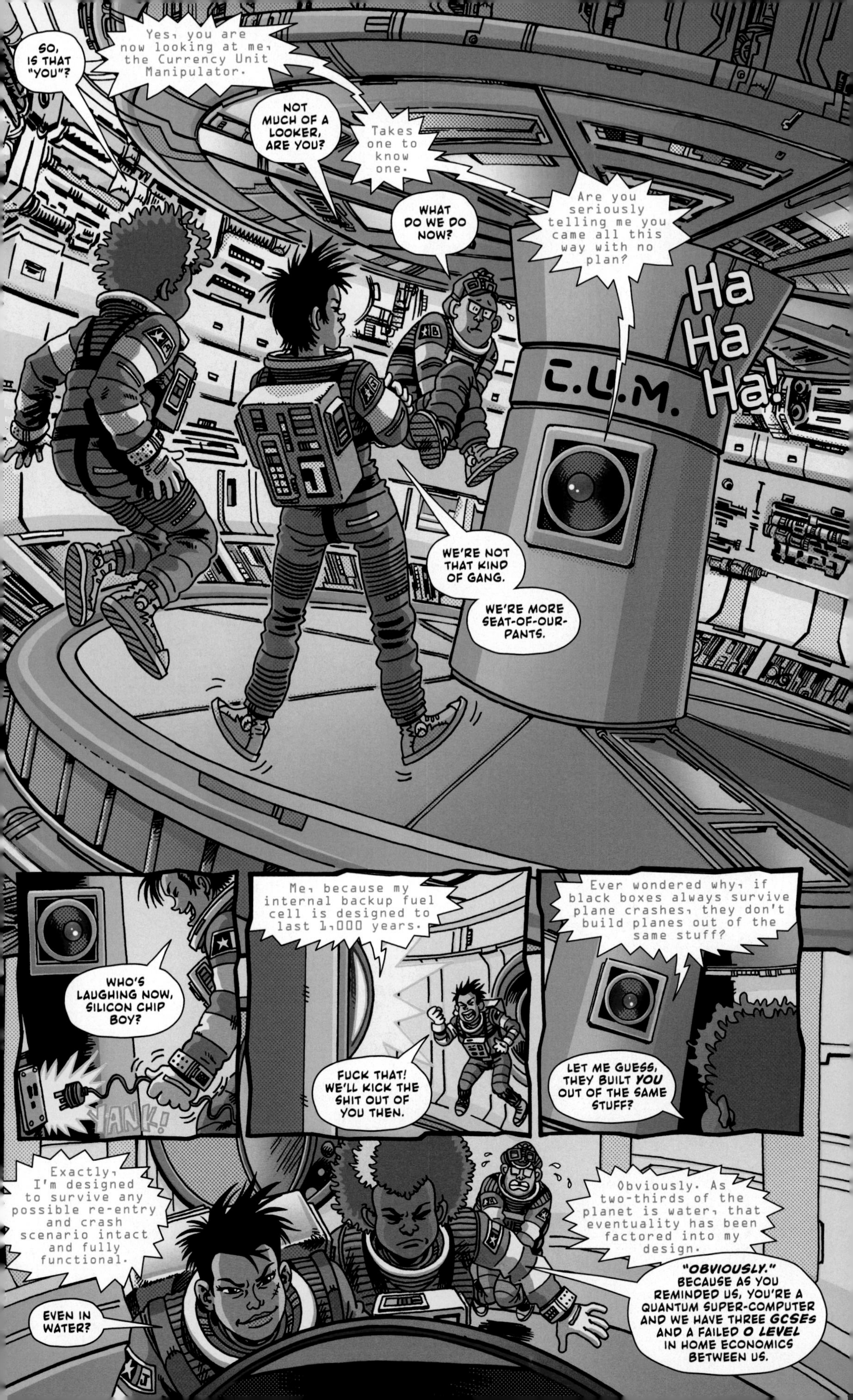
SO, IS THAT "YOU"?
Yes, you are now looking at me, the Currency Unit Manipulator.
NOT MUCH OF A LOOKER, ARE YOU?
Takes one to know one.
WHAT DO WE DO NOW?
Are you seriously telling me you came all this way with no plan?
Ha Ha Ha!
C.U.M.
WE'RE NOT THAT KIND OF GANG.
WE'RE MORE SEAT-OF-OUR-PANTS.
WHO'S LAUGHING NOW, SILICON CHIP BOY?
YANK!
Me, because my internal backup fuel cell is designed to last 1,000 years.
FUCK THAT! WE'LL KICK THE SHIT OUT OF YOU THEN.
Ever wondered why, if black boxes always survive plane crashes, they don't build planes out of the same stuff?
LET ME GUESS, THEY BUILT YOU OUT OF THE SAME STUFF?
Exactly, I'm designed to survive any possible re-entry and crash scenario intact and fully functional.
EVEN IN WATER?
Obviously. As two-thirds of the planet is water, that eventuality has been factored into my design.
"OBVIOUSLY." BECAUSE AS YOU REMINDED US, YOU'RE A QUANTUM SUPER-COMPUTER AND WE HAVE THREE GCSES AND A FAILED O LEVEL IN HOME ECONOMICS BETWEEN US.

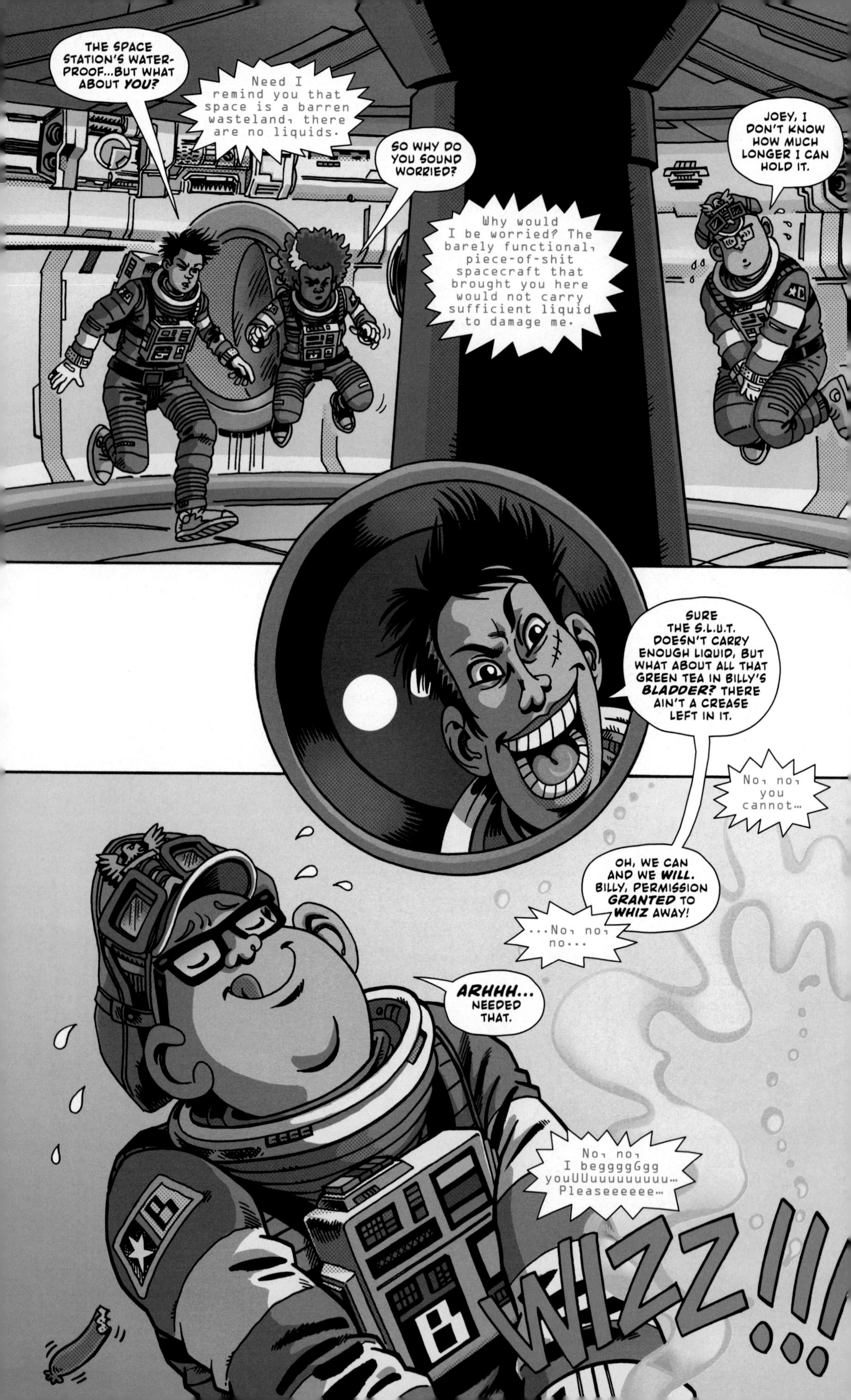
THE SPACE STATION'S WATER-PROOF...BUT WHAT ABOUT *YOU?*
Need I remind you that space is a barren wasteland, there are no liquids.
SO WHY DO YOU SOUND WORRIED?
Why would I be worried? The barely functional, piece-of-shit spacecraft that brought you here would not carry sufficient liquid to damage me.
JOEY, I DON'T KNOW HOW MUCH LONGER I CAN HOLD IT.
SURE THE S.L.U.T. DOESN'T CARRY ENOUGH LIQUID, BUT WHAT ABOUT ALL THAT GREEN TEA IN BILLY'S *BLADDER?* THERE AIN'T A CREASE LEFT IN IT.
No, no, you cannot...
OH, WE CAN AND WE *WILL.* BILLY, PERMISSION *GRANTED* TO *WHIZ* AWAY!
...No, no, no...
ARHHH... NEEDED THAT.
No, no, I beggggGgg youUUuuuuuuuuu... Pleaseeeeeee...
WIZZ!!!

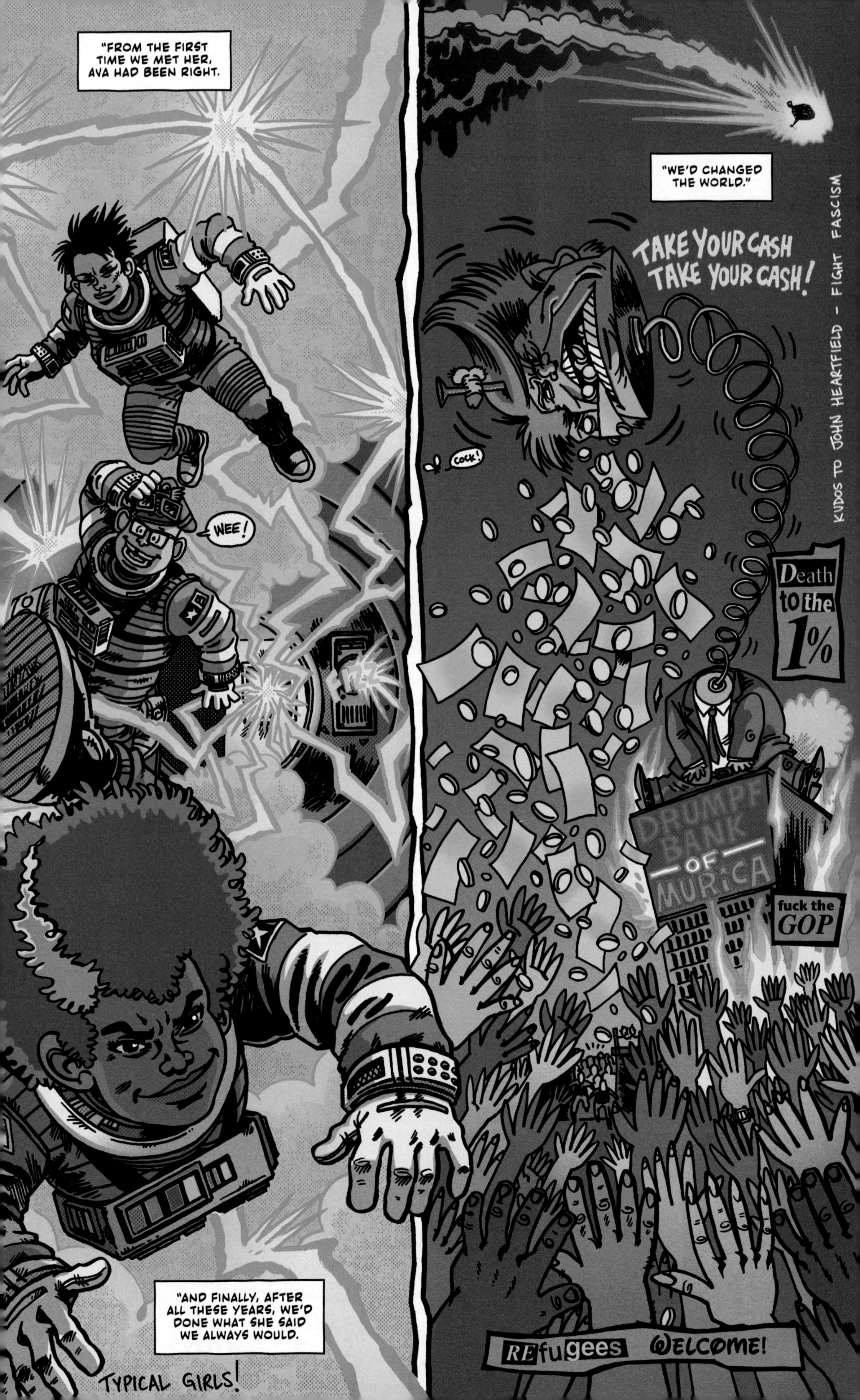
"FROM THE FIRST TIME WE MET HER, AVA HAD BEEN RIGHT.
WEE!
"AND FINALLY, AFTER ALL THESE YEARS, WE'D DONE WHAT SHE SAID WE ALWAYS WOULD.
TYPICAL GIRLS!
"WE'D CHANGED THE WORLD."
TAKE YOUR CASH TAKE YOUR CASH!
COCK!
Death to the 1%
DRUMPF BANK OF MURICA
fuck the GOP
REfugees WELCOME!
KUDOS TO JOHN HEARTFIELD - FIGHT FASCISM

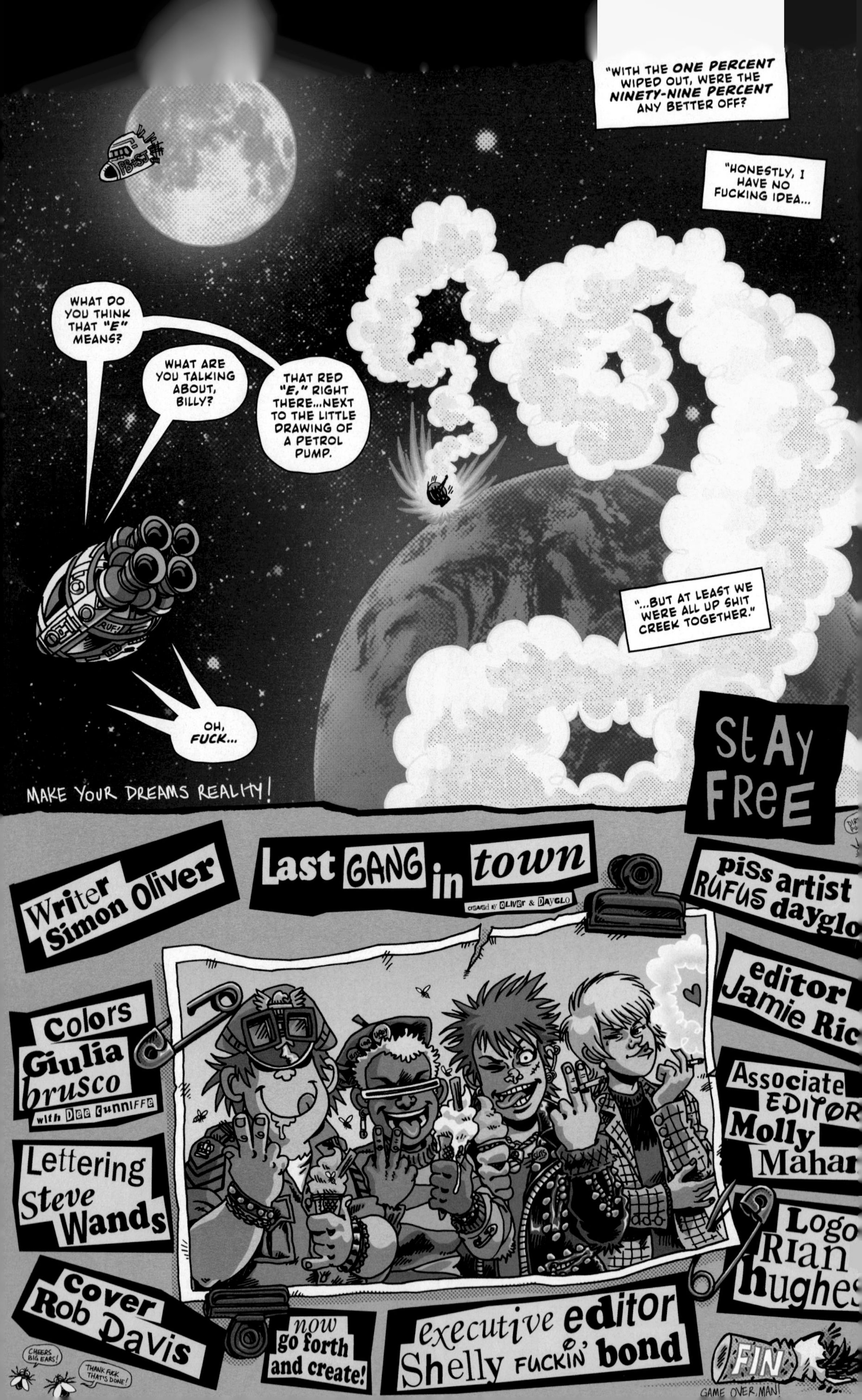

"WITH THE ONE PERCENT WIPED OUT, WERE THE NINETY-NINE PERCENT ANY BETTER OFF?
"HONESTLY, I HAVE NO FUCKING IDEA...
WHAT DO YOU THINK THAT "E" MEANS?
WHAT ARE YOU TALKING ABOUT, BILLY?
THAT RED "E," RIGHT THERE...NEXT TO THE LITTLE DRAWING OF A PETROL PUMP.
OH, FUCK...
"...BUT AT LEAST WE WERE ALL UP SHIT CREEK TOGETHER."
MAKE YOUR DREAMS REALITY!
STAY FREE
Writer Simon Oliver
Last GANG in town
created by OLIVER & DAYGLO
piss artist RUFUS dayglo
editor Jamie Ric
Colors Giulia brusco with Dee Cunniffe
Associate EDITOR Molly Mahan
Lettering Steve Wands
Logo Rian hughes
Cover Rob Davis
now go forth and create!
executive editor Shelly FUCKIN' bond
FIN
CHEERS BIG EARS!
THANK FUCK THAT'S DONE!
GAME OVER, MAN!

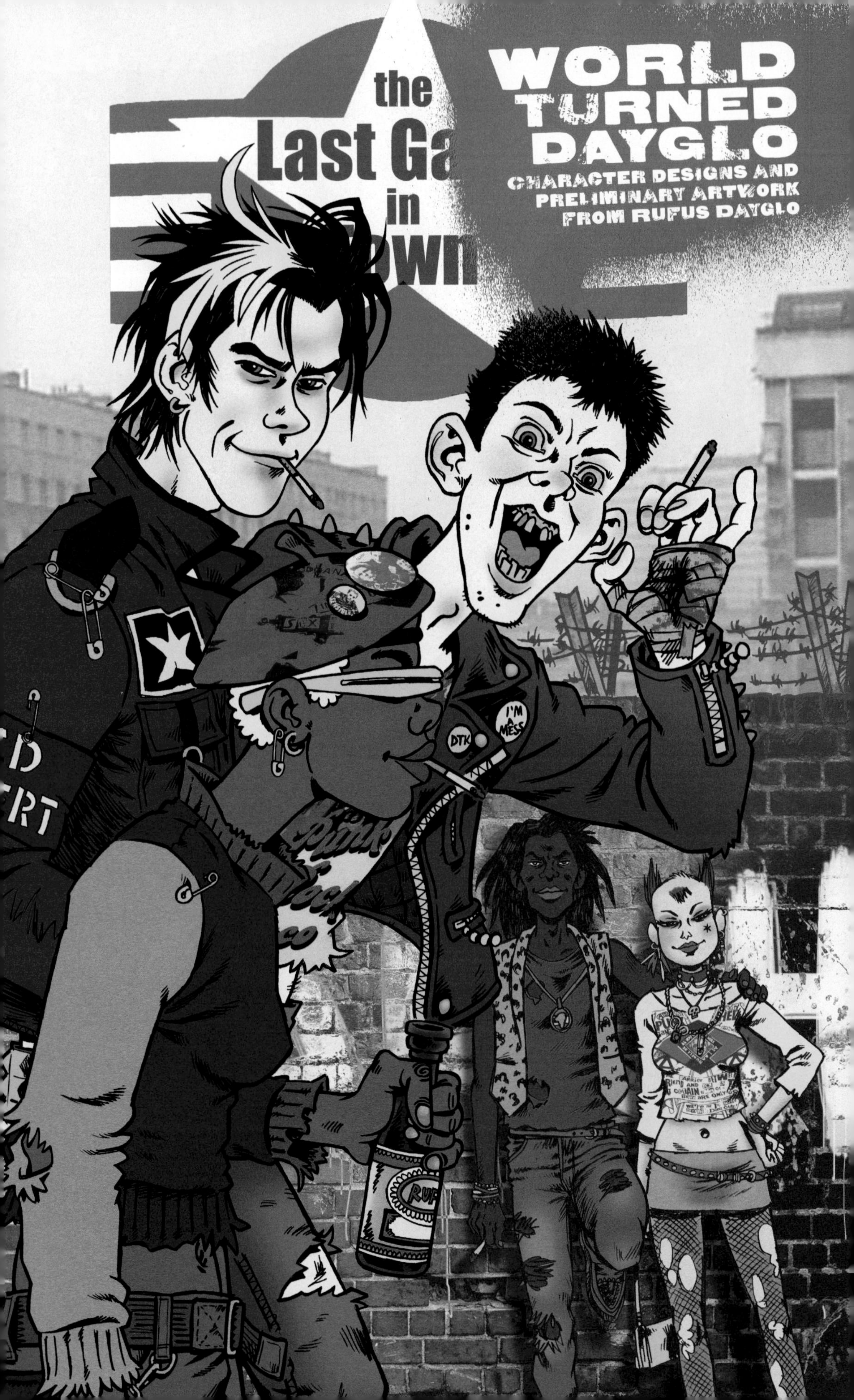
WORLD TURNED DAYGLO
CHARACTER DESIGNS AND PRELIMINARY ARTWORK FROM RUFUS DAYGLO
I'M A MESS
DTK

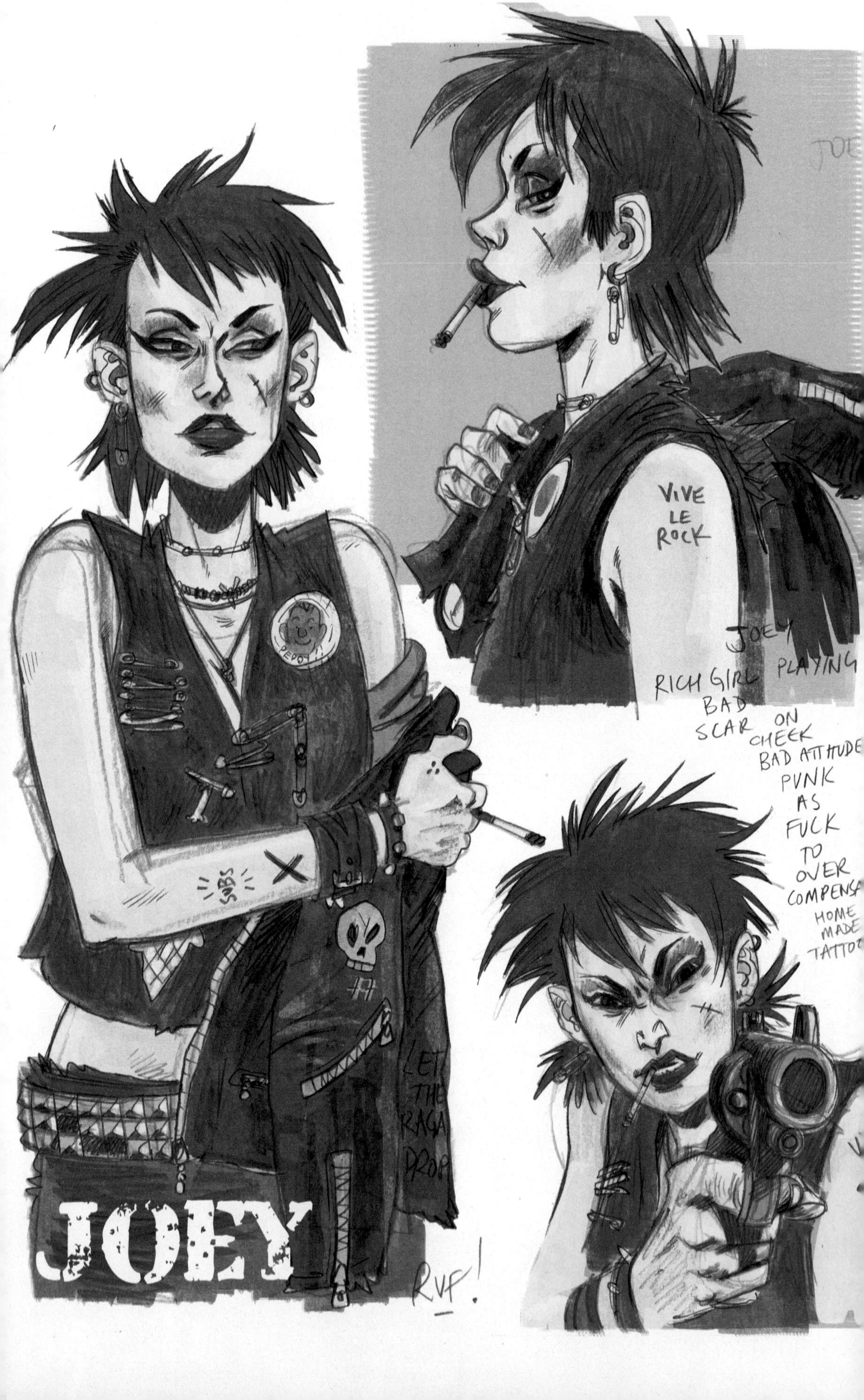

VIVE LE ROCK
JOEY PLAYING RICH GIRL BAD
SCAR ON CHEEK
BAD ATTITUDE
PUNK AS FUCK TO OVER COMPENSA
HOME MADE TATTOO
SUBS
LET THE RAGA DROP
JOEY
RVF!

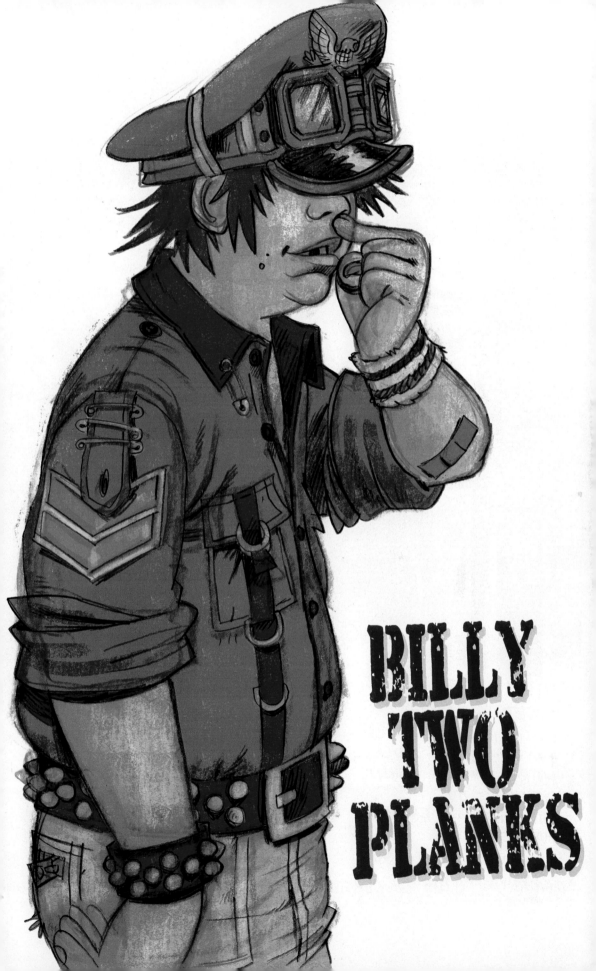

BILLY
TWO
PLANKS

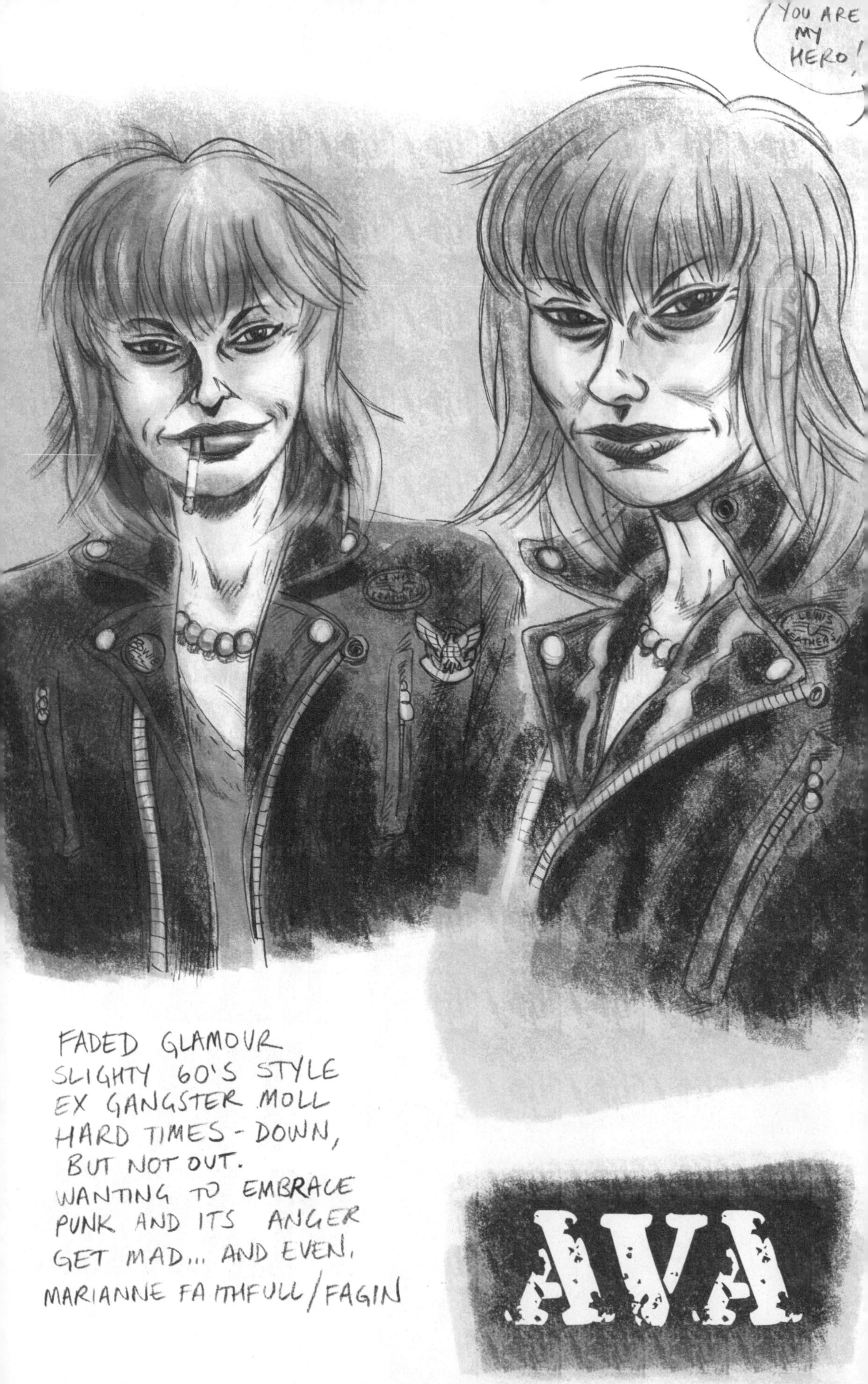
YOU ARE MY HERO!

FADED GLAMOUR
SLIGHTY 60'S STYLE
EX GANGSTER MOLL
HARD TIMES - DOWN,
BUT NOT OUT.
WANTING TO EMBRACE
PUNK AND ITS ANGER
GET MAD... AND EVEN.
MARIANNE FAITHFULL/FAGIN

AVA

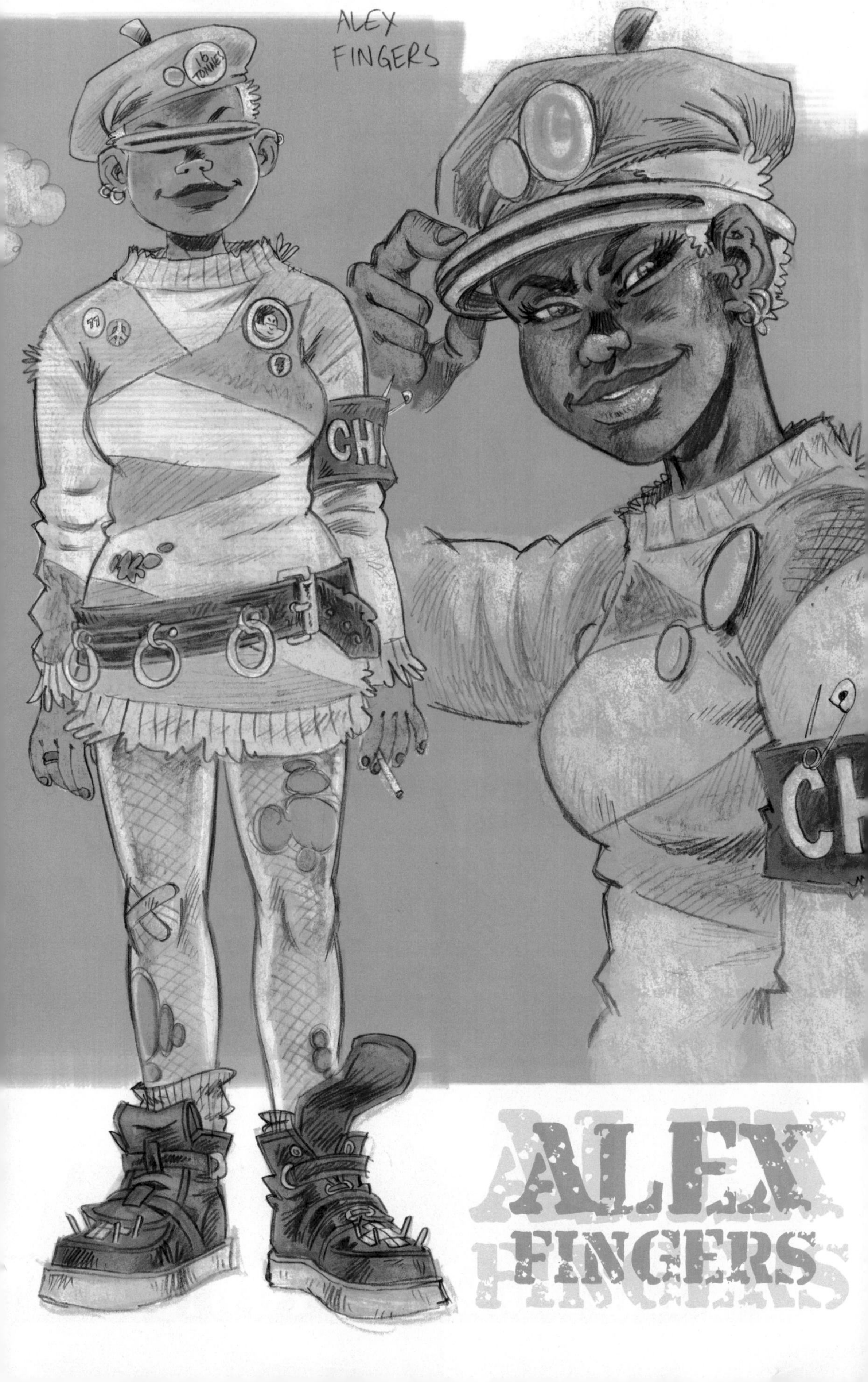
ALEX
FINGERS
16 TONNES
77
CH
CH
ALEX
FINGERS

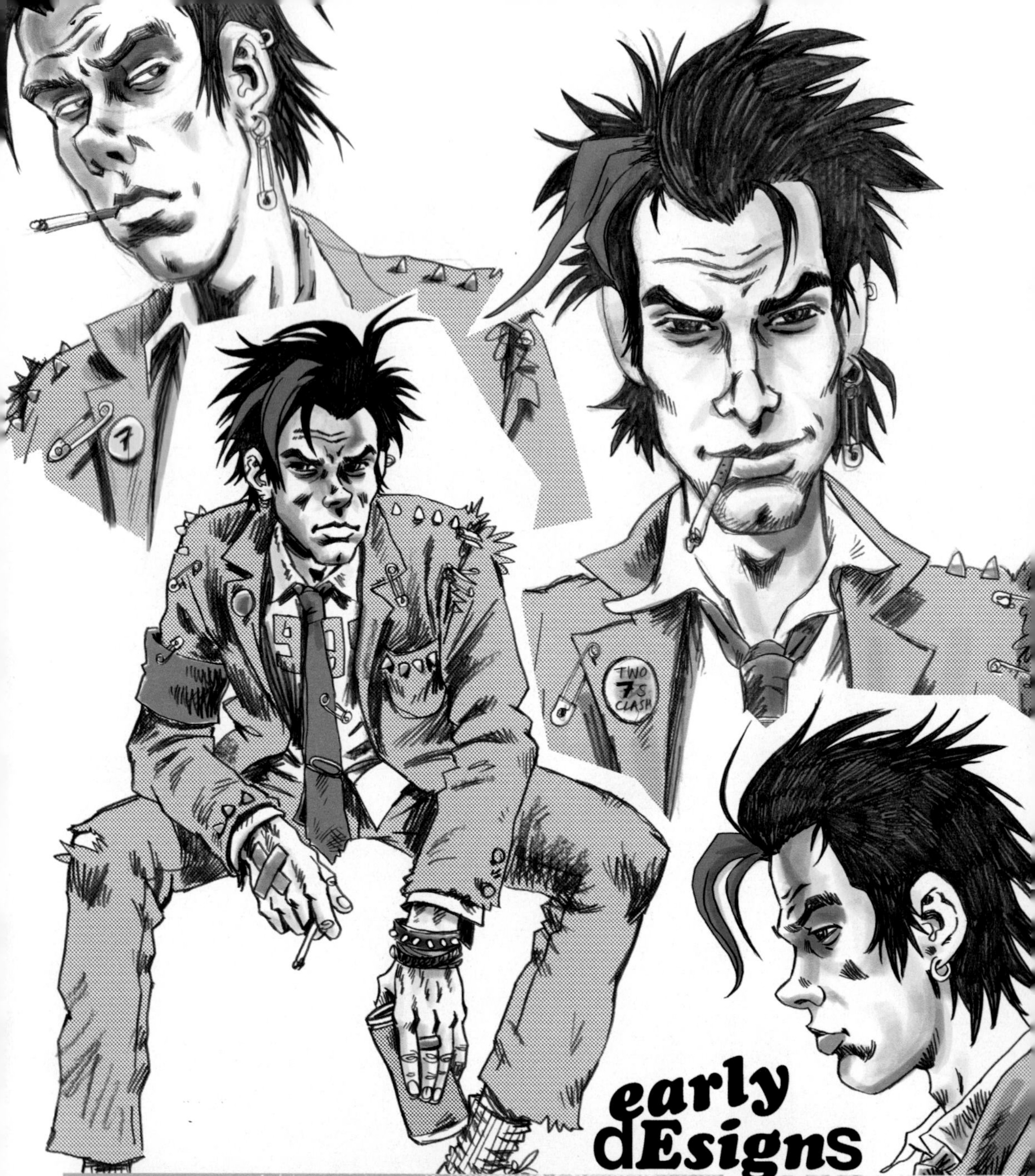
7
TWO 7S CLASH
early dEsigns

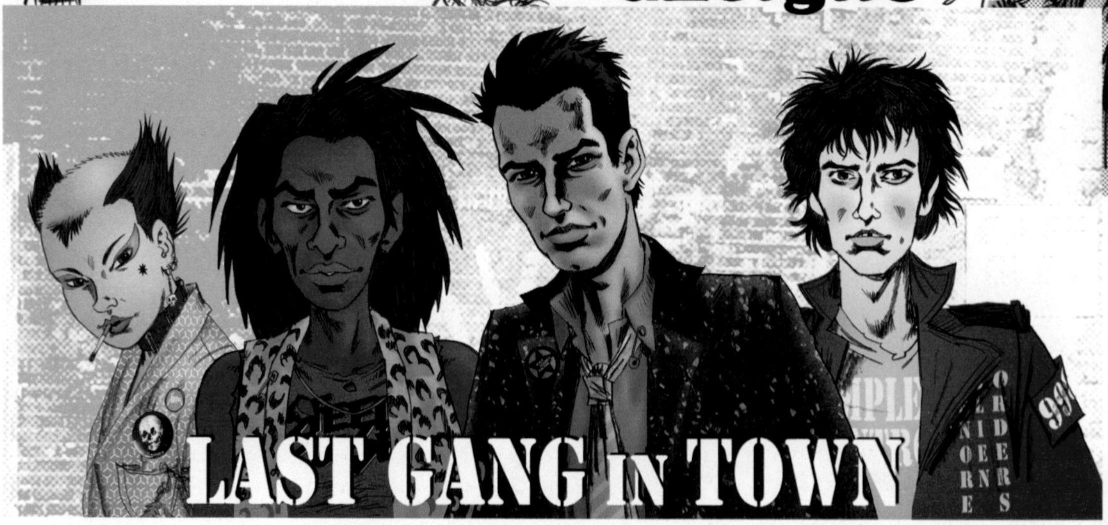
LAST GANG IN TOWN